THE COMPLETE POEMS OF

Emily Dickinson

THE COMPLETE POEMS OF

Emily Dickinson

EDITED BY

Thomas H. Johnson

BACK BAY BOOKS

LITTLE, BROWN AND COMPANY
NEW YORK • BOSTON

Back Bay Books / Little, Brown and Company
Time Warner Book Group
1271 Avenue of the Americas, New York, NY 10020
Visit our Web site at www.twbookmark.com

Originally published in hardcover by Little, Brown and Company, 1960
First paperback edition, 1961

ISBN 0-316-18413-6

LIBRARY OF CONGRESS CONTROL NUMBER 60-11646

40 39 38 37 36 35 34

Q-FF

Introduction

THERE are certain significant dates in American literary history during the nineteenth century. One was August 21, 1837, when Emerson, before the Phi Beta Kappa Society at Cambridge, Massachusetts, delivered in the presence of Thoreau's graduating class his "American Scholar" address, immediately hailed by young Oliver Wendell Holmes as "our intellectual Declaration of Independence." One was the day early in July, 1855, when Whitman "for the convenience of private reading only" began circulating printed copies of his *Leaves of Grass*. A third is surely April 15, 1862, when Thomas Wentworth Higginson received a letter from Emily Dickinson enclosing four of her poems.

Emily Dickinson, then thirty-one years old, was writing a professional man of letters to inquire whether her verses "breathed." Higginson was still living at Worcester, Massachusetts, where he had recently resigned his pastorate of a "free" church, and was beginning to establish a reputation as essayist and a lecturer in the cause of reforms. She dared bring herself to his attention because she had just read his "Letter to a Young Contributor," practical advice for those wishing to break into print, and the lead article in the current issue of the *Atlantic Monthly*. "Charge your style with life," he commented, and went on to declare that the privilege of bringing forward "new genius" was fascinating. His article happened to appear exactly at the moment that Emily Dickinson was ready to seek criticism. She knew him to be a liberal thinker, interested in the status of women in general and women writers in particular. Though the article drew responses, all of which Higginson judged "not for publication," he sensed some quality in the enclosures of the letter posted at Amherst which elicited a reply. He asked for more verses, inquired her age, her reading and her companionships.

The importance of the correspondence with Higginson thus initiated, and continuing throughout Emily Dickinson's life, cannot be exaggerated. In the first place, the four poems she initially selected reveal that in 1862 the poet was no longer a novice but an artist whose strikingly original talent was fully developed. She enclosed "Safe in their Alabaster Chambers" (216), "I'll tell you how the Sun rose" (318), "The nearest Dream recedes – unrealized" (319), and "We play at Paste" (320). What embarrassed Higginson about the poems was his inability to classify them. In 1891 he wrote an article describing this early correspondence. "The impression of a wholly new and original poetic genius," he said, "was as distinct on my mind at the first reading of these four poems as it is now, after thirty years of further knowledge; and with it came the problem never yet solved, what place ought to be assigned in literature to what is so remarkable, yet so elusive of criticism." Higginson's problem was compounded by the fact that during Emily Dickinson's lifetime he was never convinced that she wrote poetry. As he phrased his opinion to a friend, her verses were "remarkable, though odd . . . *too delicate* — not strong enough to publish."

A representative mid-nineteenth-century traditionalist was being asked to judge the work of a "wholly new" order of craftsman. His reply to the first letter (implied in her second letter to him — his letters do not survive) must have told her that the "Alabaster" poem lacked form, that it was imperfectly rhymed and its metric beat spasmodic, a judgment which would have been shared at the time by most of the fraternity of literary appraisers. The unorthodoxy of melodic pattern controlled by key words, wherein the parts express the whole, the altering of metric beat to slow or speed the nature of time itself (the theme of the "Alabaster" poem), give it dimensions which he was not equipped to estimate. He was trying to measure a cube by the rules of plane geometry.

The first weeks of this letter exchange were critical in Emily Dickinson's literary life. Putting aside for the moment the issue whether she wished to see her poetry published (though the fact that she wrote in response to an article on how to contribute to magazines suggests the possibility), one sees that she clearly is asking whether a professional critic thinks her way of writing poetry is valid. His answer must have implied that it was scarcely comprehensible. The nature of decisions thus forced upon her becomes clear. In the first place, when she wrote the letter, she had composed no fewer than three hundred poems. (Her comment to Higginson that she had written "no verse — but one or two — until this winter" was her answer to his query about her age!) She was so possessed by creative forces that within another year she had doubled that number. For the moment she is pausing to inquire whether she is alone in believing that what she has been striving for is worth attempting.

The second letter to Higginson, written ten days later, enclosed three poems: "South Winds jostle them" (86), "Of all the Sounds despatched abroad" (321), and "There came a Day at Summer's full" (322). Like the previous four they were selected for their range of theme and prosodic variety. The lapse of six weeks before she wrote again, in view of the nature of the third letter, suggests that between April 25 and June 7 she accepted her destiny as an artist who in her lifetime would remain unknown, for in assenting to his verdict she unwaveringly charts her course:

> I smile when you suggest that I delay "to publish" — that being foreign to my thought, as Firmament to Fin.
> If fame belonged to me, I could not escape her — if she did not, the longest day would pass me on the chase — and the approbation of my Dog, would forsake me — then. My Barefoot-Rank is better.
> You think my gait "spasmodic." I am in danger, Sir.
> You think me "uncontrolled." I have no Tribunal. . . .
> The Sailor cannot see the North, but knows the Needle can.

Though Emily Dickinson kept up the fiction of being Higginson's "scholar" for the rest of her life, she would never expect Higginson or anyone else to think her a poet, or do more than thank her, as at one time he pointedly did, for her "beautiful thoughts and words." Thenceforth she contented herself by enclosing or incorporating verses from time to time in letters to friends. The number thus communicated was but a minuscule fraction of what she was writing, and since the selections were made for particular occasions, they seldom reveal the intellectual and emotional depths she could plumb. Her growing preoccupation with the subject of fame is a striking characteristic of the poems written between 1862 and 1865. The dedication to her art had begun before she wrote to Higginson. It was a dedication that led to renunciation of fame in her lifetime and, as the wellsprings of her creativeness dried up after 1865, to increasing seclusion. There is strong evidence, nonetheless, that she came to think of herself as a public name in the fact that six times, between the years 1866 and 1872, she signed letters to Higginson simply "Dickinson." Among the most interesting of her poems on the subject of renown are "Some work for Immortality" (406), "Publication is the Auction/ Of the Mind of Man" (709), and "Fame of Myself, to justify" (713).

Marshaling the data, one observes a pattern somewhat as follows: From her youth Emily Dickinson had been writing poetry, and the realization of her destiny as a poet who must during her lifetime expect to maintain a "Barefoot-Rank" came in 1862. Meanwhile, probably in 1858, she winnowed her earlier verses, transcribing those she chose to save into the earliest of the famous packets. Always in ink, the packets are gatherings of four, five, or six sheets of folded stationery loosely held together by thread looped through them in the spine, at two points equidistant from the top and bottom. Of the forty-nine packets, forty-six appear to include all the verses written beween 1858 and 1865, the years of great creativeness. Three were assembled later (about 1866, 1871, and 1872). All of the packet poems are either fair copies or semifinal drafts (mostly fair copies), and they constitute two thirds of the entire body of her poetry. The increasing momentum after 1860 reached its peak in 1862 and sustained its full power for three more years.* Thereafter throughout her life Emily Dickinson continued to write poetry, but never again with the urgency she experienced in the early 1860's, when she fully developed her "flood subjects" on the themes of living and dying. With paradoxes of extraor-

---

* The assigning of packets to a given year must always remain tentative, for, in want of other evidence, it is based upon a study of the characteristic changes of the handwriting, analyzed fully in the introduction to *The Poems of Emily Dickinson* (3 vols., 1955). The number of packet poems for the years 1858-1865 at present is estimated as follows:

1858	51
1859	93
1860	63
1861	85
1862	366
1863	140
1864	172
1865	84

dinary insight she repeatedly gives relationship to the ideas and experi-
ence which exist in time but never are a part of it.

AT the time of her death in 1886, Emily Dickinson left in manuscript
a body of verse far more extensive than anyone imagined. Cared for
by a servant, Emily and her sister Lavinia had been living together in
the Amherst house built by their grandfather Dickinson, alone after
their mother's death in 1882. On going through her sister's effects,
Lavinia discovered a small box containing about 900 poems. These
were the sixty little "volumes," as Lavinia called them, "tied together
with twine," that constitute the packets. Determined that she must
find a publisher for them, she persuaded Mabel Loomis Todd, the
wife of an Amherst professor, to undertake the task of transcribing
them. Mrs. Todd enlisted the aid of Thomas Wentworth Higginson,
and together they made a selection of 115 poems for publication. But
Colonel Higginson was apprehensive about the willingness of the
public to accept the poems as they stood. Therefore in preparing copy
for the printer he undertook to smooth rhymes, regularize the meter,
delete provincialisms, and substitute "sensible" metaphors. Thus
"folks" became "those," "heft" became "weight," and occasionally line
arrangement was altered.

The publication of *Poems by Emily Dickinson* by Roberts Brothers
of Boston nevertheless proved to be one of the literary events of 1890,
and the reception of the slender volume encouraged the editors to
select 166 more verses, issued a year later as *Poems, Second Series*.
These likewise were warmly received. In 1896 Mrs. Todd alone
edited *Poems, Third Series*, bringing the total number published to
449, and together with 102 additional poems and parts of poems in-
cluded in Mrs. Todd's edition of *Letters of Emily Dickinson* (1894),
they constituted the Dickinson canon until 1914, when Emily Dickin-
son's niece and literary heir, Martha Dickinson Bianchi, issued *The
Single Hound*.

By now the public had come to appreciate the quality of Dickinson's
originalities, and alterations in the text of *The Single Hound* are re
freshingly few. But Mrs. Bianchi sometimes had trouble reading the
manuscripts, and on occasion words or phrases were misread, in that
volume and in the two later ones which completed publication of all
the verses in Mrs. Bianchi's possession: *Further Poems* (1929) and

Unpublished Poems (1935). The appearance of *Bolts of Melody* (1945), from texts prepared by Mrs. Todd and her daughter, Millicent Todd Bingham, virtually completed publication of all the Dickinson poetry, and marked a new era in textual fidelity. It presented 668 poems and fragments, deriving from transcripts made by Mrs. Todd, or from manuscripts which had remained among her papers.

Clearly the time had come to present the Dickinson poetry in an unreconstructed text and with some degree of chronological arrangement, and that opportunity was presented in 1950 when ownership of Emily Dickinson's literary estate was transferred to Harvard University. Editing then began on the variorum text of *The Poems of Emily Dickinson,* which I prepared for the Belknap Press of Harvard University Press (3 vols., 1955), comprising a total of 1775 poems and fragments.

The text for this edition of *The Complete Poems of Emily Dickinson* reproduces solely and completely that of the 1955 variorum edition, but intended as a reading text, it selects but one form of each poem. Inevitably therefore one is forced to make some editorial decisions about a text which never was prepared by the author as copy for the printer. Rare instances exist, notably in the poem "Blazing in gold" (228), where no text can be called "final." That poem describes a sunset which in one version stoops as low as "the kitchen window"; in another, as low as an "oriel window"; in a third, as low as "the Otter's Window." These copies were made over a period of five years, from 1861 to 1866, and one text is apparently as "final" as another. The reader may make the choice.

Selection becomes mandatory for the semifinal drafts. Though by far the largest number of packet copies exist in but a single fair-copy version, several exist in semifinal form: those for which marginally the poet suggested an alternate reading for one word or more. In order to keep editorial construction to a bare minimum, I have followed the policy of adopting such suggestions only when they are underlined, presumably Emily Dickinson's method of indicating her own preference.

Rough drafts, of which there are relatively few, are allowed to stand as such, with no editorial tinkering.

I have silently corrected obvious misspelling (*witheld, visiter,* etc.), and misplaced apostrophes (*does'nt*). Punctuation and capitalization remain unaltered. Dickinson used dashes as a musical device, and though some may be elongated end stops, any "correction" would be gratuitous. Capitalization, though often capricious, is likewise untouched.

The date at the left, following each poem, is that conjectured for the earliest known manuscript; that to the right is the date of first publication. The order of the poems is that of the Harvard (variorum) edition. There, where all copies of poems are reproduced, fair copies to recipients are chosen for principal representation. Thus, in this volume, for instance, the poems sent to T. W. Higginson in 1862 (nos. 318-327) range in date from 1858 to 1862. This seeming irregularity is necessary to preserve the numerical order of the poems.

Contents

INTRODUCTION   V

POEMS   3

ACKNOWLEDGMENTS   717

PREVIOUS COLLECTIONS   719

SUBJECT INDEX   723

INDEX OF FIRST LINES   737

THE COMPLETE POEMS OF
Emily Dickinson

Valentine week, 1850

Awake ye muses nine, sing me a strain divine,
Unwind the solemn twine, and tie my Valentine!

Oh the Earth was *made* for lovers, for damsel, and hopeless swain,
For sighing, and gentle whispering, and *unity* made of *twain.*
All things do go a courting, in earth, or sea, or air,
God hath made nothing single but *thee* in His world so fair!
The *bride,* and then the *bridegroom,* the *two,* and then the *one,*
Adam, and Eve, his consort, the moon, and then the sun;
The life doth prove the precept, who obey shall happy be,
Who will not serve the sovereign, be hanged on fatal tree.
The high do seek the lowly, the great do seek the small,
None cannot find who *seeketh,* on this terrestrial ball;
The bee doth court the flower, the flower his suit receives,
And they make merry wedding, whose guests are hundred leaves;
The wind doth woo the branches, the branches they are won,
And the father fond demandeth the maiden for his son.
The storm doth walk the seashore humming a mournful tune,
The wave with eye so pensive, looketh to see the moon,
Their spirits meet together, they make them solemn vows,
No more he singeth mournful, her sadness she doth lose.
The *worm* doth woo the *mortal,* death claims a living bride,
Night unto day is married, morn unto eventide;
Earth is a merry damsel, and *heaven* a knight so true,
And Earth is quite coquettish, and beseemeth in vain to sue.
Now to the *application,* to the reading of the roll,
To bringing thee to justice, and marshalling thy soul:
Thou art a *human* solo, a being cold, and lone,
Wilt have no kind companion, thou *reap'st* what thou hast *sown.*
Hast never silent hours, and minutes all too long,
And a deal of sad reflection, and *wailing* instead of song?

There's *Sarah,* and *Eliza,* and *Emeline* so fair,
And *Harriet,* and *Susan,* and she with *curling hair!*
Thine eyes are sadly blinded, but yet thou mayest see
Six true, and comely maidens sitting upon the tree;
Approach that tree with caution, then up it boldly climb,
And seize the one thou lovest, nor care for *space,* or *time!*
Then bear her to the greenwood, and build for her a bower,
And give her what she asketh, jewel, or bird, or flower –
And bring the fife, and trumpet, and beat upon the drum –
And bid the world Goodmorrow, and go to glory home!

1850   *1894*

2

There is another sky,
Ever serene and fair,
And there is another sunshine,
Though it be darkness there;
Never mind faded forests, Austin,
Never mind silent fields –
Here is a little forest,
Whose leaf is ever green;
Here is a brighter garden,
Where not a frost has been;
In its unfading flowers
I hear the bright bee hum;
Prithee, my brother,
Into *my* garden come!

1851   *1894*

3

"Sic transit gloria mundi,"
    "How doth the busy bee,"
"Dum vivimus vivamus,"
    I stay mine enemy!

Oh "veni, vidi, vici!"
    Oh caput cap-a-pie!

[4]

And oh "memento mori"
　　When I am *far* from thee!

Hurrah for Peter Parley!
　　Hurrah for Daniel Boone!
Three cheers, sir, for the gentleman
　　Who first observed the moon!

Peter, put up the sunshine;
　　Patti, arrange the stars;
Tell Luna, *tea* is waiting,
　　And call your brother Mars!

Put down the apple, Adam,
　　And come away with me,
So shalt thou have a *pippin*
　　From off my father's tree!

I climb the "Hill of Science,"
　　I "view the landscape o'er;"
Such transcendental prospect,
　　I ne'er beheld before!

Unto the Legislature
　　My country bids me go;
I'll take my *india rubbers*,
　　In case the *wind* should blow!

During my education,
　　It was announced to me
That *gravitation*, *stumbling*,
　　Fell from an *apple* tree!

The earth upon an axis
　　Was once supposed to turn,
By way of a *gymnastic*
　　In honor of the sun!

It *was* the brave Columbus,
　　A sailing o'er the tide,
Who notified the nations
　　Of where I would reside!

Mortality is fatal –
   Gentility is fine,
Rascality, heroic,
   Insolvency, sublime!

Our Fathers being weary,
   Laid down on Bunker Hill;
And tho' full many a morning,
   Yet they are sleeping still, –

The trumpet, sir, shall wake them,
   In dreams I see them rise,
Each with a solemn musket
   A marching to the skies!

A coward will remain, Sir,
   Until the fight is done;
But an *immortal hero*
   Will take his hat, and run!

Good bye, Sir, I am going;
   My country calleth me;
Allow me, Sir, at parting,
   To wipe my weeping e'e.

In token of our friendship
   Accept this "Bonnie Doon,"
And when the hand that plucked it
   Hath passed beyond the moon,

The memory of my ashes
   Will consolation be;
Then, farewell, Tuscarora,
   And farewell, Sir, to thee!

St. Valentine – '52   *1852*

4

   On this wondrous sea
   Sailing silently,
   Ho! Pilot, ho!

[6]

Knowest thou the shore
Where no breakers roar –
Where the storm is o'er?

In the peaceful west
Many the sails at rest –
The anchors fast –
Thither I pilot *thee* –
Land Ho! Eternity!
Ashore at last!

1853   *1896*

5

I have a Bird in spring
Which for myself doth sing –
The spring decoys.
And as the summer nears –
And as the Rose appears,
Robin is gone.

Yet do I not repine
Knowing that Bird of mine
Though flown –
Learneth beyond the sea
Melody new for me
And will return.

Fast in a safer hand
Held in a truer Land
Are mine –
And though they now depart,
Tell I my doubting heart
They're thine.

In a serener Bright,
In a more golden light
I see
Each little doubt and fear,
Each little discord here
Removed.

[7]

Then will I not repine,
Knowing that Bird of mine
Though flown
Shall in a distant tree
Bright melody for me
Return.

1854   1932

6

Frequently the woods are pink –
Frequently are brown.
Frequently the hills undress
Behind my native town.
Oft a head is crested
I was wont to see –
And as oft a cranny
Where it used to be –
And the Earth – they tell me –
On its Axis turned!
Wonderful Rotation!
By but *twelve* performed!

c. 1858   1891

7

The feet of people walking home
With gayer sandals go –
The Crocus – till she rises
The Vassal of the snow –
The lips at Hallelujah
Long years of practise bore
Till bye and bye these Bargemen
Walked singing on the shore.

Pearls are the Diver's farthings
Extorted from the Sea –
Pinions – the Seraph's wagon
Pedestrian once – as we –

[8]

Night is the morning's Canvas
Larceny – legacy –
Death, but our rapt attention
To Immortality.

My figures fail to tell me
How far the Village lies –
Whose peasants are the Angels –
Whose Cantons dot the skies –
My Classics veil their faces –
My faith that Dark adores –
Which from its solemn abbeys
Such resurrection pours.

c. 1858   *1914*

8

There is a word
Which bears a sword
Can pierce an armed man –
It hurls its barbed syllables
And is mute again –
But where it fell
The saved will tell
On patriotic day,
Some epauletted Brother
Gave his breath away.

Wherever runs the breathless sun –
Wherever roams the day –
There is its noiseless onset –
There is its victory!
Behold the keenest marksman!
The most accomplished shot!
Time's sublimest target
Is a soul "forgot!"

c. 1858   *1896*

Through lane it lay – through bramble –
Through clearing and through wood –
Banditti often passed us
Upon the lonely road.

The wolf came peering curious –
The owl looked puzzled down –
The serpent's satin figure
Glid stealthily along –

The tempests touched our garments –
The lightning's poinards gleamed –
Fierce from the Crag above us
The hungry Vulture screamed –

The satyr's fingers beckoned –
The valley murmured "Come" –
These were the mates –
This was the road
These children fluttered home.

c. 1858   *1924*

My wheel is in the dark!
I cannot see a spoke
Yet know its dripping feet
Go round and round.

My foot is on the Tide!
An unfrequented road –
Yet have all roads
A clearing at the end –

Some have resigned the Loom –
Some in the busy tomb
Find quaint employ –

Some with new – stately feet –
Pass royal through the gate –

Flinging the problem back
At you and I!

c. 1858

1914

11

I never told the buried gold
Upon the hill – that lies –
I saw the sun – his plunder done
Crouch low to guard his prize.

He stood as near
As stood you here –
A pace had been between –
Did but a snake bisect the brake
My life had forfeit been.

That was a wondrous booty –
I hope 'twas honest gained.
Those were the fairest ingots
That ever kissed the spade!

Whether to keep the secret –
Whether to reveal –
Whether as I ponder
Kidd will sudden sail –

Could a shrewd advise me
We might e'en divide –
Should a shrewd betray me –
Atropos decide!

c. 1858

1914

12

The morns are meeker than they were –
The nuts are getting brown –
The berry's cheek is plumper –
The Rose is out of town.

The Maple wears a gayer scarf –
The field a scarlet gown –

Lest I should be old fashioned
I'll put a trinket on.

c. 1858   *1890*

13

Sleep is supposed to be
By souls of sanity
The shutting of the eye.

Sleep is the station grand
Down which, on either hand
The hosts of witness stand!

Morn is supposed to be
By people of degree
The breaking of the Day.

Morning has not occurred!

That shall Aurora be –
East of Eternity –
One with the banner gay –
One in the red array –
That is the break of Day!

c. 1858   *1890*

14

One Sister have I in our house,
And one, a hedge away.
There's only one recorded,
But both belong to me.

One came the road that I came –
And wore my last year's gown –
The other, as a bird her nest,
Builded our hearts among.

She did not sing as we did –
It was a different tune –

Herself to her a music
As Bumble bee of June.

Today is far from Childhood –
But up and down the hills
I held her hand the tighter –
Which shortened all the miles –

And still her hum
The years among,
Deceives the Butterfly;
Still in her Eye
The Violets lie
Mouldered this many May.

I spilt the dew –
But took the morn –
I chose this single star
From out the wide night's numbers –
Sue – forevermore!

1858   *1914*

15

The Guest is gold and crimson –
An Opal guest and gray –
Of Ermine is his doublet –
His Capuchin gay –

He reaches town at nightfall –
He stops at every door –
Who looks for him at morning
I pray him too – explore
The Lark's pure territory –
Or the Lapwing's shore!

c. 1858   *1932*

16

I would distil a cup,
And bear to all my friends,

Drinking to her no more astir,
By beck, or burn, or moor!

c. 1858   1894

17

Baffled for just a day or two –
Embarrassed – not afraid –
Encounter in my garden
An unexpected Maid.

She beckons, and the woods start –
She nods, and all begin –
Surely, such a country
I was never in!

c. 1858   1945

18

The Gentian weaves her fringes –
The Maple's loom is red –
My departing blossoms
        Obviate parade.

A brief, but patient illness –
An hour to prepare,
And one below this morning
Is where the angels are –
It was a short procession,
The Bobolink was there –
An aged Bee addressed us –
And then we knelt in prayer –
We trust that she was willing –
We ask that we may be.
Summer – Sister – Seraph!
Let us go with thee!

In the name of the Bee –
And of the Butterfly –
And of the Breeze – Amen!

c. 1858   1891

A sepal, petal, and a thorn
Upon a common summer's morn –
A flask of Dew – A Bee or two –
A Breeze – a caper in the trees –
And I'm a Rose!

c. 1858

1896

20

Distrustful of the Gentian –
And just to turn away,
The fluttering of her fringes
Chid my perfidy –
Weary for my –––––––
I will singing go –
I shall not feel the sleet – then –
I shall not fear the snow.

Flees so the phantom meadow
Before the breathless Bee –
So bubble brooks in deserts
On Ears that dying lie –
Burn so the Evening Spires
To Eyes that Closing go –
Hangs so distant Heaven –
To a hand below.

c. 1858

1945

21

We lose – because we win –
Gamblers – recollecting which
Toss their dice again!

c. 1858

1945

All these my banners be.
I sow my pageantry
In May –
It rises train by train –
Then sleeps in state again –
My chancel – all the plain
    Today.

To lose – if one can find again –
To miss – if one shall meet –
The Burglar cannot rob – then –
The Broker cannot cheat.
So build the hillocks gaily
Thou little spade of mine
Leaving nooks for Daisy
And for Columbine –
You and I the secret
Of the Crocus know –
Let us chant it softly –
"*There* is no more snow!"

To him who keeps an Orchis' heart –
The swamps are pink with June.

c. 1858   1945

23

I had a guinea golden –
I lost it in the sand –
And tho' the sum was simple
And pounds were in the land –
Still, had it such a value
Unto my frugal eye –
That when I could not find it –
I sat me down to sigh.

I had a crimson Robin –
Who sang full many a day
But when the woods were painted,
He, too, did fly away –

[16]

Time brought me other Robins –
Their ballads were the same –
Still, for my missing Troubadour
I kept the "house at hame."

I had a star in heaven –
One "Pleiad" was its name –
And when I was not heeding,
It wandered from the same.
And tho' the skies are crowded –
And all the night ashine –
I do not care about it –
Since none of them are mine.

My story has a moral –
I have a missing friend –
"Pleiad" its name, and Robin,
And guinea in the sand.
And when this mournful ditty
Accompanied with tear –
Shall meet the eye of traitor
In country far from here –
Grant that repentance solemn
May seize upon his mind –
And he no consolation
Beneath the sun may find.

c. 1858   *1896*

24

There is a morn by men unseen –
Whose maids upon remoter green
Keep their Seraphic May –
And all day long, with dance and game,
And gambol I may never name –
Employ their holiday.

Here to light measure, move the feet
Which walk no more the village street –
Nor by the wood are found –

[17]

Here are the birds that sought the sun
When last year's distaff idle hung
And summer's brows were bound.

Ne'er saw I such a wondrous scene –
Ne'er such a ring on such a green –
Nor so serene array –
As if the stars some summer night
Should swing their cups of Chrysolite –
And revel till the day –

Like thee to dance – like thee to sing –
People upon the mystic green –
I ask, each new May Morn.
I wait thy far, fantastic bells –
Announcing me in other dells –
Unto the different dawn!

c. 1858   *1945*

25

She slept beneath a tree –
Remembered but by me.
I touched her Cradle mute –
She recognized the foot –
Put on her carmine suit
            And see!

c. 1858   *1896*

26

It's all I have to bring today –
This, and my heart beside –
This, and my heart, and all the fields –
And all the meadows wide –
Be sure you count – should I forget
Some one the sum could tell –

This, and my heart, and all the Bees
Which in the Clover dwell.

c. *1858*

1896

27

Morns like these – we parted –
Noons like these – she rose –
Fluttering first – then firmer
To her fair repose.

Never did she lisp it –
It was not for me –
She – was mute from transport –
I – from agony –

Till – the evening nearing
One the curtains drew –
Quick! A Sharper rustling!
And this linnet flew!

c. *1858*

1891

28

So has a Daisy vanished
From the fields today –
So tiptoed many a slipper
To Paradise away –

Oozed so in crimson bubbles
Day's departing tide –
Blooming – tripping – flowing –
Are ye then with God?

c. *1858*

1945

29

If those I loved were lost
The Crier's voice would tell me –
If those I loved were found
The bells of Ghent would ring –

Did those I loved repose
The Daisy would impel me.
Philip – when bewildered
Bore his riddle in!

c. 1858

1945

30

Adrift! A little boat adrift!
And night is coming down!
Will *no* one guide a little boat
Unto the nearest town?

So Sailors say – on yesterday –
Just as the dusk was brown
One little boat gave up its strife
And gurgled down and down.

So angels say – on yesterday –
Just as the dawn was red
One little boat – o'erspent with gales –
Retrimmed its masts – redecked its sails –
And shot – exultant on!

c. 1858

1896

31

Summer for thee, grant I may be
When Summer days are flown!
Thy music still, when Whippoorwill
And Oriole – are done!

For thee to bloom, I'll skip the tomb
And row my blossoms o'er!
Pray gather me –
Anemone –
Thy flower – forevermore!

c. 1858

1896

When Roses cease to bloom, Sir,
And Violets are done –
When Bumblebees in solemn flight
Have passed beyond the Sun –
The hand that paused to gather
Upon this Summer's day
Will idle lie – in Auburn –
Then take my flowers – pray!

c. 1858   *1896*

33

If recollecting were forgetting,
Then I remember not.
And if forgetting, recollecting,
How near I had forgot.
And if to miss, were merry,
And to mourn, were gay,
How very blithe the fingers
That gathered this, Today!

c. 1858   *1894*

34

Garlands for Queens, may be –
Laurels – for rare degree
Of soul or sword.
Ah – but remembering me –
Ah – but remembering thee –
Nature in chivalry –
Nature in charity –
Nature in equity –
The Rose ordained!

c. 1858   *1945*

35

Nobody knows this little Rose –
It might a pilgrim be
Did I not take it from the ways
And lift it up to thee.
Only a Bee will miss it –
Only a Butterfly,
Hastening from far journey –
On its breast to lie –
Only a Bird will wonder –
Only a Breeze will sigh –
Ah Little Rose – how easy
For such as thee to die!

c. 1858   *1891*

36

Snow flakes.

I counted till they danced so
Their slippers leaped the town,
And then I took a pencil
To note the rebels down.
And then they grew so jolly
I did resign the prig,
And ten of my once stately toes
Are marshalled for a jig!

c. 1858   *1945*

37

Before the ice is in the pools –
Before the skaters go,
Or any cheek at nightfall
Is tarnished by the snow –

Before the fields have finished,
Before the Christmas tree,
Wonder upon wonder
Will arrive to me!

What we touch the hems of
On a summer's day –
What is only walking
Just a bridge away –

That which sings so – speaks so –
When there's no one here –
Will the frock I wept in
Answer me to wear?

c. *1858*   *1896*

38

By such and such an offering
To Mr. So and So,
The web of life woven –
So martyrs albums show!

c. *1858*   *1945*

39

It did not surprise me –
So I said – or thought –
She will stir her pinions
And the nest forgot,

Traverse broader forests –
Build in gayer boughs,
Breathe in Ear more modern
God's old fashioned vows –

This was but a Birdling –
What and if it be
One within my bosom
Had departed me?

This was but a story –
What and if indeed
There were just such coffin
In the heart instead?

c. *1858*   *1945*

40

When I count the seeds
That are sown beneath,
To bloom so, bye and bye –

When I con the people
Lain so low,
To be received as high –

When I believe the garden
Mortal shall not see –
Pick by faith its blossom
And avoid its Bee,
I can spare this summer, unreluctantly.

c. 1858   *1945*

41

I robbed the Woods –
The trusting Woods.
The unsuspecting Trees
Brought out their Burs and mosses
My fantasy to please.
I scanned their trinkets curious –
I grasped – I bore away –
What will the solemn Hemlock –
What will the Oak tree say?

c. 1858   *1955*

42

A Day! Help! Help! Another Day!
Your prayers, oh Passer by!
From such a common ball as this
Might date a Victory!
From marshallings as simple
The flags of nations swang.
Steady – my soul: What issues
Upon thine arrow hang!

c. 1858   *1945*

Could live – *did* live –
Could die – *did* die –
Could smile upon the whole
Through faith in one he met not,
To introduce his soul.

Could go from scene familiar
To an untraversed spot –
Could contemplate the journey
With unpuzzled heart –

Such trust had one among us,
Among us *not* today –
We who saw the launching
Never sailed the Bay!

c. 1858   *1945*

If she had been the Mistletoe
And I had been the Rose –
How gay upon your table
My velvet life to close –
Since I am of the Druid,
And she is of the dew –
I'll deck Tradition's buttonhole –
And send the Rose to you.

c. 1858   *1894*

There's something quieter than sleep
Within this inner room!
It wears a sprig upon its breast –
And will not tell its name.

Some touch it, and some kiss it –
Some chafe its idle hand –

[25]

It has a simple gravity
I do not understand!

I would not weep if I were they –
How rude in one to sob!
Might scare the quiet fairy
Back to her native wood!

While simple-hearted neighbors
Chat of the "Early dead" –
We – prone to periphrasis,
Remark that Birds have fled!

c. 1858   *1896*

46

I keep my pledge.
I was not called –
Death did not notice me.
I bring my Rose.
I plight again,
By every sainted Bee –
By Daisy called from hillside –
By Bobolink from lane.
Blossom and I –
Her oath, and mine –
Will surely come again.

c. 1858   *1945*

47

Heart! We will forget him!
You and I – tonight!
You may forget the warmth he gave –
I will forget the light!

When you have done, pray tell me
That I may straight begin!
Haste! lest while you're lagging
I remember him!

c. 1858   *1896*

48

Once more, my now bewildered Dove
Bestirs her puzzled wings
Once more her mistress, on the deep
Her troubled question flings –

Thrice to the floating casement
The Patriarch's bird returned,
Courage! My brave Columba!
There may yet be *Land*!

c. 1858

1945

49

I never lost as much but twice,
And that was in the sod.
Twice have I stood a beggar
Before the door of God!

Angels – twice descending
Reimbursed my store –
Burglar! Banker – Father!
I am poor once more!

c. 1858

1890

50

I haven't told my garden yet –
Lest that should conquer me.
I haven't quite the strength now
To break it to the Bee –

I will not name it in the street
For shops would stare at me –
That one so shy – so ignorant
Should have the face to die.

The hillsides must not know it –
Where I have rambled so –
Nor tell the loving forests
The day that I shall go –

Nor lisp it at the table –
Nor heedless by the way
Hint that within the Riddle
One will walk today –

c. *1858*   *1891*

51

I often passed the village
When going home from school –
And wondered what they did there –
And why it was so still –

I did not know the year then –
In which my call would come –
Earlier, by the Dial,
Than the rest have gone.

It's stiller than the sundown.
It's cooler than the dawn –
The Daisies dare to come here –
And birds can flutter down –

So when you are tired –
Or perplexed – or cold –
Trust the loving promise
Underneath the mould,
Cry "it's I," "take Dollie,"
And I will enfold!

c. *1858*   *1945*

52

Whether my bark went down at sea –
Whether she met with gales –
Whether to isles enchanted
She bent her docile sails –

By what mystic mooring
She is held today –

This is the errand of the eye
Out upon the Bay.

c. 1858   *1890*

53

Taken from men – this morning –
Carried by men today –
Met by the Gods with banners –
Who marshalled her away –

One little maid – from playmates –
One little mind from school –
There must be guests in Eden –
All the rooms are full –

Far – as the East from Even –
Dim – as the border star –
Courtiers quaint, in Kingdoms
Our departed are.

c. 1858   *1891*

54

If I should die,
And you should live –
And time should gurgle on –
And morn should beam –
And noon should burn –
As it has usual done –
If Birds should build as early
And Bees as bustling go –
One might depart at option
From enterprise below!
'Tis sweet to know that stocks will stand
When we with Daisies lie –
That Commerce will continue –
And Trades as briskly fly –
It makes the parting tranquil
And keeps the soul serene –

That gentlemen so sprightly
Conduct the pleasing scene!

c. *1858*   *1891*

55

By Chivalries as tiny,
A Blossom, or a Book,
The seeds of smiles are planted –
Which blossom in the dark.

c. *1858*   *1945*

56

If I should cease to bring a Rose
Upon a festal day,
'Twill be because *beyond* the Rose
I have been called away –

If I should cease to take the names
My buds commemorate –
'Twill be because *Death's* finger
Claps my murmuring lip!

c. *1858*   *1945*

57

To venerate the simple days
Which lead the seasons by,
Needs but to remember
That from you or I,
They may take the trifle
Termed *mortality*!

c. *1858*   *1896*

58

Delayed till she had ceased to know –
Delayed till in its vest of snow
Her loving bosom lay –

An hour behind the fleeting breath –
Later by just an hour than Death –
Oh lagging Yesterday!

Could she have guessed that it would be –
Could but a crier of the joy
Have climbed the distant hill –
Had not the bliss so slow a pace
Who knows but this surrendered face
Were undefeated still?

Oh if there may departing be
Any forgot by Victory
In her imperial round –
Show them this meek appareled thing
That could not stop to be a king –
Doubtful if it be crowned!

c. 1859   *1890*

59

A little East of Jordan,
Evangelists record,
A Gymnast and an Angel
Did wrestle long and hard –

Till morning touching mountain –
And Jacob, waxing strong,
The Angel begged permission
To Breakfast – to return –

Not so, said cunning Jacob!
"I will not let thee go
Except thou bless me" – Stranger!
The which acceded to –

Light swung the silver fleeces
"Peniel" Hills beyond,
And the bewildered Gymnast
Found he had worsted God!

c. 1859   *1914*

Like her the Saints retire,
In their Chapeaux of fire,
Martial as she!

Like her the Evenings steal
Purple and Cochineal
After the Day!

"Departed" – both – they say!
i.e. gathered away,
Not found,

Argues the Aster still –
Reasons the Daffodil
Profound!

c. 1859   *1932*

Papa above!
Regard a Mouse
O'erpowered by the Cat!
Reserve within thy kingdom
A "Mansion" for the Rat!

Snug in seraphic Cupboards
To nibble all the day,
While unsuspecting Cycles
Wheel solemnly away!

c. 1859   *1914*

"Sown in dishonor"!
Ah! Indeed!
May *this* "dishonor" be?
If I were half so fine myself
I'd notice nobody!

[32]

"Sown in corruption"!
Not so fast!
Apostle is askew!
Corinthians 1. 15. narrates
A Circumstance or two!

c. *1859*   *1914*

63

If pain for peace prepares
Lo, what "Augustan" years
Our feet await!

If springs from winter rise,
Can the Anemones
Be reckoned up?

If night stands first – *then* noon
To gird us for the sun,
What gaze!

When from a thousand skies
On our *developed* eyes
Noons blaze!

c. *1859*   *1914*

64

Some Rainbow – coming from the Fair!
Some Vision of the World Cashmere –
I confidently see!
Or else a Peacock's purple Train
Feather by feather – on the plain
Fritters itself away!

The dreamy Butterflies bestir!
Lethargic pools resume the whir
Of last year's sundered tune!
From some old Fortress on the sun
Baronial Bees – march – one by one –
In murmuring platoon!

[33]

The Robins stand as thick today
As flakes of snow stood yesterday –
On fence – and Roof – and Twig!
The Orchis binds her feather on
For her old lover – Don the Sun!
Revisiting the Bog!

Without Commander! Countless! Still!
The Regiments of Wood and Hill
In bright detachment stand!
Behold! Whose Multitudes are these?
The children of whose turbaned seas –
Or what Circassian Land?

c. 1859   *1890*

65

I can't tell you – but you feel it –
Nor can you tell me –
Saints, with ravished slate and pencil
Solve our April Day!

Sweeter than a vanished frolic
From a vanished green!
Swifter than the hoofs of Horsemen
Round a Ledge of dream!

Modest, let us walk among it
With our faces veiled –
As they say polite Archangels
Do in meeting God!

Not for me – to prate about it!
Not for you – to say
To some fashionable Lady
"Charming April Day"!

Rather – Heaven's "Peter Parley"!
By which Children slow
To sublimer Recitation
Are prepared to go!

c. 1859   *1914*

So from the mould
Scarlet and Gold
Many a Bulb will rise –
Hidden away, cunningly,
From sagacious eyes.

So from Cocoon
Many a Worm
Leap so Highland gay,
Peasants like me,
Peasants like Thee
Gaze perplexedly!

c. *1859*   *1914*

Success is counted sweetest
By those who ne'er succeed.
To comprehend a nectar
Requires sorest need.

Not one of all the purple Host
Who took the Flag today
Can tell the definition
So clear of Victory

As he defeated – dying –
On whose forbidden ear
The distant strains of triumph
Burst agonized and clear!

c. *1859*   *1878*

Ambition cannot find him.
Affection doesn't know
How many leagues of nowhere
Lie between them now.

Yesterday, undistinguished!
Eminent Today
For our mutual honor,
Immortality!

c. 1859   1914

69

Low at my problem bending,
Another problem comes –
Larger than mine – Serener –
Involving statelier sums.

I check my busy pencil,
My figures file away.
Wherefore, my baffled fingers
Thy perplexity?

c. 1859   1914

70

"Arcturus" is his other name –
I'd rather call him "Star."
It's very mean of Science
To go and interfere!

I slew a worm the other day –
A "Savant" passing by
Murmured "Resurgam" – "Centipede"!
"Oh Lord – how frail are we"!

I pull a flower from the woods –
A monster with a glass
Computes the stamens in a breath –
And has her in a "class"!

Whereas I took the Butterfly
Aforetime in my hat –
He sits erect in "Cabinets" –
The Clover bells forgot.

What once was "Heaven"
Is "*Zenith*" now –
Where I proposed to go
When Time's brief masquerade was done
Is mapped and charted too.

What if the poles should frisk about
And stand upon their heads!
I hope I'm ready for "the worst" –
Whatever prank betides!

Perhaps the "Kingdom of Heaven's" changed –
I hope the "Children" there
Won't be "new fashioned" when I come –
And laugh at me – and stare –

I hope the Father in the skies
Will lift his little girl –
Old fashioned – naughty – everything –
Over the stile of "Pearl."

c. 1859   *1891*

71

A throe upon the features –
A hurry in the breath –
An ecstasy of parting
Denominated "Death" –

An anguish at the mention
Which when to patience grown,
I've known permission given
To rejoin its own.

c. 1859   *1891*

72

Glowing is her Bonnet,
Glowing is her Cheek,
Glowing is her Kirtle,
Yet she cannot speak.

[37]

Better as the Daisy
From the Summer hill
Vanish unrecorded
Save by tearful rill –

Save by loving sunrise
Looking for her face.
Save by feet unnumbered
Pausing at the place.

c. 1859   *1914*

73

Who never lost, are unprepared
A Coronet to find!
Who never thirsted
Flagons, and Cooling Tamarind!

Who never climbed the weary league –
Can such a foot explore
The purple territories
On Pizarro's shore?

How many Legions overcome –
The Emperor will say?
How many *Colors* taken
On Revolution Day?

How many *Bullets* bearest?
Hast Thou the Royal scar?
Angels! Write "Promoted"
On this Soldier's brow!

c. 1859   *1891*

74

A Lady red – amid the Hill
Her annual secret keeps!
A Lady white, within the Field
In placid Lily sleeps!

The tidy Breezes, with their Brooms
Sweep vale – and hill – and tree!
Prithee, My pretty Housewives!
Who may expected be?

The Neighbors do not yet suspect!
The Woods exchange a smile!
Orchard, and Buttercup, and Bird –
In such a little while!

And yet, how still the Landscape stands!
How nonchalant the Hedge!
As if the "Resurrection"
Were nothing very strange!

c. 1859   1896

75

She died at play,
Gambolled away
Her lease of spotted hours,
Then sank as gaily as a Turk
Upon a Couch of flowers.

Her ghost strolled softly o'er the hill
Yesterday, and Today,
Her vestments as the silver fleece –
Her countenance as spray.

c. 1859   1914

76

Exultation is the going
Of an inland soul to sea,
Past the houses – past the headlands –
Into deep Eternity –

Bred as we, among the mountains,
Can the sailor understand

The divine intoxication
Of the first league out from land?

c. 1859   *1890*

77

I never hear the word "escape"
Without a quicker blood,
A sudden expectation,
A flying attitude!

I never hear of prisons broad
By soldiers battered down,
But I tug childish at my bars
Only to fail again!

c. 1859   *1891*

78

A poor – torn heart – a tattered heart –
That sat it down to rest –
Nor noticed that the Ebbing Day
Flowed silver to the West –
Nor noticed Night did soft descend –
Nor Constellation burn –
Intent upon the vision
Of latitudes unknown.

The angels – happening that way
This dusty heart espied –
Tenderly took it up from toil
And carried it to God –
There – sandals for the Barefoot –
There – gathered from the gales –
Do the blue havens by the hand
Lead the wandering Sails.

c. 1859   *1891*

Going to Heaven!
I don't know when –
Pray do not ask me how!
Indeed I'm too astonished
To think of answering you!
Going to Heaven!
How dim it sounds!
And yet it will be done
As sure as flocks go home at night
Unto the Shepherd's arm!

Perhaps you're going too!
Who knows?
If you should get there first
Save just a little space for me
Close to the two I lost –
The smallest "Robe" will fit me
And just a bit of "Crown" –
For you know we do not mind our dress
When we are going home –

I'm glad I don't believe it
For it would stop my breath –
And I'd like to look a little more
At such a curious Earth!
I'm glad they did believe it
Whom I have never found
Since the mighty Autumn afternoon
I left them in the ground.

c. 1859   *1891*

80

Our lives are Swiss –
So still – so Cool –
Till some odd afternoon
The Alps neglect their Curtains
And we look farther on!

Italy stands the other side!
While like a guard between –
The solemn Alps –
The siren Alps
Forever intervene!

c. 1859   *1896*

81

We should not mind so small a flower –
Except it quiet bring
Our little garden that we lost
Back to the Lawn again.

So spicy her Carnations nod –
So drunken, reel her Bees –
So silver steal a hundred flutes
From out a hundred trees –

That whoso sees this little flower
By faith may clear behold
The Bobolinks around the throne
And Dandelions gold.

c. 1859   *1914*

82

Whose cheek is this?
What rosy face
Has lost a blush today?
I found her – "pleiad" – in the woods
And bore her safe away.

Robins, in the tradition
Did cover such with leaves,
But which the cheek –
And which the pall
My scrutiny deceives.

c. 1859   *1932*

Heart, not so heavy as mine
Wending late home –
As it passed my window
Whistled itself a tune –
A careless snatch – a ballad –
A ditty of the street –
Yet to my irritated Ear
An Anodyne so sweet –
It was as if a Bobolink
Sauntering this way
Carolled, and paused, and carolled –
Then bubbled slow away!
It was as if a chirping brook
Upon a dusty way –
Set bleeding feet to minuets
Without the knowing why!
Tomorrow, night will come again –
Perhaps, weary and sore –
Ah Bugle! By my window
I pray you pass once more.

c. 1859   *1891*

84

Her breast is fit for pearls,
But I was not a "Diver" –
Her brow is fit for thrones
But I have not a crest.
Her heart is fit for *home* –
I – a Sparrow – build there
Sweet of twigs and twine
My perennial nest.

c. 1859   *1894*

85

"They have not chosen me," he said,
"But I have chosen them!"

Brave – Broken hearted statement –
Uttered in Bethlehem!

I could not have told it,
But since *Jesus dared* –
Sovereign! Know a Daisy
Thy dishonor shared!

c. *1859*   *1894*

86

South Winds jostle them –
Bumblebees come –
Hover – hesitate –
Drink, and are gone –

Butterflies pause
On their passage Cashmere –
I – softly plucking,
Present them here!

c. *1859*   *1891*

87

A darting fear – a pomp – a tear –
A waking on a morn
To find that what one waked for,
Inhales the different dawn.

c. *1859*   *1945*

88

As by the dead we love to sit,
Become so wondrous dear –
As for the lost we grapple
Tho' all the rest are here –

In broken mathematics
We estimate our prize

Vast – in its fading ratio
To our penurious eyes!

c. 1859   1891

89

Some things that fly there be –
Birds – Hours – the Bumblebee –
Of these no Elegy.

Some things that stay there be –
Grief – Hills – Eternity –
Nor this behooveth me.

There are that resting, rise.
Can I expound the skies?
How still the Riddle lies!

c. 1859   1890

90

Within my reach!
I could have touched!
I might have chanced that way!
Soft sauntered thro' the village –
Sauntered as soft away!
So unsuspected Violets
Within the meadows go –
Too late for striving fingers
That passed, an hour ago!

c. 1859   1890

91

So bashful when I spied her!
So pretty – so ashamed!
So hidden in her leaflets
Lest anybody find –

So breathless till I passed her –
So helpless when I turned

[45]

And bore her struggling, blushing,
Her simple haunts beyond!

For whom I robbed the Dingle –
For whom betrayed the Dell –
Many, will doubtless ask me,
But I shall never tell!

c. 1859   1890

92

My friend must be a Bird –
Because it flies!
Mortal, my friend must be,
Because it dies!
Barbs has it, like a Bee!
Ah, curious friend!
Thou puzzlest me!

c. 1859   1896

93

Went up a year this evening!
I recollect it well!
Amid no bells nor bravoes
The bystanders will tell!
Cheerful – as to the village –
Tranquil – as to repose –
Chastened – as to the Chapel
This humble Tourist rose!
Did not talk of returning!
Alluded to no time
When, were the gales propitious –
We might look for him!
Was grateful for the Roses
In life's diverse bouquet –
Talked softly of new species
To pick another day;
Beguiling thus the wonder
The *wondrous* nearer drew –

Hands bustled at the moorings –
The crowd respectful grew –
Ascended from our vision
To Countenances new!
A Difference – A Daisy –
Is all the rest I knew!

c. 1859

1891

94

Angels, in the early morning
May be seen the Dews among,
Stooping – plucking – smiling – flying –
Do the Buds to them belong?

Angels, when the sun is hottest
May be seen the sands among,
Stooping – plucking – sighing – flying –
Parched the flowers they bear along.

c. 1859

1890

95

My nosegays are for Captives –
Dim – long expectant eyes,
Fingers denied the plucking,
Patient till Paradise.

To such, if they should whisper
Of morning and the moor,
They bear no other errand,
And I, no other prayer.

c. 1859

1891

96

Sexton! My Master's sleeping here.
Pray lead me to his bed!
I came to build the Bird's nest,
And sow the Early seed –

That when the snow creeps slowly
From off his chamber door –
Daisies point the way there –
And the Troubadour.

c. 1859   *1935*

97

The rainbow never tells me
That gust and storm are by,
Yet is she more convincing
Than Philosophy.

My flowers turn from Forums –
Yet eloquent declare
What Cato couldn't prove me
Except the *birds* were here!

c. 1859   *1929*

98

One dignity delays for all –
One mitred Afternoon –
None can avoid this purple –
None evade this Crown!

Coach, it insures, and footmen –
Chamber, and state, and throng –
Bells, also, in the village
As we ride grand along!

What dignified Attendants!
What service when we pause!
How loyally at parting
Their hundred hats they raise!

How pomp surpassing ermine
When simple You, and I,
Present our meek escutcheon
And claim the rank to die!

c. 1859   *1890*

New feet within my garden go –
New fingers stir the sod –
A Troubadour upon the Elm
Betrays the solitude.

New children play upon the green –
New Weary sleep below –
And still the pensive Spring returns –
And still the punctual snow!

c. 1859   *1890*

100

A science – so the Savants say,
"Comparative Anatomy" –
By which a single bone –
Is made a secret to unfold
Of some rare tenant of the mold,
Else perished in the stone –

So to the eye prospective led,
This meekest flower of the mead
Upon a winter's day,
Stands representative in gold
Of Rose and Lily, manifold,
And countless Butterfly!

c. 1859   *1929*

101

Will there really be a "Morning"?
Is there such a thing as "Day"?
Could I see it from the mountains
If I were as tall as they?

Has it feet like Water lilies?
Has it feathers like a Bird?
Is it brought from famous countries
Of which I have never heard?

Oh some Scholar! Oh some Sailor!
Oh some Wise Man from the skies!
Please to tell a little Pilgrim
Where the place called "Morning" lies!

c. 1859   1891

102

Great Caesar! Condescend
The Daisy, to receive,
Gathered by Cato's Daughter,
With your majestic leave!

c. 1859   1932

103

I have a King, who does not speak –
So – wondering – thro' the hours meek
I trudge the day away –
Half glad when it is night, and sleep,
If, haply, thro' a dream, to peep
In parlors, shut by day.

And if I do – when morning comes –
It is as if a hundred drums
Did round my pillow roll,
And shouts fill all my Childish sky,
And Bells keep saying "Victory"
From steeples in my soul!

And if I don't – the little Bird
Within the Orchard, is not heard,
And I omit to pray
"Father, thy will be done" today
For my will goes the other way,
And it were perjury!

c. 1859   1896

Where I have lost, I softer tread –
I sow sweet flower from garden bed –
I pause above that vanished head
     And mourn.

Whom I have lost, I pious guard
From accent harsh, or ruthless word –
Feeling as if their pillow heard,
     Though stone!

When I have lost, you'll know by this –
A Bonnet black – A dusk surplice –
A little tremor in my voice
     Like this!

Why, I have lost, the people know
Who dressed in frocks of purest snow
Went home a century ago
     Next Bliss!

c. 1859   1932

To hang our head – ostensibly –
And subsequent, to find
That such was not the posture
Of our immortal mind –

Affords the sly presumption
That in so dense a fuzz –
You – too – take Cobweb attitudes
Upon a plane of Gauze!

c. 1859   1896

The Daisy follows soft the Sun –
And when his golden walk is done –
Sits shyly at his feet –

He – waking – finds the flower there –
Wherefore – Marauder – art thou here?
Because, Sir, love is sweet!

We are the Flower – Thou the Sun!
Forgive us, if as days decline –
We nearer steal to Thee!
Enamored of the parting West –
The peace – the flight – the Amethyst –
Night's possibility!

c. *1859*   *1890*

107

'Twas such a little – little boat
That toddled down the bay!
'Twas such a gallant – gallant sea
That beckoned it away!

'Twas such a greedy, greedy wave
That licked it from the Coast –
Nor ever guessed the stately sails
My little craft was *lost*!

c. *1859*   *1890*

108

Surgeons must be very careful
When they take the knife!
Underneath their fine incisions
Stirs the Culprit – *Life*!

c. *1859*   *1891*

109

By a flower – By a letter –
By a nimble love –
If I weld the Rivet faster –
Final fast – above –

Never mind my breathless Anvil!
Never mind Repose!

[52]

Never mind the sooty faces
Tugging at the Forge!

c. *1859*

1932

110

Artists wrestled here!
Lo, a tint Cashmere!
Lo, a Rose!
Student of the Year!
For the easel here
Say Repose!

c. *1859*

1945

111

The Bee is not afraid of me.
I know the Butterfly.
The pretty people in the Woods
Receive me cordially –

The Brooks laugh louder when I come –
The Breezes madder play;
Wherefore mine eye thy silver mists,
Wherefore, Oh Summer's Day?

c. *1859*

1890

112

Where bells no more affright the morn –
Where scrabble never comes –
Where very nimble Gentlemen
Are forced to keep their rooms –

Where tired Children placid sleep
Thro' Centuries of noon
This place is Bliss – this town is Heaven –
Please, Pater, pretty soon!

"Oh could we climb where Moses stood,
And view the Landscape o'er"

Not Father's bells – nor Factories,
Could scare us any more!

c. 1859   *1945*

113

Our share of night to bear –
Our share of morning –
Our blank in bliss to fill
Our blank in scorning –

Here a star, and there a star,
Some lose their way!
Here a mist, and there a mist,
Afterwards – Day!

c. 1859   *1890*

114

Good night, because we must,
How intricate the dust!
I would go, to know!
Oh incognito!
Saucy, Saucy Seraph
To elude me so!
Father! they won't tell me,
Won't you tell them to?

c. 1859   *1945*

115

What Inn is this
Where for the night
Peculiar Traveller comes?
Who is the Landlord?
Where the maids?
Behold, what curious rooms!
No ruddy fires on the hearth –
No brimming Tankards flow –

Necromancer! Landlord!
Who are these below?

c. *1859*   *1891*

116

I had some things that I called mine –
And God, that he called his,
Till, recently a rival Claim
Disturbed these amities.

The property, my garden,
Which having sown with care,
He claims the pretty acre,
And sends a Bailiff there.

The station of the parties
Forbids publicity,
But Justice is sublimer
Than arms, or pedigree.

I'll institute an "Action" –
I'll vindicate the law –
Jove! Choose your counsel –
I retain "Shaw"!

c. *1859*   *1945*

117

In rags mysterious as these
The shining Courtiers go –
Veiling the purple, and the plumes –
Veiling the ermine so.

Smiling, as they request an alms –
At some imposing door!
Smiling when we walk barefoot
Upon their golden floor!

c. *1859*   *1945*

My friend attacks my friend!
Oh Battle picturesque!
Then I turn Soldier too,
And he turns Satirist!
How martial is this place!
Had I a mighty gun
I think I'd shoot the human race
And then to glory run!

c. *1859*

1945

119

Talk with prudence to a Beggar
Of "Potosi," and the mines!
Reverently, to the Hungry
Of your viands, and your wines!

Cautious, hint to any Captive
You have passed enfranchised feet!
Anecdotes of air in Dungeons
Have sometimes proved deadly sweet!

c. *1859*

1891

120

If this is "fading"
Oh let me immediately "fade"!
If this is "dying"
Bury me, in such a shroud of red!
If this is "sleep,"
On such a night
How proud to shut the eye!
Good Evening, gentle Fellow men!
Peacock presumes to die!

c. *1859*

1945

As Watchers hang upon the East,
As Beggars revel at a feast
By savory Fancy spread –
As brooks in deserts babble sweet
On ear too far for the delight,
Heaven beguiles the tired.

As that same watcher, when the East
Opens the lid of Amethyst
And lets the morning go –
That Beggar, when an honored Guest,
Those thirsty lips to flagons pressed,
Heaven to us, if true.

c. 1859   *1945*

A something in a summer's Day
As slow her flambeaux burn away
Which solemnizes me.

A something in a summer's noon –
A depth – an Azure – a perfume –
Transcending ecstasy.

And still within a summer's night
A something so transporting bright
I clap my hands to see –

Then veil my too inspecting face
Lest such a subtle – shimmering grace
Flutter too far for me –

The wizard fingers never rest –
The purple brook within the breast
Still chafes its narrow bed –

Still rears the East her amber Flag –
Guides still the Sun along the Crag
His Caravan of Red –

So looking on – the night – the morn
Conclude the wonder gay –
And I meet, coming thro' the dews
Another summer's Day!

c. 1859   *1890*

123

Many cross the Rhine
In this cup of mine.
Sip old Frankfort air
From my brown Cigar.

c. 1859   *1945*

124

In lands I never saw – they say
Immortal Alps look down –
Whose Bonnets touch the firmament –
Whose Sandals touch the town –

Meek at whose everlasting feet
A Myriad Daisy play –
Which, Sir, are you and which am I
Upon an August day?

c. 1859   *1891*

125

For each ecstatic instant
We must an anguish pay
In keen and quivering ratio
To the ecstasy.

For each beloved hour
Sharp pittances of years –
Bitter contested farthings –
And Coffers heaped with Tears!

c. 1859   *1891*

To fight aloud, is very brave –
But *gallanter*, I know
Who charge within the bosom
The Cavalry of Woe –

Who win, and nations do not see –
Who fall – and none observe –
Whose dying eyes, no Country
Regards with patriot love –

We trust, in plumed procession
For such, the Angels go –
Rank after Rank, with even feet –
And Uniforms of Snow.

c. 1859   *1890*

"Houses" – so the Wise Men tell me –
"Mansions"! Mansions must be warm!
Mansions cannot let the tears in,
Mansions must exclude the storm!

"Many Mansions," by "his Father,"
I don't know him; snugly built!
Could the Children find the way there –
Some, would even trudge tonight!

c. 1859   *1945*

Bring me the sunset in a cup,
Reckon the morning's flagons up
And say how many Dew,
Tell me how far the morning leaps –
Tell me what time the weaver sleeps
Who spun the breadths of blue!

Write me how many notes there be
In the new Robin's ecstasy
Among astonished boughs –
How many trips the Tortoise makes –
How many cups the Bee partakes,
The Debauchee of Dews!

Also, who laid the Rainbow's piers,
Also, who leads the docile spheres
By withes of supple blue?
Whose fingers string the stalactite –
Who counts the wampum of the night
To see that none is due?

Who built this little Alban House
And shut the windows down so close
My spirit cannot see?
Who'll let me out some gala day
With implements to fly away,
Passing Pomposity?

c. 1859   *1891*

129

Cocoon above! Cocoon below!
Stealthy Cocoon, why hide you so
What all the world suspect?
An hour, and gay on every tree
Your secret, perched in ecstasy
Defies imprisonment!

An hour in Chrysalis to pass,
Then gay above receding grass
A Butterfly to go!
A moment to interrogate,
Then wiser than a "Surrogate,"
The Universe to know!

c. 1859   *1935*

These are the days when Birds come back –
A very few – a Bird or two –
To take a backward look.

These are the days when skies resume
The old – old sophistries of June –
A blue and gold mistake.

Oh fraud that cannot cheat the Bee –
Almost thy plausibility
Induces my belief.

Till ranks of seeds their witness bear –
And softly thro' the altered air
Hurries a timid leaf.

Oh Sacrament of summer days,
Oh Last Communion in the Haze –
Permit a child to join.

Thy sacred emblems to partake –
Thy consecrated bread to take
And thine immortal wine!

c. 1859   *1890*

Besides the Autumn poets sing
A few prosaic days
A little this side of the snow
And that side of the Haze –

A few incisive Mornings –
A few Ascetic Eves –
Gone – Mr. Bryant's "Golden Rod" –
And Mr. Thomson's "sheaves."

Still, is the bustle in the Brook –
Sealed are the spicy valves –
Mesmeric fingers softly touch
The Eyes of many Elves –

Perhaps a squirrel may remain –
My sentiments to share –
Grant me, Oh Lord, a sunny mind –
Thy windy will to bear!

c. 1859   *1891*

132

I bring an unaccustomed wine
To lips long parching
Next to mine,
And summon them to drink;

Crackling with fever, they Essay,
I turn my brimming eyes away,
And come next hour to look.

The hands still hug the tardy glass –
The lips I would have cooled, alas –
Are so superfluous Cold –

I would as soon attempt to warm
The bosoms where the frost has lain
Ages beneath the mould –

Some other thirsty there may be
To whom this would have pointed me
Had it remained to speak –

And so I always bear the cup
If, haply, mine may be the drop
Some pilgrim thirst to slake –

If, haply, any say to me
"Unto the little, unto me,"
When I at last awake.

c. 1859   *1891*

133

As Children bid the Guest "Good Night"
And then reluctant turn –

[62]

My flowers raise their pretty lips –
Then put their nightgowns on.

As children caper when they wake
Merry that it is Morn –
My flowers from a hundred cribs
Will peep, and prance again.

c. 1859

1890

134

Perhaps you'd like to buy a flower,
But I could never sell –
If you would like to *borrow*,
Until the Daffodil

Unties her yellow Bonnet
Beneath the village door,
Until the Bees, from Clover rows
Their Hock, and Sherry, draw,

Why, I will lend until just then,
But not an hour more!

c. 1859

1890

135

Water, is taught by thirst.
Land – by the Oceans passed.
Transport – by throe –
Peace – by its battles told –
Love, by Memorial Mold –
Birds, by the Snow.

c. 1859

1896

136

Have you got a Brook in your little heart,
Where bashful flowers blow,
And blushing birds go down to drink,
And shadows tremble so –

And nobody knows, so still it flows,
That any brook is there,
And yet your little draught of life
Is daily drunken there –

Why, look out for the little brook in March,
When the rivers overflow,
And the snows come hurrying from the hills,
And the bridges often go –

And *later*, in *August* it may be –
When the meadows parching lie,
Beware, lest this little brook of life,
Some burning noon go dry!

c. 1859   *1890*

137

Flowers – Well – if anybody
Can the ecstasy define –
Half a transport – half a trouble –
With which flowers humble men:
Anybody find the fountain
From which floods so contra flow –
I will give him all the Daisies
Which upon the hillside blow.

Too much pathos in their faces
For a simple breast like mine –
Butterflies from St. Domingo
Cruising round the purple line –
Have a system of aesthetics –
Far superior to mine.

c. 1859   *1945*

138

Pigmy seraphs – gone astray –
Velvet people from Vevay –
Belles from some lost summer day –
Bees exclusive Coterie –

[64]

Paris could not lay the fold
Belted down with Emerald –
Venice could not show a cheek
Of a tint so lustrous meek –
Never such an Ambuscade
As of briar and leaf displayed
For my little damask maid –

I had rather wear her grace
Than an Earl's distinguished face –
I had rather dwell like her
Than be "Duke of Exeter" –
Royalty enough for me
To subdue the Bumblebee.

c. *1859*   *1891*

139

Soul, Wilt thou toss again?
By just such a hazard
Hundreds have lost indeed –
But tens have won an all –

Angel's breathless ballot
Lingers to record thee –
Imps in eager Caucus
Raffle for my Soul!

c. *1859*   *1890*

140

An altered look about the hills –
A Tyrian light the village fills –
A wider sunrise in the morn –
A deeper twilight on the lawn –
A print of a vermillion foot –
A purple finger on the slope –
A flippant fly upon the pane –
A spider at his trade again –
An added strut in Chanticleer –
A flower expected everywhere –

An axe shrill singing in the woods –
Fern odors on untravelled roads –
All this and more I cannot tell –
A furtive look you know as well –
And Nicodemus' Mystery
Receives its annual reply!

c. *1859*   *1891*

141

Some, too fragile for winter winds
The thoughtful grave encloses –
Tenderly tucking them in from frost
Before their feet are cold.

Never the treasures in her nest
The cautious grave exposes,
Building where schoolboy dare not look,
And sportsman is not bold.

This covert have all the children
Early aged, and often cold,
Sparrows, unnoticed by the Father –
Lambs for whom time had not a fold.

c. *1859*   *1891*

142

Whose are the little beds, I asked
Which in the valleys lie?
Some shook their heads, and others smiled –
And no one made reply.

Perhaps they did not hear, I said,
I will inquire again –
Whose are the beds – the tiny beds
So thick upon the plain?

'Tis Daisy, in the shortest –
A little further on –

[66]

Nearest the door – to wake the 1st –
Little Leontodon.

'Tis Iris, Sir, and Aster –
Anemone, and Bell –
Bartsia, in the blanket red –
And chubby Daffodil.

Meanwhile, at many cradles
Her busy foot she plied –
Humming the quaintest lullaby
That ever rocked a child.

Hush! Epigea wakens!
The Crocus stirs her lids –
Rhodora's cheek is crimson,
She's dreaming of the woods!

Then turning from them reverent –
Their bedtime 'tis, she said –
The Bumble bees will wake them
When April woods are red.

c. 1859   *1891*

143

For every Bird a Nest –
Wherefore in timid quest
Some little Wren goes seeking round –

Wherefore when boughs are free –
Households in every tree –
Pilgrim be found?

Perhaps a home too high –
Ah Aristocracy!
The little Wren desires –

Perhaps of twig so fine –
Of twine e'en superfine,
Her pride aspires –

The Lark is not ashamed
To build upon the ground
Her modest house –

Yet who of all the throng
Dancing around the sun
Does so rejoice?

c. *1859*   *1929*

144

She bore it till the simple veins
Traced azure on her hand –
Till pleading, round her quiet eyes
The purple Crayons stand.

Till Daffodils had come and gone
I cannot tell the sum,
And then she ceased to bear it –
And with the Saints sat down.

No more her patient figure
At twilight soft to meet –
No more her timid bonnet
Upon the village street –

But Crowns instead, and Courtiers –
And in the midst so fair,
Whose but her shy – immortal face
Of whom we're whispering here?

c. *1859*   *1935*

145

This heart that broke so long –
These feet that never flagged –
This faith that watched for star in vain,
Give gently to the dead –

Hound cannot overtake the Hare
That fluttered panting, here –

Nor any schoolboy rob the nest
Tenderness builded there.

c. 1859   *1935*

146

On such a night, or such a night,
Would anybody care
If such a little figure
Slipped quiet from its chair –

So quiet – Oh how quiet,
That nobody might know
But that the little figure
Rocked softer – to and fro –

On such a dawn, or such a dawn –
Would anybody sigh
That such a little figure
Too sound asleep did lie

For Chanticleer to wake it –
Or stirring house below –
Or giddy bird in orchard –
Or early task to do?

There was a little figure plump
For every little knoll –
Busy needles, and spools of thread –
And trudging feet from school –

Playmates, and holidays, and nuts –
And visions vast and small –
Strange that the feet so precious charged
Should reach so small a goal!

c. 1859   *1891*

147

Bless God, he went as soldiers,
His musket on his breast –

Grant God, he charge the bravest
Of all the martial blest!

Please God, might I behold him
In epauletted white –
I should not fear the foe then –
I should not fear the fight!

c. *1859*   *1896*

148

All overgrown by cunning moss,
All interspersed with weed,
The little cage of "Currer Bell"
In quiet "Haworth" laid.

Gathered from many wanderings –
Gethsemane can tell
Thro' what transporting anguish
She reached the Asphodel!

Soft fall the sounds of Eden
Upon her puzzled ear –
Oh what an afternoon for Heaven,
When "Bronte" entered there!

c. *1859*   *1896*

149

She went as quiet as the Dew
From an Accustomed flower.
Not like the Dew, did she return
At the Accustomed hour!

She dropt as softly as a star
From out my summer's Eve –
Less skillful than Le Verriere
It's sorer to believe!

c. *1859*   *1890*

She died – *this* was the way she died.
And when her breath was done
Took up her simple wardrobe
And started for the sun.
Her little figure at the gate
The Angels must have spied,
Since I could never find her
Upon the mortal side.

c. *1859*   *1891*

Mute thy Coronation –
Meek my Vive le roi,
Fold a tiny courtier
In thine Ermine, Sir,
There to rest revering
Till the pageant by,
I can murmur broken,
Master, It was I –

c. *1859*   *1945*

The Sun kept stooping – stooping – low!
The Hills to meet him rose!
On his side, what Transaction!
On their side, what Repose!

Deeper and deeper grew the stain
Upon the window pane –
Thicker and thicker stood the feet
Until the Tyrian

Was crowded dense with Armies –
So gay, so Brigadier –
That *I* felt martial stirrings
Who once the Cockade wore –

Charged, from my chimney corner –
But Nobody was there!

c. 1860   1945

153

Dust is the only Secret –
Death, the only One
You cannot find out all about
In his "native town."

Nobody knew "his Father" –
Never was a Boy –
Hadn't any playmates,
Or "Early history" –

Industrious! Laconic!
Punctual! Sedate!
Bold as a Brigand!
Stiller than a Fleet!

Builds, like a Bird, too!
Christ robs the Nest –
Robin after Robin
Smuggled to Rest!

c. 1860   1914

154

Except to Heaven, she is nought.
Except for Angels – lone.
Except to some wide-wandering Bee
A flower superfluous blown.

Except for winds – provincial.
Except by Butterflies
Unnoticed as a single dew
That on the Acre lies.

The smallest Housewife in the grass,
Yet take her from the Lawn

And somebody has lost the face
That made Existence – Home!

c. 1860

1890

155

The Murmur of a Bee
A Witchcraft – yieldeth me –
If any ask me why –
'Twere easier to die –
Than tell –

The Red upon the Hill
Taketh away my will –
If anybody sneer –
Take care – for God is here –
That's all.

The Breaking of the Day
Addeth to my Degree –
If any ask me how –
Artist – who drew me so –
Must tell!

c. 1860

1890

156

You love me – you are sure –
I shall not fear mistake –
I shall not *cheated* wake –
Some grinning morn –
To find the Sunrise left –
And Orchards – unbereft –
And Dollie – gone!

I need not start – you're sure –
That night will never be –
When frightened – home to Thee I run –
To find the windows dark –
And no more Dollie – mark –
Quite none?

Be sure you're sure – you know –
I'll bear it better now –
If you'll just tell me so –
Than when – a little dull Balm grown –
Over this pain of mine –
You sting – again!

c. 1860   1945

157

Musicians wrestle everywhere –
All day – among the crowded air
I hear the silver strife –
And – waking – long before the morn –
Such transport breaks upon the town
I think it that "New Life"!

It is not Bird – it has no nest –
Nor "Band" – in brass and scarlet – drest –
Nor Tamborin – nor Man –
It is not Hymn from pulpit read –
The "Morning Stars" the Treble led
On Time's first Afternoon!

Some – say – it is "the Spheres" – at play!
Some say that bright Majority
Of vanished Dames – and Men!
Some – think it service in the place
Where we – with late – celestial face –
Please God – shall Ascertain!

c. 1860   1891

158

Dying! Dying in the night!
Won't somebody bring the light
So I can see which way to go
Into the everlasting snow?

And "Jesus"! Where is *Jesus* gone?
They said that Jesus – always came –

Perhaps he doesn't know the House –
This way, Jesus, Let him pass!

Somebody run to the great gate
And see if Dollie's coming! Wait!
I hear her feet upon the stair!
Death won't hurt – now Dollie's here!

c. 1860   1945

159

A little bread – a crust – a crumb –
A little trust – a demijohn –
Can keep the soul alive –
Not portly, mind! but breathing – warm –
Conscious – as old Napoleon,
The night before the Crown!

A modest lot – A fame petite –
A brief Campaign of sting and sweet
Is plenty! Is enough!
A *Sailor's* business is *the shore*!
A *Soldier's* – *balls*! Who asketh more,
Must seek the neighboring life!

c. 1860   1896

160

Just lost, when I was saved!
Just felt the world go by!
Just girt me for the onset with Eternity,
When breath blew back,
And on the other side
I heard recede the disappointed tide!

Therefore, as One returned, I feel
Odd secrets of the line to tell!
Some Sailor, skirting foreign shores –
Some pale Reporter, from the awful doors
Before the Seal!

[75]

Next time, to stay!
Next time, the things to see
By Ear unheard,
Unscrutinized by Eye –

Next time, to tarry,
While the Ages steal –
Slow tramp the Centuries,
And the Cycles wheel!

c. 1860   *1891*

161

A feather from the Whippoorwill
That everlasting – sings!
Whose galleries – are Sunrise –
Whose Opera – the Springs –
Whose Emerald Nest the Ages spin
Of mellow – murmuring thread –
Whose Beryl Egg, what Schoolboys hunt
In "Recess" – Overhead!

c. 1860   *1894*

162

My River runs to thee –
Blue Sea! Wilt welcome me?
My River waits reply –
Oh Sea – look graciously –
I'll fetch thee Brooks
From spotted nooks –
Say – Sea – Take *Me*!

c. 1860   *1890*

163

Tho' my destiny be Fustian –
Hers be damask fine –
Tho' she wear a silver apron –
I, a less divine –

Still, my little Gypsy being
I would far prefer,
Still, my little sunburnt bosom
To her Rosier,

For, when Frosts, their punctual fingers
On her forehead lay,
You and I, and Dr. Holland,
Bloom Eternally!

Roses of a steadfast summer
In a steadfast land,
Where no Autumn lifts her pencil –
And no Reapers stand!

c. 1860   1894

164

Mama never forgets her birds,
Though in another tree –
She looks down just as often
And just as tenderly
As when her little mortal nest
With cunning care she wove –
If either of her "sparrows fall,"
She "notices," above.

c. 1860   1945

165

A *Wounded* Deer – leaps highest –
I've heard the Hunter tell –
'Tis but the Ecstasy of *death* –
And then the Brake is still!

The *Smitten* Rock that gushes!
The *trampled* Steel that springs!
A Cheek is always redder
Just where the Hectic stings!

[77]

Mirth is the Mail of Anguish –
In which it Cautious Arm,
Lest anybody spy the blood
And "you're hurt" exclaim!

c. 1860   1890

166

I met a King this afternoon!
He had not on a Crown indeed,
A little Palmleaf Hat was all,
And he was barefoot, I'm afraid!

But sure I am he Ermine wore
Beneath his faded Jacket's blue –
And sure I am, the crest he bore
Within that Jacket's pocket too!

For 'twas too stately for an Earl –
A Marquis would not go so grand!
'Twas possibly a Czar petite –
A Pope, or something of that kind!

If I must tell you, of a Horse
My freckled Monarch held the rein –
Doubtless an estimable Beast,
But not at all disposed to run!

And such a wagon! While I live
Dare I presume to see
Another such a vehicle
As then transported me!

Two other ragged Princes
His royal state partook!
Doubtless the first excursion
These sovereigns ever took!

I question if the Royal Coach
Round which the Footmen wait

Has the significance, on high,
Of this Barefoot Estate!

c. *1860*   *1893*

167

To learn the Transport by the Pain –
As Blind Men learn the sun!
To die of thirst – suspecting
That Brooks in Meadows run!

To stay the homesick – homesick feet
Upon a foreign shore –
Haunted by native lands, the while –
And blue – beloved air!

This is the Sovereign Anguish!
This – the signal woe!
These are the patient "Laureates"
Whose voices – trained – below –

Ascend in ceaseless Carol –
Inaudible, indeed,
To us – the duller scholars
Of the Mysterious Bard!

c. *1860*   *1891*

168

If the foolish, call them *"flowers"* –
Need the wiser, *tell?*
If the Savants "Classify" them
It is just as well!

Those who read the "Revelations"
Must not criticize
Those who read the same Edition –
With beclouded Eyes!

Could we stand with that Old "Moses" –
"Canaan" denied –

[79]

Scan like him, the stately landscape
On the other side –

Doubtless, we should deem superfluous
Many Sciences,
Not pursued by learned Angels
In scholastic skies!

Low amid that glad Belles lettres
Grant that we may stand,
Stars, amid profound *Galaxies* –
At that grand "Right hand"!

c. *1860*   *1896*

169

In Ebon Box, when years have flown
To reverently peer,
Wiping away the velvet dust
Summers have sprinkled there!

To hold a letter to the light –
Grown Tawny now, with time –
To con the faded syllables
That quickened us like Wine!

Perhaps a Flower's shrivelled cheek
Among its stores to find –
Plucked far away, some morning –
By gallant – mouldering hand!

A curl, perhaps, from foreheads
Our Constancy forgot –
Perhaps, an Antique trinket –
In vanished fashions set!

And then to lay them quiet back –
And go about its care –
As if the little Ebon Box
Were none of our affair!

c. *1860*   *1935*

Portraits are to daily faces
As an Evening West,
To a fine, pedantic sunshine –
In a satin Vest!

c. 1860

1891

171

Wait till the Majesty of Death
Invests so mean a brow!
Almost a powdered Footman
Might dare to touch it now!

Wait till in Everlasting Robes
That Democrat is dressed,
Then prate about "Preferment" –
And "Station," and the rest!

Around this quiet Courtier
Obsequious Angels wait!
Full royal is his Retinue!
Full purple is his state!

A Lord, might dare to lift the Hat
To such a Modest Clay
Since that My Lord, "the Lord of Lords"
Receives unblushingly!

c. 1860

1891

172

'Tis so much joy! 'Tis so much joy!
If I should fail, what poverty!
And yet, as poor as I,
Have ventured all upon a throw!
Have gained! Yes! Hesitated so –
This side the Victory!

Life is but Life! And Death, but Death!
Bliss is, but Bliss, and Breath but Breath!
And if indeed I fail,

At least, to know the worst, is sweet!
Defeat means nothing *but* Defeat,
No drearier, can befall!

And if I gain! Oh Gun at Sea!
Oh Bells, that in the Steeples be!
At first, repeat it slow!
For Heaven is a different thing,
Conjectured, and waked sudden in –
And might extinguish me!

c. 1860   *1890*

173

A fuzzy fellow, without feet,
Yet doth exceeding run!
Of velvet, is his Countenance,
And his Complexion, dun!

Sometime, he dwelleth in the grass!
Sometime, upon a bough,
From which he doth descend in plush
Upon the Passer-by!

All this in summer.
But when winds alarm the Forest Folk,
He taketh *Damask* Residence –
And struts in sewing silk!

Then, finer than a Lady,
Emerges in the spring!
A Feather on each shoulder!
You'd scarce recognize him!

By Men, yclept Caterpillar!
By me! But who am I,
To tell the pretty secret
Of the Butterfly!

c. 1860   *1929*

At last, to be identified!
At last, the lamps upon thy side
The rest of Life to *see*!

Past Midnight! Past the Morning Star!
Past Sunrise!
Ah, What leagues there *were*
Between our feet, and Day!

c. 1860   1890

I have never seen "Volcanoes" –
But, when Travellers tell
How those old – phlegmatic mountains
Usually so still –

Bear within – appalling Ordnance,
Fire, and smoke, and gun,
Taking Villages for breakfast,
And appalling Men –

If the stillness is Volcanic
In the human face
When upon a pain Titanic
Features keep their place –

If at length the smouldering anguish
Will not overcome –
And the palpitating Vineyard
In the dust, be thrown?

If some loving Antiquary,
On Resumption Morn,
Will not cry with joy "Pompeii"!
To the Hills return!

c. 1860   1945

I'm the little "Heart's Ease"!
I don't care for pouting skies!
If the Butterfly delay
Can I, therefore, stay away?

If the Coward Bumble Bee
In his chimney corner stay,
I, must resoluter be!
Who'll apologize for me?

Dear, Old fashioned, little flower!
Eden is old fashioned, too!
Birds are antiquated fellows!
Heaven does not change her blue.
Nor will I, the little Heart's Ease –
Ever be induced to do!

c. 1860   *1893*

Ah, Necromancy Sweet!
Ah, Wizard erudite!
Teach me the skill,

That I instil the pain
Surgeons assuage in vain,
Nor Herb of all the plain
Can heal!

c. 1860   *1929*

I cautious, scanned my little life –
I winnowed what would fade
From what would last till Heads like mine
Should be a-dreaming laid.

I put the latter in a Barn –
The former, blew away.

I went one winter morning
And lo – my priceless Hay

Was not upon the "Scaffold" –
Was not upon the "Beam" –
And from a thriving Farmer –
A Cynic, I became.

Whether a Thief did it –
Whether it was the wind –
Whether Deity's guiltless –
My business is, to find!

So I begin to ransack!
How is it Hearts, with Thee?
Art thou within the little Barn
Love provided Thee?

c. 1860   1929

179

If I could bribe them by a Rose
I'd bring them every flower that grows
From Amherst to Cashmere!
I would not stop for night, or storm –
Or frost, or death, or anyone –
My business were so dear!

If they would linger for a Bird
My Tambourin were soonest heard
Among the April Woods!
Unwearied, all the summer long,
Only to break in wilder song
When Winter shook the boughs!

What if they hear me!
Who shall say
That such an importunity
May not at last avail?

[85]

That, weary of this Beggar's face –
They may not finally say, Yes –
To drive her from the Hall?

c. 1860

1935

180

As if some little Arctic flower
Upon the polar hem –
Went wandering down the Latitudes
Until it puzzled came
To continents of summer –
To firmaments of sun –
To strange, bright crowds of flowers –
And birds, of foreign tongue!
I say, As if this little flower
To Eden, wandered in –
What then? Why nothing,
Only, your inference therefrom!

c. 1860

1890

181

I lost a World – the other day!
Has Anybody found?
You'll know it by the Row of Stars
Around its forehead bound.

A Rich man – might not notice it –
Yet – to my frugal Eye,
Of more Esteem than Ducats –
Oh find it – Sir – for me!

c. 1860

1890

182

If I shouldn't be alive
When the Robins come,
Give the one in Red Cravat,
A Memorial crumb.

If I couldn't thank you,
Being fast asleep,
You will know I'm trying
With my Granite lip!

c. 1860 *1890*

183

I've heard an Organ talk, sometimes
In a Cathedral Aisle,
And understood no word it said –
Yet held my breath, the while –

And risen up – and gone away,
A more Bernardine Girl –
Yet – know not what was done to me
In that old Chapel Aisle.

c. 1860 *1935*

184

A transport one cannot contain
May yet a transport be –
Though God forbid it lift the lid –
Unto its Ecstasy!

A Diagram – of Rapture!
A sixpence at a Show –
With Holy Ghosts in Cages!
The *Universe* would go!

c. 1860 *1935*

185

"Faith" is a fine invention
When Gentlemen can *see* –
But *Microscopes* are prudent
In an Emergency.

c. 1860 *1891*

What shall I do – it whimpers so –
This little Hound within the Heart
All day and night with bark and start –
And yet, it will not go –
Would you *untie* it, were you me –
Would it stop whining – if to Thee –
I sent it – even now?

It should not tease you –
By your chair – or, on the mat –
Or if it dare – to climb your dizzy knee –
Or – sometimes at your side to run –
When you were willing –
Shall it come?
Tell Carlo –
He'll tell *me*!

c. 1860   1945

How many times these low feet staggered –
Only the soldered mouth can tell –
Try – can you stir the awful rivet –
Try – can you lift the hasps of steel!

Stroke the cool forehead – hot so often –
Lift – if you care – the listless hair –
Handle the adamantine fingers
Never a thimble – more – shall wear –

Buzz the dull flies – on the chamber window –
Brave – shines the sun through the freckled pane –
Fearless – the cobweb swings from the ceiling –
Indolent Housewife – in Daisies – lain!

c. 1860   1890

Make me a picture of the sun –
So I can hang it in my room –
And make believe I'm getting warm
When others call it "Day"!

Draw me a Robin – on a stem –
So I am hearing him, I'll dream,
And when the Orchards stop their tune –
Put my pretense – away –

Say if it's really – warm at noon –
Whether it's Buttercups – that "skim" –
Or Butterflies – that "bloom"?
Then – skip – the frost – upon the lea –
And skip the Russet – on the tree –
Let's play those – never come!

c. 1860   1945

It's such a little thing to weep –
So short a thing to sigh –
And yet – by Trades – the size of *these*
We men and women die!

c. 1860   1896

He was weak, and I was strong – then –
So He let me lead him in –
I was weak, and He was strong then –
So I let him lead me – Home.

'Twasn't far – the door was near –
'Twasn't dark – for He went – too –
'Twasn't loud, for He said nought –
That was all I cared to know.

Day knocked – and we must part –
Neither – was strongest – now –

He strove – and I strove – too –
We didn't do it – tho'!

c. 1860 1945

191

The Skies can't keep their secret!
They tell it to the Hills –
The Hills just tell the Orchards –
And they – the Daffodils!

A Bird – by chance – that goes that way –
Soft overhears the whole –
If I should bribe the little Bird –
Who knows but *she* would tell?

I think I won't – however –
It's finer – not to know –
If Summer were *an Axiom* –
What sorcery had *Snow?*

So keep your secret – Father!
I would not – if I could,
Know what the Sapphire Fellows, do,
In your new-fashioned world!

c. 1860 1891

192

Poor little Heart!
Did they forget thee?
Then dinna care! Then dinna care!

Proud little Heart!
Did they forsake thee?
Be debonnaire! Be debonnaire!

Frail little Heart!
I would not break thee –
Could'st credit *me?* Could'st credit me?

[90]

Gay little Heart –
Like Morning Glory!
Wind and Sun – wilt thee array!

c. *1860*   *1896*

193

I shall know why – when Time is over –
And I have ceased to wonder why –
Christ will explain each separate anguish
In the fair schoolroom of the sky –

He will tell me what "Peter" promised –
And I – for wonder at his woe –
I shall forget the drop of Anguish
That scalds me now – that scalds me now!

c. *1860*   *1890*

194

On this long storm the Rainbow rose –
On this late Morn – the Sun –
The clouds – like listless Elephants –
Horizons – straggled down –

The Birds rose smiling, in their nests –
The gales – indeed – were done –
Alas, how heedless were the eyes –
On whom the summer shone!

The quiet nonchalance of death –
No Daybreak – can bestir –
The slow – Archangel's syllables
Must awaken *her*!

c. *1860*   *1890*

195

For this – accepted Breath –
Through it – compete with Death –
The fellow cannot touch this Crown –

By it – my title take –
Ah, what a royal sake
To my necessity – stooped down!

No Wilderness – can be
Where this attendeth me –
No Desert Noon –
No fear of frost to come
Haunt the perennial bloom –
But Certain June!

Get Gabriel – to tell – the royal syllable –
Get Saints – with new – unsteady tongue –
To say what trance below
Most like their glory show –
Fittest the Crown!

c. 1860   *1935*

196

We don't cry – Tim and I,
We are far too grand –
But we bolt the door tight
To prevent a friend –

Then we hide our brave face
Deep in our hand –
Not to cry – Tim and I –
We are far too grand –

Nor to dream – he and me –
Do we condescend –
We just shut our brown eye
To see to the end –

Tim – see Cottages –
But, Oh, so high!
Then – we shake – Tim and I –
And lest I – cry –

Tim – reads a little Hymn –
And we both pray –

Please, Sir, I and Tim –
Always lost the way!

We must die – by and by –
Clergymen say –
Tim – shall – if I – do –
I – too – if he –

How shall we arrange it –
Tim – was – so – shy?
Take us simultaneous – Lord –
I – "Tim" – and – Me!

c. 1860   1945

197

Morning – is the place for Dew –
Corn – is made at Noon –
After dinner light – for flowers –
Dukes – for Setting Sun!

c. 1860   1896

198

An awful Tempest mashed the air –
The clouds were gaunt, and few –
A Black – as of a Spectre's Cloak
Hid Heaven and Earth from view.

The creatures chuckled on the Roofs –
And whistled in the air –
And shook their fists –
And gnashed their teeth –
And swung their frenzied hair.

The morning lit – the Birds arose –
The Monster's faded eyes
Turned slowly to his native coast –
And peace – was Paradise!

c. 1860   1891

I'm "wife" – I've finished that –
That other state –
I'm Czar – I'm "Woman" now –
It's safer so –

How odd the Girl's life looks
Behind this soft Eclipse –
I think that Earth feels so
To folks in Heaven – now –

This being comfort – then
That other kind – was pain –
But why compare?
I'm "Wife"! Stop there!

c. 1860   *1890*

200

I stole them from a Bee –
Because – Thee –
Sweet plea –
He pardoned me!

c. 1860   *1894*

201

Two swimmers wrestled on the spar –
Until the morning sun –
When One – turned smiling to the land –
Oh God! the Other One!

The stray ships – passing –
Spied a face –
Upon the waters borne –
With eyes in death – still begging raised –
And hands – beseeching – thrown!

c. 1860   *1890*

My Eye is fuller than my vase –
Her Cargo – is of Dew –
And still – my Heart – my Eye outweighs –
East India – for you!

c. 1860   1945

He forgot – and I – remembered –
'Twas an everyday affair –
Long ago as Christ and Peter –
"Warmed them" at the "Temple fire."

"Thou wert with him" – quoth "the Damsel"?
"No" – said Peter, 'twasn't me –
Jesus merely "looked" at Peter –
Could I do aught else – to Thee?

c. 1860   1945

A slash of Blue –
A sweep of Gray –
Some scarlet patches on the way,
Compose an Evening Sky –
A little purple – slipped between –
Some Ruby Trousers hurried on –
A Wave of Gold –
A Bank of Day –
This just makes out the Morning Sky.

c. 1860   1935

I should not dare to leave my friend,
Because – because if he should die
While I was gone – and I – too late –
Should reach the Heart that wanted me –

If I should disappoint the eyes
That hunted – hunted so – to see –
And could not bear to shut until
They "noticed" me – they noticed me –

If I should stab the patient faith
So sure I'd come – so sure I'd come –
It *listening* – listening – went to sleep –
Telling my tardy name –

My Heart would wish it broke before –
Since breaking then – since breaking then –
Were useless as next morning's sun –
Where midnight frosts – had lain!

c. 1860   *1891*

206

The Flower must not blame the Bee –
That seeketh his felicity
Too often at her door –

But teach the Footman from Vevay –
Mistress is "not at home" – to say –
To people – any more!

c. 1860   *1935*

207

Tho' I get home how late – how late –
So I get home – 'twill compensate –
Better will be the Ecstasy
That they have done expecting me –
When Night – descending – dumb – and dark –
They hear my unexpected knock –
Transporting must the moment be –
Brewed from decades of Agony!

To think just how the fire will burn –
Just how long-cheated eyes will turn –
To wonder what myself will say,

And what itself, will say to me –
Beguiles the Centuries of way!

c. 1860   1891

208

The Rose did caper on her cheek –
Her Bodice rose and fell –
Her pretty speech – like drunken men –
Did stagger pitiful –

Her fingers fumbled at her work –
Her needle would not go –
What ailed so smart a little Maid –
It puzzled me to know –

Till opposite – I spied a cheek
That bore *another* Rose –
Just opposite – Another speech
That like the Drunkard goes –

A Vest that like her Bodice, danced –
To the immortal tune –
Till those two troubled – little Clocks
Ticked softly into one.

c. 1860   1891

209

With thee, in the Desert –
With thee in the thirst –
With thee in the Tamarind wood –
Leopard breathes – at last!

c. 1860   1945

210

The thought beneath so slight a film –
Is more distinctly seen –

As laces just reveal the surge –
Or Mists – the Apennine

c. *1860*   *1891*

211

Come slowly – Eden!
Lips unused to Thee –
Bashful – sip thy Jessamines –
As the fainting Bee –

Reaching late his flower,
Round her chamber hums –
Counts his nectars –
Enters – and is lost in Balms.

c. *1860*   *1890*

212

Least Rivers – docile to some sea.
My Caspian – thee.

c. *1860*   *1945*

213

Did the Harebell loose her girdle
To the lover Bee
Would the Bee the Harebell *hallow*
Much as formerly?

Did the "Paradise" – persuaded –
Yield her moat of pearl –
Would the Eden *be* an Eden,
Or the Earl – an *Earl*?

c. *1860*   *1891*

214

I taste a liquor never brewed –
From Tankards scooped in Pearl –

Not all the Vats upon the Rhine
Yield such an Alcohol!

Inebriate of Air – am I –
And Debauchee of Dew –
Reeling – thro endless summer days –
From inns of Molten Blue –

When "Landlords" turn the drunken Bee
Out of the Foxglove's door –
When Butterflies – renounce their "drams" –
I shall but drink the more!

Till Seraphs swing their snowy Hats –
And Saints – to windows run –
To see the little Tippler
Leaning against the – Sun –

c. 1860   *1861*

215

What is – "Paradise" –
Who live there –
Are they "Farmers" –
Do they "hoe" –
Do they know that this is "Amherst" –
And that I – am coming – too –

Do they wear "new shoes" – in "Eden" –
Is it always pleasant – there –
Won't they scold us – when we're homesick –
Or tell God – how cross we are –

You are sure there's such a person
As "a Father" – in the sky –
So if I get lost – there – ever –
Or do what the Nurse calls "die" –
I shan't walk the "Jasper" – barefoot –
Ransomed folks – won't laugh at me –
Maybe – "Eden" a'n't so lonesome
As New England used to be!

c. 1860   *1945*

Safe in their Alabaster Chambers –
Untouched by Morning
And untouched by Noon –
Sleep the meek members of the Resurrection –
Rafter of satin,
And Roof of stone.

Light laughs the breeze
In her Castle above them –
Babbles the Bee in a stolid Ear,
Pipe the Sweet Birds in ignorant cadence –
Ah, what sagacity perished here!

version of 1859   1862

Safe in their Alabaster Chambers –
Untouched by Morning –
And untouched by Noon –
Lie the meek members of the Resurrection –
Rafter of Satin – and Roof of Stone!

Grand go the Years – in the Crescent – above them –
Worlds scoop their Arcs –
And Firmaments – row –
Diadems – drop – and Doges – surrender –
Soundless as dots – on a Disc of Snow –

version of 1861   1890

Savior! I've no one else to tell –
And so I trouble *thee*.
I am the one forgot thee so –
Dost thou remember me?
Nor, for myself, I came so far –
That were the little load –
I brought thee the imperial Heart
I had not strength to hold –

The Heart I carried in my own –
Till mine too heavy grew –
Yet – strangest – *heavier* since it went –
Is it too large for *you*?

1861   *1929*

218

Is it true, dear Sue?
Are there *two*?
I shouldn't like to come
For fear of joggling Him!
If I could shut him up
In a Coffee Cup,
Or tie him to a pin
Till I got in –
Or make him fast
To "Toby's" fist –
Hist! Whist! I'd come!

1861   *1924*

219

She sweeps with many-colored Brooms –
And leaves the Shreds behind –
Oh Housewife in the Evening West –
Come back, and dust the Pond!

You dropped a Purple Ravelling in –
You dropped an Amber thread –
And now you've littered all the East
With Duds of Emerald!

And still, she plies her spotted Brooms,
And still the Aprons fly,
Till Brooms fade softly into stars –
And then I come away –

c. 1861   *1891*

Could *I* – then – shut the door –
Lest *my* beseeching face – at last –
Rejected – be – of *Her*?

c. 1861   *1932*

221

It can't be "Summer"!
That – got through!
It's early – yet – for "Spring"!
There's that long town of White – to cross –
Before the Blackbirds sing!
It can't be "Dying"!
It's too Rouge –
The Dead shall go in White –
So Sunset shuts my question down
With Cuffs of Chrysolite!

c. 1861   *1891*

222

When Katie walks, this simple pair accompany her side,
When Katie runs unwearied they follow on the road,
When Katie kneels, their loving hands still clasp her pious knee –
Ah! Katie! Smile at Fortune, with *two* so *knit to thee*!

c. 1861?   *1931*

223

I Came to buy a smile – today –
But just a single smile –
The smallest one upon your face
Will suit me just as well –
The one that no one else would miss
It shone so very small –
I'm pleading at the "counter" – sir –
Could you afford to sell –

I've *Diamonds* – on my fingers –
You know what *Diamonds* are?
I've Rubies – like the Evening Blood –
And Topaz – like the star!
'Twould be "a Bargain" for a *Jew*!
Say – may I have it – Sir?

c. *1861*   *1929*

224

I've nothing else – to bring, You know –
So I keep bringing These –
Just as the Night keeps fetching Stars
To our familiar eyes –

Maybe, we shouldn't mind them –
Unless they didn't come –
Then – maybe, it would puzzle us
To find our way Home –

c. *1861*   *1929*

225

Jesus! thy Crucifix
Enable thee to guess
The smaller size!

Jesus! thy second face
Mind thee in Paradise
Of ours!

c. *1861*   *1945*

226

Should you but fail at – Sea –
In sight of me –
Or doomed lie –
Next Sun – to die –
Or rap – at Paradise – unheard

I'd *harass God*
Until he let you in!

1861   *1955*

227

Teach Him – When He makes the *names* –
Such an one – to say –
On his babbling – Berry – lips –
As should sound – to me –
Were my Ear – as near his nest –
As my *thought* – today –
As should sound –
"Forbid us not" –
Some like "Emily."

1861   *1894*

228

Blazing in Gold and quenching in Purple
Leaping like Leopards to the Sky
Then at the feet of the old Horizon
Laying her spotted Face to die
Stooping as low as the Otter's Window
Touching the Roof and tinting the Barn
Kissing her Bonnet to the Meadow
And the Juggler of Day is gone

c. 1861   *1864*

229

A Burdock – clawed my Gown –
Not *Burdock's* – blame –
But *mine* –
Who went too near
The Burdock's *Den* –

A *Bog* – affronts my shoe –
What *else* have Bogs – *to do* –

The only Trade they *know* –
The *splashing Men*!
Ah, *pity – then*!

'Tis *Minnows can despise*!
The *Elephant's* – calm eyes
Look *further on*!

1861   1945

230

We – Bee and I – live by the quaffing –
'Tisn't *all Hock* – with us –
Life has its *Ale* –
But it's many a lay of the Dim Burgundy –
We chant – for cheer – when the Wines – fail –

Do we "get drunk"?
Ask the jolly Clovers!
Do we "beat" our "Wife"?
I – never wed –
Bee – pledges *his* – in minute flagons –
Dainty – as the tress – on her deft Head –

While runs the Rhine –
He and I – revel –
First – at the vat – and latest at the Vine –
Noon – our last Cup –
"Found dead" – "of Nectar" –
By a humming Coroner –
In a By-Thyme!

c. 1861   1929

231

God permits industrious Angels –
Afternoons – to play –
I met one – forgot my Schoolmates –
All – for Him – straightway –

[105]

God calls home – the Angels – promptly –
At the Setting Sun –
I missed mine – how *dreary – Marbles –*
After playing *Crown!*

c. 1861   *1890*

232

The *Sun – just touched* the Morning –
The *Morning –* Happy thing –
Supposed that He had come to *dwell –*
And Life would all be *Spring!*

She felt herself *supremer –*
A *Raised – Ethereal Thing!*
Henceforth – for Her – *What Holiday!*
Meanwhile – Her wheeling King –
Trailed – slow – along the Orchards –
His *haughty – spangled* Hems –
Leaving a *new necessity!*
The *want* of *Diadems!*

The Morning – *fluttered – staggered –*
Felt feebly – for Her *Crown –*
Her *unanointed forehead –*
Henceforth – Her *only* One!

c. 1861   *1891*

233

The Lamp burns sure – within –
Tho' Serfs – supply the Oil –
It matters not the busy Wick –
At her phosphoric toil!

The Slave – forgets – to fill –
The Lamp – burns golden – on –
Unconscious that the oil is out –
As that the Slave – is gone.

c. 1861   *1935*

You're right – "the way *is* narrow" –
And "difficult the Gate" –
And "few there be" – Correct again –
That "enter in – thereat" –

'*Tis* Costly – So are *purples*!
'Tis just the price of *Breath* –
With but the "Discount" of the *Grave* –
Termed by the *Brokers* – "*Death*"!

And after *that* – there's Heaven –
The *Good* Man's – "*Dividend*" –
And *Bad* Men – "go to Jail" –
I guess –

c. 1861   *1945*

The Court is far away –
No Umpire – have I –
My Sovereign is offended –
To gain his grace – I'd die!

I'll seek his royal feet –
I'll say – Remember – King –
Thou shalt – thyself – one day – a Child –
Implore a *larger* – thing –

That Empire – is of Czars –
As small – they say – as I –
Grant *me* – that day – the royalty –
To *intercede* – for *Thee* –

c. 1861   *1945*

If *He* dissolve – then – there is *nothing* – *more* –
Eclipse – at *Midnight* –
It was *dark* – *before* –

Sunset – at *Easter* –
Blindness – on the *Dawn* –
Faint Star of Bethlehem –
Gone down!

Would but some *God* – *inform* Him –
Or it be *too late*!
Say – that the pulse *just lisps* –
The *Chariots wait* –

Say – that a *little life* – for *His* –
Is *leaking* – *red* –
His little *Spaniel* – tell Him!
Will He heed?

c. *1861*   *1935*

237

I think just how my shape will rise –
When I shall be *"forgiven"* –
Till Hair – and Eyes – and timid Head –
Are *out of sight* – in Heaven –

I think just how my lips will weigh –
With shapeless – quivering – prayer –
That you – *so late* – *"Consider"* me –
The *"Sparrow"* of your Care –

I mind me that of Anguish – sent –
Some drifts were moved away –
Before my simple bosom – broke –
And why not *this* – if *they*?

And so I con that thing – *"forgiven"* –
Until – delirious – borne –
By my long bright – and *longer* – *trust* –
I *drop* my Heart – *unshriven*!

c. *1861*   *1891*

Kill your Balm – and its Odors bless you –
Bare your Jessamine – to the storm –
And she will fling her maddest perfume –
Haply – your Summer night to Charm –

Stab the Bird – that built in your bosom –
Oh, could you catch her last Refrain –
Bubble! "forgive" – "Some better" – Bubble!
"Carol for Him – when I am gone"!

c. 1861   *1945*

"Heaven" – is what I cannot reach!
The Apple on the Tree –
Provided it do hopeless – hang –
That – "Heaven" is – to Me!

The Color, on the Cruising Cloud –
The interdicted Land –
Behind the Hill – the House behind –
There – Paradise – is found!

Her teasing Purples – Afternoons –
The credulous – decoy –
Enamored – of the Conjuror –
That spurned us – Yesterday!

c. 1861   *1896*

Ah, Moon – and Star!
You are very far –
But were no one
Farther than you –
Do you think I'd stop
For a Firmament –
Or a Cubit – or so?

I could borrow a Bonnet
Of the Lark –
And a Chamois' Silver Boot –
And a stirrup of an Antelope –
And be with you – Tonight!

But, Moon, and Star,
Though you're very far –
There is one – farther than you –
He – is more than a firmament – from Me –
So I can never go!

c. *1861*

1935

241

I like a look of Agony,
Because I know it's true –
Men do not sham Convulsion,
Nor simulate, a Throe –

The Eyes glaze once – and that is Death –
Impossible to feign
The Beads upon the Forehead
By homely Anguish strung.

c. *1861*

1890

242

When we stand on the tops of Things –
And like the Trees, look down –
The smoke all cleared away from it –
And Mirrors on the scene –

Just laying light – no soul will wink
Except it have the flaw –
The Sound ones, like the Hills – shall stand –
No Lightning, scares away –

The Perfect, nowhere be afraid –
They bear their dauntless Heads,

Where others, dare not go at Noon,
Protected by their deeds –

The Stars dare shine occasionally
Upon a spotted World –
And Suns, go surer, for their Proof,
As if an Axle, held –

c. *1861*   *1945*

243

I've known a Heaven, like a Tent –
To wrap its shining Yards –
Pluck up its stakes, and disappear –
Without the sound of Boards
Or Rip of Nail – Or Carpenter –
But just the miles of Stare –
That signalize a Show's Retreat –
In North America –

No Trace – no Figment of the Thing
That dazzled, Yesterday,
No Ring – no Marvel –
Men, and Feats –
Dissolved as utterly –
As Bird's far Navigation
Discloses just a Hue –
A plash of Oars, a Gaiety -
Then swallowed up, of View.

c. *1861*   *1929*

244

It is easy to work when the soul is at play –
But when the soul is in pain –
The hearing him put his playthings up
Makes work difficult – then –

It is simple, to ache in the Bone, or the Rind –
But Gimlets – among the nerve –

Mangle daintier – terribler –
Like a Panther in the Glove –

c. *1861*   *1945*

245

I held a Jewel in my fingers –
And went to sleep –
The day was warm, and winds were prosy –
I said " 'Twill keep" –

I woke – and chid my honest fingers,
The Gem was gone –
And now, an Amethyst remembrance
Is all I own –

c. *1861*   *1891*

246

Forever at His side to walk –
The smaller of the two!
Brain of His Brain –
Blood of His Blood –
Two lives – One Being – now –

Forever of His fate to taste –
If grief – the largest part –
If joy – to put my piece away
For that beloved Heart –

All life – to know each other –
Whom we can never learn –
And bye and bye – a Change –
Called Heaven –
Rapt Neighborhoods of Men –
Just finding out – what puzzled us –
Without the lexicon!

c. *1861*   *1929*

What would I give to see his face?
I'd give – I'd give my life – of course –
But *that* is not enough!
Stop just a minute – let me think!
I'd give my biggest Bobolink!
That makes *two* – *Him* – and *Life*!
You know who *"June"* is –
I'd give *her* –
Roses a day from Zanzibar –
And Lily tubes – like Wells –
Bees – by the furlong –
Straits of Blue
Navies of Butterflies – sailed thro' –
And dappled Cowslip Dells –

Then I have "shares" in Primrose "Banks" –
Daffodil Dowries – spicy "Stocks" –
Dominions – broad as Dew –
Bags of Doubloons – adventurous Bees
Brought me – from firmamental seas –
And Purple – from Peru –

Now – have I bought it –
"Shylock"? Say!
Sign me the Bond!
"I vow to pay
To Her – who pledges *this* –
One hour – of her Sovereign's face"!
Ecstatic Contract!
Niggard Grace!
My *Kingdom's worth* of Bliss!

c. *1861*   *1929*

Why – do they shut Me out of Heaven?
Did I sing – too loud?
But – I can say a little "Minor"
Timid as a Bird!

Wouldn't the Angels try me –
Just – once – more –
Just – see – if I troubled them –
But don't – shut the door!

Oh, if I – were the Gentleman
In the "White Robe" –
And they – were the little Hand – that knocked –
Could – I – forbid?

c. *1861*   *1929*

249

Wild Nights – Wild Nights!
Were I with thee
Wild Nights should be
Our luxury!

Futile – the Winds –
To a Heart in port –
Done with the Compass –
Done with the Chart!

Rowing in Eden –
Ah, the Sea!
Might I but moor – Tonight –
In Thee!

c. *1861*   *1891*

250

I shall keep singing!
Birds will pass me
On their way to Yellower Climes –
Each – with a Robin's expectation –
I – with my Redbreast –
And my Rhymes –

Late – when I take my place in summer –
But – I shall bring a fuller tune –

Vespers – are sweeter than Matins – Signor –
Morning – only the seed of Noon –

c. 1861   1935

251

Over the fence –
Strawberries – grow –
Over the fence –
I could climb – if I tried, I know –
Berries are nice!

But – if I stained my Apron –
God would certainly scold!
Oh, dear, – I guess if He were a Boy –
He'd – climb – if He could!

c. 1861   1945

252

I can wade Grief –
Whole Pools of it –
I'm used to that –
But the least push of Joy
Breaks up my feet –
And I tip – drunken –
Let no Pebble – smile –
'Twas the New Liquor –
That was all!

Power is only Pain –
Stranded, thro' Discipline,
Till Weights – will hang –
Give Balm – to Giants –
And they'll wilt, like Men –
Give Himmaleh –
They'll Carry – Him!

c. 1861   1891

You see I cannot see – your lifetime –
I must guess –
How many times it ache for me – today – Confess –
How many times for my far sake
The brave eyes film –
But I guess guessing hurts –
Mine – get so dim!

Too vague – the face –
My own – so patient – covers –
Too far – the strength –
My timidness enfolds –
Haunting the Heart –
Like her translated faces –
Teasing the want –
It – only – can suffice!

c. 1861   *1929*

254

"Hope" is the thing with feathers –
That perches in the soul –
And sings the tune without the words –
And never stops – at all –

And sweetest – in the Gale – is heard –
And sore must be the storm –
That could abash the little Bird
That kept so many warm –

I've heard it in the chillest land –
And on the strangest Sea –
Yet, never, in Extremity,
It asked a crumb – of Me.

c. 1861   *1891*

255

To die – takes just a little while –
They say it doesn't hurt –

It's only fainter – by degrees –
And then – it's out of sight –

A darker Ribbon – for a Day –
A Crape upon the Hat –
And then the pretty sunshine comes –
And helps us to forget –

The absent – mystic – creature –
That but for love of us –
Had gone to sleep – that soundest time –
Without the weariness –

c. 1861   1935

256

If I'm lost – now
That I was found –
Shall still my transport be –
That once – on me – those Jasper Gates
Blazed open – suddenly –

That in my awkward – gazing – face –
The Angels – softly peered –
And touched me with their fleeces,
Almost as if they cared –
I'm banished – now – you know it –
How foreign that can be –
You'll know – Sir – when the Savior's face
Turns so – away from you –

c. 1861   1945

257

Delight is as the flight –
Or in the Ratio of it,
As the Schools would say –
The Rainbow's way –
A Skein
Flung colored, after Rain,

Would suit as bright,
Except that flight
Were Aliment –

"If it would last"
I asked the East,
When that Bent Stripe
Struck up my childish
Firmament –
And I, for glee,
Took Rainbows, as the common way,
And empty Skies
The Eccentricity –

And so with Lives –
And so with Butterflies –
Seen magic – through the fright
That they will cheat the sight –
And Dower latitudes far on –
Some sudden morn –
Our portion – in the fashion –
Done –

c. 1861   1929

258

There's a certain Slant of light,
Winter Afternoons –
That oppresses, like the Heft
Of Cathedral Tunes –

Heavenly Hurt, it gives us –
We can find no scar,
But internal difference,
Where the Meanings, are –

None may teach it – Any –
'Tis the Seal Despair –
An imperial affliction
Sent us of the Air –

When it comes, the Landscape listens –
Shadows – hold their breath –
When it goes, 'tis like the Distance
On the look of Death –

c. 1861

1890

259

Good Night! Which put the Candle out?
A jealous Zephyr – not a doubt –
Ah, friend, you little knew
How long at that celestial wick
The Angels – labored diligent –
Extinguished – now – for you!

It might – have been the Light House spark –
Some Sailor – rowing in the Dark –
Had importuned to see!
It might – have been the waning lamp
That lit the Drummer from the Camp
To purer Reveille!

c. 1861

1891

260

Read – Sweet – how others – strove –
Till we – are stouter –
What they – renounced –
Till we – are less afraid –
How many times they – bore the faithful witness –
Till we – are helped –
As if a Kingdom – cared!

Read then – of faith –
That shone above the fagot –
Clear strains of Hymn
The River could not drown –
Brave names of Men –
And Celestial Women –

Passed out – of Record
Into – Renown!

c. *1861*   *1890*

261

Put up my lute!
What of – my Music!
Since the sole ear I cared to charm –
Passive – as Granite – laps My Music –
Sobbing – will suit – as well as psalm!

Would but the "Memnon" of the Desert –
Teach me the strain
That vanquished Him –
When He – surrendered to the Sunrise –
Maybe – that – would awaken – them!

c. *1861*   *1935*

262

The lonesome for they know not What –
The Eastern Exiles – be –
Who strayed beyond the Amber line
Some madder Holiday –

And ever since – the purple Moat
They strive to climb – in vain –
As Birds – that tumble from the clouds
Do fumble at the strain –

The Blessed Ether – taught them –
Some Transatlantic Morn –
When Heaven – was too common – to miss –
Too sure – to dote upon!

c. *1861*   *1929*

263

A single Screw of Flesh
Is all that pins the Soul

That stands for Deity, to Mine,
Upon my side the Veil –

Once witnessed of the Gauze –
Its name is put away
As far from mine, as if no plight
Had printed yesterday,

In tender – solemn Alphabet,
My eyes just turned to see,
When it was smuggled by my sight
Into Eternity –

More Hands – to hold – These are but Two –
One more new-mailed Nerve
Just granted, for the Peril's sake –
Some striding – Giant – Love –

So greater than the Gods can show,
They slink before the Clay,
That not for all their Heaven can boast
Will let its Keepsake – go

c. 1861   *1935*

264

A Weight with Needles on the pounds –
To push, and pierce, besides –
That if the Flesh resist the Heft –
The puncture – coolly tries –

That not a pore be overlooked
Of all this Compound Frame –
As manifold for Anguish –
As Species – be – for name –

c. 1861   *1935*

265

Where Ships of Purple – gently toss –
On Seas of Daffodil –

Fantastic Sailors – mingle –
And then – the Wharf is still!

c. 1861   *1891*

266

This – is the land – the Sunset washes –
These – are the Banks of the Yellow Sea –
Where it rose – or whither it rushes –
These – are the Western Mystery!

Night after Night
Her purple traffic
Strews the landing with Opal Bales –
Merchantmen – poise upon Horizons –
Dip – and vanish like Orioles!

c. 1861   *1890*

267

Did we disobey Him?
Just one time!
Charged us to forget Him –
But we couldn't learn!

Were Himself – such a Dunce –
What would we – do?
Love the dull lad – best –
Oh, wouldn't you?

c. 1861   *1945*

268

Me, change! Me, alter!
Then I will, when on the Everlasting Hill
A Smaller Purple grows –
At sunset, or a lesser glow
Flickers upon Cordillera –
At Day's superior close!

c. 1861   *1945*

Bound – a trouble –
And lives can bear it!
Limit – how deep a bleeding go!
So – many – drops – of vital scarlet –
Deal with the soul
As with Algebra!

Tell it the Ages – to a cypher –
And it will ache – contented – on –
Sing – at its pain – as any Workman –
Notching the fall of the Even Sun!

c. 1861

1935

One Life of so much Consequence!
Yet I – for it – would pay –
My Soul's *entire income* –
In ceaseless – salary –

One Pearl – to me – so signal –
That I would instant dive –
Although – I *knew* – to *take* it –
Would *cost* me – *just a life*!

The Sea is full – I know it!
That – does not blur *my Gem*!
It burns – distinct from all the row –
Intact – *in Diadem*!

The life is thick – I know it!
Yet – not so dense a crowd –
But *Monarchs* – are *perceptible* –
Far down the dustiest Road!

c. 1861

1929

A solemn thing – it was – I said –
A woman – white – to be –

And wear – if God should count me fit –
Her blameless mystery –

A hallowed thing – to drop a life
Into the purple well –
Too plummetless – that it return –
Eternity – until –

I pondered how the bliss would look –
And would it feel as big –
When I could take it in my hand –
As hovering – seen – through fog –

And then – the size of this "small" life –
The Sages – call it small –
Swelled – like Horizons – in my vest –
And I sneered – softly – "small"!

c. 1861   *1896*

272

I breathed enough to take the Trick –
And now, removed from Air –
I simulate the Breath, so well –
That One, to be quite sure –

The Lungs are stirless – must descend
Among the Cunning Cells –
And touch the Pantomime – Himself,
How numb, the Bellows feels!

c. 1861   *1896*

273

He put the Belt around my life –
I heard the Buckle snap –
And turned away, imperial,
My Lifetime folding up –
Deliberate, as a Duke would do
A Kingdom's Title Deed –

Henceforth, a Dedicated sort –
A Member of the Cloud.

Yet not too far to come at call –
And do the little Toils
That make the Circuit of the Rest –
And deal occasional smiles
To lives that stoop to notice mine –
And kindly ask it in –
Whose invitation, know you not
For Whom I must decline?

c. 1861   1891

274

The only Ghost I ever saw
Was dressed in Mechlin – so –
He wore no sandal on his foot –
And stepped like flakes of snow –

His Gait – was soundless, like the Bird –
But rapid – like the Roe –
His fashions, quaint, Mosaic –
Or haply, Mistletoe –

His conversation – seldom –
His laughter, like the Breeze –
That dies away in Dimples
Among the pensive Trees –

Our interview – was transient –
Of me, himself was shy –
And God forbid I look behind –
Since that appalling Day!

c. 1861   1891

275

Doubt Me! My Dim Companion!
Why, God, would be content
With but a fraction of the Life –
Poured thee, without a stint –

[125]

The whole of me – forever –
What more the Woman can,
Say quick, that I may dower thee
With last Delight I own!

It cannot be my Spirit –
For that was thine, before –
I ceded all of Dust I knew –
What Opulence the more
Had I – a freckled Maiden,
Whose farthest of Degree,
Was – that she might –
Some distant Heaven,
Dwell timidly, with thee!

Sift her, from Brow to Barefoot!
Strain till your last Surmise –
Drop, like a Tapestry, away,
Before the Fire's Eyes –
Winnow her finest fondness –
But hallow just the snow
Intact, in Everlasting flake—
Oh, Caviler, for you!

c. 1861   *1890*

276

Many a phrase has the English language –
I have heard but one –
Low as the laughter of the Cricket,
Loud, as the Thunder's Tongue –

Murmuring, like old Caspian Choirs,
When the Tide's a' lull –
Saying itself in new inflection –
Like a Whippoorwill –

Breaking in bright Orthography
On my simple sleep –

Thundering its Prospective –
Till I stir, and weep –

Not for the Sorrow, done me –
But the push of Joy –
Say it again, Saxon!
Hush – Only to me!

c. *1861*   *1935*

277

What if I say I shall not wait!
What if I burst the fleshly Gate –
And pass escaped – to thee!

What if I file this Mortal – off –
See where it hurt me – That's enough –
And wade in Liberty!

They cannot take me – any more!
Dungeons can call – and Guns implore
Unmeaning – now – to me –

As laughter – was – an hour ago –
Or Laces – or a Travelling Show –
Or who died – yesterday!

c. *1861*   *1891*

278

A shady friend – for Torrid days –
Is easier to find –
Than one of higher temperature
For Frigid – hour of Mind –

The Vane a little to the East –
Scares Muslin souls – away –
If Broadcloth Hearts are firmer –
Than those of Organdy –

Who is to blame? The Weaver?
Ah, the bewildering thread!

The Tapestries of Paradise
So notelessly – are made!

c. *1861*

1891

279

Tie the Strings to my Life, My Lord,
Then, I am ready to go!
Just a look at the Horses –
Rapid! That will do!

Put me in on the firmest side –
So I shall never fall –
For we must ride to the Judgment –
And it's partly, down Hill –

But never I mind the steepest –
And never I mind the Sea –
Held fast in Everlasting Race –
By my own Choice, and Thee –

Goodbye to the Life I used to live –
And the World I used to know –
And kiss the Hills, for me, just once –
Then – I am ready to go!

c. *1861*

1896

280

I felt a Funeral, in my Brain,
And Mourners to and fro
Kept treading – treading – till it seemed
That Sense was breaking through –

And when they all were seated,
A Service, like a Drum –
Kept beating – beating – till I thought
My Mind was going numb –

And then I heard them lift a Box
And creak across my Soul

With those same Boots of Lead, again,
Then Space – began to toll,

As all the Heavens were a Bell,
And Being, but an Ear,
And I, and Silence, some strange Race
Wrecked, solitary, here –

And then a Plank in Reason, broke,
And I dropped down, and down –
And hit a World, at every plunge,
And Finished knowing – then –

c. 1861   *1896*

281

'Tis so appalling – it exhilarates –
So over Horror, it half Captivates –
The Soul stares after it, secure –
A Sepulchre, fears frost, no more –

To scan a Ghost, is faint –
But grappling, conquers it –
How easy, Torment, now –
Suspense kept sawing so –

The Truth, is Bald, and Cold –
But that will hold –
If any are not sure –
We show them – prayer –
But we, who know,
Stop hoping, now –

Looking at Death, is Dying –
Just let go the Breath –
And not the pillow at your Cheek
So Slumbereth –

Others, Can wrestle –
Yours, is done –
And so of Woe, bleak dreaded – come,
It sets the Fright at liberty –

And Terror's free –
Gay, Ghastly, Holiday!

c. *1861*   *1935*

282

How noteless Men, and Pleiads, stand,
Until a sudden sky
Reveals the fact that One is rapt
Forever from the Eye –

Members of the Invisible,
Existing, while we stare,
In Leagueless Opportunity,
O'ertakeless, as the Air –

Why didn't we detain Them?
The Heavens with a smile,
Sweep by our disappointed Heads
Without a syllable –

c. *1861*   *1929*

283

A Mien to move a Queen –
Half Child – Half Heroine –
An Orleans in the Eye
That puts its manner by
For humbler Company
When none are near
Even a Tear –
Its frequent Visitor –

A Bonnet like a Duke –
And yet a Wren's Peruke
Were not so shy
Of Goer by –
And Hands – so slight –
They would elate a Sprite
With Merriment –

A Voice that Alters – Low
And on the Ear can go
Like Let of Snow –
Or shift supreme –
As tone of Realm
On Subjects Diadem –

Too small – to fear –
Too distant – to endear –
And so Men Compromise –
And just – revere –

c. *1861*   *1935*

284

The Drop, that wrestles in the Sea –
Forgets her own locality –
As I – toward Thee –

She knows herself an incense small –
Yet *small* – she sighs – if *All* – is *All* –
How *larger* – be?

The Ocean – smiles – at her Conceit –
But *she*, forgetting Amphitrite –
Pleads – "Me"?

c. *1861*   *1945*

285

The Robin's my Criterion for Tune –
Because I grow – where Robins do –
But, were I Cuckoo born –
I'd swear by him –
The ode familiar – rules the Noon –
The Buttercup's, my Whim for Bloom –
Because, we're Orchard sprung –
But, were I Britain born,
I'd Daisies spurn –
None but the Nut – October fit –
Because, through dropping it,

The Seasons flit – I'm taught –
Without the Snow's Tableau
Winter, were lie – to me –
Because I see – New Englandly –
The Queen, discerns like me –
Provincially –

c. 1861   *1929*

286

That after Horror – that 'twas *us* –
That passed the mouldering Pier –
Just as the Granite Crumb let go –
Our Savior, by a Hair –

A second more, had dropped too deep
For Fisherman to plumb –
The very profile of the Thought
Puts Recollection numb –

The possibility – to pass
Without a Moment's Bell –
Into Conjecture's presence –
Is like a Face of Steel –
That suddenly looks into ours
With a metallic grin –
The Cordiality of Death –
Who drills his Welcome in –

c. 1861   *1935*

287

A Clock stopped –
Not the Mantel's –
Geneva's farthest skill
Can't put the puppet bowing –
That just now dangled still –

An awe came on the Trinket!
The Figures hunched, with pain –

Then quivered out of Decimals –
Into Degreeless Noon –

It will not stir for Doctors –
This Pendulum of snow –
This Shopman importunes it –
While cool – concernless No –

Nods from the Gilded pointers –
Nods from the Seconds slim –
Decades of Arrogance between
The Dial life –
And Him –

c. 1861   1896

288

I'm Nobody! Who are you?
Are you – Nobody – Too?
Then there's a pair of us!
Don't tell! they'd advertise – you know!

How dreary – to be – Somebody!
How public – like a Frog –
To tell one's name – the livelong June –
To an admiring Bog!

c. 1861   1891

289

I know some lonely Houses off the Road
A Robber'd like the look of –
Wooden barred,
And Windows hanging low,
Inviting to –
A Portico,
Where two could creep –
One – hand the Tools –
The other peep –
To make sure All's Asleep –

[133]

Old fashioned eyes –
Not easy to surprise!

How orderly the Kitchen'd look, by night,
With just a Clock –
But they could gag the Tick –
And Mice won't bark –
And so the Walls – don't tell –
None – will –

A pair of Spectacles ajar just stir –
An Almanac's aware –
Was it the Mat – winked,
Or a Nervous Star?
The Moon – slides down the stair,
To see who's there!

There's plunder – where –
Tankard, or Spoon –
Earring – or Stone –
A Watch – Some Ancient Brooch
To match the Grandmama –
Staid sleeping – there –

Day – rattles – too
Stealth's – slow –
The Sun has got as far
As the third Sycamore –
Screams Chanticleer
"Who's there"?

And Echoes – Trains away,
Sneer – "Where"!
While the old Couple, just astir,
Fancy the Sunrise – left the door ajar!

c. 1861   *1890*

290

Of Bronze – and Blaze –
The North – Tonight –
So adequate – it forms –

[134]

So preconcerted with itself –
So distant – to alarms –
An Unconcern so sovereign
To Universe, or me –
Infects my simple spirit
With Taints of Majesty –
Till I take vaster attitudes –
And strut upon my stem –
Disdaining Men, and Oxygen,
For Arrogance of them –

My Splendors, are Menagerie –
But their Competeless Show
Will entertain the Centuries
When I, am long ago,
An Island in dishonored Grass –
Whom none but Beetles – know.

c. 1861   1896

291

How the old Mountains drip with Sunset
How the Hemlocks burn –
How the Dun Brake is draped in Cinder
By the Wizard Sun –

How the old Steeples hand the Scarlet
Till the Ball is full –
Have I the lip of the Flamingo
That I dare to tell?

Then, how the Fire ebbs like Billows –
Touching all the Grass
With a departing – Sapphire – feature –
As a Duchess passed –

How a small Dusk crawls on the Village
Till the Houses blot
And the odd Flambeau, no men carry
Glimmer on the Street –

How it is Night – in Nest and Kennel –
And where was the Wood –
Just a Dome of Abyss is Bowing
Into Solitude –

These are the Visions flitted Guido –
Titian – never told –
Domenichino dropped his pencil –
Paralyzed, with Gold –

c. 1861   1896

292

If your Nerve, deny you –
Go above your Nerve –
He can lean against the Grave,
If he fear to swerve –

That's a steady posture –
Never any bend
Held of those Brass arms –
Best Giant made –

If your Soul seesaw –
Lift the Flesh door –
The Poltroon wants Oxygen –
Nothing more –

c. 1861   1935

293

I got so I could take his name –
Without – Tremendous gain –
That Stop-sensation – on my Soul –
And Thunder – in the Room –

I got so I could walk across
That Angle in the floor,
Where he turned so, and I turned – how –
And all our Sinew tore –

I got so I could stir the Box –
In which his letters grew
Without that forcing, in my breath –
As Staples – driven through –

Could dimly recollect a Grace –
I think, they call it "God" –
Renowned to ease Extremity –
When Formula, had failed –

And shape my Hands –
Petition's way,
Tho' ignorant of a word
That Ordination – utters –

My Business, with the Cloud,
If any Power behind it, be,
Not subject to Despair –
It care, in some remoter way,
For so minute affair
As Misery –
Itself, too vast, for interrupting – more –

c 1861   1929

294

The Doomed – regard the Sunrise
With different Delight –
Because – when next it burns abroad
They doubt to witness it –

The Man – to die – tomorrow –
Harks for the Meadow Bird –
Because its Music stirs the Axe
That clamors for his head –

Joyful – to whom the Sunrise
Precedes Enamored – Day –
Joyful – for whom the Meadow Bird
Has ought but Elegy!

c. 1861   1929

Unto like Story – Trouble has enticed me –
How Kinsmen fell –
Brothers and Sister – who preferred the Glory –
And their young will
Bent to the Scaffold, or in Dungeons – chanted –
Till God's full time –
When they let go the ignominy – smiling –
And Shame went still –

Unto guessed Crests, my moaning fancy, leads me,
Worn fair
By Heads rejected – in the lower country –
Of honors there –
Such spirit makes her perpetual mention,
That I – grown bold –
Step martial – at my Crucifixion –
As Trumpets – rolled –

Feet, small as mine – have marched in Revolution
Firm to the Drum –
Hands – not so stout – hoisted them – in witness –
When Speech went numb –
Let me not shame their sublime deportments –
Drilled bright –
Beckoning – Etruscan invitation –
Toward Light –

c. 1861   1935

One Year ago – jots what?
God – spell the word! I – can't –
Was't Grace? Not that –
Was't Glory? That – will do –
Spell slower – Glory –

Such Anniversary shall be –
Sometimes – not often – in Eternity –
When farther Parted, than the Common Woe –

Look – feed upon each other's faces – so –
In doubtful meal, if it be possible
Their Banquet's true –

I tasted – careless – then –
I did not know the Wine
Came once a World – Did you?
Oh, had you told me so –
This Thirst would blister – easier – now –
You said it hurt you – most –
Mine – was an Acorn's Breast –
And could not know how fondness grew
In Shaggier Vest –
Perhaps – I couldn't –
But, had you looked in –
A Giant – eye to eye with you, had been –
No Acorn – then –

So – Twelve months ago –
We breathed –
Then dropped the Air –
Which bore it best?
Was this – the patientest –
Because it was a Child, you know –
And could not value – Air?

If to be "Elder" – mean most pain –
I'm old enough, today, I'm certain – then –
As old as thee – how soon?
One – Birthday more – or Ten?
Let me – choose!
Ah, Sir, None!

c. 1861   1945

297

It's like the Light –
A fashionless Delight –
It's like the Bee –
A dateless – Melody –

[139]

It's like the Woods –
Private – Like the Breeze –
Phraseless – yet it stirs
The proudest Trees –

It's like the Morning –
Best – when it's done –
And the Everlasting Clocks –
Chime – Noon!

c. 1861   *1896*

298

Alone, I cannot be –
For Hosts – do visit me –
Recordless Company –
Who baffle Key –

They have no Robes, nor Names –
No Almanacs – nor Climes –
But general Homes
Like Gnomes –

Their Coming, may be known
By Couriers within –
Their going – is not –
For they're never gone –

c. 1861   *1932*

299

Your Riches – taught me – Poverty.
Myself – a Millionaire
In little Wealths, as Girls could boast
Till broad as Buenos Ayre –

You drifted your Dominions –
A Different Peru –
And I esteemed All Poverty
For Life's Estate with you –

Of Mines, I little know – myself –
But just the names, of Gems –
The Colors of the Commonest –
And scarce of Diadems –

So much, that did I meet the Queen –
Her Glory I should know –
But this, must be a different Wealth –
To miss it – beggars so –

I'm sure 'tis India – all Day –
To those who look on You –
Without a stint – without a blame,
Might I – but be the Jew –

I'm sure it is Golconda –
Beyond my power to deem –
To have a smile for Mine – each Day,
How better, than a Gem!

At least, it solaces to know
That there exists – a Gold –
Altho' I prove it, just in time
Its distance – to behold –

Its far – far Treasure to surmise –
And estimate the Pearl –
That slipped my simple fingers through –
While just a Girl at School.

1862   *1891*

300

"Morning" – means "Milking" – to the Farmer –
Dawn – to the Teneriffe –
Dice – to the Maid –
Morning means just Risk – to the Lover –
Just revelation – to the Beloved –

Epicures – date a Breakfast – by it –
Brides – an Apocalypse –
Worlds – a Flood –

Faint-going Lives – Their Lapse from Sighing –
Faith – The Experiment of Our Lord –

c. 1862   *1914*

301

I reason, Earth is short –
And Anguish – absolute –
And many hurt,
But, what of that?

I reason, we could die –
The best Vitality
Cannot excel Decay,
But, what of that?

I reason, that in Heaven –
Somehow, it will be even –
Some new Equation, given –
But, what of that?

c. 1862   *1890*

302

Like Some Old fashioned Miracle
When Summertime is done –
Seems Summer's Recollection
And the Affairs of June

As infinite Tradition
As Cinderella's Bays –
Or Little John – of Lincoln Green –
Or Blue Beard's Galleries –

Her Bees have a fictitious Hum –
Her Blossoms, like a Dream –
Elate us – till we almost weep –
So plausible – they seem –

Her Memories like Strains – Review –
When Orchestra is dumb –

The Violin in Baize replaced –
And Ear – and Heaven – numb –

c. 1862

1914

303

The Soul selects her own Society –
Then – shuts the Door –
To her divine Majority –
Present no more –

Unmoved – she notes the Chariots – pausing –
At her low Gate –
Unmoved – an Emperor be kneeling
Upon her Mat –

I've known her – from an ample nation –
Choose One –
Then – close the Valves of her attention –
Like Stone –

c. 1862

1890

304

The Day came slow – till Five o'clock –
Then sprang before the Hills
Like Hindered Rubies – or the Light
A Sudden Musket – spills –

The Purple could not keep the East –
The Sunrise shook abroad
Like Breadths of Topaz – packed a Night –
The Lady just unrolled –

The Happy Winds – their Timbrels took –
The Birds – in docile Rows
Arranged themselves around their Prince
The Wind – is Prince of Those –

The Orchard sparkled like a Jew –
How mighty 'twas – to be

A Guest in this stupendous place –
The Parlor – of the Day –

c. 1862   1891

305

The difference between Despair
And Fear – is like the One
Between the instant of a Wreck –
And when the Wreck has been –

The Mind is smooth – no Motion –
Contented as the Eye
Upon the Forehead of a Bust –
That knows – it cannot see –

c. 1862   1914

306

The Soul's Superior instants
Occur to Her – alone –
When friend – and Earth's occasion
Have infinite withdrawn –

Or She – Herself – ascended
To too remote a Height
For lower Recognition
Than Her Omnipotent –

This Mortal Abolition
Is seldom – but as fair
As Apparition – subject
To Autocratic Air –

Eternity's disclosure
To favorites – a few –
Of the Colossal substance
Of Immortality

c. 1862   1914

The One who could repeat the Summer day –
Were greater than itself – though He
Minutest of Mankind should be –

And He – could reproduce the Sun –
At period of going down –
The Lingering – and the Stain – I mean –

When Orient have been outgrown –
And Occident – become Unknown –
His Name – remain –

c. 1862   *1891*

I send Two Sunsets –
Day and I – in competition ran –
I finished Two – and several Stars –
While He – was making One –

His own was ampler – but as I
Was saying to a friend –
Mine – is the more convenient
To Carry in the Hand –

c. 1862   *1914*

For largest Woman's Heart I knew –
'Tis little I can do –
And yet the largest Woman's Heart
Could hold an Arrow – too –
And so, instructed by my own,
I tenderer, turn Me to.

c. 1862   *1932*

Give little Anguish –
Lives will fret –

Give Avalanches –
And they'll slant –
Straighten – look cautious for their Breath –
But make no syllable – like Death –
Who only shows his Marble Disc –
Sublimer sort – than Speech –

c. 1862   1924

311

It sifts from Leaden Sieves –
It powders all the Wood.
It fills with Alabaster Wool
The Wrinkles of the Road –

It makes an Even Face
Of Mountain, and of Plain –
Unbroken Forehead from the East
Unto the East again –

It reaches to the Fence –
It wraps it Rail by Rail
Till it is lost in Fleeces –
It deals Celestial Vail

To Stump, and Stack – and Stem –
A Summer's empty Room –
Acres of Joints, where Harvests were,
Recordless, but for them –

It Ruffles Wrists of Posts
As Ankles of a Queen –
Then stills its Artisans – like Ghosts –
Denying they have been –

c. 1862   1891

312

Her – "last Poems" –
Poets – ended –
Silver – perished – with her Tongue –

Not on Record – bubbled other,
Flute – or Woman –
So divine –
Not unto its Summer – Morning
Robin – uttered Half the Tune –
Gushed too free for the Adoring –
From the Anglo-Florentine –
Late – the Praise –
'Tis dull – conferring
On the Head too High to Crown –
Diadem – or Ducal Showing –
Be its Grave – sufficient sign –
Nought – that We – No Poet's Kinsman –
Suffocate – with easy woe –
What, and if, Ourself a Bridegroom –
Put Her down – in Italy?

c. 1862   *1914*

313

I should have been too glad, I see –
Too lifted – for the scant degree
Of Life's penurious Round –
My little Circuit would have shamed
This new Circumference – have blamed –
The homelier time behind.

I should have been too saved – I see –
Too rescued – Fear too dim to me
That I could spell the Prayer
I knew so perfect – yesterday –
That Scalding One – Sabachthani –
Recited fluent – here –

Earth would have been too much – I see –
And Heaven – not enough for me –
I should have had the Joy
Without the Fear – to justify –
The Palm – without the Calvary –
So Savior – Crucify –

Defeat – whets Victory – they say –
The Reefs – in old Gethsemane –
Endear the Coast – beyond!
'Tis Beggars – Banquets – can define –
'Tis Parching – vitalizes Wine –
"Faith" bleats – to understand!

c. 1862   1891

314

Nature – sometimes sears a Sapling –
Sometimes – scalps a Tree –
Her Green People recollect it
When they do not die –

Fainter Leaves – to Further Seasons –
Dumbly testify –
We – who have the Souls –
Die oftener – Not so vitally –

c. 1862   1945

315

He fumbles at your Soul
As Players at the Keys
Before they drop full Music on –
He stuns you by degrees –
Prepares your brittle Nature
For the Ethereal Blow
By fainter Hammers – further heard –
Then nearer – Then so slow
Your Breath has time to straighten –
Your Brain – to bubble Cool –
Deals – One – imperial – Thunderbolt –
That scalps your naked Soul –

When Winds take Forests in their Paws –
The Universe – is still –

c. 1862   1896

The Wind didn't come from the Orchard – today –
Further than that –
Nor stop to play with the Hay –
Nor joggle a Hat –
He's a transitive fellow – very –
Rely on that –

If He leave a Bur at the door
We know He has climbed a Fir –
But the Fir is Where – Declare –
Were you ever there?

If He brings Odors of Clovers –
And that is His business – not Ours –
Then He has been with the Mowers –
Whetting away the Hours
To sweet pauses of Hay –
His Way – of a June Day –

If He fling Sand, and Pebble –
Little Boys Hats – and Stubble –
With an occasional Steeple –
And a hoarse "Get out of the way, I say,"
Who'd be the fool to stay?
Would you – Say –
Would you be the fool to stay?

c. 1862   1932

Just so – Jesus – raps –
He – doesn't weary –
Last – at the Knocker –
And first – at the Bell.
Then – on divinest tiptoe – standing –
Might He but spy the lady's soul –
When He – retires –
Chilled – or weary –
It will be ample time for – me –

Patient – upon the steps – *until* then –
Heart! I am knocking – low at thee.

c. 1861   1914

318

I'll tell you how the Sun rose –
A Ribbon at a time –
The Steeples swam in Amethyst –
The news, like Squirrels, ran –
The Hills untied their Bonnets –
The Bobolinks – begun –
Then I said softly to myself –
"That must have been the Sun"!
But how he set – I know not –
There seemed a purple stile
That little Yellow boys and girls
Were climbing all the while –
Till when they reached the other side,
A Dominie in Gray –
Put gently up the evening Bars –
And led the flock away –

c. 1860   1890

319

The nearest Dream recedes – unrealized –
The Heaven we chase,
Like the June Bee – before the School Boy,
Invites the Race –
Stoops – to an easy Clover –
Dips – evades – teases – deploys –
Then – to the Royal Clouds
Lifts his light Pinnace –
Heedless of the Boy –
Staring – bewildered – at the mocking sky –

Homesick for steadfast Honey –
Ah, the Bee flies not
That brews that rare variety!

c. *1861*   *1891*

320

We play at Paste –
Till qualified, for Pearl –
Then, drop the Paste –
And deem ourself a fool –

The Shapes – though – were similar –
And our new Hands
Learned *Gem*-Tactics –
Practicing *Sands* –

c. *1862*   *1891*

321

Of all the Sounds despatched abroad,
There's not a Charge to me
Like that old measure in the Boughs –
That phraseless Melody –
The Wind does – working like a Hand,
Whose fingers Comb the Sky –
Then quiver down – with tufts of Tune –
Permitted Gods, and me –

Inheritance, it is, to us –
Beyond the Art to Earn –
Beyond the trait to take away
By Robber, since the Gain
Is gotten not of fingers –
And inner than the Bone –
Hid golden, for the whole of Days,
And even in the Urn,
I cannot vouch the merry Dust
Do not arise and play
In some odd fashion of its own,
Some quainter Holiday,

When Winds go round and round in Bands –
And thrum upon the door,
And Birds take places, overhead,
To bear them Orchestra.

I crave Him grace of Summer Boughs,
If such an Outcast be –
Who never heard that fleshless Chant –
Rise – solemn – on the Tree,
As if some Caravan of Sound
Off Deserts, in the Sky,
Had parted Rank,
Then knit, and swept –
In Seamless Company –

c. 1862   1890

322

There came a Day at Summer's full,
Entirely for me –
I thought that such were for the Saints,
Where Resurrections – be –

The Sun, as common, went abroad,
The flowers, accustomed, blew,
As if no soul the solstice passed
That maketh all things new –

The time was scarce profaned, by speech –
The symbol of a word
Was needless, as at Sacrament,
The Wardrobe – of our Lord –

Each was to each The Sealed Church,
Permitted to commune this – time –
Lest we too awkward show
At Supper of the Lamb.

The Hours slid fast – as Hours will,
Clutched tight, by greedy hands –

So faces on two Decks, look back,
Bound to opposing lands –

And so when all the time had leaked,
Without external sound
Each bound the Other's Crucifix –
We gave no other Bond –

Sufficient troth, that we shall rise –
Deposed – at length, the Grave –
To that new Marriage,
Justified – through Calvaries of Love –

c. 1861   1890

323

As if I asked a common Alms,
And in my wondering hand
A Stranger pressed a Kingdom,
And I, bewildered, stand –
As if I asked the Orient
Had it for me a Morn –
And it should lift its purple Dikes,
And shatter me with Dawn!

c. 1858   1891

324

Some keep the Sabbath going to Church –
I keep it, staying at Home –
With a Bobolink for a Chorister –
And an Orchard, for a Dome –

Some keep the Sabbath in Surplice –
I just wear my Wings –
And instead of tolling the Bell, for Church,
Our little Sexton – sings.

God preaches, a noted Clergyman –
And the sermon is never long,

[153]

So instead of getting to Heaven, at last –
I'm going, all along.

c. 1860 1864

325

Of Tribulation, these are They,
Denoted by the White –
The Spangled Gowns, a lesser Rank
Of Victors – designate –

All these – did conquer –
But the ones who overcame most times –
Wear nothing commoner than Snow –
No Ornament, but Palms –

Surrender – is a sort unknown –
On this superior soil –
Defeat – an outgrown Anguish –
Remembered, as the Mile

Our panting Ankle barely passed –
When Night devoured the Road –
But we – stood whispering in the House –
And all we said – was "Saved"!

c. 1861 1891

326

I cannot dance upon my Toes –
No Man instructed me –
But oftentimes, among my mind,
A Glee possesseth me,

That had I Ballet knowledge –
Would put itself abroad
In Pirouette to blanch a Troupe –
Or lay a Prima, mad,

And though I had no Gown of Gauze –
No Ringlet, to my Hair,

Nor hopped to Audiences – like Birds,
One Claw upon the Air,

Nor tossed my shape in Eider Balls,
Nor rolled on wheels of snow
Till I was out of sight, in sound,
The House encore me so –

Nor any know I know the Art
I mention – easy – Here –
Nor any Placard boast me –
It's full as Opera –

c. 1862   1929

327

Before I got my eye put out
I liked as well to see –
As other Creatures, that have Eyes
And know no other way –

But were it told to me – Today –
That I might have the sky
For mine – I tell you that my Heart
Would split, for size of me –

The Meadows – mine –
The Mountains – mine –
All Forests – Stintless Stars –
As much of Noon as I could take
Between my finite eyes –

The Motions of the Dipping Birds –
The Morning's Amber Road –
For mine – to look at when I liked –
The News would strike me dead –

So safer – guess – with just my soul
Upon the Window pane –
Where other Creatures put their eyes –
Incautious – of the Sun –

c. 1862   1891

A Bird came down the Walk –
He did not know I saw –
He bit an Angleworm in halves
And ate the fellow, raw,

And then he drank a Dew
From a convenient Grass –
And then hopped sidewise to the Wall
To let a Beetle pass –

He glanced with rapid eyes
That hurried all around –
They looked like frightened Beads, I thought –
He stirred his Velvet Head

Like one in danger, Cautious,
I offered him a Crumb
And he unrolled his feathers
And rowed him softer home –

Than Oars divide the Ocean,
Too silver for a seam –
Or Butterflies, off Banks of Noon
Leap, plashless as they swim.

c. *1862*   *1891*

So glad we are – a Stranger'd deem
'Twas sorry, that we were –
For where the Holiday should be
There publishes a Tear –
Nor how Ourselves be justified –
Since Grief and Joy are done
So similar – An Optizan
Could not decide between –

c. *1862*   *1894*

330

The Juggler's *Hat* her Country is –
The Mountain Gorse – the *Bee's*!

c. 1861   *1894*

331

While Asters –
On the Hill –
Their Everlasting fashions – set –
And Covenant Gentians – Frill!

c. 1861   *1894*

332

There are two Ripenings – one – of sight –
Whose forces Spheric wind
Until the Velvet product
Drop spicy to the ground –
A homelier maturing –
A process in the Bur –
That teeth of Frosts alone disclose
In far October Air.

c. 1862   *1894*

333

The Grass so little has to do –
A Sphere of simple Green –
With only Butterflies to brood
And Bees to entertain –

And stir all day to pretty Tunes
The Breezes fetch along –
And hold the Sunshine in its lap
And bow to everything –

And thread the Dews, all night, like Pearls –
And make itself so fine

A Duchess were too common
For such a noticing –

And even when it dies – to pass
In Odors so divine –
Like Lowly spices, lain to sleep –
Or Spikenards, perishing –

And then, in Sovereign Barns to dwell –
And dream the Days away,
The Grass so little has to do
I wish I were a Hay –

c. 1862   1890

334

All the letters I can write
Are not fair as this –
Syllables of Velvet –
Sentences of Plush,
Depths of Ruby, undrained,
Hid, Lip, for Thee –
Play it were a Humming Bird –
And just sipped – me –

1862   1929

335

'Tis not that Dying hurts us so –
'Tis Living – hurts us more –
But Dying – is a different way –
A Kind behind the Door –

The Southern Custom – of the Bird –
That ere the Frosts are due –
Accepts a better Latitude –
We – are the Birds – that stay.

The Shiverers round Farmers' doors –
For whose reluctant Crumb –

We stipulate – till pitying Snows
Persuade our Feathers Home.

c. 1862

1945

336

The face I carry with me – last –
When I go out of Time –
To take my Rank – by – in the West –
That face – will just be thine –

I'll hand it to the Angel –
That – Sir – was my Degree –
In Kingdoms – you have heard the Raised –
Refer to – possibly.

He'll take it – scan it – step aside –
Return – with such a crown
As Gabriel – never capered at –
And beg me put it on –

And then – he'll turn me round and round –
To an admiring sky –
As one that bore her Master's name –
Sufficient Royalty!

c. 1862

1945

337

I know a place where Summer strives
With such a practised Frost –
She – each year – leads her Daisies back –
Recording briefly – "Lost" –

But when the South Wind stirs the Pools
And struggles in the lanes –
Her Heart misgives Her, for Her Vow –
And she pours soft Refrains

Into the lap of Adamant –
And spices – and the Dew –

That stiffens quietly to Quartz –
Upon her Amber Shoe –

c. 1862   1891

338

I know that He exists.
Somewhere – in Silence –
He has hid his rare life
From our gross eyes.

'Tis an instant's play.
'Tis a fond Ambush –
Just to make Bliss
Earn her own surprise!

But – should the play
Prove piercing earnest –
Should the glee – glaze –
In Death's – stiff – stare –

Would not the fun
Look too expensive!
Would not the jest –
Have crawled too far!

c. 1862   1891

339

I tend my flowers for thee –
Bright Absentee!
My Fuchsia's Coral Seams
Rip – while the Sower – dreams –

Geraniums – tint – and spot –
Low Daisies – dot –
My Cactus – splits her Beard
To show her throat –

Carnations – tip their spice –
And Bees – pick up –
A Hyacinth – I hid –

[160]

Puts out a Ruffled Head –
And odors fall
From flasks – so small –
You marvel how they held –

Globe Roses – break their satin flake –
Upon my Garden floor –
Yet – thou – not there –
I had as lief they bore
No Crimson – more –

Thy flower – be gay –
Her Lord – away!
It ill becometh me –
I'll dwell in Calyx – Gray –
How modestly – alway –
Thy Daisy –
Draped for thee!

c. 1862   1929

340

Is Bliss then, such Abyss,
I must not put my foot amiss
For fear I spoil my shoe?

I'd rather suit my foot
Than save my Boot –
For yet to buy another Pair
Is possible,
At any store –

But Bliss, is sold just once.
The Patent lost
None buy it any more –
Say, Foot, decide the point –
The Lady cross, or not?
Verdict for Boot!

c. 1862   1896

After great pain, a formal feeling comes –
The Nerves sit ceremonious, like Tombs –
The stiff Heart questions was it He, that bore,
And Yesterday, or Centuries before?

The Feet, mechanical, go round –
Of Ground, or Air, or Ought –
A Wooden way
Regardless grown,
A Quartz contentment, like a stone –

This is the Hour of Lead –
Remembered, if outlived,
As Freezing persons, recollect the Snow –
First – Chill – then Stupor – then the letting go –

c. 1862   1929

It will be Summer – eventually.
Ladies – with parasols –
Sauntering Gentlemen – with Canes –
And little Girls – with Dolls –

Will tint the pallid landscape –
As 'twere a bright Bouquet –
Tho' drifted deep, in Parian –
The Village lies – today –

The Lilacs – bending many a year –
Will sway with purple load –
The Bees – will not despise the tune –
Their Forefathers – have hummed –

The Wild Rose – redden in the Bog –
The Aster – on the Hill
Her everlasting fashion – set –
And Covenant Gentians – frill –

Till Summer folds her miracle –
As Women – do – their Gown –

Or Priests – adjust the Symbols –
When Sacrament – is done –

c. 1862   1929

343

My Reward for Being, was This.
My premium – My Bliss –
An Admiralty, less –
A Sceptre – penniless –
And Realms – just Dross –

When Thrones accost my Hands –
With "Me, Miss, Me" –
I'll unroll Thee –
Dominions dowerless – beside this Grace –
Election – Vote –
The Ballots of Eternity, will show just that.

c. 1862   1945

344

'Twas the old – road – through pain –
That unfrequented – one –
With many a turn – and thorn –
That stops – at Heaven –

This – was the Town – she passed –
There – where she – rested – last –
Then – stepped more fast –
The little tracks – close prest –
Then – not so swift –
Slow – slow – as feet did weary – grow –
Then – stopped – no other track!

Wait! Look! Her little Book –
The leaf – at love – turned back –
Her very Hat –
And this worn shoe just fits the track –
Herself – though – fled!

Another bed – a short one –
Women make – tonight –
In Chambers bright –
Too out of sight – though –
For our hoarse Good Night –
To touch her Head!

c. 1862   *1929*

345

Funny – to be a Century –
And see the People – going by –
I – should die of the Oddity –
But then – I'm not so staid – as He –

He keeps His Secrets safely – very –
Were He to tell – extremely sorry
This Bashful Globe of Ours would be –
So dainty of Publicity –

c. 1862   *1929*

346

Not probable – The barest Chance –
A smile too few – a word too much
And far from Heaven as the Rest –
The Soul so close on Paradise –

What if the Bird from journey far –
Confused by Sweets – as Mortals – are –
Forget the secret of His wing
And perish – but a Bough between –
Oh, Groping feet –
Oh Phantom Queen!

c. 1862   *1935*

347

When Night is almost done –
And Sunrise grows so near

That we can touch the Spaces –
It's time to smooth the Hair –

And get the Dimples ready –
And wonder we could care
For that old – faded Midnight –
That frightened – but an Hour –

c. 1862   *1890*

348

I dreaded that first Robin, so,
But He is mastered, now,
I'm some accustomed to Him grown,
He hurts a little, though –

I thought if I could only live
Till that first Shout got by –
Not all Pianos in the Woods
Had power to mangle me –

I dared not meet the Daffodils –
For fear their Yellow Gown
Would pierce me with a fashion
So foreign to my own –

I wished the Grass would hurry –
So – when 'twas time to see –
He'd be too tall, the tallest one
Could stretch – to look at me –

I could not bear the Bees should come,
I wished they'd stay away
In those dim countries where they go,
What word had they, for me?

They're here, though; not a creature failed –
No Blossom stayed away
In gentle deference to me –
The Queen of Calvary –

Each one salutes me, as he goes,
And I, my childish Plumes,

Lift, in bereaved acknowledgment
Of their unthinking Drums –

c. 1862   1891

349

I had the Glory – that will do –
An Honor, Thought can turn her to
When lesser Fames invite –
With one long "Nay" –
Bliss' early shape
Deforming – Dwindling – Gulfing up –
Time's possibility.

c. 1862   1945

350

They leave us with the Infinite.
But He – is not a man –
His fingers are the size of fists –
His fists, the size of men –

And whom he foundeth, with his Arm
As Himmaleh, shall stand –
Gibraltar's Everlasting Shoe
Poised lightly on his Hand,

So trust him, Comrade –
You for you, and I, for you and me
Eternity is ample,
And quick enough, if true.

c. 1862   1945

351

I felt my life with both my hands
To see if it was there –
I held my spirit to the Glass,
To prove it possibler –

I turned my Being round and round
And paused at every pound
To ask the Owner's name –
For doubt, that I should know the Sound –

I judged my features – jarred my hair –
I pushed my dimples by, and waited –
If they – twinkled back –
Conviction might, of me –

I told myself, "Take Courage, Friend –
That – was a former time –
But we might learn to like the Heaven,
As well as our Old Home!"

c. 1862   1945

352

Perhaps I asked too large –
I take – no less than skies –
For Earths, grow thick as
Berries, in my native town –

My Basket holds – just – Firmaments –
Those – dangle easy – on my arm,
But smaller bundles – Cram.

c. 1862   1945

353

A happy lip – breaks sudden –
It doesn't state you how
It contemplated – smiling –
Just consummated – now –
But this one, wears its merriment
So patient – like a pain –
Fresh gilded – to elude the eyes
Unqualified, to scan –

c. 1862   1955

From Cocoon forth a Butterfly
As Lady from her Door
Emerged – a Summer Afternoon –
Repairing Everywhere –

Without Design – that I could trace
Except to stray abroad
On Miscellaneous Enterprise
The Clovers – understood –

Her pretty Parasol be seen
Contracting in a Field
Where Men made Hay –
Then struggling hard
With an opposing Cloud –

Where Parties – Phantom as Herself –
To Nowhere – seemed to go
In purposeless Circumference –
As 'twere a Tropic Show –

And notwithstanding Bee – that worked –
And Flower – that zealous blew –
This Audience of Idleness
Disdained them, from the Sky –

Till Sundown crept – a steady Tide –
And Men that made the Hay –
And Afternoon – and Butterfly –
Extinguished – in the Sea –

c. 1862   1891

'Tis Opposites – entice –
Deformed Men – ponder Grace –
Bright fires – the Blanketless –
The Lost – Day's face –

The Blind – esteem it be
Enough Estate – to see –

The Captive – strangles new –
For deeming – Beggars – play –

To lack – enamor Thee –
Tho' the Divinity –
Be only
Me –

c. 1862

1929

356

The Day that I was crowned
Was like the other Days –
Until the Coronation came –
And then – 'twas Otherwise –

As Carbon in the Coal
And Carbon in the Gem
Are One – and yet the former
Were dull for Diadem –

I rose, and all was plain –
But when the Day declined
Myself and It, in Majesty
Were equally – adorned –

The Grace that I – was chose –
To Me – surpassed the Crown
That was the Witness for the Grace –
'Twas even that 'twas Mine –

c. 1862

1935

357

God is a distant – stately Lover –
Woos, as He states us – by His Son –
Verily, a Vicarious Courtship –
"Miles", and "Priscilla", were such an One –

But, lest the Soul – like fair "Priscilla"
Choose the Envoy – and spurn the Groom –

Vouches, with hyperbolic archness –
"Miles", and "John Alden" were Synonym –

c. *1862*   *1891*

358

If any sink, assure that this, now standing –
Failed like Themselves – and conscious that it rose –
Grew by the Fact, and not the Understanding
How Weakness passed – or Force – arose –

Tell that the Worst, is easy in a Moment –
Dread, but the Whizzing, before the Ball –
When the Ball enters, enters Silence –
Dying – annuls the power to kill.

c. 1862   *1935*

359

I gained it so –
By Climbing slow –
By Catching at the Twigs that grow
Between the Bliss – and me –
It hung so high
As well the Sky
Attempt by Strategy –

I said I gained it –
This – was all –
Look, how I clutch it
Lest it fall –
And I a Pauper go –
Unfitted by an instant's Grace
For the Contented – Beggar's face
I wore – an hour ago –

c. 1862   *1891*

360

Death sets a Thing significant
The Eye had hurried by

Except a perished Creature
Entreat us tenderly

To ponder little Workmanships
In Crayon, or in Wool,
With "This was last Her fingers did" –
Industrious until –

The Thimble weighed too heavy –
The stitches stopped – themselves –
And then 'twas put among the Dust
Upon the Closet shelves –

A Book I have – a friend gave –
Whose Pencil – here and there –
Had notched the place that pleased Him –
At Rest – His fingers are –

Now – when I read – I read not –
For interrupting Tears –
Obliterate the Etchings
Too Costly for Repairs.

c. 1862   1891

361

What I can do – I will –
Though it be little as a Daffodil –
That I cannot – must be
Unknown to possibility –

c. 1862   1929

362

It struck me – every Day –
The Lightning was as new
As if the Cloud that instant slit
And let the Fire through –

It burned Me – in the Night –
It Blistered to My Dream –

It sickened fresh upon my sight –
With every Morn that came –

I thought that Storm – was brief –
The Maddest – quickest by –
But Nature lost the Date of This –
And left it in the Sky –

c. 1862   1896

363

I went to thank Her –
But She Slept –
Her Bed – a funneled Stone –
With Nosegays at the Head and Foot –
That Travellers – had thrown –

Who went to thank Her –
But She Slept –
'Twas Short – to cross the Sea –
To look upon Her like – alive –
But turning back – 'twas slow –

c. 1862   1890

364

The Morning after Woe –
'Tis frequently the Way –
Surpasses all that rose before –
For utter Jubilee –

As Nature did not care –
And piled her Blossoms on –
And further to parade a Joy
Her Victim stared upon –

The Birds declaim their Tunes –
Pronouncing every word
Like Hammers – Did they know they fell
Like Litanies of Lead –

[172]

On here and there – a creature –
They'd modify the Glee
To fit some Crucifixal Clef –
Some Key of Calvary –

c. 1862 *1935*

365

Dare you see a Soul *at the White Heat*?
Then crouch within the door –
Red – is the Fire's common tint –
But when the vivid Ore
Has vanquished Flame's conditions,
It quivers from the Forge
Without a color, but the light
Of unanointed Blaze.
Least Village has its Blacksmith
Whose Anvil's even ring
Stands symbol for the finer Forge
That soundless tugs – within –
Refining these impatient Ores
With Hammer, and with Blaze
Until the Designated Light
Repudiate the Forge –

c. 1862 *1891*

366

Although I put away his life –
An Ornament too grand
For Forehead low as mine, to wear,
This might have been the Hand

That sowed the flower, he preferred –
Or smoothed a homely pain,
Or pushed the pebble from his path –
Or played his chosen tune –

On Lute the least – the latest –
But just his Ear could know

That whatsoe'er delighted it,
I never would let go –

The foot to bear his errand –
A little Boot I know –
Would leap abroad like Antelope –
With just the grant to do –

His weariest Commandment –
A sweeter to obey,
Than "Hide and Seek" –
Or skip to Flutes –
Or All Day, chase the Bee –

Your Servant, Sir, will weary –
The Surgeon, will not come –
The World, will have its own – to do –
The Dust, will vex your Fame –

The Cold will force your tightest door
Some February Day,
But say my apron bring the sticks
To make your Cottage gay –

That I may take that promise
To Paradise, with me –
To teach the Angels, avarice,
You, Sir, taught first – to me.

c. 1862   1929

367

Over and over, like a Tune –
The Recollection plays –
Drums off the Phantom Battlements
Cornets of Paradise –

Snatches, from Baptized Generations –
Cadences too grand
But for the Justified Processions
At the Lord's Right hand.

c. 1862   1929

How sick – to wait – in any place – but thine –
I knew last night – when someone tried to twine –
Thinking – perhaps – that I looked tired – or alone –
Or breaking – almost – with unspoken pain –

And I turned – ducal –
That right – was thine –
One port – suffices – for a Brig – like *mine* –

Ours be the tossing – wild though the sea –
Rather than a Mooring – unshared by thee.
Ours be the Cargo – *unladen – here* –
Rather than the *"spicy isles –"*
And thou – not there –

c. 1862   1945

She lay as if at play
Her life had leaped away –
Intending to return –
But not so soon –

Her merry Arms, half dropt –
As if for lull of sport –
An instant had forgot –
The Trick to start –

Her dancing Eyes – ajar –
As if their Owner were
Still sparkling through
For fun – at you –

Her Morning at the door –
Devising, I am sure –
To force her sleep –
So light – so deep –

c. 1862   1935

Heaven is so far of the Mind
That were the Mind dissolved –
The Site – of it – by Architect
Could not again be proved –

'Tis vast – as our Capacity –
As fair – as our idea –
To Him of adequate desire
No further 'tis, than Here –

c. 1862   1929

A precious – mouldering pleasure – 'tis –
To meet an Antique Book –
In just the Dress his Century wore –
A privilege – I think –

His venerable Hand to take –
And warming in our own –
A passage back – or two – to make –
To Times when he – was young –

His quaint opinions – to inspect –
His thought to ascertain
On Themes concern our mutual mind –
The Literature of Man –

What interested Scholars – most –
What Competitions ran –
When Plato – was a Certainty –
And Sophocles – a Man –

When Sappho – was a living Girl –
And Beatrice wore
The Gown that Dante – deified –
Facts Centuries before

He traverses – familiar –
As One should come to Town –

And tell you all your Dreams – were true –
He lived – where Dreams were born –

His presence is Enchantment –
You beg him not to go –
Old Volumes shake their Vellum Heads
And tantalize – just so –

c. *1862*   *1890*

372

I know lives, I could miss
Without a Misery –
Others – whose instant's wanting –
Would be Eternity –

The last – a scanty Number –
'Twould scarcely fill a Two –
The first – a Gnat's Horizon
Could easily outgrow –

c. *1862*   *1929*

373

I'm saying every day
"If I should be a Queen, tomorrow" –
I'd do this way –
And so I deck, a little,

If it be, I wake a Bourbon,
None on me, bend supercilious –
With "This was she –
Begged in the Market place –
Yesterday."

Court is a stately place –
I've heard men say –
So I loop my apron, against the Majesty
With bright Pins of Buttercup –
That not too plain –
Rank – overtake me –

And perch my Tongue
On Twigs of singing – rather high –
But this, might be my brief Term
To qualify –

Put from my simple speech all plain word –
Take other accents, as such I heard
Though but for the Cricket – just,
And but for the Bee –
Not in all the Meadow –
One accost me –

Better to be ready –
Than did next morn
Meet me in Aragon –
My old Gown – on –

And the surprised Air
Rustics – wear –
Summoned – unexpectedly –
To Exeter –

c. 1862   *1935*

374

I went to Heaven –
'Twas a small Town –
Lit – with a Ruby –
Lathed – with Down –

Stiller – than the fields
At the full Dew –
Beautiful – as Pictures –
No Man drew.
People – like the Moth –
Of Mechlin – frames –
Duties – of Gossamer –
And Eider – names –
Almost – contented –
I – could be –

'Mong such unique
Society –

c. 1862   1891

375

The Angle of a Landscape –
That every time I wake –
Between my Curtain and the Wall
Upon an ample Crack –

Like a Venetian – waiting –
Accosts my open eye –
Is just a Bough of Apples –
Held slanting, in the Sky –

The Pattern of a Chimney –
The Forehead of a Hill –
Sometimes – a Vane's Forefinger –
But that's – Occasional –

The Seasons – shift – my Picture –
Upon my Emerald Bough,
I wake – to find no – Emeralds –
Then – Diamonds – which the Snow

From Polar Caskets – fetched me –
The Chimney – and the Hill –
And just the Steeple's finger –
These – never stir at all –

c. 1862   1945

376

Of Course – I prayed –
And did God Care?
He cared as much as on the Air
A Bird – had stamped her foot –
And cried "Give Me" –
My Reason – Life –
I had not had – but for Yourself –

[179]

'Twere better Charity
To leave me in the Atom's Tomb –
Merry, and Nought, and gay, and numb –
Than this smart Misery.

c. 1862   *1929*

377

To lose one's faith – surpass
The loss of an Estate –
Because Estates can be
Replenished – faith cannot –

Inherited with Life –
Belief – but once – can be –
Annihilate a single clause –
And Being's – Beggary –

c. 1862   *1896*

378

I saw no Way – The Heavens were stitched –
I felt the Columns close –
The Earth reversed her Hemispheres –
I touched the Universe –

And back it slid – and I alone –
A Speck upon a Ball –
Went out upon Circumference –
Beyond the Dip of Bell –

c. 1862   *1935*

379

Rehearsal to Ourselves
Of a Withdrawn Delight –
Affords a Bliss like Murder –
Omnipotent – Acute –

We will not drop the Dirk –
Because We love the Wound

The Dirk Commemorate – Itself
Remind Us that we died.

380

There is a flower that Bees prefer –
And Butterflies – desire –
To gain the Purple Democrat
The Humming Bird – aspire –

And Whatsoever Insect pass –
A Honey bear away
Proportioned to his several dearth
And her – capacity –

Her face be rounder than the Moon
And ruddier than the Gown
Of Orchis in the Pasture –
Or Rhododendron – worn –

She doth not wait for June –
Before the World be Green –
Her sturdy little Countenance
Against the Wind – be seen –

Contending with the Grass –
Near Kinsman to Herself –
For Privilege of Sod and Sun –
Sweet Litigants for Life –

And when the Hills be full –
And newer fashions blow –
Doth not retract a single spice
For pang of jealousy –

Her Public – be the Noon –
Her Providence – the Sun –
Her Progress – by the Bee – proclaimed –
In sovereign – Swerveless Tune –

The Bravest – of the Host –
Surrendering – the last –

Nor even of Defeat – aware –
When cancelled by the Frost –

c. 1862   1890

381

A Secret told –
Ceases to be a Secret – then –
A Secret – kept –
That – can appal but One –

Better of it – continual be afraid –
Than it –
And Whom you told it to – beside –

c. 1862   1929

382

For Death – or rather
For the Things 'twould buy –
This – put away
Life's Opportunity –

The Things that Death will buy
Are Room –
Escape from Circumstances –
And a Name –

With Gifts of Life
How Death's Gifts may compare –
We know not –
For the Rates – lie Here –

c. 1862   1914

383

Exhilaration – is within –
There can no Outer Wine
So royally intoxicate
As that diviner Brand

The Soul achieves – Herself –
To drink – or set away
For Visitor – Or Sacrament –
'Tis not of Holiday

To stimulate a Man
Who hath the Ample Rhine
Within his Closet – Best you can
Exhale in offering.

c. 1862   *1935*

384

No Rack can torture me –
My Soul – at Liberty –
Behind this mortal Bone
There knits a bolder One –

You cannot prick with saw –
Nor pierce with Scimitar –
Two Bodies – therefore be –
Bind One – The Other fly –

The Eagle of his Nest
No easier divest –
And gain the Sky
Than mayest Thou –

Except Thyself may be
Thine Enemy –
Captivity is Consciousness –
So's Liberty.

c. 1862   *1890*

385

Smiling back from Coronation
May be Luxury –
On the Heads that started with us –
Being's Peasantry –

Recognizing in Procession
Ones We former knew –
When Ourselves were also dusty –
Centuries ago –

Had the Triumph no Conviction
Of how many be –
Stimulated – by the Contrast –
Unto Misery –

c. 1862   *1945*

386

Answer July –
Where is the Bee –
Where is the Blush –
Where is the Hay?

Ah, said July –
Where is the Seed –
Where is the Bud –
Where is the May –
Answer Thee – Me –

Nay – said the May –
Show me the Snow –
Show me the Bells –
Show me the Jay!

Quibbled the Jay –
Where be the Maize –
Where be the Haze –
Where be the Bur?
Here – said the Year –

c. 1862   *1935*

387

The Sweetest Heresy received
That Man and Woman know –

Each Other's Convert –
Though the Faith accommodate but Two –

The Churches are so frequent –
The Ritual – so small –
The Grace so unavoidable –
To fail – is Infidel –

c. 1862   1929

388

Take Your Heaven further on –
This – to Heaven divine Has gone –
Had You earlier blundered in
Possibly, e'en You had seen
An Eternity – put on –
Now – to ring a Door beyond
Is the utmost of Your Hand –
To the Skies – apologize –
Nearer to Your Courtesies
Than this Sufferer polite –
Dressed to meet You –
See – in White!

c. 1862   1935

389

There's been a Death, in the Opposite House,
As lately as Today –
I know it, by the numb look
Such Houses have – alway –

The Neighbors rustle in and out –
The Doctor – drives away –
A Window opens like a Pod –
Abrupt – mechanically –

Somebody flings a Mattress out –
The Children hurry by –
They wonder if it died – on that –
I used to – when a Boy –

The Minister – goes stiffly in –
As if the House were His –
And He owned all the Mourners – now –
And little Boys – besides –

And then the Milliner – and the Man
Of the Appalling Trade –
To take the measure of the House –

There'll be that Dark Parade –

Of Tassels – and of Coaches – soon –
It's easy as a Sign –
The Intuition of the News –
In just a Country Town –

c. 1862   1896

390

It's coming – the postponeless Creature –
It gains the Block – and now – it gains the Door –
Chooses its latch, from all the other fastenings –
Enters – with a "You know Me – Sir"?

Simple Salute – and certain Recognition –
Bold – were it Enemy – Brief – were it friend –
Dresses each House in Crape, and Icicle –
And carries one – out of it – to God –

c. 1862   1929

391

A Visitor in Marl –
Who influences Flowers –
Till they are orderly as Busts –
And Elegant – as Glass –

Who visits in the Night –
And just before the Sun –
Concludes his glistening interview –
Caresses – and is gone –

But whom his fingers touched –
And where his feet have run –
And whatsoever Mouth he kissed –
Is as it had not been –

c. 1862   1935

392

Through the Dark Sod – as Education –
The Lily passes sure –
Feels her white foot – no trepidation –
Her faith – no fear –

Afterward – in the Meadow –
Swinging her Beryl Bell –
The Mold-life – all forgotten – now –
In Ecstasy – and Dell –

c. 1862   1929

393

Did Our Best Moment last –
'Twould supersede the Heaven –
A few – and they by Risk – procure –
So this Sort – are not given –

Except as stimulants – in
Cases of Despair –
Or Stupor – The Reserve –
These Heavenly Moments are –

A Grant of the Divine –
That Certain as it Comes –
Withdraws – and leaves the dazzled Soul
In her unfurnished Rooms

c. 1862   1933

394

'Twas Love – not me –
Oh punish – pray –

[187]

The Real one died for Thee –
Just Him – not me –

Such Guilt – to love Thee – most!
Doom it beyond the Rest –
Forgive it – last –
'Twas base as Jesus – most!

Let Justice not mistake –
We Two – looked so alike –
Which was the Guilty Sake –
'Twas Love's – Now Strike!

c. 1862   *1945*

395

Reverse cannot befall
That fine Prosperity
Whose Sources are interior –
As soon – Adversity

A Diamond – overtake
In far – Bolivian Ground –
Misfortune hath no implement
Could mar it – if it found –

c. 1862   *1914*

396

There is a Languor of the Life
More imminent than Pain –
'Tis Pain's Successor – When the Soul
Has suffered all it can –

A Drowsiness – diffuses –
A Dimness like a Fog
Envelops Consciousness –
As Mists – obliterate a Crag.

The Surgeon – does not blanch – at pain –
His Habit – is severe –

But tell him that it ceased to feel —
The Creature lying there —

And he will tell you — skill is late —
A Mightier than He —
Has ministered before Him —
There's no Vitality.

c. 1862

1929

397

When Diamonds are a Legend,
And Diadems — a Tale —
I Brooch and Earrings for Myself,
Do sow, and Raise for sale —

And tho' I'm scarce accounted,
My Art, a Summer Day — had Patrons —
Once — it was a Queen —
And once — a Butterfly —

c. 1862

1935

398

I had not minded — Walls —
Were Universe — one Rock —
And far I heard his silver Call
The other side the Block —

I'd tunnel — till my Groove
Pushed sudden thro' to his —
Then my face take her Recompense —
The looking in his Eyes —

But 'tis a single Hair —
A filament — a law —
A Cobweb — wove in Adamant —
A Battlement — of Straw —

A limit like the Veil
Unto the Lady's face —

But every Mesh – a Citadel –
And Dragons – in the Crease –

c. 1862   1929

399

A House upon the Height –
That Wagon never reached –
No Dead, were ever carried down –
No Peddler's Cart – approached –

Whose Chimney never smoked –
Whose Windows – Night and Morn –
Caught Sunrise first – and Sunset – last –
Then – held an Empty Pane –

Whose fate – Conjecture knew –
No other neighbor – did –
And what it was – we never lisped –
Because He – never told –

c. 1862   1945

400

A Tongue – to tell Him I am true!
Its fee – to be of Gold –
Had Nature – in Her monstrous House
A single Ragged Child –

To earn a Mine – would run
That Interdicted Way,
And tell Him – Charge thee speak it plain –
That so far – Truth is True?

And answer What I do –
Beginning with the Day
That Night – begun –
Nay – Midnight – 'twas –
Since Midnight – happened – say –

If once more – Pardon – Boy –
The Magnitude thou may

Enlarge my Message – If too vast
Another Lad – help thee –

Thy Pay – in Diamonds – be –
And His – in solid Gold –
Say Rubies – if He hesitate –
My Message – must be told –

Say – last I said – was This –
That when the Hills – come down –
And hold no higher than the Plain –
My Bond – have just begun –

And when the Heavens – disband –
And Deity conclude –
Then – look for me. Be sure you say –
Least Figure – on the Road –

c. 1862   *1945*

401

What Soft – Cherubic Creatures –
These Gentlewomen are –
One would as soon assault a Plush –
Or violate a Star –

Such Dimity Convictions –
A Horror so refined
Of freckled Human Nature –
Of Deity – ashamed –

It's such a common – Glory –
A Fisherman's – Degree –
Redemption – Brittle Lady –
Be so – ashamed of Thee –

c. 1862   *1896*

402

I pay – in Satin Cash –
You did not state – your price –

[191]

A Petal, for a Paragraph
Is near as I can guess –

c. 1862   1929

403

The Winters are so short –
I'm hardly justified
In sending all the Birds away –
And moving into Pod –

Myself – for scarcely settled –
The Phoebes have begun –
And then – it's time to strike my Tent –
And open House – again –

It's mostly, interruptions –
My Summer – is despoiled –
Because there was a Winter – once –
And all the Cattle – starved –

And so there was a Deluge –
And swept the World away –
But Ararat's a Legend – now –
And no one credits Noah –

c. 1862   1935

404

How many Flowers fail in Wood –
Or perish from the Hill –
Without the privilege to know
That they are Beautiful –

How many cast a nameless Pod
Upon the nearest Breeze –
Unconscious of the Scarlet Freight –
It bear to Other Eyes –

c. 1862   1929

It might be lonelier
Without the Loneliness –
I'm so accustomed to my Fate –
Perhaps the Other – Peace –

Would interrupt the Dark –
And crowd the little Room –
Too scant – by Cubits – to contain
The Sacrament – of Him –

I am not used to Hope –
It might intrude upon –
Its sweet parade – blaspheme the place –
Ordained to Suffering –

It might be easier
To fail – with Land in Sight –
Than gain – My Blue Peninsula –
To perish – of Delight –

c. 1862

1935

Some – Work for Immortality –
The Chiefer part, for Time –
He – Compensates – immediately –
The former – Checks – on Fame –

Slow Gold – but Everlasting –
The Bullion of Today –
Contrasted with the Currency
Of Immortality –

A Beggar – Here and There –
Is gifted to discern
Beyond the Broker's insight –
One's – Money – One's – the Mine –

c. 1862

1929

If What we could – were what we would –
Criterion – be small –
It is the Ultimate of Talk –
The Impotence to Tell –

c. 1862   *1914*

Unit, like Death, for Whom?
True, like the Tomb,
Who tells no secret
Told to Him –
The Grave is strict –
Tickets admit
Just two – the Bearer –
And the Borne –
And seat – just One –
The Living – tell –
The Dying – but a Syllable –
The Coy Dead – None –
No Chatter – here – no tea –
So Babbler, and Bohea – stay there –
But Gravity – and Expectation – and Fear –
A tremor just, that All's not sure.

c. 1862   *1947*

They dropped like Flakes –
They dropped like Stars –
Like Petals from a Rose –
When suddenly across the June
A wind with fingers – goes –

They perished in the Seamless Grass –
No eye could find the place –

But God can summon every face
On his Repealless – List.

c. 1862

1891

410

The first Day's Night had come –
And grateful that a thing
So terrible – had been endured –
I told my Soul to sing –

She said her Strings were snapt –
Her Bow – to Atoms blown –
And so to mend her – gave me work
Until another Morn –

And then – a Day as huge
As Yesterdays in pairs,
Unrolled its horror in my face –
Until it blocked my eyes –

My Brain – begun to laugh –
I mumbled – like a fool –
And tho' 'tis Years ago – that Day –
My Brain keeps giggling – still.

And Something's odd – within –
That person that I was –
And this One – do not feel the same –
Could it be Madness – this?

c. 1862

1947

411

The Color of the Grave is Green –
The Outer Grave – I mean –
You would not know it from the Field –
Except it own a Stone –

To help the fond – to find it –
Too infinite asleep

To stop and tell them where it is –
But just a Daisy – deep –

The Color of the Grave is white –
The outer Grave – I mean –
You would not know it from the Drifts –
In Winter – till the Sun –

Has furrowed out the Aisles –
Then – higher than the Land
The little Dwelling Houses rise
Where each – has left a friend –

The Color of the Grave within –
The Duplicate – I mean –
Not all the Snows could make it white –
Not all the Summers – Green –

You've seen the Color – maybe –
Upon a Bonnet bound –
When that you met it with before –
The Ferret – cannot find –

c. 1862   1935

412

I read my sentence – steadily –
Reviewed it with my eyes,
To see that I made no mistake
In its extremest clause –
The Date, and manner, of the shame –
And then the Pious Form
That "God have mercy" on the Soul
The Jury voted Him –
I made my soul familiar – with her extremity –
That at the last, it should not be a novel Agony –
But she, and Death, acquainted –
Meet tranquilly, as friends –
Salute, and pass, without a Hint –
And there, the Matter ends –

c. 1862   1891

I never felt at Home – Below –
And in the Handsome Skies
I shall not feel at Home – I know –
I don't like Paradise –

Because it's Sunday – all the time –
And Recess – never comes –
And Eden'll be so lonesome
Bright Wednesday Afternoons –

If God could make a visit –
Or ever took a Nap –
So not to see us – but they say
Himself – a Telescope

Perennial beholds us –
Myself would run away
From Him – and Holy Ghost – and All –
But there's the "Judgment Day"!

c. 1862   1929

'Twas like a Maelstrom, with a notch,
That nearer, every Day,
Kept narrowing its boiling Wheel
Until the Agony

Toyed coolly with the final inch
Of your delirious Hem –
And you dropt, lost,
When something broke –
And let you from a Dream –

As if a Goblin with a Gauge –
Kept measuring the Hours –
Until you felt your Second
Weigh, helpless, in his Paws –

And not a Sinew – stirred – could help,
And sense was setting numb –

When God – remembered – and the Fiend
Let go, then, Overcome –

As if your Sentence stood – pronounced –
And you were frozen led
From Dungeon's luxury of Doubt
To Gibbets, and the Dead –

And when the Film had stitched your eyes
A Creature gasped "Reprieve"!
Which Anguish was the utterest – then –
To perish, or to live?

c. 1862

1945

415

Sunset at Night – is natural –
But Sunset on the Dawn
Reverses Nature – Master –
So Midnight's – due – at Noon.

Eclipses be – predicted –
And Science bows them in –
But do one face us suddenly –
Jehovah's Watch – is wrong.

c. 1862

1929

416

A Murmur in the Trees – to note –
Not loud enough – for Wind –
A Star – not far enough to seek –
Nor near enough – to find –

A long – long Yellow – on the Lawn –
A Hubbub – as of feet –
Not audible – as Ours – to Us –
But dapperer – More Sweet –

A Hurrying Home of little Men
To Houses unperceived –

All this – and more – if I should tell –
Would never be believed –

Of Robins in the Trundle bed
How many I espy
Whose Nightgowns could not hide the Wings –
Although I heard them try –

But then I promised ne'er to tell –
How could I break My Word?
So go your Way – and I'll go Mine –
No fear you'll miss the Road.

c. 1862   *1896*

417

It is dead – Find it –
Out of sound – Out of sight –
"Happy"? Which is wiser –
You, or the Wind?
"Conscious"? Won't you ask that –
Of the low Ground?

"Homesick"? Many met it –
Even through them – This
Cannot testify –
Themself – as dumb –

c. 1862   *1929*

418

Not in this World to see his face –
Sounds long – until I read the place
Where this – is said to be
But just the Primer – to a life –
Unopened – rare – Upon the Shelf –
Clasped yet – to Him – and me –

And yet – My Primer suits me so
I would not choose – a Book to know
Than that – be sweeter wise –

Might some one else – so learned – be –
And leave me – just my A – B – C –
Himself – could have the Skies –

c. 1862   1890

419

We grow accustomed to the Dark –
When Light is put away –
As when the Neighbor holds the Lamp
To witness her Goodbye –

A Moment – We uncertain step
For newness of the night –
Then – fit our Vision to the Dark –
And meet the Road – erect –

And so of larger – Darknesses –
Those Evenings of the Brain –
When not a Moon disclose a sign –
Or Star – come out – within –

The Bravest – grope a little –
And sometimes hit a Tree
Directly in the Forehead –
But as they learn to see –

Either the Darkness alters –
Or something in the sight
Adjusts itself to Midnight –
And Life steps almost straight.

c. 1862   1935

420

You'll know it – as you know 'tis Noon –
By Glory –
As you do the Sun –
By Glory –
As you will in Heaven –
Know God the Father – and the Son.

By intuition, Mightiest Things
Assert themselves – and not by terms –
"I'm Midnight" – need the Midnight say –
"I'm Sunrise" – Need the Majesty?

Omnipotence – had not a Tongue –
His lisp – is Lightning – and the Sun –
His Conversation – with the Sea –
"How shall you know"?
Consult your Eye!

c. 1862   *1935*

421

A Charm invests a face
Imperfectly beheld –
The Lady dare not lift her Veil
For fear it be dispelled –

But peers beyond her mesh –
And wishes – and denies –
Lest Interview – annul a want
That Image – satisfies –

c. 1862   *1891*

422

More Life – went out – when He went
Than Ordinary Breath –
Lit with a finer Phosphor –
Requiring in the Quench –

A Power of Renowned Cold,
The Climate of the Grave
A Temperature just adequate
So Anthracite, to live –

For some – an Ampler Zero –
A Frost more needle keen
Is necessary, to reduce
The Ethiop within.

[201]

Others – extinguish easier –
A Gnat's minutest Fan
Sufficient to obliterate
A Tract of Citizen –

Whose Peat lift – amply vivid –
Ignores the solemn News
That Popocatapel exists –
Or Etna's Scarlets, Choose –

c. 1862   *1935*

423

The Months have ends – the Years – a knot –
No Power can untie
To stretch a little further
A Skein of Misery –

The Earth lays back these tired lives
In her mysterious Drawers –
Too tenderly, that any doubt
An ultimate Repose –

The manner of the Children –
Who weary of the Day –
Themself – the noisy Plaything
They cannot put away –

c. 1862   *1935*

424

Removed from Accident of Loss
By Accident of Gain
Befalling not my simple Days –
Myself had just to earn –

Of Riches – as unconscious
As is the Brown Malay
Of Pearls in Eastern Waters,
Marked His – What Holiday

Would stir his slow conception –
Had he the power to dream
That but the Dower's fraction –
Awaited even – Him –

c. 1862   *1935*

425

Good Morning – Midnight –
I'm coming Home –
Day – got tired of Me –
How could I – of Him?

Sunshine was a sweet place –
I liked to stay –
But Morn – didn't want me – now –
So – Goodnight – Day!

I can look – can't I –
When the East is Red?
The Hills – have a way – then –
That puts the Heart – abroad –

You – are not so fair – Midnight –
I chose – Day –
But – please take a little Girl –
He turned away!

c. 1862   *1929*

426

It don't sound so terrible – quite – as it did –
I run it over – "Dead", Brain, "Dead."
Put it in Latin – left of my school –
Seems it don't shriek so – under rule.

Turn it, a little – full in the face
A Trouble looks bitterest –
Shift it – just –
Say "When Tomorrow comes this way –
I shall have waded down one Day."

[203]

I suppose it will interrupt me some
Till I get accustomed – but then the Tomb
Like other new Things – shows largest – then –
And smaller, by Habit –

It's shrewder then
Put the Thought in advance – a Year –
How like "a fit" – then –
Murder – wear!

c. *1862* *1945*

427

I'll clutch – and clutch –
Next – One – Might be the golden touch –
Could take it –
Diamonds – Wait –
I'm diving – just a little late –
But stars – go slow – for night –

I'll string you – in fine Necklace –
Tiaras – make – of some –
Wear you on Hem –
Loop up a Countess – with you –
Make – a Diadem – and mend my old One –
Count – Hoard – then lose –
And doubt that you are mine –
To have the joy of feeling it – again –

I'll show you at the Court –
Bear you – for Ornament
Where Women breathe –
That every sigh – may lift you
Just as high – as I –

And – when I die –
In meek array – display you –
Still to show – how rich I go –
Lest Skies impeach a wealth so wonderful –
And banish me –

c. *1862* *1945*

Taking up the fair Ideal,
Just to cast her down
When a fracture – we discover –
Or a splintered Crown –
Makes the Heavens portable –
And the Gods – a lie –
Doubtless – "Adam" – scowled at Eden –
For *his* perjury!

Cherishing – our poor Ideal –
Till in purer dress –
We behold her – glorified –
Comforts – search – like this –
Till the broken creatures –
We adored – for whole –
Stains – all washed –
Transfigured – mended –
Meet us – with a smile –

c. 1862   *1945*

The Moon is distant from the Sea –
And yet, with Amber Hands –
She leads Him – docile as a Boy –
Along appointed Sands –

He never misses a Degree –
Obedient to Her Eye
He comes just so far – toward the Town –
Just so far – goes away –

Oh, Signor, Thine, the Amber Hand –
And mine – the distant Sea –
Obedient to the least command
Thine eye impose on me –

c. 1862   *1891*

It would never be Common – more – I said –
Difference – had begun –
Many a bitterness – had been –
But that old sort – was done –

Or – if it sometime – showed – as 'twill –
Upon the Downiest – Morn –
Such bliss – had I – for all the years –
'Twould give an Easier – pain –

I'd so much joy – I told it – Red –
Upon my simple Cheek –
I felt it publish – in my Eye –
'Twas needless – any speak –

I walked – as wings – my body bore –
The feet – I former used –
Unnecessary – now to me –
As boots – would be – to Birds –

I put my pleasure all abroad –
I dealt a word of Gold
To every Creature – that I met –
And Dowered – all the World –

When – suddenly – my Riches shrank –
A Goblin – drank my Dew –
My Palaces – dropped tenantless –
Myself – was beggared – too –

I clutched at sounds –
I groped at shapes –
I touched the tops of Films –
I felt the Wilderness roll back
Along my Golden lines –

The Sackcloth – hangs upon the nail –
The Frock I used to wear –
But where my moment of Brocade –
My – drop – of India?

c. 1862   *1935*

Me – come! My dazzled face
In such a shining place!
Me – hear! My foreign Ear
The sounds of Welcome – there!

The Saints forget
Our bashful feet –

My Holiday, shall be
That They – remember me –
My Paradise – the fame
That They – pronounce my name –

c. 1862   1896

Do People moulder equally,
They bury, in the Grave?
I do believe a Species
As positively live

As I, who testify it
Deny that I – am dead –
And fill my Lungs, for Witness –
From Tanks – above my Head –

I say to you, said Jesus –
That there be standing here –
A Sort, that shall not taste of Death –
If Jesus was sincere –

I need no further Argue –
That statement of the Lord
Is not a controvertible –
He told me, Death was dead –

c. 1862   1945

Knows how to forget!
But could It teach it?

Easiest of Arts, they say
When one learn how

Dull Hearts have died
In the Acquisition
Sacrifice for Science
Is common, though, now –

I went to School
But was not wiser
Globe did not teach it
Nor Logarithm Show

"How to forget"!
Say – some – Philosopher!
Ah, to be erudite
Enough to know!

Is it in a Book?
So, I could buy it –
Is it like a Planet?
Telescopes would know –

If it be invention
It must have a Patent.
Rabbi of the Wise Book
Don't you know?

c. 1865   1945

434

To love thee Year by Year –
May less appear
Than sacrifice, and cease –
However, dear,
Forever might be short, I thought to show –
And so I pieced it, with a flower, now.

c. 1862   1914

Much Madness is divinest Sense –
To a discerning Eye –
Much Sense – the starkest Madness –
'Tis the Majority
In this, as All, prevail –
Assent – and you are sane –
Demur – you're straightway dangerous –
And handled with a Chain –

c. 1862   1890

The Wind – tapped like a tired Man –
And like a Host – "Come in"
I boldly answered – entered then
My Residence within

A Rapid – footless Guest –
To offer whom a Chair
Were as impossible as hand
A Sofa to the Air –

No Bone had He to bind Him –
His Speech was like the Push
Of numerous Humming Birds at once
From a superior Bush –

His Countenance – a Billow –
His Fingers, as He passed
Let go a music – as of tunes
Blown tremulous in Glass –

He visited – still flitting –
Then like a timid Man
Again, He tapped – 'twas flurriedly –
And I became alone –

c. 1862   1891

Prayer is the little implement
Through which Men reach
Where Presence – is denied them.
They fling their Speech

By means of it – in God's Ear –
If then He hear –
This sums the Apparatus
Comprised in Prayer –

c. 1862   *1891*

438

Forget! The lady with the Amulet
Forget she wore it at her Heart
Because she breathed against
Was Treason twixt?

Deny! Did Rose her Bee –
For Privilege of Play
Or Wile of Butterfly
Or Opportunity – Her Lord away?

The lady with the Amulet – will fade –
The Bee – in Mausoleum laid –
Discard his Bride –
But longer than the little Rill –
That cooled the Forehead of the Hill –
While Other – went the Sea to fill –
And Other – went to turn the Mill –
I'll do thy Will –

c. 1862   *1935*

439

Undue Significance a starving man attaches
To Food –
Far off – He sighs – and therefore – Hopeless –
And therefore – Good –

Partaken – it relieves – indeed –
But proves us
That Spices fly
In the Receipt – It was the Distance –
Was Savory –

c. 1862   1891

440

'Tis customary as we part
A trinket – to confer –
It helps to stimulate the faith
When Lovers be afar –

'Tis various – as the various taste –
Clematis – journeying far –
Presents me with a single Curl
Of her Electric Hair –

c. 1862   1945

441

This is my letter to the World
That never wrote to Me –
The simple News that Nature told –
With tender Majesty

Her Message is committed
To Hands I cannot see –
For love of Her – Sweet – countrymen –
Judge tenderly – of Me

c. 1862   1890

442

God made a little Gentian –
It tried – to be a Rose –
And failed – and all the Summer laughed –
But just before the Snows

There rose a Purple Creature –
That ravished all the Hill –
And Summer hid her Forehead –
And Mockery – was still –

The Frosts were her condition –
The Tyrian would not come
Until the North – invoke it –
Creator – Shall I – bloom?

c. 1862

1891

443

I tie my Hat – I crease my Shawl –
Life's little duties do – precisely –
As the very least
Were infinite – to me –

I put new Blossoms in the Glass –
And throw the old – away –
I push a petal from my Gown
That anchored there – I weigh
The time 'twill be till six o'clock
I have so much to do –
And yet – Existence – some way back –
Stopped – struck – my ticking – through –
We cannot put Ourself away
As a completed Man
Or Woman – When the Errand's done
We came to Flesh – upon –
There may be – Miles on Miles of Nought –
Of Action – sicker far –
To simulate – is stinging work –
To cover what we are
From Science – and from Surgery –
Too Telescopic Eyes
To bear on us unshaded –
For their – sake – not for Ours –

'Twould start them –
We – could tremble –
But since we got a Bomb –
And held it in our Bosom –
Nay – Hold it – it is calm –

Therefore – we do life's labor –
Though life's Reward – be done –
With scrupulous exactness –
To hold our Senses – on –

c. 1862   1929

444

It feels a shame to be Alive –
When Men so brave – are dead –
One envies the Distinguished Dust –
Permitted – such a Head –

The Stone – that tells defending Whom
This Spartan put away
What little of Him we – possessed
In Pawn for Liberty –

The price is great – Sublimely paid –
Do we deserve – a Thing –
That lives – like Dollars – must be piled
Before we may obtain?

Are we that wait – sufficient worth –
That such Enormous Pearl
As life – dissolved be – for Us –
In Battle's – horrid Bowl?

It may be – a Renown to live –
I think the Man who die –
Those unsustained – Saviors –
Present Divinity –

c. 1862   1929

'Twas just this time, last year, I died.
I know I heard the Corn,
When I was carried by the Farms –
It had the Tassels on –

I thought how yellow it would look –
When Richard went to mill –
And then, I wanted to get out,
But something held my will.

I thought just how Red – Apples wedged
The Stubble's joints between –
And the Carts stooping round the fields
To take the Pumpkins in –

I wondered which would miss me, least,
And when Thanksgiving, came,
If Father'd multiply the plates –
To make an even Sum –

And would it blur the Christmas glee
My Stocking hang too high
For any Santa Claus to reach
The Altitude of me –

But this sort, grieved myself,
And so, I thought the other way,
How just this time, some perfect year –
Themself, should come to me –

c. 1862

1896

I showed her Heights she never saw –
"Would'st Climb," I said?
She said – "Not so" –
"With *me* –" I said – With *me*?
I showed her Secrets – Morning's Nest –
The Rope the Nights were put across –
And *now* – "Would'st have me for a Guest?"

She could not find her Yes –
And then, I brake my life – And Lo,
A Light, for her, did solemn glow,
The larger, as her face withdrew –
And *could* she, further, "No"?

c. 1862   *1914*

447

Could – I do more – for Thee –
Wert Thou a Bumble Bee –
Since for the Queen, have I –
Nought but Bouquet?

c. 1862   *1929*

448

This was a Poet – It is That
Distills amazing sense
From ordinary Meanings –
And Attar so immense

From the familiar species
That perished by the Door –
We wonder it was not Ourselves
Arrested it – before –

Of Pictures, the Discloser –
The Poet – it is He –
Entitles Us – by Contrast –
To ceaseless Poverty –

Of Portion – so unconscious –
The Robbing – could not harm –
Himself – to Him – a Fortune –
Exterior – to Time –

c. 1862   *1929*

I died for Beauty – but was scarce
Adjusted in the Tomb
When One who died for Truth, was lain
In an adjoining Room –

He questioned softly "Why I failed"?
"For Beauty", I replied –
"And I – for Truth – Themself are One –
We Brethren, are", He said –

And so, as Kinsmen, met a Night –
We talked between the Rooms –
Until the Moss had reached our lips –
And covered up – our names –

c. 1862   *1890*

Dreams – are well – but Waking's better,
If One wake at Morn –
If One wake at Midnight – better –
Dreaming – of the Dawn –

Sweeter – the Surmising Robins –
Never gladdened Tree –
Than a Solid Dawn – confronting –
Leading to no Day –

c. 1862   *1935*

The Outer – from the Inner
Derives its Magnitude –
'Tis Duke, or Dwarf, according
As is the Central Mood –

The fine – unvarying Axis
That regulates the Wheel –
Though Spokes – spin – more conspicuous
And fling a dust – the while.

The Inner – paints the Outer –
The Brush without the Hand –
Its Picture publishes – precise –
As is the inner Brand –

On fine – Arterial Canvas –
A Cheek – perchance a Brow –
The Star's whole Secret – in the Lake –
Eyes were not meant to know.

c. 1862   *1935*

452

The Malay – took the Pearl –
Not – I – the Earl –
I – feared the Sea – too much
Unsanctified – to touch –

Praying that I might be
Worthy – the Destiny –
The Swarthy fellow swam –
And bore my Jewel – Home –

Home to the Hut! What lot
Had I – the Jewel – got –
Borne on a Dusky Breast –
I had not deemed a Vest
Of Amber – fit –

The Negro never knew
I – wooed it – too –
To gain, or be undone –
Alike to Him – One –

c. 1862   *1945*

453

Love – thou art high –
I cannot climb thee –
But, were it Two –
Who knows but we –

Taking turns – at the Chimborazo –
Ducal – at last – stand up by thee –

Love – thou art deep –
I cannot cross thee –
But, were there Two
Instead of One –
Rower, and Yacht – some sovereign Summer –
Who knows – but we'd reach the Sun?

Love – thou art Veiled –
A few – behold thee –
Smile – and alter – and prattle – and die –
Bliss – were an Oddity – without thee –
Nicknamed by God –
Eternity –

c. 1862   1929

454

It was given to me by the Gods –
When I was a little Girl –
They give us Presents most – you know –
When we are new – and small.
I kept it in my Hand –
I never put it down –
I did not dare to eat – or sleep –
For fear it would be gone –
I heard such words as "Rich" –
When hurrying to school –
From lips at Corners of the Streets –
And wrestled with a smile.
Rich! 'Twas Myself – was rich –
To take the name of Gold –
And Gold to own – in solid Bars –
The Difference – made me bold –

c. 1862   1945

Triumph – may be of several kinds –
There's Triumph in the Room
When that Old Imperator – Death –
By Faith – be overcome –

There's Triumph of the finer Mind
When Truth – affronted long –
Advance unmoved – to Her Supreme –
Her God – Her only Throng –

A Triumph – when Temptation's Bribe
Be slowly handed back –
One eye upon the Heaven renounced –
And One – upon the Rack –

Severer Triumph – by Himself
Experienced – who pass
Acquitted – from that Naked Bar –
Jehovah's Countenance –

c. 1862   *1891*

So well that I can live without –
I love thee – then How well is that?
As well as Jesus?
Prove it me
That He – loved Men –
As I – love thee –

c. 1862   *1929*

Sweet – safe – Houses –
Glad – gay – Houses –
Sealed so stately tight –
Lids of Steel – on Lids of Marble –
Locking Bare feet out –

Brooks of Plush – in Banks of Satin
Not so softly fall
As the laughter – and the whisper –
From their People Pearl –

No Bald Death – affront their Parlors –
No Bold Sickness come
To deface their Stately Treasures –
Anguish – and the Tomb –

Hum by – in Muffled Coaches –
Lest they – wonder Why –
Any – for the Press of Smiling –
Interrupt – to die –

c. 1862   1945

458

Like Eyes that looked on Wastes –
Incredulous of Ought
But Blank – and steady Wilderness –
Diversified by Night –

Just Infinites of Nought –
As far as it could see –
So looked the face I looked upon –
So looked itself – on Me –

I offered it no Help –
Because the Cause was Mine –
The Misery a Compact
As hopeless – as divine –

Neither – would be absolved –
Neither would be a Queen
Without the Other – Therefore –
We perish – tho' We reign –

c. 1862   1945

A Tooth upon Our Peace
The Peace cannot deface –
Then Wherefore be the Tooth?
To vitalize the Grace –

The Heaven hath a Hell –
Itself to signalize –
And every sign before the Place
Is Gilt with Sacrifice –

c. 1862   *1935*

I know where Wells grow – Droughtless Wells –
Deep dug – for Summer days –
Where Mosses go no more away –
And Pebble – safely plays –

It's made of Fathoms – and a Belt –
A Belt of jagged Stone –
Inlaid with Emerald – half way down –
And Diamonds – jumbled on –

It has no Bucket – Were I rich
A Bucket I would buy –
I'm often thirsty – but my lips
Are so high up – You see –

I read in an Old fashioned Book
That People "thirst no more" –
The Wells have Buckets to them there –
It must mean that – I'm sure –

Shall We remember Parching – then?
Those Waters sound so grand –
I think a little Well – like Mine –
Dearer to understand –

c. 1862   *1935*

461

A Wife – at Daybreak I shall be –
Sunrise – Hast thou a Flag for me?
At Midnight, I am but a Maid,
How short it takes to make a Bride –
Then – Midnight, I have passed from thee
Unto the East, and Victory –

Midnight – Good Night! I hear them call,
The Angels bustle in the Hall –
Softly my Future climbs the Stair,
I fumble at my Childhood's prayer
So soon to be a Child no more –
Eternity, I'm coming – Sir,
Savior – I've seen the face – before!

c. 1862   *1929*

462

Why make it doubt – it hurts it so –
So sick – to guess –
So strong – to know –
So brave – upon its little Bed
To tell the very last They said
Unto Itself – and smile – And shake –
For that dear – distant – dangerous – Sake –
But – the Instead – the Pinching fear
That Something – it did do – or dare –
Offend the Vision – and it flee –
And They no more remember me –
Nor ever turn to tell me why –
Oh, Master, This is Misery –

c. 1862   *1929*

463

I live with Him – I see His face –
I go no more away

[222]

For Visitor – or Sundown –
Death's single privacy

The Only One – forestalling Mine –
And that – by Right that He
Presents a Claim invisible –
No wedlock – granted Me –

I live with Him – I hear His Voice –
I stand alive – Today –
To witness to the Certainty
Of Immortality –

Taught Me – by Time – the lower Way –
Conviction – Every day –
That Life like This – is stopless –
Be Judgment – what it may –

c. 1862   1896

464

The power to be true to You,
Until upon my face
The Judgment push His Picture –
Presumptuous of Your Place –

Of This – Could Man deprive Me –
Himself – the Heaven excel –
Whose invitation – Yours reduced
Until it showed too small –

c. 1862   1929

465

I heard a Fly buzz – when I died –
The Stillness in the Room
Was like the Stillness in the Air –
Between the Heaves of Storm –

The Eyes around – had wrung them dry –
And Breaths were gathering firm

For that last Onset – when the King
Be witnessed – in the Room –

I willed my Keepsakes – Signed away
What portion of me be
Assignable – and then it was
There interposed a Fly –

With Blue – uncertain stumbling Buzz –
Between the light – and me –
And then the Windows failed – and then
I could not see to see –

c. 1862   1896

466

'Tis little I – could care for Pearls –
Who own the ample sea –
Or Brooches – when the Emperor –
With Rubies – pelteth me –

Or Gold – who am the Prince of Mines –
Or Diamonds – when have I
A Diadem to fit a Dome –
Continual upon me –

c. 1862   1896

467

We do not play on Graves –
Because there isn't Room –
Besides – it isn't even – it slants
And People come –

And put a Flower on it –
And hang their faces so –
We're fearing that their Hearts will drop –
And crush our pretty play –

And so we move as far
As Enemies – away –

[224]

Just looking round to see how far
It is – Occasionally –

c. 1862

1945

468

The Manner of its Death
When Certain it must die –
'Tis deemed a privilege to choose –
'Twas Major André's Way –

When Choice of Life – is past –
There yet remains a Love
Its little Fate to stipulate –

How small in those who live –

The Miracle to tease
With Babble of the styles –
How "they are Dying mostly – now" –
And Customs at "St. James"!

c. 1862

1945

469

The Red – Blaze – is the Morning –
The Violet – is Noon –
The Yellow – Day – is falling –
And after that – is none –

But Miles of Sparks – at Evening –
Reveal the Width that burned –
The Territory Argent – that
Never yet – consumed –

c. 1862

1945

470

I am alive – I guess –
The Branches on my Hand

Are full of Morning Glory –
And at my finger's end –

The Carmine – tingles warm –
And if I hold a Glass
Across my Mouth – it blurs it –
Physician's – proof of Breath –

I am alive – because
I am not in a Room –
The Parlor – Commonly – it is –
So Visitors may come –

And lean – and view it sidewise –
And add "How cold – it grew" –
And "Was it conscious – when it stepped
In Immortality?"

I am alive – because
I do not own a House –
Entitled to myself – precise –
And fitting no one else –

And marked my Girlhood's name –
So Visitors may know
Which Door is mine – and not mistake –
And try another Key –

How good – to be alive!
How infinite – to be
Alive – two-fold – The Birth I had –
And this – besides, in – Thee!

c. 1862   1945

471

A Night – there lay the Days between –
The Day that was Before –
And Day that was Behind – were one –
And now – 'twas Night – was here –

Slow – Night – that must be watched away –
As Grains upon a shore –

Too imperceptible to note –
Till it be night – no more –

c. 1862   *1945*

472

Except the Heaven had come so near –
So seemed to choose My Door –
The Distance would not haunt me so –
I had not hoped – before –

But just to hear the Grace depart –
I never thought to see –
Afflicts me with a Double loss –
'Tis lost – And lost to me –

c. 1862   *1891*

473

I am ashamed – I hide –
What right have I – to be a Bride –
So late a Dowerless Girl –
Nowhere to hide my dazzled Face –
No one to teach me that new Grace –
Nor introduce – my Soul –

Me to adorn – How – tell –
Trinket – to make Me beautiful –
Fabrics of Cashmere –
Never a Gown of Dun – more –
Raiment instead – of Pompadour –
For Me – My soul – to wear –

Fingers – to frame my Round Hair
Oval – as Feudal Ladies wore –
Far Fashions – Fair –
Skill – to hold my Brow like an Earl –
Plead – like a Whippoorwill –
Prove – like a Pearl –
Then, for Character –

Fashion My Spirit quaint – white –
Quick – like a Liquor –
Gay – like Light –
Bring Me my best Pride –
No more ashamed –
No more to hide –
Meek – let it be – too proud – for Pride –
Baptized – this Day – A Bride –

c. *1862*   *1929*

474

They put Us far apart –
As separate as Sea
And Her unsown Peninsula –
We signified "These see" –

They took away our Eyes –
They thwarted Us with Guns –
"I see Thee" each responded straight
Through Telegraphic Signs –

With Dungeons – They devised –
But through their thickest skill –
And their opaquest Adamant –
Our Souls saw – just as well –

They summoned Us to die –
With sweet alacrity
We stood upon our stapled feet –
Condemned – but just – to see –

Permission to recant –
Permission to forget –
We turned our backs upon the Sun
For perjury of that –

Not Either – noticed Death –
Of Paradise – aware –
Each other's Face – was all the Disc
Each other's setting – saw –

c. *1862*   *1935*

Doom is the House without the Door –
'Tis entered from the Sun –
And then the Ladder's thrown away,
Because Escape – is done –

'Tis varied by the Dream
Of what they do outside –
Where Squirrels play – and Berries die –
And Hemlocks – bow – to God –

c. 1862   *1929*

I meant to have but modest needs –
Such as Content – and Heaven –
Within my income – these could lie
And Life and I – keep even –

But since the last – included both –
It would suffice my Prayer
But just for One – to stipulate –
And Grace would grant the Pair –

And so – upon this wise – I prayed –
Great Spirit – Give to me
A Heaven not so large as Yours,
But large enough – for me –

A Smile suffused Jehovah's face –
The Cherubim – withdrew –
Grave Saints stole out to look at me –
And showed their dimples – too –

I left the Place, with all my might –
I threw my Prayer away –
The Quiet Ages picked it up –
And Judgment – twinkled – too –
That one so honest – be extant –
It take the Tale for true –

That "Whatsoever Ye shall ask –
Itself be given You" –

But I, grown shrewder – scan the Skies
With a suspicious Air –
As Children – swindled for the first
All Swindlers – be – infer –

c. 1862   1891

477

No Man can compass a Despair –
As round a Goalless Road
No faster than a Mile at once
The Traveller proceed –

Unconscious of the Width –
Unconscious that the Sun
Be setting on His progress –
So accurate the One

At estimating Pain –
Whose own – has just begun –
His ignorance – the Angel
That pilot Him along –

c. 1862   1935

478

I had no time to Hate –
Because
The Grave would hinder Me –
And Life was not so
Ample I
Could finish – Enmity –

Nor had I time to Love –
But since
Some Industry must be –

The little Toil of Love –
I thought
Be large enough for Me –

c. 1862   1890

479

She dealt her pretty words like Blades –
How glittering they shone –
And every One unbared a Nerve
Or wantoned with a Bone –

She never deemed – she hurt –
That – is not Steel's Affair –
A vulgar grimace in the Flesh –
How ill the Creatures bear –

To Ache is human – not polite –
The Film upon the eye
Mortality's old Custom –
Just locking up – to Die.

c. 1862   1929

480

"Why do I love" You, Sir?
Because –
The Wind does not require the Grass
To answer – Wherefore when He pass
She cannot keep Her place.

Because He knows – and
Do not You –
And We know not –
Enough for Us
The Wisdom it be so –

The Lightning – never asked an Eye
Wherefore it shut – when He was by –
Because He knows it cannot speak –
And reasons not contained –

– Of Talk –
There be – preferred by Daintier Folk –

The Sunrise – Sir – compelleth Me –
Because He's Sunrise – and I see –
Therefore – Then –
I love Thee –

c. 1862   *1929*

481

The Himmaleh was known to stoop
Unto the Daisy low –
Transported with Compassion
That such a Doll should grow
Where Tent by Tent – Her Universe
Hung out its Flags of Snow –

c. 1862   *1935*

482

We Cover Thee – Sweet Face –
Not that We tire of Thee –
But that Thyself fatigue of Us –
Remember – as Thou go –
We follow Thee until
Thou notice Us – no more –
And then – reluctant – turn away
To Con Thee o'er and o'er –

And blame the scanty love
We were Content to show –
Augmented – Sweet – a Hundred fold –
If Thou would'st take it – now –

c. 1862   *1896*

483

A Solemn thing within the Soul
To feel itself get ripe –

And golden hang – while farther up –
The Maker's Ladders stop –
And in the Orchard far below –
You hear a Being – drop –

A Wonderful – to feel the Sun
Still toiling at the Cheek
You thought was finished –
Cool of eye, and critical of Work –
He shifts the stem – a little –
To give your Core – a look –

But solemnest – to know
Your chance in Harvest moves
A little nearer – Every Sun
The Single – to some lives.

c. 1862   *1945*

484

My Garden – like the Beach –
Denotes there be – a Sea –
That's Summer –
Such as These – the Pearls
She fetches – such as Me

c. 1862   *1935*

485

To make One's Toilette – after Death
Has made the Toilette cool
Of only Taste we cared to please
Is difficult, and still –

That's easier – than Braid the Hair –
And make the Bodice gay –
When eyes that fondled it are wrenched
By Decalogues – away –

c. 1862   *1935*

I was the slightest in the House –
I took the smallest Room –
At night, my little Lamp, and Book –
And one Geranium –

So stationed I could catch the Mint
That never ceased to fall –
And just my Basket –
Let me think – I'm sure
That this was all –

I never spoke – unless addressed –
And then, 'twas brief and low –
I could not bear to live – aloud –
The Racket shamed me so –

And if it had not been so far –
And any one I knew
Were going – I had often thought
How noteless – I could die –

c. 1862   *1945*

You love the Lord – you cannot see –
You write Him – every day –
A little note – when you awake –
And further in the Day.

An Ample Letter – How you miss –
And would delight to see –
But then His House – is but a Step –
And Mine's – in Heaven – You see.

c. 1862   *1945*

Myself was formed – a Carpenter –
An unpretending time

[234]

My Plane – and I, together wrought
Before a Builder came –

To measure our attainments –
Had we the Art of Boards
Sufficiently developed – He'd hire us
At Halves –

My Tools took Human – Faces –
The Bench, where we had toiled –
Against the Man – persuaded –
We – Temples build – I said –

c. 1862   1935

489

We pray – to Heaven –
We prate – of Heaven –
Relate – when Neighbors die –
At what o'clock to Heaven – they fled –
Who saw them – Wherefore fly?

Is Heaven a Place – a Sky – a Tree?
Location's narrow way is for Ourselves –
Unto the Dead
There's no Geography –

But State – Endowal – Focus –
Where – Omnipresence – fly?

c. 1862   1929

490

To One denied to drink
To tell what Water is
Would be acuter, would it not
Than letting Him surmise?

To lead Him to the Well
And let Him hear it drip

Remind Him, would it not, somewhat
Of His condemned lip?

c. 1862

1945

491

While it is alive
Until Death touches it
While it and I lap one Air
Dwell in one Blood
Under one Sacrament
Show me Division can split or pare –

Love is like Life – merely longer
Love is like Death, during the Grave
Love is the Fellow of the Resurrection
Scooping up the Dust and chanting "Live"!

c. 1862

1945

492

Civilization – spurns – the Leopard!
Was the Leopard – bold?
Deserts – never rebuked her Satin –
Ethiop – her Gold –
Tawny – her Customs –
She was Conscious –
Spotted – her Dun Gown –
This was the Leopard's nature – Signor –
Need – a keeper – frown?

Pity – the Pard – that left her Asia –
Memories – of Palm –
Cannot be stifled – with Narcotic –
Nor suppressed – with Balm –

c. 1862

1945

The World – stands – solemner – to me –
Since I was wed – to Him –
A modesty befits the soul
That bears another's – name –
A doubt – if it be fair – indeed –
To wear that perfect – pearl –
The Man – upon the Woman – binds –
To clasp her soul – for all –
A prayer, that it more angel – prove –
A whiter Gift – within –
To that munificence, that chose –
So unadorned – a Queen –
A Gratitude – that such be true –
It had esteemed the Dream –
Too beautiful – for Shape to prove –
Or posture – to redeem!

c. 1862   1945

Going to Him! Happy letter!
Tell Him –
Tell Him the page I didn't write –
Tell Him – I only said the Syntax –
And left the Verb and the pronoun out –
Tell Him just how the fingers hurried –
Then – how they waded – slow – slow –
And then you wished you had eyes in your pages –
So you could see what moved them so –

Tell Him – it wasn't a Practised Writer –
You guessed – from the way the sentence toiled –
You could hear the Bodice tug, behind you –
As if it held but the might of a child –
You almost pitied it – you – it worked so –
Tell Him – no – you may quibble there –
For it would split His Heart, to know it –
And then you and I, were silenter.

[237]

Tell Him – Night finished – before we finished –
And the Old Clock kept neighing "Day"!
And you – got sleepy – and begged to be ended –
What could it hinder so – to say?
Tell Him – just how she sealed you – Cautious!
But – if He ask where you are hid
Until tomorrow – Happy letter!
Gesture Coquette – and shake your Head!

Version I
c. 1862   *1891*

Going – to – Her!
Happy – Letter! Tell Her –
Tell Her – the page I never wrote!
Tell Her, I only said – the Syntax –
And left the Verb and the Pronoun – out!
Tell Her just how the fingers – hurried –
Then – how they – stammered – slow – slow –
And then – you wished you had eyes – in your pages –
So you could see – what moved – them – so –

Tell Her – it wasn't a practised writer –
You guessed –
From the way the sentence – toiled –
You could hear the Bodice – tug – behind you –
As if it held but the might of a child!
You almost pitied – it – you – it worked so –
Tell Her – No – you may quibble – there –
For it would split Her Heart – to know it –
And then – you and I – were silenter!

Tell Her – Day – finished – before we – finished –
And the old Clock kept neighing – "Day"!
And you – got sleepy – and begged to be ended –
What could – it hinder so – to say?
Tell Her – just how she sealed – you – Cautious!
But – if she ask "where you are hid" – until the evening –
Ah! Be bashful!

Gesture Coquette –
And shake your Head!

Version II
c. 1862

1955

495

It's thoughts – and just One Heart –
And Old Sunshine – about –
Make frugal – Ones – Content –
And two or three – for Company –
Upon a Holiday –
Crowded – as Sacrament –

Books – when the Unit –
Spare the Tenant – long eno' –
A Picture – if it Care –
Itself – a Gallery too rare –
For needing more –

Flowers – to keep the Eyes – from going awkward –
When it snows –
A Bird – if they – prefer –
Though Winter fire – sing clear as Plover –
To our – ear –

A Landscape – not so great
To suffocate the Eye –
A Hill – perhaps –
Perhaps – the profile of a Mill
Turned by the Wind –
Tho' *such* – are *luxuries* –

It's thoughts – and just two Heart –
And Heaven – about –
At least – a Counterfeit –
We would not have Correct –
And Immortality – can be almost –
Not quite – Content –

c. 1862

1935

As far from pity, as complaint –
As cool to speech – as stone –
As numb to Revelation
As if my Trade were Bone –

As far from Time – as History –
As near yourself – Today –
As Children, to the Rainbow's scarf –
Or Sunset's Yellow play

To eyelids in the Sepulchre –
How dumb the Dancer lies –
While Color's Revelations break –
And blaze – the Butterflies!

c. 1862   1896

He strained my faith –
Did he find it supple?
Shook my strong trust –
Did it then – yield?

Hurled my belief –
But – did he shatter – it?
Racked – with suspense –
Not a nerve failed!

Wrung me – with Anguish –
But I never doubted him –
'Tho' for what wrong
He did never say –

Stabbed – while I sued
His sweet forgiveness –
Jesus – it's your little "John"!
Don't you know – me?

c. 1862   1945

I envy Seas, whereon He rides –
I envy Spokes of Wheels
Of Chariots, that Him convey –
I envy Crooked Hills

That gaze upon His journey –
How easy All can see
What is forbidden utterly
As Heaven – unto me!

I envy Nests of Sparrows –
That dot His distant Eaves –
The wealthy Fly, upon His Pane –
The happy – happy Leaves –

That just abroad His Window
Have Summer's leave to play –
The Ear Rings of Pizarro
Could not obtain for me –

I envy Light – that wakes Him –
And Bells – that boldly ring
To tell Him it is Noon, abroad –
Myself – be Noon to Him –

Yet interdict – my Blossom –
And abrogate – my Bee –
Lest Noon in Everlasting Night –
Drop Gabriel – and Me –

c. 1862   *1896*

Those fair – fictitious People –
The Women – plucked away
From our familiar Lifetime –
The Men of Ivory –

Those Boys and Girls, in Canvas –
Who stay upon the Wall

In Everlasting Keepsake –
Can Anybody tell?

We trust – in places perfecter –
Inheriting Delight
Beyond our faint Conjecture –
Our dizzy Estimate –

Remembering ourselves, we trust –
Yet Blesseder – than We –
Through Knowing – where We only hope –
Receiving – where we – pray –

Of Expectation – also –
Anticipating us
With transport, that would be a pain
Except for Holiness –

Esteeming us – as Exile –
Themself – admitted Home –
Through easy Miracle of Death –
The Way ourself, must come –

c. 1862   *1929*

500

Within my Garden, rides a Bird
Upon a single Wheel –
Whose spokes a dizzy Music make
As 'twere a travelling Mill –

He never stops, but slackens
Above the Ripest Rose –
Partakes without alighting
And praises as he goes,

Till every spice is tasted –
And then his Fairy Gig
Reels in remoter atmospheres –
And I rejoin my Dog,

And He and I, perplex us
If positive, 'twere we –

[242]

Or bore the Garden in the Brain
This Curiosity –

But He, the best Logician,
Refers my clumsy eye –
To just vibrating Blossoms!
An Exquisite Reply!

c. *1862*   *1929*

501

This World is not Conclusion.
A Species stands beyond –
Invisible, as Music –
But positive, as Sound –
It beckons, and it baffles –
Philosophy – don't know –
And through a Riddle, at the last –
Sagacity, must go –
To guess it, puzzles scholars –
To gain it, Men have borne
Contempt of Generations
And Crucifixion, shown –
Faith slips – and laughs, and rallies –
Blushes, if any see –
Plucks at a twig of Evidence –
And asks a Vane, the way –
Much Gesture, from the Pulpit –
Strong Hallelujahs, roll –
Narcotics cannot still the Tooth
That nibbles at the soul –

c. *1862*   *1896*

502

At least – to pray – is left – is left –
Oh Jesus – in the Air –
I know not which thy chamber is –
I'm knocking – everywhere –

[243]

Thou settest Earthquake in the South –
And Maelstrom, in the Sea –
Say, Jesus Christ of Nazareth –
Hast thou no Arm for Me?

c. 1862   1891

503

Better – than Music! For I – who heard it –
I was used – to the Birds – before –
This – was different – 'Twas Translation –
Of all tunes I knew – and more –

'Twasn't contained – like other stanza –
No one could play it – the second time –
But the Composer – perfect Mozart –
Perish with him – that Keyless Rhyme!

So – Children – told how Brooks in Eden –
Bubbled a better – Melody –
Quaintly infer – Eve's great surrender –
Urging the feet – that would – not – fly –

Children – matured – are wiser – mostly –
Eden – a legend – dimly told –
Eve – and the Anguish – Grandame's story –
But – I was telling a tune – I heard –

Not such a strain – the Church – baptizes –
When the last Saint – goes up the Aisles –
Not such a stanza splits the silence –
When the Redemption strikes her Bells –

Let me not spill – its smallest cadence –
Humming – for promise – when alone –
Humming – until my faint Rehearsal –
Drop into tune – around the Throne –

c. 1862   1945

[244]

You know that Portrait in the Moon –
So tell me who 'tis like –
The very Brow – the stooping eyes –
A-fog for – Say – Whose Sake?

The very Pattern of the Cheek –
It varies – in the Chin –
But – Ishmael – since we met – 'tis long –
And fashions – intervene –

When Moon's at full – 'Tis Thou – I say –
My lips just hold the name –
When crescent – Thou art worn – I note –
But – there – the Golden Same –

And when – Some Night – Bold – slashing Clouds
Cut Thee away from Me –
That's easier – than the other film
That glazes Holiday –

c. 1862

1935

I would not paint – a picture –
I'd rather be the One
Its bright impossibility
To dwell – delicious – on –
And wonder how the fingers feel
Whose rare – celestial – stir –
Evokes so sweet a Torment –
Such sumptuous – Despair –

I would not talk, like Cornets –
I'd rather be the One
Raised softly to the Ceilings –
And out, and easy on –
Through Villages of Ether –
Myself endued Balloon
By but a lip of Metal –
The pier to my Pontoon –

Nor would I be a Poet –
It's finer – own the Ear –
Enamored – impotent – content –
The License to revere,
A privilege so awful
What would the Dower be,
Had I the Art to stun myself
With Bolts of Melody!

c. 1862   *1945*

506

He touched me, so I live to know
That such a day, permitted so,
I groped upon his breast –
It was a boundless place to me
And silenced, as the awful sea
Puts minor streams to rest.

And now, I'm different from before,
As if I breathed superior air –
Or brushed a Royal Gown –
My feet, too, that had wandered so –
My Gypsy face – transfigured now –
To tenderer Renown –

Into this Port, if I might come,
Rebecca, to Jerusalem,
Would not so ravished turn –
Nor Persian, baffled at her shrine
Lift such a Crucifixal sign
To her imperial Sun.

c. 1862 ·   *1896*

507

She sights a Bird – she chuckles –
She flattens – then she crawls –
She runs without the look of feet –
Her eyes increase to Balls –

[246]

Her Jaws stir – twitching – hungry –
Her Teeth can hardly stand –
She leaps, but Robin leaped the first –
Ah, Pussy, of the Sand,

The Hopes so juicy ripening –
You almost bathed your Tongue –
When Bliss disclosed a hundred Toes –
And fled with every one –

c. 1862   *1945*

508

I'm ceded – I've stopped being Theirs –
The name They dropped upon my face
With water, in the country church
Is finished using, now,
And They can put it with my Dolls,
My childhood, and the string of spools,
I've finished threading – too –

Baptized, before, without the choice,
But this time, consciously, of Grace –
Unto supremest name –
Called to my Full – The Crescent dropped –
Existence's whole Arc, filled up,
With one small Diadem.

My second Rank – too small the first –
Crowned – Crowing – on my Father's breast –
A half unconscious Queen –
But this time – Adequate – Erect,
With Will to choose, or to reject,
And I choose, just a Crown –

c. 1862   *1890*

509

If anybody's friend be dead
It's sharpest of the theme

The thinking how they walked alive –
At such and such a time –

Their costume, of a Sunday,
Some manner of the Hair –
A prank nobody knew but them
Lost, in the Sepulchre –

How warm, they were, on such a day,
You almost feel the date –
So short way off it seems –
And now – they're Centuries from that –

How pleased they were, at what you said –
You try to touch the smile
And dip your fingers in the frost –
When was it – Can you tell –

You asked the Company to tea –
Acquaintance – just a few –
And chatted close with this Grand Thing
That don't remember you –

Past Bows, and Invitations –
Past Interview, and Vow –
Past what Ourself can estimate –
That – makes the Quick of Woe!

c. 1862   *1891*

510

It was not Death, for I stood up,
And all the Dead, lie down –
It was not Night, for all the Bells
Put out their Tongues, for Noon.

It was not Frost, for on my Flesh
I felt Siroccos – crawl –
Nor Fire – for just my Marble feet
Could keep a Chancel, cool –

And yet, it tasted, like them all,
The Figures I have seen

[248]

Set orderly, for Burial,
Reminded me, of mine –

As if my life were shaven,
And fitted to a frame,
And could not breathe without a key,
And 'twas like Midnight, some –

When everything that ticked – has stopped –
And Space stares all around –
Or Grisly frosts – first Autumn morns,
Repeal the Beating Ground –

But, most, like Chaos – Stopless – cool –
Without a Chance, or Spar –
Or even a Report of Land –
To justify – Despair.

c. 1862   *1891*

511

If you were coming in the Fall,
I'd brush the Summer by
With half a smile, and half a spurn,
As Housewives do, a Fly.

If I could see you in a year,
I'd wind the months in balls –
And put them each in separate Drawers,
For fear the numbers fuse –

If only Centuries, delayed,
I'd count them on my Hand,
Subtracting, till my fingers dropped
Into Van Dieman's Land.

If certain, when this life was out –
That yours and mine, should be
I'd toss it yonder, like a Rind,
And take Eternity –

But, now, uncertain of the length
Of this, that is between,

[249]

It goads me, like the Goblin Bee –
That will not state – its sting.

c. 1862   *1890*

512

The Soul has Bandaged moments –
When too appalled to stir –
She feels some ghastly Fright come up
And stop to look at her –

Salute her – with long fingers –
Caress her freezing hair –
Sip, Goblin, from the very lips
The Lover – hovered – o'er –
Unworthy, that a thought so mean
Accost a Theme – so – fair –

The soul has moments of Escape –
When bursting all the doors –
She dances like a Bomb, abroad,
And swings upon the Hours,

As do the Bee – delirious borne –
Long Dungeoned from his Rose –
Touch Liberty – then know no more,
But Noon, and Paradise –

The Soul's retaken moments –
When, Felon led along,
With shackles on the plumed feet,
And staples, in the Song,

The Horror welcomes her, again,
These, are not brayed of Tongue –

c. 1862   *1945*

513

Like Flowers, that heard the news of Dews,
But never deemed the dripping prize
Awaited their – low Brows –

Or Bees – that thought the Summer's name
Some rumor of Delirium,
No Summer – could – for Them –

Or Arctic Creatures, dimly stirred –
By Tropic Hint – some Travelled Bird
Imported to the Wood –

Or Wind's bright signal to the Ear –
Making that homely, and severe,
Contented, known, before –

The Heaven – unexpected come,
To Lives that thought the Worshipping
A too presumptuous Psalm –

c. 1862   1890

514

Her smile was shaped like other smiles –
The Dimples ran along –
And still it hurt you, as some Bird
Did hoist herself, to sing,
Then recollect a Ball, she got –
And hold upon the Twig,
Convulsive, while the Music broke –
Like Beads – among the Bog –

c. 1862   1935

515

No Crowd that has occurred
Exhibit – I suppose
That General Attendance
That Resurrection – does –

Circumference be full –
The long restricted Grave
Assert her Vital Privilege –
The Dust – connect – and live –

On Atoms – features place –
All Multitudes that were
Efface in the Comparison –
As Suns – dissolve a star –

Solemnity – prevail –
Its Individual Doom
Possess each separate Consciousness –
August – Absorbed – Numb –

What Duplicate – exist –
What Parallel can be –
Of the Significance of This –
To Universe – and Me?

c. 1862   1929

516

Beauty – be not caused – It Is –
Chase it, and it ceases –
Chase it not, and it abides –

Overtake the Creases

In the Meadow – when the Wind
Runs his fingers thro' it –
Deity will see to it
That You never do it –

c. 1862   1929

517

He parts Himself – like Leaves –
And then – He closes up –
Then stands upon the Bonnet
Of Any Buttercup –

And then He runs against
And oversets a Rose –
And then does Nothing –
Then away upon a Jib – He goes –

And dangles like a Mote
Suspended in the Noon –
Uncertain – to return Below –
Or settle in the Moon –

What come of Him – at Night –
The privilege to say
Be limited by Ignorance –
What come of Him – That Day –

The Frost – possess the World –
In Cabinets – be shown –
A Sepulchre of quaintest Floss –
An Abbey – a Cocoon –

c. 1862 *1935*

518

Her sweet Weight on my Heart a Night
Had scarcely deigned to lie –
When, stirring, for Belief's delight,
My Bride had slipped away –

If 'twas a Dream – made solid – just
The Heaven to confirm –
Or if Myself were dreamed of Her –
The power to presume –

With Him remain – who unto Me –
Gave – even as to All –
A Fiction superseding Faith –
By so much – as 'twas real –

c. 1862 *1945*

519

'Twas warm – at first – like Us –
Until there crept upon
A Chill – like frost upon a Glass –
Till all the scene – be gone.

The Forehead copied Stone –
The Fingers grew too cold
To ache – and like a Skater's Brook –
The busy eyes – congealed –

It straightened – that was all –
It crowded Cold to Cold –
It multiplied indifference –
As Pride were all it could –

And even when with Cords –
'Twas lowered, like a Weight –
It made no Signal, nor demurred,
But dropped like Adamant.

c. 1862   1929

520

I started Early – Took my Dog –
And visited the Sea –
The Mermaids in the Basement
Came out to look at me –

And Frigates – in the Upper Floor
Extended Hempen Hands –
Presuming Me to be a Mouse –
Aground – upon the Sands –

But no Man moved Me – till the Tide
Went past my simple Shoe –
And past my Apron – and my Belt
And past my Bodice – too –

And made as He would eat me up –
As wholly as a Dew
Upon a Dandelion's Sleeve –
And then – I started – too –

And He – He followed – close behind –
I felt His Silver Heel
Upon my Ankle – Then my Shoes
Would overflow with Pearl –

Until We met the Solid Town –
No One He seemed to know –
And bowing – with a Mighty look –
At me – The Sea withdrew –

c. 1862

1891

521

Endow the Living – with the Tears –
You squander on the Dead,
And They were Men and Women – now,
Around Your Fireside –

Instead of Passive Creatures,
Denied the Cherishing
Till They – the Cherishing deny –
With Death's Ethereal Scorn –

c. 1862

1945

522

Had I presumed to hope –
The loss had been to Me
A Value – for the Greatness' Sake –
As Giants – gone away –

Had I presumed to gain
A Favor so remote –
The failure but confirm the Grace
In further Infinite –

'Tis failure – not of Hope –
But Confident Despair –
Advancing on Celestial Lists –
With faint – Terrestrial power –

'Tis Honor – though I die –
For That no Man obtain
Till He be justified by Death –
This – is the Second Gain –

c. 1862

1929

523

Sweet – You forgot – but I remembered
Every time – for Two –
So that the Sum be never hindered
Through Decay of You –

Say if I erred? Accuse my Farthings –
Blame the little Hand
Happy it be for You – a Beggar's –
Seeking More – to spend –

Just to be Rich – to waste my Guineas
On so Best a Heart –
Just to be Poor – for Barefoot Vision
You – Sweet – Shut me out –

c. 1862   1945

524

Departed – to the Judgment –
A Mighty Afternoon –
Great Clouds – like Ushers – leaning –
Creation – looking on –

The Flesh – Surrendered – Cancelled –
The Bodiless – begun –
Two Worlds – like Audiences – disperse –
And leave the Soul – alone –

c. 1862   1890

525

I think the Hemlock likes to stand
Upon a Marge of Snow –
It suits his own Austerity –
And satisfies an awe

That men, must slake in Wilderness –
And in the Desert – cloy –
An instinct for the Hoar, the Bald –
Lapland's – necessity –

The Hemlock's nature thrives – on cold –
The Gnash of Northern winds
Is sweetest nutriment – to him –
His best Norwegian Wines –

To satin Races – he is nought –
But Children on the Don,
Beneath his Tabernacles, play,
And Dnieper Wrestlers, run.

c. 1862   1890

526

To hear an Oriole sing
May be a common thing –
Or only a divine.

It is not of the Bird
Who sings the same, unheard,
As unto Crowd –

The Fashion of the Ear
Attireth that it hear
In Dun, or fair –

So whether it be Rune,
Or whether it be none
Is of within.

The "Tune is in the Tree – "
The Skeptic – showeth me –
"No Sir! In Thee!"

c. 1862   1891

527

To put this World down, like a Bundle –
And walk steady, away,
Requires Energy – possibly Agony –
'Tis the Scarlet way

Trodden with straight renunciation
By the Son of God –

[257]

Later, his faint Confederates
Justify the Road –

Flavors of that old Crucifixion –
Filaments of Bloom, Pontius Pilate sowed –
Strong Clusters, from Barabbas' Tomb –

Sacrament, Saints partook before us –
Patent, every drop,
With the Brand of the Gentile Drinker
Who indorsed the Cup –

c. 1862   *1935*

528

Mine – by the Right of the White Election!
Mine – by the Royal Seal!
Mine – by the Sign in the Scarlet prison –
Bars – cannot conceal!

Mine – here – in Vision – and in Veto!
Mine – by the Grave's Repeal –
Titled – Confirmed –
Delirious Charter!
Mine – long as Ages steal!

c. 1862   *1890*

529

I'm sorry for the Dead – Today –
It's such congenial times
Old Neighbors have at fences –
It's time o' year for Hay.

And Broad – Sunburned Acquaintance
Discourse between the Toil –
And laugh, a homely species
That makes the Fences smile –

It seems so straight to lie away
From all the noise of Fields –

The Busy Carts – the fragrant Cocks –
The Mower's Metre – Steals

A Trouble lest they're homesick –
Those Farmers – and their Wives –
Set separate from the Farming –
And all the Neighbors' lives –

A Wonder if the Sepulchre
Don't feel a lonesome way –
When Men – and Boys – and Carts – and June,
Go down the Fields to "Hay" –

c. 1862   1929

530

You cannot put a Fire out –
A Thing that can ignite
Can go, itself, without a Fan –
Upon the slowest Night –

You cannot fold a Flood –
And put it in a Drawer –
Because the Winds would find it out –
And tell your Cedar Floor –

c. 1862   1896

531

We dream – it is good we are dreaming –
It would hurt us – were we awake –
But since it is playing – kill us,
And we are playing – shriek –

What harm? Men die – externally –
It is a truth – of Blood –
But we – are dying in Drama –
And Drama – is never dead –

Cautious – We jar each other –
And either – open the eyes –

[259]

Lest the Phantasm – prove the Mistake –
And the livid Surprise

Cool us to Shafts of Granite –
With just an Age – and Name –
And perhaps a phrase in Egyptian –
It's prudenter – to dream –

c. 1862   1935

532

I tried to think a lonelier Thing
Than any I had seen –
Some Polar Expiation – An Omen in the Bone
Of Death's tremendous nearness –

I probed Retrieveless things
My Duplicate – to borrow –
A Haggard Comfort springs

From the belief that Somewhere –
Within the Clutch of Thought –
There dwells one other Creature
Of Heavenly Love – forgot –

I plucked at our Partition
As One should pry the Walls –
Between Himself – and Horror's Twin –
Within Opposing Cells –

I almost strove to clasp his Hand,
Such Luxury – it grew –
That as Myself – could pity Him –
Perhaps he – pitied me –

c. 1862   1945

533

Two Butterflies went out at Noon –
And waltzed upon a Farm –
Then stepped straight through the Firmament
And rested, on a Beam –

And then – together bore away
Upon a shining Sea –
Though never yet, in any Port –
Their coming, mentioned – be –

If spoken by the distant Bird –
If met in Ether Sea
By Frigate, or by Merchantman –
No notice – was – to me –

c. 1862   1891

534

We see – Comparatively –
The Thing so towering high
We could not grasp its segment
Unaided – Yesterday –

This Morning's finer Verdict –
Makes scarcely worth the toil –
A furrow – Our Cordillera –
Our Apennine – a Knoll –

Perhaps 'tis kindly – done us –
The Anguish – and the loss –
The wrenching – for His Firmament
The Thing belonged to us –

To spare these Striding Spirits
Some Morning of Chagrin –
The waking in a Gnat's – embrace –
Our Giants – further on –

c. 1862   1929

535

She's happy, with a new Content –
That feels to her – like Sacrament –
She's busy – with an altered Care –
As just apprenticed to the Air –

[261]

She's tearful – if she weep at all –
For blissful Causes – Most of all
That Heaven permit so meek as her –
To such a Fate – to Minister.

c. 1862   1935

536

The Heart asks Pleasure – first –
And then – Excuse from Pain –
And then – those little Anodynes
That deaden suffering –

And then – to go to sleep –
And then – if it should be
The will of its Inquisitor
The privilege to die –

c. 1862   1890

537

Me prove it now – Whoever doubt
Me stop to prove it – now –
Make haste – the Scruple! Death be scant
For Opportunity –

The River reaches to my feet –
As yet – My Heart be dry –
Oh Lover – Life could not convince –
Might Death – enable Thee –

The River reaches to My Breast –
Still – still – My Hands above
Proclaim with their remaining Might –
Dost recognize the Love?

The River reaches to my Mouth –
Remember – when the Sea
Swept by my searching eyes – the last –
Themselves were quick – with Thee!

c. 1862   1935

538

'Tis true – They shut me in the Cold –
But then – Themselves were warm
And could not know the feeling 'twas –
Forget it – Lord – of Them –

Let not my Witness hinder Them
In Heavenly esteem –
No Paradise could be – Conferred
Through Their beloved Blame –

The Harm They did – was short – And since
Myself – who bore it – do –
Forgive Them – Even as Myself –
Or else – forgive not me –

c. 1862   1945

539

The Province of the Saved
Should be the Art – To save –
Through Skill obtained in Themselves –
The Science of the Grave

No Man can understand
But He that hath endured
The Dissolution – in Himself –
That Man – be qualified

To qualify Despair
To Those who failing new –
Mistake Defeat for Death – Each time –
Till acclimated – to –

c. 1862   1935

540

I took my Power in my Hand –
And went against the World –
'Twas not so much as David – had –
But I – was twice as bold –

I aimed my Pebble – but Myself
Was all the one that fell –
Was it Goliah – was too large –
Or was myself – too small?

c. 1862   *1891*

541

Some such Butterfly be seen
On Brazilian Pampas –
Just at noon – no later – Sweet –
Then – the License closes –

Some such Spice – express and pass –
Subject to Your Plucking –
As the Stars – You knew last Night –
Foreigners – This Morning –

c. 1862   *1935*

542

I had no Cause to be awake –
My Best – was gone to sleep –
And Morn a new politeness took –
And failed to wake them up –

But called the others – clear –
And passed their Curtains by –
Sweet Morning – When I oversleep –
Knock – Recollect – to Me –

I looked at Sunrise – Once –
And then I looked at Them –
And wishfulness in me arose –
For Circumstance the same –

'Twas such an Ample Peace –
It could not hold a Sigh –
'Twas Sabbath – with the Bells divorced –
'Twas Sunset – all the Day –

So choosing but a Gown –
And taking but a Prayer –
The only Raiment I should need –
I struggled – and was There –

c. 1862   *1891*

543

I fear a Man of frugal Speech –
I fear a Silent Man –
Haranguer – I can overtake –
Or Babbler – entertain –

But He who weigheth – While the Rest –
Expend their furthest pound –
Of this Man – I am wary –
I fear that He is Grand –

c. 1862   *1929*

544

The Martyr Poets – did not tell –
But wrought their Pang in syllable –
That when their mortal name be numb –
Their mortal fate – encourage Some –

The Martyr Painters – never spoke –
Bequeathing – rather – to their Work –
That when their conscious fingers cease –
Some seek in Art – the Art of Peace –

c. 1862   *1935*

545

'Tis One by One – the Father counts –
And then a Tract between
Set Cypherless – to teach the Eye
The Value of its Ten –

Until the peevish Student
Acquire the Quick of Skill –

'Then Numerals are dowered back –
Adorning all the Rule –

'Tis mostly Slate and Pencil –
And Darkness on the School
Distracts the Children's fingers –
Still the Eternal Rule

Regards least Cypherer alike
With Leader of the Band –
And every separate Urchin's Sum –
Is fashioned for his hand –

c. 1862   *1945*

546

To fill a Gap
Insert the Thing that caused it –
Block it up
With Other – and 'twill yawn the more –
You cannot solder an Abyss
With Air.

c. 1862   *1929*

547

I've seen a Dying Eye
Run round and round a Room –
In search of Something – as it seemed –
Then Cloudier become –
And then – obscure with Fog –
And then – be soldered down
Without disclosing what it be
'Twere blessed to have seen –

c. 1862   *1890*

548

Death is potential to that Man
Who dies – and to his friend –

[266]

Beyond that – unconspicuous
To Anyone but God –

Of these Two – God remembers
The longest – for the friend –
Is integral – and therefore
Itself dissolved – of God –

c. 1862   *1945*

549

That I did always love
I bring thee Proof
That till I loved
I never lived – Enough –

That I shall love alway –
I argue thee
That love is life –
And life hath Immortality –

This – dost thou doubt – Sweet –
Then have I
Nothing to show
But Calvary –

c. 1862   *1890*

550

I cross till I am weary
A Mountain – in my mind –
More Mountains – then a Sea –
More Seas – And then
A Desert – find –

And My Horizon blocks
With steady – drifting – Grains
Of unconjectured quantity –
As Asiatic Rains –

Nor this – defeat my Pace –
It hinder from the West

But as an Enemy's Salute
One hurrying to Rest –

What merit had the Goal –
Except there intervene
Faint Doubt – and far Competitor –
To jeopardize the Gain?

At last – the Grace in sight –
I shout unto my feet –
I offer them the Whole of Heaven
The instant that we meet –

They strive – and yet delay –
They perish – Do we die –
Or is this Death's Experiment –
Reversed – in Victory?

c. 1862   1935

551

There is a Shame of Nobleness –
Confronting Sudden Pelf –
A finer Shame of Ecstasy –
Convicted of Itself –

A best Disgrace – a Brave Man feels –
Acknowledged – of the Brave –
One More – "Ye Blessed" – to be told –
But that's – Behind the Grave –

c. 1862   1891

552

An ignorance a Sunset
Confer upon the Eye –
Of Territory – Color –
Circumference – Decay –

Its Amber Revelation
Exhilarate – Debase –

[268]

Omnipotence' inspection
Of Our inferior face –

And when the solemn features
Confirm – in Victory –
We start – as if detected
In Immortality –

c. 1862   1935

553

One Crucifixion is recorded – only –
How many be
Is not affirmed of Mathematics –
Or History –

One Calvary – exhibited to Stranger –
As many be
As persons – or Peninsulas –
Gethsemane –

Is but a Province – in the Being's Centre –
Judea –
For Journey – or Crusade's Achieving –
Too near –

Our Lord – indeed – made Compound Witness –
And yet –
There's newer – nearer Crucifixion
Than That –

c. 1862   1945

554

The Black Berry – wears a Thorn in his side –
But no Man heard Him cry –
He offers His Berry, just the same
To Partridge – and to Boy –

He sometimes holds upon the Fence –
Or struggles to a Tree –

[269]

Or clasps a Rock, with both His Hands –
But not for Sympathy –

We – tell a Hurt – to cool it –
This Mourner – to the Sky
A little further reaches – instead –
Brave Black Berry –

c. 1862   *1945*

555

Trust in the Unexpected –
By this – was William Kidd
Persuaded of the Buried Gold –
As One had testified –

Through this – the old Philosopher –
His Talismanic Stone
Discernéd – still withholden
To effort undivine –

'Twas this – allured Columbus –
When Genoa – withdrew
Before an Apparition
Baptized America –

The Same – afflicted Thomas –
When Deity assured
'Twas better – the perceiving not –
Provided it believed –

c. 1862   *1935*

556

The Brain, within its Groove
Runs evenly – and true –
But let a Splinter swerve –
'Twere easier for You –

To put a Current back –
When Floods have slit the Hills –

And scooped a Turnpike for Themselves –
And trodden out the Mills –

c. 1862   1890

557

She hideth Her the last –
And is the first, to rise –
Her Night doth hardly recompense
The Closing of Her eyes –

She doth Her Purple Work –
And putteth Her away
In low Apartments in the Sod –
As Worthily as We.

To imitate Her life
As impotent would be
As make of Our imperfect Mints,
The Julep – of the Bee –

c. 1862   1935

558

But little Carmine hath her face –
Of Emerald scant – her Gown –
Her Beauty – is the love she doth –
Itself – exhibit – Mine –

c. 1862   1935

559

It knew no Medicine –
It was not Sickness – then –
Nor any need of Surgery –
And therefore – 'twas not Pain –

It moved away the Cheeks –
A Dimple at a time –
And left the Profile – plainer –
And in the place of Bloom

It left the little Tint
That never had a Name –
You've seen it on a Cast's face –
Was Paradise – to blame –

If momently ajar –
Temerity – drew near –
And sickened – ever afterward
For Somewhat that it saw?

c. 1862   1935

560

It knew no lapse, nor Diminution –
But large – serene –
Burned on – until through Dissolution –
It failed from Men –

I could not deem these Planetary forces
Annulled –
But suffered an Exchange of Territory –
Or World –

c. 1862   1945

561

I measure every Grief I meet
With narrow, probing, Eyes –
I wonder if It weighs like Mine –
Or has an Easier size.

I wonder if They bore it long –
Or did it just begin –
I could not tell the Date of Mine –
It feels so old a pain –

I wonder if it hurts to live –
And if They have to try –
And whether – could They choose between –
It would not be – to die –

[272]

I note that Some – gone patient long –
At length, renew their smile –
An imitation of a Light
That has so little Oil –

I wonder if when Years have piled –
Some Thousands – on the Harm –
That hurt them early – such a lapse
Could give them any Balm –

Or would they go on aching still
Through Centuries of Nerve –
Enlightened to a larger Pain –
In Contrast with the Love –

The Grieved – are many – I am told –
There is the various Cause –
Death – is but one – and comes but once –
And only nails the eyes –

There's Grief of Want – and Grief of Cold –
A sort they call "Despair" –
There's Banishment from native Eyes –
In sight of Native Air –

And though I may not guess the kind –
Correctly – yet to me
A piercing Comfort it affords
In passing Calvary –

To note the fashions – of the Cross –
And how they're mostly worn –
Still fascinated to presume
That Some – are like My Own –

c. 1862   *1896*

562

Conjecturing a Climate
Of unsuspended Suns –
Adds poignancy to Winter –
The Shivering Fancy turns

[273]

To a fictitious Country
To palliate a Cold –
Not obviated of Degree –
Nor eased – of Latitude –

c. 1862   1929

563

I could not prove the Years had feet –
Yet confident they run
Am I, from symptoms that are past
And Series that are done –

I find my feet have further Goals –
I smile upon the Aims
That felt so ample – Yesterday –
Today's – have vaster claims –

I do not doubt the self I was
Was competent to me –
But something awkward in the fit –
Proves that – outgrown – I see –

c. 1862   1945

564

My period had come for Prayer –
No other Art – would do –
My Tactics missed a rudiment –
Creator – Was it you?

God grows above – so those who pray
Horizons – must ascend –
And so I stepped upon the North
To see this Curious Friend –

His House was not – no sign had He –
By Chimney – nor by Door
Could I infer his Residence –
Vast Prairies of Air

Unbroken by a Settler –
Were all that I could see –
Infinitude – Had'st Thou no Face
That I might look on Thee?

The Silence condescended –
Creation stopped – for Me –
But awed beyond my errand –
I worshipped – did not "pray" –

c. 1862   1929

565

One Anguish – in a Crowd –
A Minor thing – it sounds –
And yet, unto the single Doe
Attempted of the Hounds

'Tis Terror as consummate
As Legions of Alarm
Did leap, full flanked, upon the Host –
'Tis Units – make the Swarm –

A Small Leech – on the Vitals –
The sliver, in the Lung –
The Bung out – of an Artery –
Are scarce accounted – Harms –

Yet mighty – by relation
To that Repealless thing –
A Being – impotent to end –
When once it has begun –

c. 1862   1945

566

A Dying Tiger – moaned for Drink –
I hunted all the Sand –
I caught the Dripping of a Rock
And bore it in my Hand –

His Mighty Balls – in death were thick –
But searching – I could see
A Vision on the Retina
Of Water – and of me –

'Twas not my blame – who sped too slow –
'Twas not his blame – who died
While I was reaching him –
But 'twas – the fact that He was dead –

c. *1862*   *1945*

567

He gave away his Life –
To Us – Gigantic Sum –
A trifle – in his own esteem –
But magnified – by Fame –

Until it burst the Hearts
That fancied they could hold –
When swift it slipped its limit –
And on the Heavens – unrolled –

'Tis Ours – to wince – and weep –
And wonder – and decay
By Blossoms gradual process –
He chose – Maturity –

And quickening – as we sowed –
Just obviated Bud –
And when We turned to note the Growth –
Broke – perfect – from the Pod –

c. *1862*   *1935*

568

We learned the Whole of Love –
The Alphabet – the Words –
A Chapter – then the mighty Book –
Then – Revelation closed –

[276]

But in Each Other's eyes
An Ignorance beheld –
Diviner than the Childhood's –
And each to each, a Child –

Attempted to expound
What Neither – understood –
Alas, that Wisdom is so large –
And Truth – so manifold!

c. 1862   1945

569

I reckon – when I count at all –
First – Poets – Then the Sun –
Then Summer – Then the Heaven of God –
And then – the List is done –

But, looking back – the First so seems
To Comprehend the Whole –
The Others look a needless Show –
So I write – Poets – All –

Their Summer – lasts a Solid Year –
They can afford a Sun
The East – would deem extravagant –
And if the Further Heaven –

Be Beautiful as they prepare
For Those who worship Them –
It is too difficult a Grace –
To justify the Dream –

c. 1862   1929

570

I could die – to know –
'Tis a trifling knowledge –
News-Boys salute the Door –
Carts – joggle by –

[277]

Morning's bold face – stares in the window –
Were but mine – the Charter of the least Fly –

Houses hunch the House
With their Brick Shoulders –
Coals – from a Rolling Load – rattle – how – near –
To the very Square – His foot is passing –
Possibly, this moment –
While I – dream – Here –

c. 1862   1935

571

Must be a Woe –
A loss or so –
To bend the eye
Best Beauty's way –

But – once aslant
It notes Delight
As difficult
As Stalactite

A Common Bliss
Were had for less –
The price – is
Even as the Grace –

Our lord – thought no
Extravagance
To pay – a Cross –

c. 1862   1935

572

Delight – becomes pictorial –
When viewed through Pain –
More fair – because impossible
That any gain –

The Mountain – at a given distance –
In Amber – lies –

[278]

Approached – the Amber flits – a little –
And That's – the Skies –

c. 1862

1891

573

The Test of Love – is Death –
Our Lord – "so loved" – it saith –
What Largest Lover – hath –
Another – doth –

If smaller Patience – be –
Through less Infinity –
If Bravo, sometimes swerve –
Through fainter Nerve –

Accept its Most –
And overlook – the Dust –
Last – Least –
The Cross' – Request –

c. 1862

1935

574

My first well Day – since many ill –
I asked to go abroad,
And take the Sunshine in my hands,
And see the things in Pod –

A'blossom just when I went in
To take my Chance with pain –
Uncertain if myself, or He,
Should prove the strongest One.

The Summer deepened, while we strove –
She put some flowers away –
And Redder cheeked Ones – in their stead –
A fond – illusive way –

To cheat Herself, it seemed she tried –
As if before a child

To fade – Tomorrow – Rainbows held
The Sepulchre, could hide.

She dealt a fashion to the Nut –
She tied the Hoods to Seeds –
She dropped bright scraps of Tint, about –
And left Brazilian Threads

On every shoulder that she met –
Then both her Hands of Haze
Put up – to hide her parting Grace
From our unfitted eyes.

My loss, by sickness – Was it Loss?
Or that Ethereal Gain
One earns by measuring the Grave –
Then – measuring the Sun –

c. 1862   *1935*

575

"Heaven" has different Signs – to me –
Sometimes, I think that Noon
Is but a symbol of the Place –
And when again, at Dawn,

A mighty look runs round the World
And settles in the Hills –
An Awe if it should be like that
Upon the Ignorance steals –

The Orchard, when the Sun is on –
The Triumph of the Birds
When they together Victory make –
Some Carnivals of Clouds –

The Rapture of a finished Day –
Returning to the West –
All these – remind us of the place
That Men call "Paradise" –

Itself be fairer – we suppose –
But how Ourself, shall be

Adorned, for a Superior Grace –
Not yet, our eyes can see –

c. 1862   *1929*

576

I prayed, at first, a little Girl,
Because they told me to –
But stopped, when qualified to guess
How prayer would feel – to me –

If I believed God looked around,
Each time my Childish eye
Fixed full, and steady, on his own
In Childish honesty –

And told him what I'd like, today,
And parts of his far plan
That baffled me –
The mingled side
Of his Divinity –

And often since, in Danger,
I count the force 'twould be
To have a God so strong as that
To hold my life for me

Till I could take the Balance
That tips so frequent, now,
It takes me all the while to poise –
And then – it doesn't stay –

c. 1862   *1929*

577

If I may have it, when it's dead,
I'll be contented – so –
If just as soon as Breath is out
It shall belong to me –

Until they lock it in the Grave,
'Tis Bliss I cannot weigh –

For tho' they lock Thee in the Grave,
Myself – can own the key –

Think of it Lover! I and Thee
Permitted – face to face to be –
After a Life – a Death – We'll say –
For Death was That –
And this – is Thee –

I'll tell Thee All – how Bald it grew –
How Midnight felt, at first – to me –
How all the Clocks stopped in the World –
And Sunshine pinched me – 'Twas so cold –

Then how the Grief got sleepy – some –
As if my Soul were deaf and dumb –
Just making signs – across – to Thee –
That this way – thou could'st notice me –

I'll tell you how I tried to keep
A smile, to show you, when this Deep
All Waded – We look back for Play,
At those Old Times – in Calvary.

Forgive me, if the Grave come slow –
For Coveting to look at Thee –
Forgive me, if to stroke thy frost
Outvisions Paradise!

c. 1862   *1896*

578

The Body grows without –
The more convenient way –
That if the Spirit – like to hide
Its Temple stands, alway,

Ajar – secure – inviting –
It never did betray
The Soul that asked its shelter
In solemn honesty

c. 1862   *1891*

579

I had been hungry, all the Years –
My Noon had Come – to dine –
I trembling drew the Table near –
And touched the Curious Wine –

'Twas this on Tables I had seen –
When turning, hungry, Home
I looked in Windows, for the Wealth
I could not hope – for Mine –

I did not know the ample Bread –
'Twas so unlike the Crumb
The Birds and I, had often shared
In Nature's – Dining Room –

The Plenty hurt me – 'twas so new –
Myself felt ill – and odd –
As Berry – of a Mountain Bush –
Transplanted – to the Road –

Nor was I hungry – so I found
That Hunger – was a way
Of Persons outside Windows –
The Entering – takes away –

c. 1862   *1891*

580

I gave myself to Him –
And took Himself, for Pay,
The solemn contract of a Life
Was ratified, this way –

The Wealth might disappoint –
Myself a poorer prove
Than this great Purchaser suspect,
The Daily Own – of Love

Depreciate the Vision –
But till the Merchant buy –

[283]

Still Fable – in the Isles of Spice –
The subtle Cargoes – lie –

At least – 'tis Mutual – Risk –
Some – found it – Mutual Gain –
Sweet Debt of Life – Each Night to owe –
Insolvent – every Noon –

c. 1862   *1891*

581

I found the words to every thought
I ever had – but One –
And that – defies me –
As a Hand did try to chalk the Sun

To Races – nurtured in the Dark –
How would your own – begin?
Can Blaze be shown in Cochineal –
Or Noon – in Mazarin?

c. 1862   *1891*

582

Inconceivably solemn!
Things so gay
Pierce – by the very Press
Of Imagery –

Their far Parades – order on the eye
With a mute Pomp –
A pleading Pageantry –

Flags, are a brave sight –
But no true Eye
Ever went by One –
Steadily –

Music's triumphant –
But the fine Ear

[284]

Winces with delight
Are Drums too near –

c. 1862   *1929*

583

A Toad, can die of Light –
Death is the Common Right
Of Toads and Men –
Of Earl and Midge
The privilege –
Why swagger, then?
The Gnat's supremacy is large as Thine –

Life – is a different Thing –
So measure Wine –
Naked of Flask – Naked of Cask –
Bare Rhine –
Which Ruby's mine?

c. 1862   *1896*

584

It ceased to hurt me, though so slow
I could not feel the Anguish go –
But only knew by looking back –
That something – had benumbed the Track –

Nor when it altered, I could say,
For I had worn it, every day,
As constant as the Childish frock –
I hung upon the Peg, at night.

But not the Grief – that nestled close
As needles – ladies softly press
To Cushions Cheeks –
To keep their place –

Nor what consoled it, I could trace –
Except, whereas 'twas Wilderness –
It's better – almost Peace –

c. 1862   *1929*

585

I like to see it lap the Miles –
And lick the Valleys up –
And stop to feed itself at Tanks –
And then – prodigious step

Around a Pile of Mountains –
And supercilious peer
In Shanties – by the sides of Roads –
And then a Quarry pare

To fit its Ribs
And crawl between
Complaining all the while
In horrid – hooting stanza –
Then chase itself down Hill –

And neigh like Boanerges –
Then – punctual as a Star
Stop – docile and omnipotent
At its own stable door –

c. 1862   1891

586

We talked as Girls do –
Fond, and late –
We speculated fair, on every subject, but the Grave –
Of ours, none affair –

We handled Destinies, as cool –
As we – Disposers – be –
And God, a Quiet Party
To our Authority –

But fondest, dwelt upon Ourself
As we eventual – be –
When Girls to Women, softly raised
We – occupy – Degree –

We parted with a contract
To cherish, and to write

[286]

But Heaven made both, impossible
Before another night.

c. 1862

1929

587

Empty my Heart, of Thee –
Its single Artery –
Begin, and leave Thee out –
Simply Extinction's Date –

Much Billow hath the Sea –
One Baltic – They –
Subtract Thyself, in play,
And not enough of me
Is left – to put away –
"Myself" meant Thee –

Erase the Root – no Tree –
Thee – then – no me –
The Heavens stripped –
Eternity's vast pocket, picked –

c. 1862

1929

588

I cried at Pity – not at Pain –
I heard a Woman say
"Poor Child" – and something in her voice
Convicted me – of me –

So long I fainted, to myself
It seemed the common way,
And Health, and Laughter, Curious things –
To look at, like a Toy –

To sometimes hear "Rich people" buy
And see the Parcel rolled –
And carried, I supposed – to Heaven,
For children, made of Gold –

But not to touch, or wish for,
Or think of, with a sigh –
And so and so – had been to me,
Had God willed differently.

I wish I knew that Woman's name –
So when she comes this way,
To hold my life, and hold my ears
For fear I hear her say

She's "sorry I am dead" – again –
Just when the Grave and I –
Have sobbed ourselves almost to sleep,
Our only Lullaby –

c. 1862   1896

589

The Night was wide, and furnished scant
With but a single Star –
That often as a Cloud it met –
Blew out itself – for fear –

The Wind pursued the little Bush –
And drove away the Leaves
November left – then clambered up
And fretted in the Eaves –

No Squirrel went abroad –
A Dog's belated feet
Like intermittent Plush, he heard
Adown the empty Street –

To feel if Blinds be fast –
And closer to the fire –
Her little Rocking Chair to draw –
And shiver for the Poor –

The Housewife's gentle Task –
How pleasanter – said she

Unto the Sofa opposite –
The Sleet – than May, no Thee –

c. 1862   1891

590

Did you ever stand in a Cavern's Mouth –
Widths out of the Sun –
And look – and shudder, and block your breath –
And deem to be alone

In such a place, what horror,
How Goblin it would be –
And fly, as 'twere pursuing you?
Then Loneliness – looks so –

Did you ever look in a Cannon's face –
Between whose Yellow eye –
And yours – the Judgment intervened –
The Question of "To die" –

Extemporizing in your ear
As cool as Satyr's Drums –
If you remember, and were saved –
It's liker so – it seems –

c. 1862   1935

591

To interrupt His Yellow Plan
The Sun does not allow
Caprices of the Atmosphere –
And even when the Snow

Heaves Balls of Specks, like Vicious Boy
Directly in His Eye –
Does not so much as turn His Head
Busy with Majesty –

'Tis His to stimulate the Earth –
And magnetize the Sea –

And bind Astronomy, in place,
Yet Any passing by

Would deem Ourselves – the busier
As the Minutest Bee
That rides – emits a Thunder –
A Bomb – to justify –

c. 1862 *1929*

592

What care the Dead, for Chanticleer –
What care the Dead for Day?
'Tis late your Sunrise vex their face –
And Purple Ribaldry – of Morning

Pour as blank on them
As on the Tier of Wall
The Mason builded, yesterday,
And equally as cool –

What care the Dead for Summer?
The Solstice had no Sun
Could waste the Snow before their Gate –
And knew One Bird a Tune –

Could thrill their Mortised Ear
Of all the Birds that be –
This One – beloved of Mankind
Henceforward cherished be –

What care the Dead for Winter?
Themselves as easy freeze –
June Noon – as January Night –
As soon the South – her Breeze

Of Sycamore – or Cinnamon –
Deposit in a Stone
And put a Stone to keep it Warm –
Give Spices – unto Men –

c. 1862 *1932*

I think I was enchanted
When first a sombre Girl –
I read that Foreign Lady –
The Dark – felt beautiful –

And whether it was noon at night –
Or only Heaven – at Noon –
For very Lunacy of Light
I had not power to tell –

The Bees – became as Butterflies –
The Butterflies – as Swans –
Approached – and spurned the narrow Grass –
And just the meanest Tunes

That Nature murmured to herself
To keep herself in Cheer –
I took for Giants – practising
Titanic Opera –

The Days – to Mighty Metres stept –
The Homeliest – adorned
As if unto a Jubilee
'Twere suddenly confirmed –

I could not have defined the change –
Conversion of the Mind
Like Sanctifying in the Soul –
Is witnessed – not explained –

'Twas a Divine Insanity –
The Danger to be Sane
Should I again experience –
'Tis Antidote to turn –

To Tomes of solid Witchcraft –
Magicians be asleep –
But Magic – hath an Element
Like Deity – to keep –

c. 1862   1935

The Battle fought between the Soul
And No Man – is the One
Of all the Battles prevalent –
By far the Greater One –

No News of it is had abroad –
Its Bodiless Campaign
Establishes, and terminates –
Invisible – Unknown –

Nor History – record it –
As Legions of a Night
The Sunrise scatters – These endure –
Enact – and terminate –

c. 1862   *1929*

Like Mighty Foot Lights – burned the Red
At Bases of the Trees –
The far Theatricals of Day
Exhibiting – to These –

'Twas Universe – that did applaud –
While Chiefest – of the Crowd –
Enabled by his Royal Dress –
Myself distinguished God –

c. 1862   *1891*

When I was small, a Woman died –
Today – her Only Boy
Went up from the Potomac –
His face all Victory

To look at her – How slowly
The Seasons must have turned
Till Bullets clipt an Angle
And He passed quickly round –

If pride shall be in Paradise –
Ourself cannot decide –
Of their imperial Conduct –
No person testified –

But, proud in Apparition –
That Woman and her Boy
Pass back and forth, before my Brain
As even in the sky –

I'm confident that Bravoes –
Perpetual break abroad
For Braveries, remote as this
In Scarlet Maryland –

c. 1862   1890

597

It always felt to me – a wrong
To that Old Moses – done –
To let him see – the Canaan –
Without the entering –

And tho' in soberer moments –
No Moses there can be
I'm satisfied – the Romance
In point of injury –

Surpasses sharper stated –
Of Stephen – or of Paul –
For these – were only put to death –
While God's adroiter will

On Moses – seemed to fasten
With tantalizing Play
As Boy – should deal with lesser Boy –
To prove ability.

The fault – was doubtless Israel's –
Myself – had banned the Tribes –
And ushered Grand Old Moses
In Pentateuchal Robes

[293]

Upon the Broad Possession
'Twas little – But titled Him – to see –
Old Man on Nebo! Late as this –
My justice bleeds – for Thee!

c. *1862*   *1929*

598

Three times – we parted – Breath – and I –
Three times – He would not go –
But strove to stir the lifeless Fan
The Waters – strove to stay.

Three Times – the Billows tossed me up –
Then caught me – like a Ball –
Then made Blue faces in my face –
And pushed away a sail

That crawled Leagues off – I liked to see –
For thinking – while I die –
How pleasant to behold a Thing
Where Human faces – be –

The Waves grew sleepy – Breath – did not –
The Winds – like Children – lulled –
Then Sunrise kissed my Chrysalis –
And I stood up – and lived –

c. *1862*   *1929*

599

There is a pain – so utter –
It swallows substance up –
Then covers the Abyss with Trance –
So Memory can step
Around – across – upon it –
As one within a Swoon –
Goes safely – where an open eye –
Would drop Him – Bone by Bone.

c. *1862*   *1929*

It troubled me as once I was –
For I was once a Child –
Concluding how an Atom – fell –
And yet the Heavens – held –

The Heavens weighed the most – by far –
Yet Blue – and solid – stood –
Without a Bolt – that I could prove –
Would Giants – understand?

Life set me larger – problems –
Some I shall keep – to solve
Till Algebra is easier –
Or simpler proved – above –

Then – too – be comprehended –
What sorer – puzzled me –
Why Heaven did not break away –
And tumble – Blue – on me –

c. 1862   1945

A still – Volcano – Life –
That flickered in the night –
When it was dark enough to do
Without erasing sight –

A quiet – Earthquake Style –
Too subtle to suspect
By natures this side Naples –
The North cannot detect

The Solemn – Torrid – Symbol –
The lips that never lie –
Whose hissing Corals part – and shut –
And Cities – ooze away –

c. 1862   1929

Of Brussels – it was not –
Of Kidderminster? Nay –
The Winds did buy it of the Woods –
They – sold it unto me

It was a gentle price –
The poorest – could afford –
It was within the frugal purse
Of Beggar – or of Bird –

Of small and spicy Yards –
In hue – a mellow Dun –
Of Sunshine – and of Sere – Composed –
But, principally – of Sun –

The Wind – unrolled it fast –
And spread it on the Ground –
Upholsterer of the Pines – is He –
Upholsterer – of the Pond –

c. 1862   *1945*

603

He found my Being – set it up –
Adjusted it to place –
Then carved his name – upon it –
And bade it to the East

Be faithful – in his absence –
And he would come again –
With Equipage of Amber –
That time – to take it Home –

c. 1862   *1945*

604

Unto my Books – so good to turn –
Far ends of tired Days –
It half endears the Abstinence –
And Pain – is missed – in Praise –

As Flavors – cheer Retarded Guests
With Banquettings to be –
So Spices – stimulate the time
Till my small Library –

It may be Wilderness – without –
Far feet of failing Men –
But Holiday – excludes the night –
And it is Bells – within –

I thank these Kinsmen of the Shelf –
Their Countenances Kid
Enamor – in Prospective –
And satisfy – obtained –

c. 1862   *1891*

605

The Spider holds a Silver Ball
In unperceived Hands –
And dancing softly to Himself
His Yarn of Pearl – unwinds –

He plies from Nought to Nought –
In unsubstantial Trade –
Supplants our Tapestries with His –
In half the period –

An Hour to rear supreme
His Continents of Light –
Then dangle from the Housewife's Broom –
His Boundaries – forgot –

c. 1862   *1945*

606

The Trees like Tassels – hit – and swung –
There seemed to rise a Tune
From Miniature Creatures
Accompanying the Sun –

[297]

Far Psalteries of Summer –
Enamoring the Ear
They never yet did satisfy –
Remotest – when most fair

The Sun shone whole at intervals –
Then Half – then utter hid –
As if Himself were optional
And had Estates of Cloud

Sufficient to enfold Him
Eternally from view –
Except it were a whim of His
To let the Orchards grow –

A Bird sat careless on the fence –
One gossipped in the Lane
On silver matters charmed a Snake
Just winding round a Stone –

Bright Flowers slit a Calyx
And soared upon a Stem
Like Hindered Flags – Sweet hoisted –
With Spices – in the Hem –

'Twas more – I cannot mention –
How mean – to those that see –
Vandyke's Delineation
Of Nature's – Summer Day!

c. 1862   1935

607

Of nearness to her sundered Things
The Soul has special times –
When Dimness – looks the Oddity –
Distinctness – easy – seems –

The Shapes we buried, dwell about,
Familiar, in the Rooms –
Untarnished by the Sepulchre,
The Mouldering Playmate comes –

[298]

In just the Jacket that he wore –
Long buttoned in the Mold
Since we – old mornings, Children – played –
Divided – by a world –

The Grave yields back her Robberies –
The Years, our pilfered Things –
Bright Knots of Apparitions
Salute us, with their wings –

As we – it were – that perished –
Themself – had just remained till we rejoin them –
And 'twas they, and not ourself
That mourned.

c. 1862   *1929*

608

Afraid! Of whom am I afraid?
Not Death – for who is He?
The Porter of my Father's Lodge
As much abasheth me!

Of Life? 'Twere odd I fear [a] thing
That comprehendeth me
In one or two existences –
As Deity decree –

Of Resurrection? Is the East
Afraid to trust the Morn
With her fastidious forehead?
As soon impeach my Crown!

c. 1862   *1890*

609

I Years had been from Home
And now before the Door
I dared not enter, lest a Face
I never saw before

Stare stolid into mine
And ask my Business there –

[299]

"My Business but a Life I left
Was such remaining there?"

I leaned upon the Awe –
I lingered with Before –
The Second like an Ocean rolled
And broke against my ear –

I laughed a crumbling Laugh
That I could fear a Door
Who Consternation compassed
And never winced before.

I fitted to the Latch
My Hand, with trembling care
Lest back the awful Door should spring
And leave me in the Floor –

Then moved my Fingers off
As cautiously as Glass
And held my ears, and like a Thief
Fled gasping from the House –

c. 1872   1891

610

You'll find – it when you try to die –
The Easier to let go –
For recollecting such as went –
You could not spare – you know.

And though their places somewhat filled –
As did their Marble names
With Moss – they never grew so full –
You chose the newer names –

And when this World – sets further back –
As Dying – say it does –
The former love – distincter grows –
And supersedes the fresh –

And Thought of them – so fair invites –
It looks too tawdry Grace

[300]

To stay behind – with just the Toys
We bought – to ease their place –

c. 1862   *1929*

611

I see thee better – in the Dark –
I do not need a Light –
The Love of Thee – a Prism be –
Excelling Violet –

I see thee better for the Years
That hunch themselves between –
The Miner's Lamp – sufficient be –
To nullify the Mine –

And in the Grave – I see Thee best –
Its little Panels be
Aglow – All ruddy – with the Light
I held so high, for Thee –

What need of Day –
To Those whose Dark – hath so – surpassing Sun –
It deem it be – Continually –
At the Meridian?

c. 1862   *1914*

612

It would have starved a Gnat –
To live so small as I –
And yet I was a living Child –
With Food's necessity

Upon me – like a Claw –
I could no more remove
Than I could coax a Leech away –
Or make a Dragon – move –

Nor like the Gnat – had I –
The privilege to fly
And seek a Dinner for myself –
How mightier He – than I –

Nor like Himself – the Art
Upon the Window Pane
To gad my little Being out –
And not begin – again –

c. 1862   1945

613

They shut me up in Prose –
As when a little Girl
They put me in the Closet –
Because they liked me "still" –

Still! Could themself have peeped –
And seen my Brain – go round –
They might as wise have lodged a Bird
For Treason – in the Pound –

Himself has but to will
And easy as a Star
Abolish his Captivity –
And laugh – No more have I –

c. 1862   1935

614

In falling Timbers buried –
There breathed a Man –
Outside – the spades – were plying –
The Lungs – within –

Could He – know – they sought Him –
Could They – know – He breathed –
Horrid Sand Partition –
Neither – could be heard –

Never slacked the Diggers –
But when Spades had done –
Oh, Reward of Anguish,
It was dying – Then –

[302]

Many Things – are fruitless –
'Tis a Baffling Earth –
But there is no Gratitude
Like the Grace – of Death –

c. 1862   1945

615

Our journey had advanced –
Our feet were almost come
To that odd Fork in Being's Road –
Eternity – by Term –

Our pace took sudden awe –
Our feet – reluctant – led –
Before – were Cities – but Between –
The Forest of the Dead –

Retreat – was out of Hope –
Behind – a Sealed Route –
Eternity's White Flag – Before –
And God – at every Gate –

c 1862   1891

616

I rose – because He sank –
I thought it would be opposite –
But when his power dropped –
My Soul grew straight.

I cheered my fainting Prince –
I sang firm – even – Chants –
I helped his Film – with Hymn –

And when the Dews drew off
That held his Forehead stiff –
I met him –
Balm to Balm –

I told him Best – must pass
Through this low Arch of Flesh –

No Casque so brave
It spurn the Grave –

I told him Worlds I knew
Where Emperors grew –
Who recollected us
If we were true –

And so with Thews of Hymn –
And Sinew from within –
And ways I knew not that I knew – till then –
I lifted Him –

c. 1862   *1929*

617

Don't put up my Thread and Needle –
I'll begin to Sew
When the Birds begin to whistle –
Better Stitches – so –

These were bent – my sight got crooked –
When my mind – is plain
I'll do seams – a Queen's endeavor
Would not blush to own –

Hems – too fine for Lady's tracing
To the sightless Knot –
Tucks – of dainty interspersion –
Like a dotted Dot –

Leave my Needle in the furrow –
Where I put it down –
I can make the zigzag stitches
Straight – when I am strong –

Till then – dreaming I am sewing
Fetch the seam I missed –
Closer – so I – at my sleeping –
Still surmise I stitch –

c. 1862   *1929*

At leisure is the Soul
That gets a Staggering Blow –
The Width of Life – before it spreads
Without a thing to do –

It begs you give it Work –
But just the placing Pins –
Or humblest Patchwork – Children do –
To Help its Vacant Hands –

c. 1862   1929

Glee – The great storm is over –
Four – have recovered the Land –
Forty – gone down together –
Into the boiling Sand –

Ring – for the Scant Salvation –
Toll – for the bonnie Souls –
Neighbor – and friend – and Bridegroom –
Spinning upon the Shoals –

How they will tell the Story –
When Winter shake the Door –
Till the Children urge –
But the Forty –
Did they – come back no more?

Then a softness – suffuse the Story –
And a silence – the Teller's eye –
And the Children – no further question –
And only the Sea – reply –

c. 1862   1890

It makes no difference abroad –
The Seasons – fit – the same –

The Mornings blossom into Noons –
And split their Pods of Flame –

Wild flowers – kindle in the Woods –
The Brooks slam – all the Day –
No Black bird bates his Banjo –
For passing Calvary –

Auto da Fe – and Judgment –
Are nothing to the Bee –
His separation from His Rose –
To Him – sums Misery –

c. 1862   *1890*

621

I asked no other thing –
No other – was denied –
I offered Being – for it –
The Mighty Merchant sneered –

Brazil? He twirled a Button –
Without a glance my way –
"But – Madam – is there nothing else –
That We can show – Today?"

c. 1862   *189*

622

To know just how He suffered – would be dear –
To know if any Human eyes were near
To whom He could entrust His wavering gaze –
Until it settled broad – on Paradise –

To know if He was patient – part content –
Was Dying as He thought – or different –
Was it a pleasant Day to die –
And did the Sunshine face His way –

What was His furthest mind – Of Home – or God –
Or what the Distant say –

[306]

At news that He ceased Human Nature
Such a Day –

And Wishes – Had He Any –
Just His Sigh – Accented –
Had been legible – to Me –
And was He Confident until
Ill fluttered out – in Everlasting Well –

And if He spoke – What name was Best –
What last
What One broke off with
At the Drowsiest –

Was He afraid – or tranquil –
Might He know
How Conscious Consciousness – could grow –
Till Love that was – and Love too best to be –
Meet – and the Junction be Eternity

c. 1862   1890

623

It was too late for Man –
But early, yet, for God –
Creation – impotent to help –
But Prayer – remained – Our Side –

How excellent the Heaven –
When Earth – cannot be had –
How hospitable – then – the face
Of our Old Neighbor – God –

c. 1862   1890

624

Forever – is composed of Nows –
'Tis not a different time –
Except for Infiniteness –
And Latitude of Home –

From this – experienced Here –
Remove the Dates – to These –
Let Months dissolve in further Months –
And Years – exhale in Years –

Without Debate – or Pause –
Or Celebrated Days –
No different Our Years would be
From Anno Domini's –

c. 1862   *1929*

625

'Twas a long Parting – but the time
For Interview – had Come –
Before the Judgment Seat of God –
The last – and second time

These Fleshless Lovers met –
A Heaven in a Gaze –
A Heaven of Heavens – the Privilege
Of one another's Eyes –

No Lifetime – on Them –
Appareled as the new
Unborn – except They had beheld –
Born infiniter – now –

Was Bridal – e'er like This?
A Paradise – the Host –
And Cherubim – and Seraphim –
The unobtrusive Guest –

c. 1862   *1890*

626

Only God – detect the Sorrow –
Only God –
The Jehovahs – are no Babblers –
Unto God –

God the Son – confide it –
Still secure –
God the Spirit's Honor –
Just as sure –

c. 1862

1935

627

The Tint I cannot take – is best –
The Color too remote
That I could show it in Bazaar –
A Guinea at a sight –

The fine – impalpable Array –
That swaggers on the eye
Like Cleopatra's Company –
Repeated – in the sky –

The Moments of Dominion
That happen on the Soul
And leave it with a Discontent
Too exquisite – to tell –

The eager look – on Landscapes –
As if they just repressed
Some Secret – that was pushing
Like Chariots – in the Vest –

The Pleading of the Summer –
That other Prank – of Snow –
That Cushions Mystery with Tulle,
For fear the Squirrels – know.

Their Graspless manners – mock us –
Until the Cheated Eye
Shuts arrogantly – in the Grave –
Another way – to see –

c. 1862

1929

628

They called me to the Window, for
" 'Twas Sunset" – Some one said –
I only saw a Sapphire Farm –
And just a Single Herd –

Of Opal Cattle – feeding far
Upon so vain a Hill –
As even while I looked – dissolved –
Nor Cattle were – nor Soil –

But in their stead – a Sea – displayed –
And Ships – of such a size
As Crew of Mountains – could afford –
And Decks – to seat the skies –

This – too – the Showman rubbed away –
And when I looked again –
Nor Farm – nor Opal Herd – was there –
Nor Mediterranean –

c. 1862   *1945*

629

I watched the Moon around the House
Until upon a Pane –
She stopped – a Traveller's privilege – for Rest –
And there upon

I gazed – as at a stranger –
The Lady in the Town
Doth think no incivility
To lift her Glass – upon –

But never Stranger justified
The Curiosity
Like Mine – for not a Foot – nor Hand –
Nor Formula – had she –

But like a Head – a Guillotine
Slid carelessly away –

[310]

Did independent, Amber –
Sustain her in the sky –

Or like a Stemless Flower –
Upheld in rolling Air
By finer Gravitations –
Than bind Philosopher –

No Hunger – had she – nor an Inn –
Her Toilette – to suffice –
Nor Avocation – nor Concern
For little Mysteries

As harass us – like Life – and Death –
And Afterwards – or Nay –
But seemed engrossed to Absolute –
With shining – and the Sky –

The privilege to scrutinize
Was scarce upon my Eyes
When, with a Silver practise –
She vaulted out of Gaze –

And next – I met her on a Cloud –
Myself too far below
To follow her superior Road –
Or its advantage – Blue –

c. 1862   *1945*

630

The Lightning playeth – all the while –
But when He singeth – then –
Ourselves are conscious He exist –
And we approach Him – stern –

With Insulators – and a Glove –
Whose short – sepulchral Bass
Alarms us – tho' His Yellow feet
May pass – and counterpass –

Upon the Ropes – above our Head –
Continual – with the News –

[311]

Nor We so much as check our speech –
Nor stop to cross Ourselves –

c. 1862   1945

631

Ourselves were wed one summer – dear –
Your Vision – was in June –
And when Your little Lifetime failed,
I wearied – too – of mine –

And overtaken in the Dark –
Where You had put me down –
By Some one carrying a Light –
I – too – received the Sign.

'Tis true – Our Futures different lay –
Your Cottage – faced the sun –
While Oceans – and the North must be –
On every side of mine

'Tis true, Your Garden led the Bloom,
For mine – in Frosts – was sown –
And yet, one Summer, we were Queens –
But You – were crowned in June –

c. 1862   1945

632

The Brain – is wider than the Sky –
For – put them side by side –
The one the other will contain
With ease – and You – beside –

The Brain is deeper than the sea –
For – hold them – Blue to Blue –
The one the other will absorb –
As Sponges – Buckets – do –

The Brain is just the weight of God –
For – Heft them – Pound for Pound –

And they will differ – if they do –
As Syllable from Sound –

c. *1862*   *1896*

633

When Bells stop ringing – Church – begins –
The Positive – of Bells –
When Cogs – stop – that's Circumference –
The Ultimate – of Wheels.

c. *1862*   *1945*

634

You'll know Her – by Her Foot –
The smallest Gamboge Hand
With Fingers – where the Toes should be –
Would more affront the Sand –

Than this Quaint Creature's Boot –
Adjusted by a Stem –
Without a Button – I could vouch –
Unto a Velvet Limb –

You'll know Her – by Her Vest –
Tight fitting – Orange – Brown –
Inside a Jacket duller –
She wore when she was born –

Her Cap is small – and snug –
Constructed for the Winds –
She'd pass for Barehead – short way off –
But as She Closer stands –

So finer 'tis than Wool –
You cannot feel the Seam –
Nor is it Clasped unto of Band –
Nor held upon – of Brim –

You'll know Her – by Her Voice –
At first – a doubtful Tone –

A sweet endeavor – but as March
To April – hurries on –

She squanders on your Ear
Such Arguments of Pearl –
You beg the Robin in your Brain
To keep the other – still –

c. 1862   1945

635

I think the longest Hour of all
Is when the Cars have come –
And we are waiting for the Coach –
It seems as though the Time

Indignant – that the Joy was come –
Did block the Gilded Hands –
And would not let the Seconds by –
But slowest instant – ends –

The Pendulum begins to count –
Like little Scholars – loud –
The steps grow thicker – in the Hall –
The Heart begins to crowd –

Then I – my timid service done –
Tho' service 'twas, of Love –
Take up my little Violin –
And further North – remove.

c. 1862   1945

636

The Way I read a Letter's – this –
'Tis first – I lock the Door –
And push it with my fingers – next –
For transport it be sure –

And then I go the furthest off
To counteract a knock –

Then draw my little Letter forth
And slowly pick the lock –

Then – glancing narrow, at the Wall –
And narrow at the floor
For firm Conviction of a Mouse
Not exorcised before –

Peruse how infinite I am
To no one that You – know –
And sigh for lack of Heaven – but not
The Heaven God bestow –

c. 1862   1891

637

The Child's faith is new –
Whole – like His Principle –
Wide – like the Sunrise
On fresh Eyes –
Never had a Doubt –
Laughs – at a Scruple –
Believes all sham
But Paradise –

Credits the World –
Deems His Dominion
Broadest of Sovereignties –
And Caesar – mean –
In the Comparison –
Baseless Emperor –
Ruler of Nought,
Yet swaying all –

Grown bye and bye
To hold mistaken
His pretty estimates
Of Prickly Things
He gains the skill
Sorrowful – as certain –

Men – to anticipate
Instead of Kings –

c. 1862   1929

638

To my small Hearth His fire came –
And all my House aglow
Did fan and rock, with sudden light –
'Twas Sunrise – 'twas the Sky –

Impanelled from no Summer brief –
With limit of Decay –
'Twas Noon – without the News of Night –
Nay, Nature, it was Day –

c. 1862   1932

639

My Portion is Defeat – today –
A paler luck than Victory –
Less Paeans – fewer Bells –
The Drums don't follow Me – with tunes –
Defeat – a somewhat slower – means –
More Arduous than Balls –

'Tis populous with Bone and stain –
And Men too straight to stoop again,
And Piles of solid Moan –
And Chips of Blank – in Boyish Eyes –
And scraps of Prayer –
And Death's surprise,
Stamped visible – in Stone –

There's somewhat prouder, over there –
The Trumpets tell it to the Air –
How different Victory
To Him who has it – and the One
Who to have had it, would have been
Contenteder – to die –

c. 1862   1929

I cannot live with You –
It would be Life –
And Life is over there –
Behind the Shelf

The Sexton keeps the Key to –
Putting up
Our Life – His Porcelain –
Like a Cup –

Discarded of the Housewife –
Quaint – or Broke –
A newer Sevres pleases –
Old Ones crack –

I could not die – with You –
For One must wait
To shut the Other's Gaze down –
You – could not –

And I – Could I stand by
And see You – freeze –
Without my Right of Frost –
Death's privilege?

Nor could I rise – with You –
Because Your Face
Would put out Jesus' –
That New Grace

Glow plain – and foreign
On my homesick Eye –
Except that You than He
Shone closer by –

They'd judge Us – How –
For You – served Heaven – You know,
Or sought to –
I could not –

Because You saturated Sight –
And I had no more Eyes

For sordid excellence
As Paradise

And were You lost, I would be –
Though My Name
Rang loudest
On the Heavenly fame –

And were You – saved –
And I – condemned to be
Where You were not –
That self – were Hell to Me –

So We must meet apart –
You there – I – here –
With just the Door ajar
That Oceans are – and Prayer –
And that White Sustenance –
Despair –

c. 1862   *1890*

641

Size circumscribes – it has no room
For petty furniture –
The Giant tolerates no Gnat
For Ease of Gianture –

Repudiates it, all the more –
Because intrinsic size
Ignores the possibility
Of Calumnies – or Flies.

c. 1862   *1935*

642

Me from Myself – to banish –
Had I Art –
Impregnable my Fortress
Unto All Heart –

[318]

But since Myself – assault Me –
How have I peace
Except by subjugating
Consciousness?

And since We're mutual Monarch
How this be
Except by Abdication –
Me – of Me?

c. *1862*   *1929*

643

I could suffice for Him, I knew –
He – could suffice for Me –
Yet Hesitating Fractions – Both
Surveyed Infinity –

"Would I be Whole" He sudden broached –
My syllable rebelled –
'Twas face to face with Nature – forced –
'Twas face to face with God –

Withdrew the Sun – to Other Wests –
Withdrew the furthest Star
Before Decision – stooped to speech –
And then – be audibler

The Answer of the Sea unto
The Motion of the Moon –
Herself adjust Her Tides – unto –
Could I – do else – with Mine?

c. *1862*   *1935*

644

You left me – Sire – two Legacies –
A Legacy of Love
A Heavenly Father would suffice
Had He the offer of –

You left me Boundaries of Pain –
Capacious as the Sea –
Between Eternity and Time –
Your Consciousness – and Me –

c. 1862   1890

645

Bereavement in their death to feel
Whom We have never seen –
A Vital Kinsmanship import
Our Soul and theirs – between –

For Stranger – Strangers do not mourn –
There be Immortal friends
Whom Death see first – 'tis news of this
That paralyze Ourselves –

Who, vital only to Our Thought –
Such Presence bear away
In dying – 'tis as if Our Souls
Absconded – suddenly –

c. 1862   1935

646

I think to Live – may be a Bliss
To those who dare to try –
Beyond my limit to conceive –
My lip – to testify –

I think the Heart I former wore
Could widen – till to me
The Other, like the little Bank
Appear – unto the Sea –

I think the Days – could every one
In Ordination stand –
And Majesty – be easier –
Than an inferior kind –

No numb alarm – lest Difference come –
No Goblin – on the Bloom –
No start in Apprehension's Ear,
No Bankruptcy – no Doom –

But Certainties of Sun –
Midsummer – in the Mind –
A steadfast South – upon the Soul –
Her Polar time – behind –

The Vision – pondered long –
So plausible becomes
That I esteem the fiction – real –
The Real – fictitious seems –

How bountiful the Dream –
What Plenty – it would be –
Had all my Life but been Mistake
Just rectified – in Thee

c. 1862   1935

647

A little Road – not made of Man –
Enabled of the Eye –
Accessible to Thill of Bee –
Or Cart of Butterfly –

If Town it have – beyond itself –
'Tis that – I cannot say –
I only know – no Curricle that rumble there
Bear Me –

c. 1862   1890

648

Promise This – When You be Dying –
Some shall summon Me –
Mine belong Your latest Sighing –
Mine – to Belt Your Eye –

[321]

Not with Coins – though they be Minted
From an Emperor's Hand –
Be my lips – the only Buckle
Your low Eyes – demand –

Mine to stay – when all have wandered –
To devise once more
If the Life be too surrendered –
Life of Mine – restore –

Poured like this – My Whole Libation –
Just that You should see
Bliss of Death – Life's Bliss extol thro'
Imitating You –

Mine – to guard Your Narrow Precinct –
To seduce the Sun
Longest on Your South, to linger,
Largest Dews of Morn

To demand, in Your low favor
Lest the Jealous Grass
Greener lean – Or fonder cluster
Round some other face –

Mine to supplicate Madonna –
If Madonna be
Could behold so far a Creature –
Christ – omitted – Me –

Just to follow Your dear feature –
Ne'er so far behind –
For My Heaven –
Had I not been
Most enough – denied?

c. 1862   1935

649

Her Sweet turn to leave the Homestead
Came the Darker Way –

Carriages – Be sure – and Guests – too –
But for Holiday

'Tis more pitiful Endeavor
Than did Loaded Sea
O'er the Curls attempt to caper
It had cast away –

Never Bride had such Assembling –
Never kinsmen kneeled
To salute so fair a Forehead –
Garland be indeed –

Fitter Feet – of Her before us –
Than whatever Brow
Art of Snow – or Trick of Lily
Possibly bestow

Of Her Father – Whoso ask Her –
He shall seek as high
As the Palm – that serve the Desert –
To obtain the Sky –

Distance – be Her only Motion –
If 'tis Nay – or Yes –
Acquiescence – or Demurral –
Whosoever guess –

He – must pass the Crystal Angle
That obscure Her face –
He – must have achieved in person
Equal Paradise –

c. 1862   1935

650

Pain – has an Element of Blank –
It cannot recollect
When it begun – or if there were
A time when it was not –

It has no Future – but itself –
Its Infinite contain

[323]

Its Past – enlightened to perceive
New Periods – of Pain.

c. 1862   *1890*

651

So much Summer
Me for showing
Illegitimate –
Would a Smile's minute bestowing
Too exorbitant

To the Lady
With the Guinea
Look – if She should know
Crumb of Mine
A Robin's Larder
Would suffice to stow –

c. 1862   *1945*

652

A Prison gets to be a friend –
Between its Ponderous face
And Ours – a Kinsmanship express –
And in its narrow Eyes –

We come to look with gratitude
For the appointed Beam
It deal us – stated as our food –
And hungered for – the same –

We learn to know the Planks –
That answer to Our feet –
So miserable a sound – at first –
Nor ever now – so sweet –

As plashing in the Pools –
When Memory was a Boy –
But a Demurer Circuit –
A Geometric Joy –

The Posture of the Key
That interrupt the Day
To Our Endeavor – Not so real
The Cheek of Liberty –

As this Phantasm Steel –
Whose features – Day and Night –
Are present to us – as Our Own –
And as escapeless – quite –

The narrow Round – the Stint –
The slow exchange of Hope –
For something passiver – Content
Too steep for looking up –

The Liberty we knew
Avoided – like a Dream –
Too wide for any Night but Heaven –
If That – indeed – redeem –

c. 1862   *1929*

653

Of Being is a Bird
The likest to the Down
An Easy Breeze do put afloat
The General Heavens – upon –

It soars – and shifts – and whirls –
And measures with the Clouds
In easy – even – dazzling pace –
No different the Birds –

Except a Wake of Music
Accompany their feet –
As did the Down emit a Tune –
For Ecstasy – of it

c. 1862   *1929*

654

A long – long Sleep – A famous – Sleep –
That makes no show for Morn –
By Stretch of Limb – or stir of Lid –
An independent One –

Was ever idleness like This?
Upon a Bank of Stone
To bask the Centuries away –
Nor once look up – for Noon?

c. 1862   1896

655

Without this – there is nought –
All other Riches be
As is the Twitter of a Bird –
Heard opposite the Sea –

I could not care – to gain
A lesser than the Whole –
For did not this include themself –
As Seams – include the Ball?

I wished a way might be
My Heart to subdivide –
'Twould magnify – the Gratitude –
And not reduce – the Gold –

c. 1862   1935

656

The name – of it – is "Autumn" –
The hue – of it – is Blood –
An Artery – upon the Hill –
A Vein – along the Road –

Great Globules – in the Alleys –
And Oh, the Shower of Stain –
When Winds – upset the Basin –
And spill the Scarlet Rain –

[326]

It sprinkles Bonnets – far below –
It gathers ruddy Pools –
Then – eddies like a Rose – away –
Upon Vermilion Wheels –

c. 1862   *1892*

657

I dwell in Possibility –
A fairer House than Prose –
More numerous of Windows –
Superior – for Doors –

Of Chambers as the Cedars –
Impregnable of Eye –
And for an Everlasting Roof
The Gambrels of the Sky –

Of Visitors – the fairest –
For Occupation – This –
The spreading wide my narrow Hands
To gather Paradise –

c. 1862   *1929*

658

Whole Gulfs – of Red, and Fleets – of Red –
And Crews – of solid Blood –
Did place about the West – Tonight –
As 'twere specific Ground –

And They – appointed Creatures –
In Authorized Arrays –
Due – promptly – as a Drama –
That bows – and disappears –

c. 1862   *1945*

659

That first Day, when you praised Me, Sweet,
And said that I was strong –

And could be mighty, if I liked –
That Day – the Days among –

Glows Central – like a Jewel
Between Diverging Golds –
The Minor One – that gleamed behind –
And Vaster – of the World's.

c. 1862

660

'Tis good – the looking back on Grief –
To re-endure a Day –
We thought the Mighty Funeral –
Of All Conceived Joy –

To recollect how Busy Grass
Did meddle – one by one –
Till all the Grief with Summer – waved
And none could see the stone.

And though the Woe you have Today
Be larger – As the Sea
Exceeds its Unremembered Drop –
They're Water – equally –

c. 1862

661

Could I but ride indefinite
As doth the Meadow Bee
And visit only where I liked
And No one visit me

And flirt all Day with Buttercups
And marry whom I may
And dwell a little everywhere
Or better, run away

With no Police to follow
Or chase Him if He do

Till He should jump Peninsulas
To get away from me –

I said "But just to be a Bee"
Upon a Raft of Air
And row in Nowhere all Day long
And anchor "off the Bar"

What Liberty! So Captives deem
Who tight in Dungeons are.

c. 1862   *1896*

662

Embarrassment of one another
And God
Is Revelation's limit,
Aloud
Is nothing that is chief,
But still,
Divinity dwells under seal.

c. 1862   *1945*

663

Again – his voice is at the door –
I feel the old *Degree* –
I hear him ask the servant
For such an one – as me –

I take a *flower* – as I go –
My face to *justify* –
He never *saw* me – *in this life* –
I might *surprise* his eye!

I cross the Hall with *mingled* steps –
I – silent – pass the door –
I look on all this world *contains* –
Just his face – nothing more!

We talk in *careless* – and in *toss* –
A kind of *plummet* strain –

Each – sounding – shyly –
Just – how – deep –
The *other's* one – had been –

We *walk* – I leave my Dog – at home –
A *tender* – *thoughtful* Moon
Goes with us – just a little way –
And – then – we are *alone* –

Alone – if *Angels* are "alone" –
First time they *try* the *sky*!
Alone – if those "veiled faces" – be –
We cannot *count* – on High!

I'd give – to live that hour – *again* –
The *purple* – *in my Vein* –
But *He* must *count the drops* – *himself* –
My price for *every stain*!

c. *1862*   *1945*

664

Of all the Souls that stand create –
I have elected – One –
When Sense from Spirit – files away –
And Subterfuge – is done –
When that which is – and that which was –
Apart – intrinsic – stand –
And this brief Drama in the flesh –
Is shifted – like a Sand –
When Figures show their royal Front –
And Mists – are carved away,
Behold the Atom – I preferred –
To all the lists of Clay!

c. *1862*   *1891*

665

Dropped into the Ether Acre –
Wearing the Sod Gown –

Bonnet of Everlasting Laces –
Brooch – frozen on –

Horses of Blonde – and Coach of Silver –
Baggage a strapped Pearl –
Journey of Down – and Whip of Diamond –
Riding to meet the Earl –

c. *1863*   *1914*

666

Ah, Teneriffe!
Retreating Mountain!
Purples of Ages – pause for *you* –
Sunset – reviews her Sapphire Regiment –
Day – drops you her Red Adieu!

Still – Clad in your Mail of ices –
Thigh of Granite – and thew – of Steel –
Heedless – alike – of pomp – or parting

Ah, Teneriffe!
I'm kneeling – still –

c. *1863*   *1914*

667

Bloom upon the Mountain – stated –
Blameless of a Name –
Efflorescence of a Sunset –
Reproduced – the same –

Seed, had I, my Purple Sowing
Should endow the Day –
Not a Tropic of a Twilight –
Show itself away –

Who for tilling – to the Mountain
Come, and disappear –
Whose be Her Renown, or fading,
Witness, is not here –

[331]

While I state – the Solemn Petals,
Far as North – and East,
Far as South and West – expanding –
Culminate – in Rest –

And the Mountain to the Evening
Fit His Countenance –
Indicating, by no Muscle –
The Experience –

c. 1863   *1914*

668

"Nature" is what we see –
The Hill – the Afternoon –
Squirrel – Eclipse – the Bumble bee –
Nay – Nature is Heaven –
Nature is what we hear –
The Bobolink – the Sea –
Thunder – the Cricket –
Nay – Nature is Harmony –
Nature is what we know –
Yet have no art to say –
So impotent Our Wisdom is
To her Simplicity.

c. 1863   *1914*

669

No Romance sold unto
Could so enthrall a Man
As the perusal of
His Individual One –
'Tis Fiction's – to dilute to Plausibility
Our Novel – When 'tis small enough
To Credit – 'Tisn't true!

c. 1863   *1914*

[332]

One need not be a Chamber – to be Haunted –
One need not be a House –
The Brain has Corridors – surpassing
Material Place –

Far safer, of a Midnight Meeting
External Ghost
Than its interior Confronting –
That Cooler Host.

Far safer, through an Abbey gallop,
The Stones a'chase –
Than Unarmed, one's a'self encounter –
In lonesome Place –

Ourself behind ourself, concealed –
Should startle most –
Assassin hid in our Apartment
Be Horror's least.

The Body – borrows a Revolver –
He bolts the Door –
O'erlooking a superior spectre –
Or More –

c. 1863   *1891*

She dwelleth in the Ground –
Where Daffodils – abide –
Her Maker – Her Metropolis –
The Universe – Her Maid –

To fetch Her Grace – and Hue –
And Fairness – and Renown –
The Firmament's – To Pluck Her –
And fetch Her Thee – be mine –

c. 1863   *1945*

The Future – never spoke –
Nor will He – like the Dumb –
Reveal by sign – a syllable
Of His Profound To Come –

But when the News be ripe –
Presents it – in the Act –
Forestalling Preparation –
Escape – or Substitute –

Indifferent to Him –
The Dower – as the Doom –
His Office – but to execute
Fate's – Telegram – to Him –

c. 1863   *1914*

The Love a Life can show Below
Is but a filament, I know,
Of that diviner thing
That faints upon the face of Noon –
And smites the Tinder in the Sun –
And hinders Gabriel's Wing –

'Tis this – in Music – hints and sways –
And far abroad on Summer days –
Distils uncertain pain –
'Tis this enamors in the East –
And tints the Transit in the West
With harrowing Iodine –

'Tis this – invites – appalls – endows –
Flits – glimmers – proves – dissolves –
Returns – suggests – convicts – enchants –
Then – flings in Paradise –

c. 1863   *1929*

674

The Soul that hath a Guest
Doth seldom go abroad –
Diviner Crowd at Home –
Obliterate the need –

And Courtesy forbid
A Host's departure when
Upon Himself be visiting
The Emperor of Men –

c. 1863   *1914*

675

Essential Oils – are wrung –
The Attar from the Rose
Be not expressed by Suns – alone –
It is the gift of Screws –

The General Rose – decay –
But this – in Lady's Drawer
Make Summer – When the Lady lie
In Ceaseless Rosemary –

c. 1863   *1891*

676

Least Bee that brew –
A Honey's Weight
The Summer multiply –
Content Her smallest fraction help
The Amber Quantity –

c. 1863   *1945*

677

To be alive – is Power –
Existence – in itself –
Without a further function –
Omnipotence – Enough –

To be alive – and Will!
'Tis able as a God –
The Maker – of Ourselves – be what –
Such being Finitude!

c. *1863*   *1914*

678

Wolfe demanded during dying
"Which obtain the Day"?
"General, the British" – "Easy"
Answered Wolfe "to die"

Montcalm, his opposing Spirit
Rendered with a smile
"Sweet" said he "my own Surrender
Liberty's beguile"

c. *1863*   *1945*

679

Conscious am I in my Chamber,
Of a shapeless friend –
He doth not attest by Posture –
Nor Confirm – by Word –

Neither Place – need I present Him –
Fitter Courtesy
Hospitable intuition
Of His Company –

Presence – is His furthest license –
Neither He to Me
Nor Myself to Him – by Accent –
Forfeit Probity –

Weariness of Him, were quainter
Than Monotony
Knew a Particle – of Space's
Vast Society –

[336]

Neither if He visit Other –
Do He dwell – or Nay – know I –
But Instinct esteem Him
Immortality –

c. 1863   1929

680

Each Life Converges to some Centre –
Expressed – or still –
Exists in every Human Nature
A Goal –

Embodied scarcely to itself – it may be –
Too fair
For Credibility's presumption
To mar –

Adored with caution – as a Brittle Heaven –
To reach
Were hopeless, as the Rainbow's Raiment
To touch –

Yet persevered toward – sure – for the Distance –
How high –
Unto the Saints' slow diligence –
The Sky –

Ungained – it may be – by a Life's low Venture –
But then –
Eternity enable the endeavoring
Again.

c. 1863   1891

681

Soil of Flint, if steady tilled –
Will refund the Hand –
Seed of Palm, by Libyan Sun
Fructified in Sand –

c. 1863   1896

'Twould ease – a Butterfly –
Elate – a Bee –
Thou'rt neither –
Neither – thy capacity –

But, Blossom, were I,
I would rather be
Thy moment
Than a Bee's Eternity –

Content of fading
Is enough for me –
Fade I unto Divinity –

And Dying – Lifetime –
Ample as the Eye –
Her least attention raise on me –

c. 1863   *1945*

The Soul unto itself
Is an imperial friend –
Or the most agonizing Spy –
An Enemy – could send –

Secure against its own –
No treason it can fear –
Itself – its Sovereign – of itself
The Soul should stand in Awe –

c. 1862   *1891*

Best Gains – must have the Losses' Test –
To constitute them – Gains –

c. 1863   *1891*

Not "Revelation" – 'tis – that waits,
But our unfurnished eyes –

c. 1863   *1891*

686

They say that "Time assuages" –
Time never did assuage –
An actual suffering strengthens
As Sinews do, with age –

Time is a Test of Trouble –
But not a Remedy –
If such it prove, it prove too
There was no Malady –

c. 1863   *1896*

687

I'll send the feather from my Hat!
Who knows – but at the sight of *that*
My Sovereign will relent?
As trinket – worn by faded Child –
Confronting eyes long – comforted –
Blisters the Adamant!

c. 1861   *1894*

688

"*Speech*" – is a prank of *Parliament* –
"*Tears*" – a trick of the *nerve* –
But the Heart with the heaviest freight on –
Doesn't – always – move –

c. 1862   *1894*

The Zeroes – taught us – Phosphorus –
We learned to like the Fire
By playing Glaciers – when a Boy –
And Tinder – guessed – by power
Of Opposite – to balance Odd –
If White – a Red – must be!
Paralysis – our Primer – dumb –
Unto Vitality!

c. *1863*   *1894*

Victory comes late –
And is held low to freezing lips –
Too rapt with frost
To take it –
How sweet it would have tasted –
Just a Drop –
Was God so economical?
His Table's spread too high for Us –
Unless We dine on tiptoe –
Crumbs – fit such little mouths –
Cherries – suit Robins –
The Eagle's Golden Breakfast strangles – Them –
God keep His Oath to Sparrows –
Who of little Love – know how to starve –

c. *1863*   *1891*

Would you like summer? Taste of ours.
Spices? Buy here!
Ill! We have berries, for the parching!
Weary! Furloughs of down!
Perplexed! Estates of violet trouble ne'er looked on!
Captive! We bring reprieve of roses!
Fainting! Flasks of air!

Even for Death, a fairy medicine.
But, which is it, sir?

1863?   *1894*

692

The Sun kept setting – setting – still
No Hue of Afternoon –
Upon the Village I perceived –
From House to House 'twas Noon –

The Dusk kept dropping – dropping – still
No Dew upon the Grass –
But only on my Forehead stopped –
And wandered in my Face –

My Feet kept drowsing – drowsing – still
My fingers were awake –
Yet why so little sound – Myself
Unto my Seeming – make?

How well I knew the Light before –
I could see it now –
'Tis Dying – I am doing – but
I'm not afraid to know –

c. 1863   *1890*

693

Shells from the Coast mistaking –
I cherished them for All –
Happening in After Ages
To entertain a Pearl –

Wherefore so late – I murmured –
My need of Thee – be done –
Therefore – the Pearl responded –
My Period begin

c. 1863   *1945*

The Heaven vests for Each
In that small Deity
It craved the grace to worship
Some bashful Summer's Day –

Half shrinking from the Glory
It importuned to see
Till these faint Tabernacles drop
In full Eternity –

How imminent the Venture –
As one should sue a Star –
For His mean sake to leave the Row
And entertain Despair –

A Clemency so common –
We almost cease to fear –
Enabling the minutest –
And furthest – to adore –

c. 1863   1935

As if the Sea should part
And show a further Sea –
And that – a further – and the Three
But a presumption be –

Of Periods of Seas –
Unvisited of Shores –
Themselves the Verge of Seas to be –
Eternity – is Those –

c. 1863   1929

Their Height in Heaven comforts not –
Their Glory – nought to me –
'Twas best imperfect – as it was –
I'm finite – I can't see –

The House of Supposition –
The Glimmering Frontier that
Skirts the Acres of Perhaps –
To Me – shows insecure –

The Wealth I had – contented me –
If 'twas a meaner size –
Then I had counted it until
It pleased my narrow Eyes –

Better than larger values –
That show however true –
This timid life of Evidence
Keeps pleading – "I don't know."

c. 1863   1891

697

I could bring You Jewels – had I a mind to –
But You have enough – of those –
I could bring You Odors from St. Domingo –
Colors – from Vera Cruz –

Berries of the Bahamas – have I –
But this little Blaze
Flickering to itself – in the Meadow –
Suits Me – more than those –

Never a Fellow matched this Topaz –
And his Emerald Swing –
Dower itself – for Bobadilo –
Better – Could I bring?

c. 1863   1945

698

Life – is what we make it –
Death – We do not know –
Christ's acquaintance with Him
Justify Him – though –

[343]

He – would trust no stranger –
Other – could betray –
Just His own endorsement –
That – sufficeth Me –

All the other Distance
He hath traversed first –
No New Mile remaineth –
Far as Paradise –

His sure foot preceding –
Tender Pioneer –
Base must be the Coward
Dare not venture – now –

c. 1863   *1929*

699

The Judge is like the Owl –
I've heard my Father tell –
And Owls do build in Oaks –
So here's an Amber Sill –

That slanted in my Path –
When going to the Barn –
And if it serve You for a House –
Itself is not in vain –

About the price – 'tis small –
I only ask a Tune
At Midnight – Let the Owl select
His favorite Refrain.

c. 1863   *1945*

700

You've seen Balloons set – Haven't You?
So stately they ascend –
It is as Swans – discarded You,
For Duties Diamond –

[344]

Their Liquid Feet go softly out
Upon a Sea of Blonde –
They spurn the Air, as 'twere too mean
For Creatures so renowned –

Their Ribbons just beyond the eye –
They struggle – some – for Breath –
And yet the Crowd applaud, below –
They would not encore – Death –

The Gilded Creature strains – and spins –
Trips frantic in a Tree –
Tears open her imperial Veins –
And tumbles in the Sea –

The Crowd – retire with an Oath –
The Dust in Streets – go down –
And Clerks in Counting Rooms
Observe – " 'Twas only a Balloon" –

c. 1863   1896

701

A Thought went up my mind today –
That I have had before –
But did not finish – some way back –
I could not fix the Year –

Nor where it went – nor why it came
The second time to me –
Nor definitely, what it was –
Have I the Art to say –

But somewhere – in my Soul – I know –
I've met the Thing before –
It just reminded me – 'twas all –
And came my way no more –

c. 1863   1891

A first Mute Coming –
In the Stranger's House –
A first fair Going –
When the Bells rejoice –

A first Exchange – of
What hath mingled – been –
For Lot – exhibited to
Faith – alone –

c. 1863   *1935*

Out of sight? What of that?
See the Bird – reach it!
Curve by Curve – Sweep by Sweep –
Round the Steep Air –
Danger! What is that to Her?
Better 'tis to fail – there –
Than debate – here –

Blue is Blue – the World through –
Amber – Amber – Dew – Dew –
Seek – Friend – and see –
Heaven is shy of Earth – that's all –
Bashful Heaven – thy Lovers small –
Hide – too – from thee –

c. 1863   *1929*

No matter – now – Sweet –
But when I'm Earl –
Won't you wish you'd spoken
To that dull Girl?

Trivial a Word – just –
Trivial – a Smile –

But won't you wish you'd spared one
When I'm Earl?

I shan't need it – then –
Crests – will do –
Eagles on my Buckles –
On my Belt – too –

Ermine – my familiar Gown –
Say – Sweet – then
Won't you wish you'd smiled – just –
Me upon?

c. 1863   *1945*

705

Suspense – is Hostiler than Death –
Death – tho'soever Broad,
Is just Death, and cannot increase –
Suspense – does not conclude –

But perishes – to live anew –
But just anew to die –
Annihilation – plated fresh
With Immortality –

c. 1863   *1929*

706

Life, and Death, and Giants –
Such as These – are still –
Minor – Apparatus – Hopper of the Mill –
Beetle at the Candle –
Or a Fife's Fame –
Maintain – by Accident that they proclaim –

c. 1863   *1896*

707

The Grace – Myself – might not obtain –
Confer upon My flower –

[347]

Refracted but a Countenance –
For I – inhabit Her –

c. *1863*

1935

708

I sometimes drop it, for a Quick –
The Thought to be alive –
Anonymous Delight to know –
And Madder – to conceive –

Consoles a Woe so monstrous
That did it tear all Day,
Without an instant's Respite –
'Twould look too far – to Die –

Delirium – diverts the Wretch
For Whom the Scaffold neighs –
The Hammock's Motion lulls the Heads
So close on Paradise –

A Reef – crawled easy from the Sea
Eats off the Brittle Line –
The Sailor doesn't know the Stroke –
Until He's past the Pain –

c. *1863*

1935

709

Publication – is the Auction
Of the Mind of Man –
Poverty – be justifying
For so foul a thing

Possibly – but We – would rather
From Our Garret go
White – Unto the White Creator –
Than invest – Our Snow –

Thought belong to Him who gave it –
Then – to Him Who bear

Its Corporeal illustration – Sell
The Royal Air –

In the Parcel – Be the Merchant
Of the Heavenly Grace –
But reduce no Human Spirit
To Disgrace of Price –

c. 1863   *1929*

710

The Sunrise runs for Both –
The East – Her Purple Troth
Keeps with the Hill –
The Noon unwinds Her Blue
Till One Breadth cover Two –
Remotest – still –

Nor does the Night forget
A Lamp for Each – to set –
Wicks wide away –
The North – Her blazing Sign
Erects in Iodine –
Till Both – can see –

The Midnight's Dusky Arms
Clasp Hemispheres, and Homes
And so
Upon Her Bosom – One –
And One upon Her Hem –
Both lie –

c. 1863   *1929*

711

Strong Draughts of Their Refreshing Minds
To drink – enables Mine
Through Desert or the Wilderness
As bore it Sealed Wine –

To go elastic – Or as One
The Camel's trait – attained –

[349]

How powerful the Stimulus
Of an Hermetic Mind –

c. 1863

1929

712

Because I could not stop for Death –
He kindly stopped for me –
The Carriage held but just Ourselves –
And Immortality.

We slowly drove – He knew no haste
And I had put away
My labor and my leisure too,
For His Civility –

We passed the School, where Children strove
At Recess – in the Ring –
We passed the Fields of Gazing Grain –
We passed the Setting Sun –

Or rather – He passed Us –
The Dews drew quivering and chill –
For only Gossamer, my Gown –
My Tippet – only Tulle –

We paused before a House that seemed
A Swelling of the Ground –
The Roof was scarcely visible –
The Cornice – in the Ground –

Since then – 'tis Centuries – and yet
Feels shorter than the Day
I first surmised the Horses' Heads
Were toward Eternity –

c. 1863

1890

713

Fame of Myself, to justify,
All other Plaudit be

[350]

Superfluous – An Incense
Beyond Necessity –

Fame of Myself to lack – Although
My Name be else Supreme –
This were an Honor honorless –
A futile Diadem –

c. *1863*   *1945*

714

Rests at Night
The Sun from shining,
Nature – and some Men –
Rest at Noon – some Men –
While Nature
And the Sun – go on –

c. *1863*   *1945*

715

The World – feels Dusty
When We stop to Die –
We want the Dew – then –
Honors – taste dry –

Flags – vex a Dying face –
But the least Fan
Stirred by a friend's Hand –
Cools – like the Rain –

Mine be the Ministry
When thy Thirst comes –
And Hybla Balms –
Dews of Thessaly, to fetch –

c. *1863*   *1929*

716

The Day undressed – Herself –
Her Garter – was of Gold –

[351]

Her Petticoat – of Purple plain –
Her Dimities – as old

Exactly – as the World –
And yet the newest Star –
Enrolled upon the Hemisphere
Be wrinkled – much as Her –

Too near to God – to pray –
Too near to Heaven – to fear –
The Lady of the Occident
Retired without a care –

Her Candle so expire
The flickering be seen
On Ball of Mast in Bosporus –
And Dome – and Window Pane –

c. *1863*   *1935*

717

The Beggar Lad – dies early –
It's Somewhat in the Cold –
And Somewhat in the Trudging feet –
And haply, in the World –

The Cruel – smiling – bowing World –
That took its Cambric Way –
Nor heard the timid cry for "Bread" –
"Sweet Lady – Charity" –

Among Redeemed Children
If Trudging feet may stand –
The Barefoot time forgotten – so –
The Sleet – the bitter Wind –

The Childish Hands that teased for Pence
Lifted adoring – then –
To Him whom never Ragged – Coat
Did supplicate in vain –

c. *1863*   *1945*

I meant to find Her when I came –
Death – had the same design –
But the Success – was His – it seems –
And the Surrender – Mine –

I meant to tell Her how I longed
For just this single time –
But Death had told Her so the first –
And she had past, with Him –

To wander – now – is my Repose –
To rest – To rest would be
A privilege of Hurricane
To Memory – and Me.

c. 1863   *1896*

A South Wind – has a pathos
Of individual Voice –
As One detect on Landings
An Emigrant's address.

A Hint of Ports and Peoples –
And much not understood –
The fairer – for the farness –
And for the foreignhood.

c. 1863   *1945*

No Prisoner be –
Where Liberty –
Himself – abide with Thee –

c. 1863   *1932*

Behind Me – dips Eternity –
Before Me – Immortality –
Myself – the Term between –

Death but the Drift of Eastern Gray,
Dissolving into Dawn away,
Before the West begin –

'Tis Kingdoms – afterward – they say –
In perfect – pauseless Monarchy –
Whose Prince – is Son of None –
Himself – His Dateless Dynasty –
Himself – Himself diversify –
In Duplicate divine –

'Tis Miracle before Me – then –
'Tis Miracle behind – between –
A Crescent in the Sea –
With Midnight to the North of Her –
And Midnight to the South of Her –
And Maelstrom – in the Sky –

c. 1863   *1929*

722

Sweet Mountains – Ye tell Me no lie –
Never deny Me – Never fly –
Those same unvarying Eyes
Turn on Me – when I fail – or feign,
Or take the Royal names in vain –
Their far – slow – Violet Gaze –

My Strong Madonnas – Cherish still –
The Wayward Nun – beneath the Hill –
Whose service – is to You –
Her latest Worship – When the Day
Fades from the Firmament away –
To lift Her Brows on You –

c. 1863   *1945*

723

It tossed – and tossed –
A little Brig I knew – o'ertook by Blast –

It spun – and spun –
And groped delirious, for Morn –

It slipped – and slipped –
As One that drunken – stept –
Its white foot tripped –
Then dropped from sight –

Ah, Brig – Good Night
To Crew and You –
The Ocean's Heart too smooth – too Blue –
To break for You –

c. 1863   1891

724

It's easy to invent a Life –
God does it – every Day –
Creation – but the Gambol
Of His Authority –

It's easy to efface it –
The thrifty Deity
Could scarce afford Eternity
To Spontaneity –

The Perished Patterns murmur –
But His Perturbless Plan
Proceed – inserting Here – a Sun –
There – leaving out a Man –

c. 1863   1929

725

Where Thou art – that – is Home –
Cashmere – or Calvary – the same –
Degree – or Shame –
I scarce esteem Location's Name –
So I may Come –

What Thou dost – is Delight –
Bondage as Play – be sweet –

Imprisonment – Content –
And Sentence – Sacrament –
Just We two – meet –

Where Thou art not – is Woe –
Tho' Bands of Spices – row –
What Thou dost not – Despair –
Tho' Gabriel – praise me – Sir –

c. 1863   1929

726

We thirst at first – 'tis Nature's Act –
And later – when we die –
A little Water supplicate –
Of fingers going by –

It intimates the finer want –
Whose adequate supply
Is that Great Water in the West –
Termed Immortality –

c. 1863   1896

727

Precious to Me – She still shall be –
Though She forget the name I bear –
The fashion of the Gown I wear –
The very Color of My Hair –

So like the Meadows – now –
I dared to show a Tress of Theirs
If haply – She might not despise
A Buttercup's Array –

I know the Whole – obscures the Part –
The fraction – that appeased the Heart
Till Number's Empery –
Remembered – as the Milliner's flower

When Summer's Everlasting Dower –
Confronts the dazzled Bee.

c. 1863

1945

728

Let Us play Yesterday –
I – the Girl at school –
You – and Eternity – the
Untold Tale –

Easing my famine
At my Lexicon –
Logarithm – had I – for Drink –
'Twas a dry Wine –

Somewhat different – must be –
Dreams tint the Sleep –
Cunning Reds of Morning
Make the Blind – leap –

Still at the Egg-life –
Chafing the Shell –
When you troubled the Ellipse –
And the Bird fell –

Manacles be dim – they say –
To the new Free –
Liberty – Commoner –
Never could – to me –

'Twas my last gratitude
When I slept – at night –
'Twas the first Miracle
Let in – with Light –

Can the Lark resume the Shell –
Easier – for the Sky –
Wouldn't Bonds hurt more
Than Yesterday?

Wouldn't Dungeons sorer grate
On the Man – free –

Just long enough to taste –
Then – doomed new –

God of the Manacle
As of the Free –
Take not my Liberty
Away from Me –

c. *1863*   *1935*

729

Alter! When the Hills do –
Falter! When the Sun
Question if His Glory
Be the Perfect One –

Surfeit! When the Daffodil
Doth of the Dew –
Even as Herself – Sir –
I will – of You –

c. *1863*   *1890*

730

Defrauded I a Butterfly –
The lawful Heir – for Thee –

c. *1863*   *1929*

731

"I want" – it pleaded – All its life –
I want – was chief it said
When Skill entreated it – the last –
And when so newly dead –

I could not deem it late – to hear
That single – steadfast sigh –
The lips had placed as with a "Please"
Toward Eternity –

c. *1863*   *1945*

732

She rose to His Requirement – dropt
The Playthings of Her Life
To take the honorable Work
Of Woman, and of Wife –

If ought She missed in Her new Day,
Of Amplitude, or Awe –
Or first Prospective – Or the Gold
In using, wear away,

It lay unmentioned – as the Sea
Develop Pearl, and Weed,
But only to Himself – be known
The Fathoms they abide –

c. 1863   *1890*

733

The Spirit is the Conscious Ear.
We actually Hear
When We inspect – that's audible –
That is admitted – Here –

For other Services – as Sound –
There hangs a smaller Ear
Outside the Castle – that Contain –
The other – only – Hear –

c. 1863   *1945*

734

If He were living – dare I ask –
And how if He be dead –
And so around the Words I went –
Of meeting them – afraid –

I hinted Changes – Lapse of Time –
The Surfaces of Years –
I touched with Caution – lest they crack –
And show me to my fears –

Reverted to adjoining Lives –
Adroitly turning out
Wherever I suspected Graves –
'Twas prudenter – I thought –

And He – I pushed – with sudden force –
In face of the Suspense –
"Was buried" – "Buried"! "He!"
My Life just holds the Trench –

c. *1863*   *1929*

735

Upon Concluded Lives
There's nothing cooler falls –
Than Life's sweet Calculations –
The mixing Bells and Palls –

Makes Lacerating Tune –
To Ears the Dying Side –
'Tis Coronal – and Funeral –
Saluting – in the Road –

c. *1863*   *1945*

736

Have any like Myself
Investigating March,
New Houses on the Hill descried –
And possibly a Church –

That were not, We are sure –
As lately as the Snow –
And are Today – if We exist –
Though how may this be so?

Have any like Myself
Conjectured Who may be
The Occupants of the Abodes –
So easy to the Sky –

[360]

'Twould seem that God should be
The nearest Neighbor to –
And Heaven – a convenient Grace
For Show, or Company –

Have any like Myself
Preserved the Charm secure
By shunning carefully the Place
All Seasons of the Year,

Excepting March – 'Tis then
My Villages be seen –
And possibly a Steeple –
Not afterward – by Men –

c. 1863   1935

737

The Moon was but a Chin of Gold
A Night or two ago –
And now she turns Her perfect Face
Upon the World below –

Her Forehead is of Amplest Blonde –
Her Cheek – a Beryl hewn –
Her Eye unto the Summer Dew
The likest I have known –

Her Lips of Amber never part –
But what must be the smile
Upon Her Friend she could confer
Were such Her Silver Will –

And what a privilege to be
But the remotest Star –
For Certainty She take Her Way
Beside Your Palace Door –

Her Bonnet is the Firmament –
The Universe – Her Shoe –

The Stars – the Trinkets at Her Belt –
Her Dimities – of Blue –

c. 1863   *1896*

738

You said that I "was Great" – one Day –
Then "Great" it be – if that please Thee –
Or Small – or any size at all –
Nay – I'm the size suit Thee –

Tall – like the Stag – would that?
Or lower – like the Wren –
Or other heights of Other Ones
I've seen?

Tell which – it's dull to guess –
And I must be Rhinoceros
Or Mouse
At once – for Thee –

So say – if Queen it be –
Or Page – please Thee –
I'm that – or nought –
Or other thing – if other thing there be –
With just this Stipulus –
I suit Thee –

c. 1863   *1945*

739

I many times thought Peace had come
When Peace was far away –
As Wrecked Men – deem they sight the Land –
At Centre of the Sea –

And struggle slacker – but to prove
As hopelessly as I –
How many the fictitious Shores –
Before the Harbor be –

c. 1863   *1891*

You taught me Waiting with Myself –
Appointment strictly kept –
You taught me fortitude of Fate –
This – also – I have learnt –

An Altitude of Death, that could
No bitterer debar
Than Life – had done – before it –
Yet – there is a Science more –

The Heaven you know – to understand
That you be not ashamed
Of Me – in Christ's bright Audience
Upon the further Hand –

c. 1863   *1929*

Drama's Vitallest Expression is the Common Day
That arise and set about Us –
Other Tragedy

Perish in the Recitation –
This – the best enact
When the Audience is scattered
And the Boxes shut –

"Hamlet" to Himself were Hamlet –
Had not Shakespeare wrote –
Though the "Romeo" left no Record
Of his Juliet,

It were infinite enacted
In the Human Heart –
Only Theatre recorded
Owner cannot shut –

c. 1863   *1929*

Four Trees – upon a solitary Acre –
Without Design
Or Order, or Apparent Action –
Maintain –

The Sun – upon a Morning meets them –
The Wind –
No nearer Neighbor – have they –
But God –

The Acre gives them – Place –
They – Him – Attention of Passer by –
Of Shadow, or of Squirrel, haply –
Or Boy –

What Deed is Theirs unto the General Nature –
What Plan
They severally – retard – or further –
Unknown –

c. 1863   1945

The Birds reported from the South –
A News express to Me –
A spicy Charge, My little Posts –
But I am deaf – Today –

The Flowers – appealed – a timid Throng –
I reinforced the Door –
Go blossom to the Bees – I said –
And trouble Me – no More –

The Summer Grace, for Notice strove –
Remote – Her best Array –
The Heart – to stimulate the Eye
Refused too utterly –

At length, a Mourner, like Myself,
She drew away austere –

Her frosts to ponder – then it was
I recollected Her –

She suffered Me, for I had mourned –
I offered Her no word –
My Witness – was the Crape I bore –
Her – Witness – was Her Dead –

Thenceforward – We – together dwelt –
I never questioned Her –
Our Contract
A Wiser Sympathy

c. *1863*   *1935*

744

Remorse – is Memory – awake –
Her Parties all astir –
A Presence of Departed Acts –
At window – and at Door –

Its Past – set down before the Soul
And lighted with a Match –
Perusal – to facilitate –
And help Belief to stretch –

Remorse is cureless – the Disease
Not even God – can heal –
For 'tis His institution – and
The Adequate of Hell –

c. *1863*   *1891*

745

Renunciation – is a piercing Virtue –
The letting go
A Presence – for an Expectation –
Not now –
The putting out of Eyes –
Just Sunrise –
Lest Day –

[365]

Day's Great Progenitor –
Outvie
Renunciation – is the Choosing
Against itself –
Itself to justify
Unto itself –
When larger function –
Make that appear –
Smaller – that Covered Vision – Here –

c. 1863   *1929*

746

Never for Society
He shall seek in vain –
Who His own acquaintance
Cultivate – Of Men
Wiser Men may weary –
But the Man within

Never knew Satiety –
Better entertain
Than could Border Ballad –
Or Biscayan Hymn –
Neither introduction
Need You – unto Him –

c. 1863   *1894*

747

It dropped so low – in my Regard –
I heard it hit the Ground –
And go to pieces on the Stones
At bottom of my Mind –

Yet blamed the Fate that flung it – *less*
Than I denounced Myself,
For entertaining Plated Wares
Upon my Silver Shelf –

c. 1863   *1896*

[366]

748

Autumn – overlooked my Knitting –
Dyes – said He – have I –
Could disparage a Flamingo –
Show Me them – said I –

Cochineal – I chose – for deeming
It resemble Thee –
And the little Border – Dusker –
For resembling Me –

c. 1863   *1929*

749

All but Death, can be Adjusted –
Dynasties repaired –
Systems – settled in their Sockets –
Citadels – dissolved –

Wastes of Lives – resown with Colors
By Succeeding Springs –
Death – unto itself – Exception –
Is exempt from Change –

c. 1863   *1929*

750

Growth of Man – like Growth of Nature –
Gravitates within –
Atmosphere, and Sun endorse it –
But it stir – alone –

Each – its difficult Ideal
Must achieve – Itself –
Through the solitary prowess
Of a Silent Life –

Effort – is the sole condition –
Patience of Itself –
Patience of opposing forces –
And intact Belief –

Looking on – is the Department
Of its Audience –
But Transaction – is assisted
By no Countenance –

c. *1863*   *1929*

751

My Worthiness is all my Doubt –
His Merit – all my fear –
Contrasting which, my quality
Do lowlier – appear –

Lest I should insufficient prove
For His beloved Need –
The Chiefest Apprehension
Upon my thronging Mind –

'Tis true – that Deity to stoop
Inherently incline –
For nothing higher than Itself
Itself can rest upon –

So I – the undivine abode
Of His Elect Content –
Conform my Soul – as 'twere a Church,
Unto Her Sacrament –

c. *1863*   *1896*

752

So the Eyes accost – and sunder
In an Audience –
Stamped – occasionally – forever –
So may Countenance

Entertain – without addressing
Countenance of One
In a Neighboring Horizon –
Gone – as soon as known –

c. *1863*   *1929*

[368]

My Soul – accused me – And I quailed –
As Tongues of Diamond had reviled
All else accused me – and I smiled –
My Soul – that Morning – was My friend –

Her favor – is the best Disdain
Toward Artifice of Time – or Men –
But Her Disdain – 'twere lighter bear
A finger of Enamelled Fire –

c. 1863

1929

My Life had stood – a Loaded Gun –
In Corners – till a Day
The Owner passed – identified –
And carried Me away –

And now We roam in Sovereign Woods –
And now We hunt the Doe –
And every time I speak for Him –
The Mountains straight reply –

And do I smile, such cordial light
Upon the Valley glow –
It is as a Vesuvian face
Had let its pleasure through –

And when at Night – Our good Day done –
I guard My Master's Head –
'Tis better than the Eider-Duck's
Deep Pillow – to have shared –

To foe of His – I'm deadly foe –
None stir the second time –
On whom I lay a Yellow Eye –
Or an emphatic Thumb –

Though I than He – may longer live
He longer must – than I –

For I have but the power to kill,
Without – the power to die –

c. *1863*

1929

755

No Bobolink – reverse His Singing
When the only Tree
Ever He minded occupying
By the Farmer be –

Clove to the Root –
His Spacious Future –
Best Horizon – gone –
Whose Music be His
Only Anodyne –
Brave Bobolink –

c. *1863*

1945

756

One Blessing had I than the rest
So larger to my Eyes
That I stopped gauging – satisfied –
For this enchanted size –

It was the limit of my Dream –
The focus of my Prayer –
A perfect – paralyzing Bliss –
Contented as Despair –

I knew no more of Want – or Cold –
Phantasms both become
For this new Value in the Soul –
Supremest Earthly Sum –

The Heaven below the Heaven above –
Obscured with ruddier Blue –
Life's Latitudes leant over – full –
The Judgment perished – too –

[370]

Why Bliss so scantily disburse –
Why Paradise defer –
Why Floods be served to Us – in Bowls –
I speculate no more –

c. 1863   1896

757

The Mountains – grow unnoticed –
Their Purple figures rise
Without attempt – Exhaustion –
Assistance – or Applause –

In Their Eternal Faces
The Sun – with just delight
Looks long – and last – and golden –
For fellowship – at night –

c. 1863   1929

758

These – saw Visions –
Latch them softly –
These – held Dimples –
Smooth them slow –
This – addressed departing accents –
Quick – Sweet Mouth – to miss thee so –

This – We stroked –
Unnumbered Satin –
These – we held among our own –
Fingers of the Slim Aurora –
Not so arrogant – this Noon –

These – adjust – that ran to meet us –
Pearl – for Stocking – Pearl for Shoe –
Paradise – the only Palace
Fit for Her reception – now –

c. 1863   1935

He fought like those Who've nought to lose –
Bestowed Himself to Balls
As One who for a further Life
Had not a further Use –

Invited Death – with bold attempt –
But Death was Coy of Him
As Other Men, were Coy of Death –
To Him – to live – was Doom –

His Comrades, shifted like the Flakes
When Gusts reverse the Snow –
But He – was left alive Because
Of Greediness to die –

c. *1863*

1935

Most she touched me by her muteness –
Most she won me by the way
She presented her small figure –
Plea itself – for Charity –

Were a Crumb my whole possession –
Were there famine in the land –
Were it my resource from starving –
Could I such a plea withstand –

Not upon her knee to thank me
Sank this Beggar from the Sky –
But the Crumb partook – departed –
And returned On High –

I supposed – when sudden
Such a Praise began
'Twas as Space sat singing
To herself – and men –

'Twas the Winged Beggar –
Afterward I learned

To her Benefactor
Making Gratitude

c. *1863*

1929

761

From Blank to Blank –
A Threadless Way
I pushed Mechanic feet –
To stop – or perish – or advance –
Alike indifferent –

If end I gained
It ends beyond
Indefinite disclosed –
I shut my eyes – and groped as well
'Twas lighter – to be Blind –

c. *1863*

1929

762

The Whole of it came not at once –
'Twas Murder by degrees –
A Thrust – and then for Life a chance –
The Bliss to cauterize –

The Cat reprieves the Mouse
She eases from her teeth
Just long enough for Hope to tease –
Then mashes it to death –

'Tis Life's award – to die –
Contenteder if once –
Than dying half – then rallying
For consciouser Eclipse –

c. *1863*

1945

763

He told a homely tale
And spotted it with tears –

Upon his infant face was set
The Cicatrice of years –

All crumpled was the cheek
No other kiss had known
Than flake of snow, divided with
The Redbreast of the Barn –

If Mother – in the Grave –
Or Father – on the Sea –
Or Father in the Firmament –
Or Brethren, had he –

If Commonwealth below,
Or Commonwealth above
Have missed a Barefoot Citizen –
I've ransomed it – alive –

c. 1863   1945

764

Presentiment – is that long Shadow – on the Lawn –
Indicative that Suns go down –

The Notice to the startled Grass
That Darkness – is about to pass –

c. 1863   1890

765

You constituted Time –
I deemed Eternity
A Revelation of Yourself –
'Twas therefore Deity

The Absolute – removed
The Relative away –
That I unto Himself adjust
My slow idolatry –

c. 1863   1945

My Faith is larger than the Hills –
So when the Hills decay –
My Faith must take the Purple Wheel
To show the Sun the way –

'Tis first He steps upon the Vane –
And then – upon the Hill –
And then abroad the World He go
To do His Golden Will –

And if His Yellow feet should miss –
The Bird would not arise –
The Flowers would slumber on their Stems –
No Bells have Paradise –

How dare I, therefore, stint a faith
On which so vast depends –
Lest Firmament should fail for me –
The Rivet in the Bands

c. 1863   *1929*

767

To offer brave assistance
To Lives that stand alone –
When One has failed to stop them –
Is Human – but Divine

To lend an Ample Sinew
Unto a Nameless Man –
Whose Homely Benediction
No other – stopped to earn –

c. 1863   *1929*

768

When I hoped, I recollect
Just the place I stood –
At a Window facing West –
Roughest Air – was good –

Not a Sleet could bite me –
Not a frost could cool –
Hope it was that kept me warm –
Not Merino shawl –

When I feared – I recollect
Just the Day it was –
Worlds were lying out to Sun –
Yet how Nature froze –

Icicles upon my soul
Prickled Blue and Cool –
Bird went praising everywhere –
Only Me – was still –

And the Day that I despaired –
This – if I forget
Nature will – that it be Night
After Sun has set –
Darkness intersect her face –
And put out her eye –
Nature hesitate – before
Memory and I –

c. 1863   *1929*

769

One and One – are One –
Two – be finished using –
Well enough for Schools –
But for Minor Choosing –

Life – just – Or Death –
Or the Everlasting –
More – would be too vast
For the Soul's Comprising –

c. 1863   *1929*

770

I lived on Dread –
To Those who know

The Stimulus there is
In Danger – Other impetus
Is numb – and Vitalless –

As 'twere a Spur – upon the Soul –
A Fear will urge it where
To go without the Spectre's aid
Were Challenging Despair.

c. 1863   *1891*

771

None can experience stint
Who Bounty – have not known –
The fact of Famine – could not be
Except for Fact of Corn –

Want – is a meagre Art
Acquired by Reverse –
The Poverty that was not Wealth –
Cannot be Indigence.

c. 1863   *1945*

772

The hallowing of Pain
Like hallowing of Heaven,
Obtains at a corporeal cost –
The Summit is not given

To Him who strives severe
At middle of the Hill –
But He who has achieved the Top –
All – is the price of All –

c. 1863   *1945*

773

Deprived of other Banquet,
I entertained Myself –

At first – a scant nutrition –
An insufficient Loaf –

But grown by slender addings
To so esteemed a size
'Tis sumptuous enough for me –
And almost to suffice

A Robin's famine able –
Red Pilgrim, He and I –
A Berry from our table
Reserve – for charity –

c. 1863   1945

774

It is a lonesome Glee –
Yet sanctifies the Mind –
With fair association –
Afar upon the Wind

A Bird to overhear
Delight without a Cause –
Arrestless as invisible –
A matter of the Skies.

c. 1863   1945

775

If Blame be my side – forfeit Me –
But doom me not to forfeit Thee –
To forfeit Thee? The very name
Is sentence from Belief – and Home –

c. 1863   1945

776

Purple –

The Color of a Queen, is this –
The Color of a Sun

At setting – this and Amber –
Beryl – and this, at Noon –

And when at night – Auroran widths
Fling suddenly on men –
'Tis this – and Witchcraft – nature keeps
A Rank – for Iodine –

c. 1863   *1945*

777

The Loneliness One dare not sound –
And would as soon surmise
As in its Grave go plumbing
To ascertain the size –

The Loneliness whose worst alarm
Is lest itself should see –
And perish from before itself
For just a scrutiny –

The Horror not to be surveyed –
But skirted in the Dark –
With Consciousness suspended –
And Being under Lock –

I fear me this – is Loneliness –
The Maker of the soul
Its Caverns and its Corridors
Illuminate – or seal –

c. 1863   *1945*

778

This that would greet – an hour ago –
Is quaintest Distance – now –
Had it a Guest from Paradise –
Nor glow, would it, nor bow –

Had it a notice from the Noon
Nor beam would it nor warm –

Match me the Silver Reticence –
Match me the Solid Calm –

c. *1863*   *1945*

779

The Service without Hope –
Is tenderest, I think –
Because 'tis unsustained
By stint – Rewarded Work –

Has impetus of Gain –
And impetus of Goal –
There is no Diligence like that
That knows not an Until –

c. *1863*   *1945*

780

The Truth – is stirless –
Other force – may be presumed to move –
This – then – is best for confidence –
When oldest Cedars swerve –

And Oaks untwist their fists –
And Mountains – feeble – lean –
How excellent a Body, that
Stands without a Bone –

How vigorous a Force
That holds without a Prop –
Truth stays Herself – and every man
That trusts Her – boldly up –

c. *1863*   *1945*

781

To wait an Hour – is long –
If Love be just beyond –

To wait Eternity – is short –
If Love reward the end –

c. 1863   *1945*

782

There is an arid Pleasure –
As different from Joy –
As Frost is different from Dew –
Like element – are they –

Yet one – rejoices Flowers –
And one – the Flowers abhor –
The finest Honey – curdled –
Is worthless – to the Bee –

c. 1863   *1945*

783

The Birds begun at Four o'clock –
Their period for Dawn –
A Music numerous as space –
But neighboring as Noon –

I could not count their Force –
Their Voices did expend
As Brook by Brook bestows itself
To multiply the Pond.

Their Witnesses were not –
Except occasional man –
In homely industry arrayed –
To overtake the Morn –

Nor was it for applause –
That I could ascertain –
But independent Ecstasy
Of Deity and Men –

By Six, the Flood had done –
No Tumult there had been

Of Dressing, or Departure –
And yet the Band was gone –

The Sun engrossed the East –
The Day controlled the World –
The Miracle that introduced
Forgotten, as fulfilled.

c. *1863*   *1945*

784

Bereaved of all, I went abroad –
No less bereaved was I
Upon a New Peninsula –
The Grave preceded me –

Obtained my Lodgings, ere myself –
And when I sought my Bed –
The Grave it was reposed upon
The Pillow for my Head –

I waked to find it first awake –
I rose – It followed me –
I tried to drop it in the Crowd –
To lose it in the Sea –

In Cups of artificial Drowse
To steep its shape away –
The Grave – was finished – but the Spade
Remained in Memory –

c. *1863*   *1896*

785

They have a little Odor – that to me
Is metre – nay – 'tis melody –
And spiciest at fading – indicate –
A Habit – of a Laureate –

c. *1863*   *1945*

Severer Service of myself
I – hastened to demand
To fill the awful Vacuum
Your life had left behind –

I worried Nature with my Wheels
When Hers had ceased to run –
When she had put away Her Work
My own had just begun.

I strove to weary Brain and Bone –
To harass to fatigue
The glittering Retinue of nerves –
Vitality to clog

To some dull comfort Those obtain
Who put a Head away
They knew the Hair to –
And forget the color of the Day –

Affliction would not be appeased –
The Darkness braced as firm
As all my stratagem had been
The Midnight to confirm –

No Drug for Consciousness – can be –
Alternative to die
Is Nature's only Pharmacy
For Being's Malady –

c. 1863

1945

Such is the Force of Happiness –
The Least – can lift a Ton
Assisted by its stimulus –

Who Misery – sustain –
No Sinew can afford –
The Cargo of Themselves –

Too infinite for Consciousness'
Slow capabilities.

c. *1863*   *1945*

788

Joy to have merited the Pain –
To merit the Release –
Joy to have perished every step –
To Compass Paradise –

Pardon – to look upon thy face –
With these old fashioned Eyes –
Better than new – could be – for that –
Though bought in Paradise –

Because they looked on thee before –
And thou hast looked on them –
Prove Me – My Hazel Witnesses
The features are the same –

So fleet thou wert, when present –
So infinite – when gone –
An Orient's Apparition –
Remanded of the Morn –

The Height I recollect –
'Twas even with the Hills –
The Depth upon my Soul was notched –
As Floods – on Whites of Wheels –

To Haunt – till Time have dropped
His last Decade away,
And Haunting actualize – to last
At least – Eternity –

c. *1863*   *1929*

789

On a Columnar Self –
How ample to rely

[384]

In Tumult – or Extremity –
How good the Certainty

That Lever cannot pry –
And Wedge cannot divide
Conviction – That Granitic Base –
Though None be on our Side –

Suffice Us – for a Crowd –
Ourself – and Rectitude –
And that Assembly – not far off
From furthest Spirit – God –

c. 1863   1929

790

Nature – the Gentlest Mother is,
Impatient of no Child –
The feeblest – or the waywardest –
Her Admonition mild –

In Forest – and the Hill –
By Traveller – be heard –
Restraining Rampant Squirrel –
Or too impetuous Bird –

How fair Her Conversation –
A Summer Afternoon –
Her Household – Her Assembly –
And when the Sun go down –

Her Voice among the Aisles
Incite the timid prayer
Of the minutest Cricket –
The most unworthy Flower –

When all the Children sleep –
She turns as long away
As will suffice to light Her lamps –
Then bending from the Sky –

With infinite Affection –
And infiniter Care –

Her Golden finger on Her lip –
Wills Silence – Everywhere –

c. 1863

1891

791

God gave a Loaf to every Bird –
But just a Crumb – to Me –
I dare not eat it – tho' I starve –
My poignant luxury –

To own it – touch it –
Prove the feat – that made the Pellet mine –
Too happy – for my Sparrow's chance –
For Ampler Coveting –

It might be Famine – all around –
I could not miss an Ear –
Such Plenty smiles upon my Board –
My Garner shows so fair –

I wonder how the Rich – may feel –
An Indiaman – An Earl –
I deem that I – with but a Crumb –
Am Sovereign of them all –

c. 1863

1891

792

Through the strait pass of suffering –
The Martyrs – even – trod.
Their feet – upon Temptation –
Their faces – upon God –

A stately – shriven – Company –
Convulsion – playing round –
Harmless – as streaks of Meteor –
Upon a Planet's Bond –

Their faith – the everlasting troth –
Their Expectation – fair –

The Needle – to the North Degree –
Wades – so – thro' polar Air!

c. 1863   1891

793

Grief is a Mouse –
And chooses Wainscot in the Breast
For His Shy House –
And baffles quest –

Grief is a Thief – quick startled –
Pricks His Ear – report to hear
Of that Vast Dark –
That swept His Being – back –

Grief is a Juggler – boldest at the Play –
Lest if He flinch – the eye that way
Pounce on His Bruises – One – say – or Three –
Grief is a Gourmand – spare His luxury –

Best Grief is Tongueless – before He'll tell –
Burn Him in the Public Square –
His Ashes – will
Possibly – if they refuse – How then know –
Since a Rack couldn't coax a syllable – now.

c. 1863   1945

794

A Drop fell on the Apple Tree –
Another – on the Roof –
A Half a Dozen kissed the Eaves –
And made the Gables laugh –

A few went out to help the Brook
That went to help the Sea –
Myself Conjectured were they Pearls –
What Necklaces could be –

The Dust replaced, in Hoisted Roads –
The Birds jocoser sung –

The Sunshine threw his Hat away –
The Bushes – spangles flung –

The Breezes brought dejected Lutes –
And bathed them in the Glee –
Then Orient showed a single Flag,
And signed the Fete away –

c. *1863*   *1890*

795

Her final Summer was it –
And yet We guessed it not –
If tenderer industriousness
Pervaded Her, We thought

A further force of life
Developed from within –
When Death lit all the shortness up
It made the hurry plain –

We wondered at our blindness
When nothing was to see
But Her Carrara Guide post –
At Our Stupidity –

When duller than our dullness
The Busy Darling lay –
So busy was she – finishing –
So leisurely – were We –

c. *1863*   *1891*

796

Who Giants know, with lesser Men
Are incomplete, and shy –
For Greatness, that is ill at ease
In minor Company –

A Smaller, could not be perturbed –
The Summer Gnat displays –

Unconscious that his single Fleet
Do not comprise the skies –

797

By my Window have I for Scenery
Just a Sea – with a Stem –
If the Bird and the Farmer – deem it a "Pine" –
The Opinion will serve – for them –

It has no Port, nor a "Line" – but the Jays –
That split their route to the Sky –
Or a Squirrel, whose giddy Peninsula
May be easier reached – this way –

For Inlands – the Earth is the under side –
And the upper side – is the Sun –
And its Commerce – if Commerce it have –
Of Spice – I infer from the Odors borne –

Of its Voice – to affirm – when the Wind is within –
Can the Dumb – define the Divine?
The Definition of Melody – is –
That Definition is none –

It – suggests to our Faith –
They – suggest to our Sight –
When the latter – is put away
I shall meet with Conviction I somewhere met
That Immortality –

Was the Pine at my Window a "Fellow
Of the Royal" Infinity?
Apprehensions – are God's introductions –
To be hallowed – accordingly –

798

She staked her Feathers – Gained an Arc –
Debated – Rose again –

This time – beyond the estimate
Of Envy, or of Men –

And now, among Circumference –
Her steady Boat be seen –
At home – among the Billows – As
The Bough where she was born –

c. 1863

1935

799

Despair's advantage is achieved
By suffering – Despair –
To be assisted of Reverse
One must Reverse have bore –

The Worthiness of Suffering like
The Worthiness of Death
Is ascertained by tasting –

As can no other Mouth

Of Savors – make us conscious –
As did ourselves partake –
Affliction feels impalpable
Until Ourselves are struck –

c. 1863

1935

800

Two – were immortal twice –
The privilege of few –
Eternity – obtained – in Time –
Reversed Divinity –

That our ignoble Eyes
The quality conceive
Of Paradise superlative –
Through their Comparative.

c. 1863

1945

I play at Riches – to appease
The Clamoring for Gold –
It kept me from a Thief, I think,
For often, overbold

With Want, and Opportunity –
I could have done a Sin
And been Myself that easy Thing
An independent Man –

But often as my lot displays
Too hungry to be borne
I deem Myself what I would be –
And novel Comforting

My Poverty and I derive –
We question if the Man –
Who own – Esteem the Opulence –
As We – Who never Can –

Should ever these exploring Hands
Chance Sovereign on a Mine –
Or in the long – uneven term
To win, become their turn –

How fitter they will be – for Want –
Enlightening so well –
I know not which, Desire, or Grant –
Be wholly beautiful –

c. 1863   *1935*

Time feels so vast that were it not
For an Eternity –
I fear me this Circumference
Engross my Finity –

To His exclusion, who prepare
By Processes of Size

For the Stupendous Vision
Of His diameters –

c. *1863*   *1935*

803

Who Court obtain within Himself
Sees every Man a King –
And Poverty of Monarchy
Is an interior thing –

No Man depose
Whom Fate Ordain –
And Who can add a Crown
To Him who doth continual
Conspire against His Own

c. *1863*   *1929*

804

No Notice gave She, but a Change –
No Message, but a Sigh –
For Whom, the Time did not suffice
That She should specify.

She was not warm, though Summer shone
Nor scrupulous of cold
Though Rime by Rime, the steady Frost
Upon Her Bosom piled –

Of shrinking ways – she did not fright
Though all the Village looked –
But held Her gravity aloft –
And met the gaze – direct –

And when adjusted like a Seed
In careful fitted Ground
Unto the Everlasting Spring
And hindered but a Mound

Her Warm return, if so she chose –
And We – imploring drew –

Removed our invitation by
As Some She never knew –

c. 1863   1935

805

This Bauble was preferred of Bees –
By Butterflies admired
At Heavenly – Hopeless Distances –
Was justified of Bird –

Did Noon – enamel – in Herself
Was Summer to a Score
Who only knew of Universe –
It had created Her.

c. 1863   1935

806

A Plated Life – diversified
With Gold and Silver Pain
To prove the presence of the Ore
In Particles – 'tis when

A Value struggle – it exist –
A Power – will proclaim
Although Annihilation pile
Whole Chaoses on Him –

c. 1863   1935

807

Expectation – is Contentment –
Gain – Satiety –
But Satiety – Conviction
Of Necessity

Of an Austere trait in Pleasure –
Good, without alarm

Is a too established Fortune –
Danger – deepens Sum –

c. *1863*

1929

808

So set its Sun in Thee
What Day be dark to me –
What Distance – far –
So I the Ships may see
That touch – how seldomly –
Thy Shore?

c. *1864*

1914

809

Unable are the Loved to die
For Love is Immortality,
Nay, it is Deity –

Unable they that love – to die
For Love reforms Vitality
Into Divinity.

c. *1864*

1932

810

Her Grace is all she has –
And that, so least displays –
One Art to recognize, must be,
Another Art, to praise.

c. *1864*

1914

811

The Veins of other Flowers
The Scarlet Flowers are
Till Nature leisure has for Terms
As "Branch," and "Jugular."

[394]

We pass, and she abides.
We conjugate Her Skill
While She creates and federates
Without a syllable.

c. 1864   *1945*

812

A Light exists in Spring
Not present on the Year
At any other period –
When March is scarcely here

A Color stands abroad
On Solitary Fields
That Science cannot overtake
But Human Nature feels.

It waits upon the Lawn,
It shows the furthest Tree
Upon the furthest Slope you know
It almost speaks to you.

Then as Horizons step
Or Noons report away
Without the Formula of sound
It passes and we stay –

A quality of loss
Affecting our Content
As Trade had suddenly encroached
Upon a Sacrament.

c. 1864   *1896*

813

This quiet Dust was Gentlemen and Ladies
And Lads and Girls –
Was laughter and ability and Sighing
And Frocks and Curls.

This Passive Place a Summer's nimble mansion
Where Bloom and Bees
Exists an Oriental Circuit
Then cease, like these –

c. 1864

1914

814

One Day is there of the Series
Termed Thanksgiving Day.
Celebrated part at Table
Part in Memory.

Neither Patriarch nor Pussy
I dissect the Play
Seems it to my Hooded thinking
Reflex Holiday.

Had there been no sharp Subtraction
From the early Sum –
Not an Acre or a Caption
Where was once a Room –

Not a Mention, whose small Pebble
Wrinkled any Sea,
Unto Such, were such Assembly
'Twere Thanksgiving Day.

c. 1864

1896

815

The Luxury to apprehend
The Luxury 'twould be
To look at Thee a single time
An Epicure of Me

In whatsoever Presence makes
Till for a further Food
I scarcely recollect to starve
So first am I supplied –

[396]

The Luxury to meditate
The Luxury it was
To banquet on thy Countenance
A Sumptuousness bestows

On plainer Days, whose Table far
As Certainty can see
Is laden with a single Crumb
The Consciousness of Thee.

r. 1864   1914

816

A Death blow is a Life blow to Some
Who till they died, did not alive become –
Who had they lived, had died but when
They died, Vitality begun.

c. 1864   1891

817

Given in Marriage unto Thee
Oh thou Celestial Host –
Bride of the Father and the Son
Bride of the Holy Ghost.

Other Betrothal shall dissolve –
Wedlock of Will, decay –
Only the Keeper of this Ring
Conquer Mortality –

c. 1864   1896

818

I could not drink it, Sweet,
Till You had tasted first,
Though cooler than the Water was
The Thoughtfulness of Thirst.

c. 1864   1932

819

All I may, if small,
Do it not display
Larger for the Totalness –
'Tis Economy

To bestow a World
And withhold a Star –
Utmost, is Munificence –
Less, tho' larger, poor.

c. *1864*   *1914*

820

All Circumstances are the Frame
In which His Face is set –
All Latitudes exist for His
Sufficient Continent –

The Light His Action, and the Dark
The Leisure of His Will –
In Him Existence serve or set
A Force illegible.

c. *1864*   *1914*

821

Away from Home are some and I –
An Emigrant to be
In a Metropolis of Homes
Is easy, possibly –

The Habit of a Foreign Sky
We – difficult – acquire
As Children, who remain in Face
The more their Feet retire.

c. *1864*   *1894*

This Consciousness that is aware
Of Neighbors and the Sun
Will be the one aware of Death
And that itself alone

Is traversing the interval
Experience between
And most profound experiment
Appointed unto Men –

How adequate unto itself
Its properties shall be
Itself unto itself and none
Shall make discovery.

Adventure most unto itself
The Soul condemned to be –
Attended by a single Hound
Its own identity.

c. 1864   *1945*

823

Not what We did, shall be the test
When Act and Will are done
But what Our Lord infers We would
Had We diviner been –

c. 1864   *1929*

824

The Wind begun to knead the Grass –
As Women do a Dough –
He flung a Hand full at the Plain –
A Hand full at the Sky –
The Leaves unhooked themselves from Trees –
And started all abroad –
The Dust did scoop itself like Hands –
And throw away the Road –

The Wagons quickened on the Street –
The Thunders gossiped low –
The Lightning showed a Yellow Head –
And then a livid Toe –
The Birds put up the Bars to Nests –
The Cattle flung to Barns –
Then came one drop of Giant Rain –
And then, as if the Hands
That held the Dams – had parted hold –
The Waters Wrecked the Sky –
But overlooked my Father's House –
Just Quartering a Tree –

first version
c. 1864   *1955*

The Wind begun to rock the Grass
With threatening Tunes and low –
He threw a Menace at the Earth –
A Menace at the Sky.

The Leaves unhooked themselves from Trees –
And started all abroad
The Dust did scoop itself like Hands
And threw away the Road.

The Wagons quickened on the Streets
The Thunder hurried slow –
The Lightning showed a Yellow Beak
And then a livid Claw.

The Birds put up the Bars to Nests –
The Cattle fled to Barns –
There came one drop of Giant Rain
And then as if the Hands

That held the Dams had parted hold
The Waters Wrecked the Sky,

But overlooked my Father's House –
Just quartering a Tree –

second version
c. 1864   *1891*

825

An Hour is a Sea
Between a few, and me –
With them would Harbor be –

c. 1864   *1915*

826

Love reckons by itself – alone –
"As large as I" – relate the Sun
To One who never felt it blaze –
Itself is all the like it has –

c. 1864   *1914*

827

The Only News I know
Is Bulletins all Day
From Immortality.

The Only Shows I see –
Tomorrow and Today –
Perchance Eternity –

The Only One I meet
Is God – The Only Street –
Existence – This traversed

If Other News there be –
Or Admirabler Show –
I'll tell it You –

c. 1864   *1929*

The Robin is the One
That interrupt the Morn
With hurried – few – express Reports
When March is scarcely on –

The Robin is the One
That overflow the Noon
With her cherubic quantity –
An April but begun –

The Robin is the One
That speechless from her Nest
Submit that Home – and Certainty
And Sanctity, are best

c. 1864   *1891*

Ample make this Bed –
Make this Bed with Awe –
In it wait till Judgment break
Excellent and Fair.

Be its Mattress straight –
Be its Pillow round –
Let no Sunrise' yellow noise
Interrupt this Ground –

c. 1864   *1891*

To this World she returned.
But with a tinge of that –
A Compound manner,
As a Sod
Espoused a Violet,
That chiefer to the Skies
Than to Himself, allied,

Dwelt hesitating, half of Dust,
And half of Day, the Bride.

1864   *1894*

831

Dying! To be afraid of thee
One must to thine Artillery
Have left exposed a Friend –
Than thine old Arrow is a Shot
Delivered straighter to the Heart
The leaving Love behind.

Not for itself, the Dust is shy,
But, enemy, Beloved be
Thy Batteries divorce.
Fight sternly in a Dying eye
Two Armies, Love and Certainty
And Love and the Reverse.

c. 1864   *1945*

832

Soto! Explore thyself!
Therein thyself shalt find
The "Undiscovered Continent" –
No Settler had the Mind.

c. 1864   *1932*

833'

Perhaps you think me stooping
I'm not ashamed of that
Christ – stooped until He touched the Grave –
Do those at Sacrament

Commemorate Dishonor
Or love annealed of love
Until it bend as low as Death
Redignified, above?

c. 1864   *1894*

834

Before He comes we weigh the Time!
'Tis Heavy and 'tis Light.
When He depart, an Emptiness
Is the prevailing Freight.

c. *1864*   *1894*

835

Nature and God – I neither knew
Yet Both so well knew me
They startled, like Executors
Of My identity.

Yet Neither told – that I could learn –
My Secret as secure
As Herschel's private interest
Or Mercury's affair –

c. *1864*   *1894*

836

Truth – is as old as God –
His Twin identity
And will endure as long as He
A Co-Eternity –

And perish on the Day
Himself is borne away
From Mansion of the Universe
A lifeless Deity.

c. *1864*   *1894*

837

How well I knew Her not
Whom not to know has been
A Bounty in prospective, now
Next Door to mine the Pain.

c. *1864*   *1894*

838

Impossibility, like Wine
Exhilarates the Man
Who tastes it; Possibility
Is flavorless – Combine

A Chance's faintest Tincture
And in the former Dram
Enchantment makes ingredient
As certainly as Doom –

c. 1864   *1945*

839

Always Mine!
No more Vacation!
Term of Light this Day begun!
Failless as the fair rotation
Of the Seasons and the Sun.

Old the Grace, but new the Subjects –
Old, indeed, the East,
Yet upon His Purple Programme
Every Dawn, is first.

c. 1864   *1945*

840

I cannot buy it – 'tis not sold –
There is no other in the World –
Mine was the only one

I was so happy I forgot
To shut the Door And it went out
And I am all alone –

If I could find it Anywhere
I would not mind the journey there
Though it took all my store

But just to look it in the Eye –
"Did'st thou?" "Thou did'st not mean," to say,
Then, turn my Face away.

c. 1864   1945

841

A Moth the hue of this
Haunts Candles in Brazil.
Nature's Experience would make
Our Reddest Second pale.

Nature is fond, I sometimes think,
Of Trinkets, as a Girl.

c. 1864   1945

842

Good to hide, and hear 'em hunt!
Better, to be found,
If one care to, that is,
The Fox fits the Hound –

Good to know, and not tell,
Best, to know and tell,
Can one find the rare Ear
Not too dull –

c. 1864   1945

843

I made slow Riches but my Gain
Was steady as the Sun
And every Night, it numbered more
Than the preceding One

All Days, I did not earn the same
But my perceiveless Gain
Inferred the less by Growing than
The Sum that it had grown.

c. 1864   1945

844

Spring is the Period
Express from God.
Among the other seasons
Himself abide,

But during March and April
None stir abroad
Without a cordial interview
With God.

c. 1864   *1945*

845

Be Mine the Doom –
Sufficient Fame –
To perish in Her Hand!

c. 1864   *1945*

846

Twice had Summer her fair Verdure
Proffered to the Plain –
Twice a Winter's silver Fracture
On the Rivers been –

Two full Autumns for the Squirrel
Bounteous prepared –
Nature, Had'st thou not a Berry
For thy wandering Bird?

c. 1864   *1945*

847

Finite – to fail, but infinite to Venture –
For the one ship that struts the shore
Many's the gallant – overwhelmed Creature
Nodding in Navies nevermore –

c. 1864   *1896*

[407]

Just as He spoke it from his Hands
This Edifice remain –
A Turret more, a Turret less
Dishonor his Design –

According as his skill prefer
It perish, or endure –
Content, soe'er, it ornament
His absent character.

c. 1864   *1945*

The good Will of a Flower
The Man who would possess
Must first present
Certificate
Of minted Holiness.

c. 1864   *1945*

I sing to use the Waiting
My Bonnet but to tie
And shut the Door unto my House
No more to do have I

Till His best step approaching
We journey to the Day
And tell each other how We sung
To Keep the Dark away.

c. 1864   *1896*

When the Astronomer stops seeking
For his Pleiad's Face –
When the lone British Lady
Forsakes the Arctic Race

When to his Covenant Needle
The Sailor doubting turns –
It will be amply early
To ask what treason means.

c. 1864

1945

852

Apology for Her
Be rendered by the Bee –
Herself, without a Parliament
Apology for Me.

c. 1864

1945

853

When One has given up One's life
The parting with the rest
Feels easy, as when Day lets go
Entirely the West

The Peaks, that lingered last
Remain in Her regret
As scarcely as the Iodine
Upon the Cataract.

c. 1864

1945

854

Banish Air from Air –
Divide Light if you dare –
They'll meet
While Cubes in a Drop
Or Pellets of Shape
Fit
Films cannot annul
Odors return whole
Force Flame
And with a Blonde push

Over your impotence
Flits Steam.

c. *1864*   *1945*

855

To own the Art within the Soul
The Soul to entertain
With Silence as a Company
And Festival maintain

Is an unfurnished Circumstance
Possession is to One
As an Estate perpetual
Or a reduceless Mine.

c. *1864*   *1945*

856

There is a finished feeling
Experienced at Graves –
A leisure of the Future –
A Wilderness of Size.

By Death's bold Exhibition
Preciser what we are
And the Eternal function
Enabled to infer.

c. *1864*   *1945*

857

Uncertain lease – develops lustre
On Time
Uncertain Grasp, appreciation
Of Sum –

The shorter Fate – is oftener the chiefest
Because

Inheritors upon a tenure
Prize –

c. 1864

1945

858

This Chasm, Sweet, upon my life
I mention it to you,
When Sunrise through a fissure drop
The Day must follow too.

If we demur, its gaping sides
Disclose as 'twere a Tomb
Ourself am lying straight wherein
The Favorite of Doom.

When it has just contained a Life
Then, Darling, it will close
And yet so bolder every Day
So turbulent it grows

I'm tempted half to stitch it up
With a remaining Breath
I should not miss in yielding, though
To Him, it would be Death –

And so I bear it big about
My Burial – before
A Life quite ready to depart
Can harass me no more –

c. 1864

1945

859

A doubt if it be Us
Assists the staggering Mind
In an extremer Anguish
Until it footing find.

An Unreality is lent,
A merciful Mirage

That makes the living possible
While it suspends the lives.

c. *1864*   *1945*

860

Absence disembodies – so does Death
Hiding individuals from the Earth
Superstition helps, as well as love –
Tenderness decreases as we prove –

c. *1864*   *1945*

861

Split the Lark – and you'll find the Music –
Bulb after Bulb, in Silver rolled –
Scantily dealt to the Summer Morning
Saved for your Ear when Lutes be old.

Loose the Flood – you shall find it patent –
Gush after Gush, reserved for you –
Scarlet Experiment! Sceptic Thomas!
Now, do you doubt that your Bird was true?

c. *1864*   *1896*

862

Light is sufficient to itself –
If Others want to see
It can be had on Window Panes
Some Hours in the Day.

But not for Compensation –
It holds as large a Glow
To Squirrel in the Himmaleh
Precisely, as to you.

c. *1864*   *1945*

863

That Distance was between Us
That is not of Mile or Main –
The Will it is that situates –
Equator – never can –

c. *1864*   *1945*

864

The Robin for the Crumb
Returns no syllable
But long records the Lady's name
In Silver Chronicle.

c. *1864*   *1945*

865

He outstripped Time with but a Bout,
He outstripped Stars and Sun
And then, unjaded, challenged God
In presence of the Throne.

And He and He in mighty List
Unto this present, run,
The larger Glory for the less
A just sufficient Ring.

c. *1864*   *1945*

866

Fame is the tint that Scholars leave
Upon their Setting Names –
The Iris not of Occident
That disappears as comes –

c. *1864*   *1945*

867

Escaping backward to perceive
The Sea upon our place –

Escaping forward, to confront
His glittering Embrace –

Retreating up, a Billow's height
Retreating blinded down
Our undermining feet to meet
Instructs to the Divine.

c. 1864   1945

868

They ask but our Delight –
The Darlings of the Soil
And grant us all their Countenance
For a penurious smile.

c. 1864   1945

869

Because the Bee may blameless hum
For Thee a Bee do I become
List even unto Me.

Because the Flowers unafraid
May lift a look on thine, a Maid
Alway a Flower would be.

Nor Robins, Robins need not hide
When Thou upon their Crypts intrude
So Wings bestow on Me
Or Petals, or a Dower of Buzz
That Bee to ride, or Flower of Furze
I that way worship Thee.

c. 1864   1945

870

Finding is the first Act
The second, loss,
Third, Expedition for
The "Golden Fleece"

Fourth, no Discovery –
Fifth, no Crew –
Finally, no Golden Fleece –
Jason – sham – too.

c. 1864   *1945*

871

The Sun and Moon must make their haste –
The Stars express around
For in the Zones of Paradise
The Lord alone is burned –

His Eye, it is the East and West –
The North and South when He
Do concentrate His Countenance
Like Glow Worms, flee away –

Oh Poor and Far –
Oh Hindered Eye
That hunted for the Day –
The Lord a Candle entertains
Entirely for Thee –

c. 1864   *1945*

872

As the Starved Maelstrom laps the Navies
As the Vulture teased
Forces the Broods in lonely Valleys
As the Tiger eased

By but a Crumb of Blood, fasts Scarlet
Till he meet a Man
Dainty adorned with Veins and Tissues
And partakes – his Tongue

Cooled by the Morsel for a moment
Grows a fiercer thing
Till he esteem his Dates and Cocoa
A Nutrition mean

I, of a finer Famine
Deem my Supper dry
For but a Berry of Domingo
And a Torrid Eye.

c. *1864*   *1945*

873

Ribbons of the Year –
Multitude Brocade –
Worn to Nature's Party once

Then, as flung aside
As a faded Bead
Or a Wrinkled Pearl
Who shall charge the Vanity
Of the Maker's Girl?

c. *1864*   *1945*

874

They won't frown always – some sweet Day
When I forget to tease –
They'll recollect how cold I looked
And how I just said "Please."

Then They will hasten to the Door
To call the little Girl
Who cannot thank Them for the Ice
That filled the lisping full.

c. *1864*   *1896*

875

I stepped from Plank to Plank
A slow and cautious way
The Stars about my Head I felt
About my Feet the Sea.

I knew not but the next
Would be my final inch –

[416]

This gave me that precarious Gait
Some call Experience.

c. *1864*

1896

876

It was a Grave, yet bore no Stone
Enclosed 'twas not of Rail
A Consciousness its Acre, and
It held a Human Soul.

Entombed by whom, for what offence
If Home or Foreign born –
Had I the curiosity
'Twere not appeased of men

Till Resurrection, I must guess
Denied the small desire
A Rose upon its Ridge to sow
Or take away a Briar.

c. *1864*

1935

877

Each Scar I'll keep for Him
Instead I'll say of Gem
In His long Absence worn
A Costlier one

But every Tear I bore
Were He to count them o'er
His own would fall so more
I'll mis sum them.

c. *1864*

1945

878

The Sun is gay or stark
According to our Deed.
If Merry, He is merrier –
If eager for the Dead

Or an expended Day
He helped to make too bright
His mighty pleasure suits Us not
It magnifies our Freight

c. 1864   *1945*

879

Each Second is the last
Perhaps, recalls the Man
Just measuring unconsciousness
The Sea and Spar between.

To fail within a Chance –
How terribler a thing
Than perish from the Chance's list
Before the Perishing!

c. 1864   *1945*

880

The Bird must sing to earn the Crumb
What merit have the Tune
No Breakfast if it guaranty

The Rose content may bloom
To gain renown of Lady's Drawer
But if the Lady come
But once a Century, the Rose
Superfluous become –

c. 1864   *1945*

881

I've none to tell me to but Thee
So when Thou failest, nobody.
It was a little tie –
It just held Two, nor those it held
Since Somewhere thy sweet Face has spilled
Beyond my Boundary –

If things were opposite – and Me
And Me it were – that ebbed from Thee
On some unanswering Shore –
Would'st Thou seek so – just say
That I the Answer may pursue
Unto the lips it eddied through –
So – overtaking Thee –

c. *1864*   *1945*

882

A Shade upon the mind there passes
As when on Noon
A Cloud the mighty Sun encloses
Remembering

That some there be too numb to notice
Oh God
Why give if Thou must take away
The Loved?

c. *1864*   *1945*

883

The Poets light but Lamps –
Themselves – go out –
The Wicks they stimulate –
If vital Light

Inhere as do the Suns –
Each Age a Lens
Disseminating their
Circumference –

c. *1864*   *1945*

884

An Everywhere of Silver
With Ropes of Sand

[419]

To keep it from effacing
The Track called Land.

c. 1864   1891

885

Our little Kinsmen – after Rain
In plenty may be seen,
A Pink and Pulpy multitude
The tepid Ground upon.

A needless life, it seemed to me
Until a little Bird
As to a Hospitality
Advanced and breakfasted.

As I of He, so God of Me
I pondered, may have judged,
And left the little Angle Worm
With Modesties enlarged.

c. 1864   1945

886

These tested Our Horizon –
Then disappeared
As Birds before achieving
A Latitude.

Our Retrospection of Them
A fixed Delight,
But our Anticipation
A Dice – a Doubt –

c. 1864   1945

887

We outgrow love, like other things
And put it in the Drawer –

Till it an Antique fashion shows –
Like Costumes Grandsires wore.

c. 1864   1896

888

When I have seen the Sun emerge
From His amazing House –
And leave a Day at every Door
A Deed, in every place –

Without the incident of Fame
Or accident of Noise –
The Earth has seemed to me a Drum,
Pursued of little Boys

c. 1864   1945

889

Crisis is a Hair
Toward which the forces creep
Past which forces retrograde
If it come in sleep

To suspend the Breath
Is the most we can
Ignorant is it Life or Death
Nicely balancing.

Let an instant push
Or an Atom press
Or a Circle hesitate
In Circumference

It – may jolt the Hand
That adjusts the Hair
That secures Eternity
From presenting – Here –

c. 1864   1945

From Us She wandered now a Year,
Her tarrying, unknown,
If Wilderness prevent her feet
Or that Ethereal Zone

No Eye hath seen and lived
We ignorant must be –
We only know what time of Year
We took the Mystery.

c. *1864*   *1896*

To my quick ear the Leaves – conferred –
The Bushes – they were Bells –
I could not find a Privacy
From Nature's sentinels –

In Cave if I presumed to hide
The Walls – begun to tell –
Creation seemed a mighty Crack –
To make me visible –

c. *1864*   *1896*

Who occupies this House?
A Stranger I must judge
Since No one knows His Circumstance –
'Tis well the name and age

Are writ upon the Door
Or I should fear to pause
Where not so much as Honest Dog
Approach encourages.

It seems a curious Town –
Some Houses very old,
Some – newly raised this Afternoon,
Were I compelled to build

It should not be among
Inhabitants so still
But where the Birds assemble
And Boys were possible.

Before Myself was born
'Twas settled, so they say,
A Territory for the Ghosts –
And Squirrels, formerly.

Until a Pioneer, as
Settlers often do
Liking the quiet of the Place
Attracted more unto –

And from a Settlement
A Capital has grown
Distinguished for the gravity
Of every Citizen.

The Owner of this House
A Stranger He must be –
Eternity's Acquaintances
Are mostly so – to me.

c. 1864   *1945*

893

Drab Habitation of Whom?
Tabernacle or Tomb –
Or Dome of Worm –
Or Porch of Gnome –
Or some Elf's Catacomb?

c. 1864   *1896*

894

Of Consciousness, her awful Mate
The Soul cannot be rid –
As easy the secreting her
Behind the Eyes of God.

[423]

The deepest hid is sighted first
And scant to Him the Crowd –
What triple Lenses burn upon
The Escapade from God –

c. 1864   1945

895

A Cloud withdrew from the Sky
Superior Glory be
But that Cloud and its Auxiliaries
Are forever lost to me

Had I but further scanned
Had I secured the Glow
In an Hermetic Memory
It had availed me now.

Never to pass the Angel
With a glance and a Bow
Till I am firm in Heaven
Is my intention now.

c. 1864   1945

896

Of Silken Speech and Specious Shoe
A Traitor is the Bee
His service to the newest Grace
Present continually

His Suit a chance
His Troth a Term
Protracted as the Breeze
Continual Ban propoundeth He
Continual Divorce.

c. 1864   1945

How fortunate the Grave –
All Prizes to obtain –
Successful certain, if at last,
First Suitor not in vain.

c. 1864   1945

898

How happy I was if I could forget
To remember how sad I am
Would be an easy adversity
But the recollecting of Bloom

Keeps making November difficult
Till I who was almost bold
Lose my way like a little Child
And perish of the cold.

c. 1864   1945

899

Herein a Blossom lies –
A Sepulchre, between –
Cross it, and overcome the Bee –
Remain – 'tis but a Rind.

c. 1864   1945

900

What did They do since I saw Them?
Were They industrious?
So many questions to put Them
Have I the eagerness

That could I snatch Their Faces
That could Their lips reply
Not till the last was answered
Should They start for the Sky.

Not if Their Party were waiting,
Not if to talk with Me
Were to Them now, Homesickness
After Eternity.

Not if the Just suspect me
And offer a Reward
Would I restore my Booty
To that Bold Person, God –

c. 1864   1945

901

Sweet, to have had them lost
For news that they be saved –
The nearer they departed Us
The nearer they, restored,

Shall stand to Our Right Hand –
Most precious and the Dead –
Next precious
Those that rose to go –
Then thought of Us, and stayed.

c. 1864   1935

902

The first Day that I was a Life
I recollect it – How still –
That last Day that I was a Life
I recollect it – as well –

'Twas stiller – though the first
Was still –
'Twas empty – but the first
Was full –

This – was my finallest Occasion –
But then
My tenderer Experiment
Toward Men –

"Which choose I"?
That – I cannot say –
"Which choose They"?
Question Memory!

c. *1864*   *1945*

903

I hide myself within my flower,
That fading from your Vase,
You, unsuspecting, feel for me –
Almost a loneliness.

c. *1864*   *1890*

904

Had I not This, or This, I said,
Appealing to Myself,
In moment of prosperity –
Inadequate – were Life –

"Thou hast not Me, nor Me" – it said,
In Moment of Reverse –
"And yet Thou art industrious –
No need – hadst Thou – of us"?

My need – was all I had – I said –
The need did not reduce –
Because the food – exterminate –
The hunger – does not cease –

But diligence – is sharper –
Proportioned to the Chance –
To feed upon the Retrograde –
Enfeebles – the Advance –

c. *1864*   *1935*

905

Between My Country – and the Others –
There is a Sea –

But Flowers – negotiate between us –
As Ministry.

c. *1864*   *1935*

906

The Admirations – and Contempts – of time –
Show justest – through an Open Tomb –
The Dying – as it were a Height
Reorganizes Estimate
And what We saw not
We distinguish clear –
And mostly – see not
What We saw before –

'Tis Compound Vision –
Light – enabling Light –
The Finite – furnished
With the Infinite –
Convex – and Concave Witness –
Back – toward Time –
And forward –
Toward the God of Him –

c. *1864*   *1929*

907

Till Death – is narrow Loving –
The scantest Heart extant
Will hold you till your privilege
Of Finiteness – be spent –

But He whose loss procures you
Such Destitution that
Your Life too abject for itself
Thenceforward imitate –

Until – Resemblance perfect –
Yourself, for His pursuit

Delight of Nature – abdicate –
Exhibit Love – somewhat –

c. *1864*   *1929*

908

'Tis Sunrise – Little Maid – Hast Thou
No Station in the Day?
'Twas not thy wont, to hinder so –
Retrieve thine industry –

'Tis Noon – My little Maid –
Alas – and art thou sleeping yet?
The Lily – waiting to be Wed –
The Bee – Hast thou forgot?

My little Maid – 'Tis Night – Alas
That Night should be to thee
Instead of Morning – Had'st thou broached
Thy little Plan to Die –
Dissuade thee, if I could not, Sweet,
I might have aided – thee –

c. *1864*   *1896*

909

I make His Crescent fill or lack –
His Nature is at Full
Or Quarter – as I signify –
His Tides – do I control –

He holds superior in the Sky
Or gropes, at my Command
Behind inferior Clouds – or round
A Mist's slow Colonnade –

But since We hold a Mutual Disc –
And front a Mutual Day –
Which is the Despot, neither knows –
Nor Whose – the Tyranny –

c. *1864*   *1929*

Experience is the Angled Road
Preferred against the Mind
By – Paradox – the Mind itself –
Presuming it to lead

Quite Opposite – How Complicate
The Discipline of Man –
Compelling Him to Choose Himself
His Preappointed Pain –

c. 1864   1929

Too little way the House must lie
From every Human Heart
That holds in undisputed Lease
A white inhabitant –

Too narrow is the Right between –
Too imminent the chance –
Each Consciousness must emigrate
And lose its neighbor once –

c. 1864   1935

Peace is a fiction of our Faith –
The Bells a Winter Night
Bearing the Neighbor out of Sound
That never did alight.

c. 1864   1945

And this of all my Hopes
This, is the silent end
Bountiful colored, my Morning rose
Early and sere, its end

Never Bud from a Stem
Stepped with so gay a Foot
Never a Worm so confident
Bored at so brave a Root

c. 1864   1929

914

I cannot be ashamed
Because I cannot see
The love you offer –
Magnitude
Reverses Modesty

And I cannot be proud
Because a Height so high
Involves Alpine
Requirements
And Services of Snow.

c. 1864   1929

915

Faith – is the Pierless Bridge
Supporting what We see
Unto the Scene that We do not –
Too slender for the eye

It bears the Soul as bold
As it were rocked in Steel
With Arms of Steel at either side –
It joins – behind the Veil

To what, could We presume
The Bridge would cease to be
To Our far, vacillating Feet
A first Necessity.

c. 1864   1929

916

His Feet are shod with Gauze –
His Helmet, is of Gold,
His Breast, a Single Onyx
With Chrysophrase, inlaid.

His Labor is a Chant –
His Idleness – a Tune –
Oh, for a Bee's experience
Of Clovers, and of Noon!

c. 1864   *1890*

917

Love – is anterior to Life –
Posterior – to Death –
Initial of Creation, and
The Exponent of Earth –

c. 1864   *1896*

918

Only a Shrine, but Mine –
I made the Taper shine –
Madonna dim, to whom all Feet may come,
Regard a Nun –

Thou knowest every Woe –
Needless to tell thee – so –
But can'st thou do
The Grace next to it – heal?
That looks a harder skill to us –
Still – just as easy, if it be thy Will
To thee – Grant me –
Thou knowest, though, so Why tell thee?

c. 1864   *1929*

[432]

919

If I can stop one Heart from breaking
I shall not live in vain
If I can ease one Life the Aching
Or cool one Pain

Or help one fainting Robin
Unto his Nest again
I shall not live in Vain.

c. 1864

1890

920

We can but follow to the Sun –
As oft as He go down
He leave Ourselves a Sphere behind –
'Tis mostly – following –

We go no further with the Dust
Than to the Earthen Door –
And then the Panels are reversed –
And we behold – no more.

c. 1864

1955

921

If it had no pencil
Would it try mine –
Worn – now – and *dull* – sweet,
Writing much to thee.
If it had no word,
Would it make the Daisy,
Most as big as I was,
When it plucked me?

c. 1864

1945

922

Those who have been in the Grave the longest –
Those who begin Today –

Equally perish from our Practise –
Death is the other way –

Foot of the Bold did least attempt it –
It – is the White Exploit –
Once to achieve, annuls the power
Once to communicate –

c. 1864   1945

923

How the Waters closed above Him
We shall never know –
How He stretched His Anguish to us
That – is covered too –

Spreads the Pond Her Base of Lilies
Bold above the Boy
Whose unclaimed Hat and Jacket
Sum the History –

c. 1864   1945

924

Love – is that later Thing than Death –
More previous – than Life –
Confirms it at its entrance – And
Usurps it – of itself –

Tastes Death – the first – to hand the sting
The Second – to its friend –
Disarms the little interval –
Deposits Him with God –

Then hovers – an inferior Guard –
Lest this Beloved Charge
Need – once in an Eternity –
A smaller than the Large –

c. 1864   1945

Struck, was I, not yet by Lightning –
Lightning – lets away
Power to perceive His Process
With Vitality.

Maimed – was I – yet not by Venture –
Stone of stolid Boy –
Nor a Sportsman's Peradventure –
Who mine Enemy?

Robbed – was I – intact to Bandit –
All my Mansion torn –
Sun – withdrawn to Recognition –
Furthest shining – done –

Yet was not the foe – of any –
Not the smallest Bird
In the nearest Orchard dwelling
Be of Me – afraid.

Most – I love the Cause that slew Me.
Often as I die
Its beloved Recognition
Holds a Sun on Me –

Best – at Setting – as is Nature's –
Neither witnessed Rise
Till the infinite Aurora
In the other's eyes.

c. 1864   1945

Patience – has a quiet Outer –
Patience – Look within –
Is an Insect's futile forces
Infinites – between –

'Scaping one – against the other
Fruitlesser to fling –

Patience – is the Smile's exertion
Through the quivering –

c. 1864

1945

927

Absent Place – an April Day –
Daffodils a-blow
Homesick curiosity
To the Souls that snow –

Drift may block within it
Deeper than without –
Daffodil delight but
Him it duplicate –

c. 1864

1945

928

The Heart has narrow Banks
It measures like the Sea
In mighty – unremitting Bass
And Blue Monotony

Till Hurricane bisect
And as itself discerns
Its insufficient Area
The Heart convulsive learns

That Calm is but a Wall
Of unattempted Gauze
An instant's Push demolishes
A Questioning – dissolves.

c. 1864

1945

929

How far is it to Heaven?
As far as Death this way –
Of River or of Ridge beyond
Was no discovery.

[436]

How far is it to Hell?
As far as Death this way –
How far left hand the Sepulchre
Defies Topography.

c. 1864   1945

930

There is a June when Corn is cut
And Roses in the Seed –
A Summer briefer than the first
But tenderer indeed

As should a Face supposed the Grave's
Emerge a single Noon
In the Vermilion that it wore
Affect us, and return –

Two Seasons, it is said, exist –
The Summer of the Just,
And this of Ours, diversified
With Prospect, and with Frost –

May not our Second with its First
So infinite compare
That We but recollect the one
The other to prefer?

c. 1864   1945

931

Noon – is the Hinge of Day –
Evening – the Tissue Door –
Morning – the East compelling the sill
Till all the World is ajar –

c. 1864   1945

932

My best Acquaintances are those
With Whom I spoke no Word –

[437]

The Stars that stated come to Town
Esteemed Me never rude
Although to their Celestial Call
I failed to make reply –
My constant – reverential Face
Sufficient Courtesy.

c. 1864   *1945*

933

Two Travellers perishing in Snow
The Forests as they froze
Together heard them strengthening
Each other with the words

That Heaven if Heaven – must contain
What Either left behind
And then the cheer too solemn grew
For language, and the wind

Long steps across the features took
That Love had touched that Morn
With reverential Hyacinth –
The taleless Days went on

Till Mystery impatient drew
And those They left behind
Led absent, were procured of Heaven
As Those first furnished, said –

c. 1864   *1945*

934

That is solemn we have ended
Be it but a Play
Or a Glee among the Garret
Or a Holiday

Or a leaving Home, or later,
Parting with a World

[438]

We have understood for better
Still to be explained.

c. 1864   *1896*

935

Death leaves Us homesick, who behind,
Except that it is gone
Are ignorant of its Concern
As if it were not born.

Through all their former Places, we
Like Individuals go
Who something lost, the seeking for
Is all that's left them, now –

c. 1863   *1945*

936

This Dust, and its Feature –
Accredited – Today –
Will in a second Future –
Cease to identify –

This Mind, and its measure –
A too minute Area
For its enlarged inspection's
Comparison – appear –

This World, and its species
A too concluded show
For its absorbed Attention's
Remotest scrutiny –

c. 1864   *1945*

937*

I felt a Cleaving in my Mind –
As if my Brain had split –
I tried to match it – Seam by Seam –
But could not make them fit.

* See poem 992.

The thought behind, I strove to join
Unto the thought before –
But Sequence ravelled out of Sound
Like Balls – upon a Floor.

c. 1864   *1896*

938

Fairer through Fading – as the Day
Into the Darkness dips away –
Half Her Complexion of the Sun –
Hindering – Haunting – Perishing –

Rallies Her Glow, like a dying Friend –
Teasing with glittering Amend –
Only to aggravate the Dark
Through an expiring – perfect – look –

c. 1864   *1945*

939

What I see not, I better see –
Through Faith – my Hazel Eye
Has periods of shutting –
But, No lid has Memory –

For frequent, all my sense obscured
I equally behold
As someone held a light unto
The Features so beloved –

And I arise – and in my Dream –
Do Thee distinguished Grace –
Till jealous Daylight interrupt –
And mar thy perfectness –

c. 1864   *1945*

940

On that dear Frame the Years had worn
Yet precious as the House

[440]

In which We first experienced Light
The Witnessing, to Us –

Precious! It was conceiveless fair
As Hands the Grave had grimed
Should softly place within our own
Denying that they died.

c. *1864*   *1945*

941

The Lady feeds Her little Bird
At rarer intervals –
The little Bird would not dissent
But meekly recognize

The Gulf between the Hand and Her
And crumbless and afar
And fainting, on Her yellow Knee
Fall softly, and adore –

c. *1864*   *1945*

942

Snow beneath whose chilly softness
Some that never lay
Make their first Repose this Winter
I admonish Thee

Blanket Wealthier the Neighbor
We so new bestow
Than thine acclimated Creature
Wilt Thou, Austere Snow?

c. *1864*   *1945*

943

A Coffin – is a small Domain,
Yet able to contain
A Citizen of Paradise
In its diminished Plane.

A Grave – is a restricted Breadth –
Yet ampler than the Sun –
And all the Seas He populates
And Lands He looks upon

To Him who on its small Repose
Bestows a single Friend –
Circumference without Relief –
Or Estimate – or End –

c. 1864   1945

944

I learned – at least – what Home could be –
How ignorant I had been
Of pretty ways of Covenant –
How awkward at the Hymn

Round our new Fireside – but for this –
This pattern – of the Way –
Whose Memory drowns me, like the Dip
Of a Celestial Sea –

What Mornings in our Garden – guessed –
What Bees – for us – to hum –
With only Birds to interrupt
The Ripple of our Theme –

And Task for Both –
When Play be done –
Your Problem – of the Brain –
And mine – some foolisher effect –
A Ruffle – or a Tune –

The Afternoons – Together spent –
And Twilight – in the Lanes –
Some ministry to poorer lives –
Seen poorest – thro' our gains –

And then Return – and Night – and Home –

And then away to You to pass –
A new – diviner – care –

Till Sunrise take us back to Scene –
Transmuted – Vivider –

This seems a Home –
And Home is not –
But what that Place could be –
Afflicts me – as a Setting Sun –
Where Dawn – knows how to be –

c. 1864

1945

945

This is a Blossom of the Brain –
A small – italic Seed
Lodged by Design or Happening
The Spirit fructified –

Shy as the Wind of his Chambers
Swift as a Freshet's Tongue
So of the Flower of the Soul
Its process is unknown.

When it is found, a few rejoice
The Wise convey it Home
Carefully cherishing the spot
If other Flower become.

When it is lost, that Day shall be
The Funeral of God,
Upon his Breast, a closing Soul
The Flower of our Lord.

c. 1864

1945

946

It is an honorable Thought
And makes One lift One's Hat
As One met sudden Gentlefolk
Upon a daily Street

That We've immortal Place
Though Pyramids decay

And Kingdoms, like the Orchard
Flit Russetly away

c. 1864 *1896*

947

Of Tolling Bell I ask the cause?
"A Soul has gone to Heaven"
I'm answered in a lonesome tone –
Is Heaven then a Prison?

That Bells should ring till all should know
A Soul had gone to Heaven
Would seem to me the more the way
A Good News should be given.

c. 1864 *1896*

948

'Twas Crisis – All the length had passed –
That dull – benumbing time
There is in Fever or Event –
And now the Chance had come –

The instant holding in its claw
The privilege to live
Or warrant to report the Soul
The other side the Grave.

The Muscles grappled as with leads
That would not let the Will –
The Spirit shook the Adamant –
But could not make it feel.

The Second poised – debated – shot –
Another had begun –
And simultaneously, a Soul
Escaped the House unseen –

c. 1864 *1945*

Under the Light, yet under,
Under the Grass and the Dirt,
Under the Beetle's Cellar
Under the Clover's Root,

Further than Arm could stretch
Were it Giant long,
Further than Sunshine could
Were the Day Year long,

Over the Light, yet over,
Over the Arc of the Bird –
Over the Comet's chimney –
Over the Cubit's Head,

Further than Guess can gallop
Further than Riddle ride –
Oh for a Disc to the Distance
Between Ourselves and the Dead!

c. 1864   *1945*

The Sunset stopped on Cottages
Where Sunset hence must be
For treason not of His, but Life's,
Gone Westerly, Today –

The Sunset stopped on Cottages
Where Morning just begun –
What difference, after all, Thou mak'st
Thou supercilious Sun?

c. 1864   *1945*

As Frost is best conceived
By force of its Result –
Affliction is inferred
By subsequent effect –

[445]

If when the sun reveal,
The Garden keep the Gash –
If as the Days resume
The wilted countenance

Cannot correct the crease
Or counteract the stain –
Presumption is Vitality
Was somewhere put in twain.

c. 1864   *1945*

952

A Man may make a Remark –
In itself – a quiet thing
That may furnish the Fuse unto a Spark
In dormant nature – lain –

Let us deport – with skill –
Let us discourse – with care –
Powder exists in Charcoal –
Before it exists in Fire.

c. 1864   *1945*

953

A Door just opened on a street –
I – lost – was passing by –
An instant's Width of Warmth disclosed –
And Wealth – and Company.

The Door as instant shut – And I –
I – lost – was passing by –
Lost doubly – but by contrast – most –
Informing – misery –

c. 1864   *1896*

954

The Chemical conviction
That Nought be lost

[446]

Enable in Disaster
My fractured Trust –

The Faces of the Atoms
If I shall see
How more the Finished Creatures
Departed me!

c. 1864   1945

955

The Hollows round His eager Eyes
Were Pages where to read
Pathetic Histories – although
Himself had not complained.
Biography to All who passed
Of Unobtrusive Pain
Except for the italic Face
Endured, unhelped – unknown.

c. 1864   1945

956

What shall I do when the Summer troubles –
What, when the Rose is ripe –
What when the Eggs fly off in Music
From the Maple Keep?

What shall I do when the Skies a'chirrup
Drop a Tune on me –
When the Bee hangs all Noon in the Buttercup
What will become of me?

Oh, when the Squirrel fills His Pockets
And the Berries stare
How can I bear their jocund Faces
Thou from Here, so far?

'Twouldn't afflict a Robin –
All His Goods have Wings –

[447]

I – do not fly, so wherefore
My Perennial Things?

c. 1864   1945

957

As One does Sickness over
In convalescent Mind,
His scrutiny of Chances
By blessed Health obscured –

As One rewalks a Precipice
And whittles at the Twig
That held Him from Perdition
Sown sidewise in the Crag

A Custom of the Soul
Far after suffering
Identity to question
For evidence 't has been –

c. 1864   1945

958

We met as Sparks – Diverging Flints
Sent various – scattered ways –
We parted as the Central Flint
Were cloven with an Adze –
Subsisting on the Light We bore
Before We felt the Dark –
A Flint unto this Day – perhaps –
But for that single Spark.

c. 1864   1945

959

A loss of something ever felt I –
The first that I could recollect
Bereft I was – of what I knew not
Too young that any should suspect

A Mourner walked among the children
I notwithstanding went about
As one bemoaning a Dominion
Itself the only Prince cast out –

Elder, Today, a session wiser
And fainter, too, as Wiseness is –
I find myself still softly searching
For my Delinquent Palaces –

And a Suspicion, like a Finger
Touches my Forehead now and then
That I am looking oppositely
For the site of the Kingdom of Heaven –

c. 1864   *1945*

960

As plan for Noon and plan for Night
So differ Life and Death
In positive Prospective –
The Foot upon the Earth

At Distance, and Achievement, strains,
The Foot upon the Grave
Makes effort at conclusion
Assisted faint of Love.

c. 1864   *1945*

961

Wert Thou but ill – that I might show thee
How long a Day I could endure
Though thine attention stop not on me
Nor the least signal, Me assure –

Wert Thou but Stranger in ungracious country –
And Mine – the Door
Thou paused at, for a passing bounty –
No More –

Accused – wert Thou – and Myself – Tribunal –
Convicted – Sentenced – Ermine – not to Me
Half the Condition, thy Reverse – to follow –
Just to partake – the infamy –

The Tenant of the Narrow Cottage, wert Thou –
Permit to be
The Housewife in thy low attendance
Contenteth Me –

No Service hast Thou, I would not achieve it –
To die – or live –
The first – Sweet, proved I, ere I saw thee –
For Life – be Love –

c. 1864   *1945*

962

Midsummer, was it, when They died –
A full, and perfect time –
The Summer closed upon itself
In Consummated Bloom –

The Corn, her furthest kernel filled
Before the coming Flail –
When These – leaned into Perfectness –
Through Haze of Burial –

c. 1864   *1929*

963

A nearness to Tremendousness –
An Agony procures –
Affliction ranges Boundlessness –
Vicinity to Laws

Contentment's quiet Suburb –
Affliction cannot stay
In Acres – Its Location
Is Illocality –

c. 1864   *1935*

964

"Unto Me?" I do not know you –
Where may be your House?

"I am Jesus – Late of Judea –
Now – of Paradise" –

Wagons – have you – to convey me?
This is far from Thence –

"Arms of Mine – sufficient Phaeton –
Trust Omnipotence" –

I am spotted – "I am Pardon" –
I am small – "The Least
Is esteemed in Heaven the Chiefest –
Occupy my House" –

c. 1864   *1929*

965

Denial – is the only fact
Perceived by the Denied –
Whose Will – a numb significance –
The Day the Heaven died –

And all the Earth strove common round –
Without Delight, or Beam –
What Comfort was it Wisdom – was –
The spoiler of Our Home?

c. 1864   *1929*

966

All forgot for recollecting
Just a paltry One –
All forsook, for just a Stranger's
New Accompanying –

Grace of Wealth, and Grace of Station
Less accounted than

An unknown Esteem possessing –
Estimate – Who can –

Home effaced – Her faces dwindled –
Nature – altered small –
Sun – if shone – or Storm – if shattered –
Overlooked I all –

Dropped – my fate – a timid Pebble –
In thy bolder Sea –
Prove – me – Sweet – if I regret it –
Prove Myself – of Thee –

c. 1864   *1929*

967

Pain – expands the Time –
Ages coil within
The minute Circumference
Of a single Brain –

Pain contracts – the Time –
Occupied with Shot
Gamuts of Eternities
Are as they were not –

c. 1864   *1929*

968

Fitter to see Him, I may be
For the long Hindrance – Grace – to Me –
With Summers, and with Winters, grow,
Some passing Year – A trait bestow

To make Me fairest of the Earth –
The Waiting – then – will seem so worth
I shall impute with half a pain
The blame that I was chosen – then –

Time to anticipate His Gaze –
It's first – Delight – and then – Surprise –

[452]

The turning o'er and o'er my face
For Evidence it be the Grace –

He left behind One Day – So less
He seek Conviction, That – be This –

I only must not grow so new
That He'll mistake – and ask for me
Of me – when first unto the Door
I go – to Elsewhere go no more –

I only must not change so fair
He'll sigh – "The Other – She – is Where?"
The Love, tho', will array me right
I shall be perfect – in His sight –

If He perceive the other Truth –
Upon an Excellenter Youth –

How sweet I shall not lack in Vain –
But gain – thro' loss – Through Grief – obtain –
The Beauty that reward Him best –
The Beauty of Demand – at Rest –

c. 1864   1930

969

He who in Himself believes –
Fraud cannot presume –
Faith is Constancy's Result –
And assumes – from Home –

Cannot perish, though it fail
Every second time –
But defaced Vicariously –
For Some Other Shame –

c. 1864   1945

970

Color – Caste – Denomination –
These – are Time's Affair –

Death's diviner Classifying
Does not know they are –

As in sleep – All Hue forgotten –
Tenets – put behind –
Death's large – Democratic fingers
Rub away the Brand –

If Circassian – He is careless –
If He put away
Chrysalis of Blonde – or Umber –
Equal Butterfly –

They emerge from His Obscuring –
What Death – knows so well –
Our minuter intuitions –
Deem unplausible –

c. 1864

1929

971

Robbed by Death – but that was easy –
To the failing Eye
I could hold the latest Glowing –
Robbed by Liberty

For Her Jugular Defences –
This, too, I endured –
Hint of Glory – it afforded –
For the Brave Beloved –

Fraud of Distance – Fraud of Danger,
Fraud of Death – to bear –
It is Bounty – to Suspense's
Vague Calamity –

Staking our entire Possession
On a Hair's result –
Then – Seesawing – coolly – on it –
Trying if it split –

c. 1864

1945

Unfulfilled to Observation –
Incomplete – to Eye –
But to Faith – a Revolution
In Locality –

Unto Us – the Suns extinguish –
To our Opposite –
New Horizons – they embellish –
Fronting Us – with Night.

c. 1864

1935

973

'Twas awkward, but it fitted me –
An Ancient fashioned Heart –
Its only lore – its Steadfastness –
In Change – unerudite –

It only moved as do the Suns –
For merit of Return –
Or Birds – confirmed perpetual
By Alternating Zone –

I only have it not Tonight
In its established place –
For technicality of Death –
Omitted in the Lease –

c. 1864

1935

974

The Soul's distinct connection
With immortality
Is best disclosed by Danger
Or quick Calamity –

As Lightning on a Landscape
Exhibits Sheets of Place –

Not yet suspected – but for Flash –
And Click – and Suddenness.

c. 1864 1929

975

The Mountain sat upon the Plain
In his tremendous Chair –
His observation omnifold,
His inquest, everywhere –

The Seasons played around his knees
Like Children round a sire –
Grandfather of the Days is He
Of Dawn, the Ancestor –

c. 1864 1890

976

Death is a Dialogue between
The Spirit and the Dust.
"Dissolve" says Death – The Spirit "Sir
I have another Trust" –

Death doubts it – Argues from the Ground –
The Spirit turns away
Just laying off for evidence
An Overcoat of Clay.

c. 1864 1890

977

Besides this May
We know
There is Another –
How fair
Our Speculations of the Foreigner!

Some know Him whom We knew –
Sweet Wonder –

A Nature be
Where Saints, and our plain going Neighbor
Keep May!

c. 1864   1945

978

It bloomed and dropt, a Single Noon –
The Flower – distinct and Red –
I, passing, thought another Noon
Another in its stead

Will equal glow, and thought no More
But came another Day
To find the Species disappeared –
The Same Locality –

The Sun in place – no other fraud
On Nature's perfect Sum –
Had I but lingered Yesterday –
Was my retrieveless blame –

Much Flowers of this and further Zones
Have perished in my Hands
For seeking its Resemblance –
But unapproached it stands –

The single Flower of the Earth
That I, in passing by
Unconscious was – Great Nature's Face
Passed infinite by Me –

c. 1864   1955

979

This Merit hath the worst –
It cannot be again –
When Fate hath taunted last
And thrown Her furthest Stone –

The Maimed may pause, and breathe,
And glance securely round –

The Deer attracts no further
Than it resists – the Hound –

c. 1864   1891

980

Purple – is fashionable twice –
This season of the year,
And when a soul perceives itself
To be an Emperor.

c. 1864   1945

981

As Sleigh Bells seem in summer
Or Bees, at Christmas show –
So fairy – so fictitious
The individuals do
Repealed from observation –
A Party that we knew –
More distant in an instant
Than Dawn in Timbuctoo.

c. 1864   1945

982

No Other can reduce
Our mortal Consequence
Like the remembering it be nought
A Period from hence
But Contemplation for
Contemporaneous Nought
Our Single Competition
Jehovah's Estimate.

c. 1865   1914

983

Ideals are the Fairy Oil
With which we help the Wheel

But when the Vital Axle turns
The Eye rejects the Oil.

c. 1865 1945

984

'Tis Anguish grander than Delight
'Tis Resurrection Pain –
The meeting Bands of smitten Face
We questioned to, again.

'Tis Transport wild as thrills the Graves
When Cerements let go
And Creatures clad in Miracle
Go up by Two and Two.

c. 1865 1945

985

The Missing All – prevented Me
From missing minor Things.
If nothing larger than a World's
Departure from a Hinge –
Or Sun's extinction, be observed –
'Twas not so large that I
Could lift my Forehead from my work
For Curiosity.

c. 1865 1914

986

A narrow Fellow in the Grass
Occasionally rides –
You may have met Him – did you not
His notice sudden is –

The Grass divides as with a Comb –
A spotted shaft is seen –
And then it closes at your feet
And opens further on –

He likes a Boggy Acre
A Floor too cool for Corn –
Yet when a Boy, and Barefoot –
I more than once at Noon
Have passed, I thought, a Whip lash
Unbraiding in the Sun
When stooping to secure it
It wrinkled, and was gone –

Several of Nature's People
I know, and they know me –
I feel for them a transport
Of cordiality –

But never met this Fellow
Attended, or alone
Without a tighter breathing
And Zero at the Bone –

c. 1865   *1866*

987

The Leaves like Women interchange
Exclusive Confidence –
Somewhat of nods and somewhat
Portentous inference.

The Parties in both cases
Enjoining secrecy –
Inviolable compact
To notoriety.

c. 1865   *1891*

988

The Definition of Beauty is
That Definition is none –
Of Heaven, easing Analysis,
Since Heaven and He are one.

c. 1865   *1924*

Gratitude – is not the mention
Of a Tenderness,
But its still appreciation
Out of Plumb of Speech.

When the Sea return no Answer
By the Line and Lead
Proves it there's no Sea, or rather
A remoter Bed?

c. 1865   *1947*

Not all die early, dying young –
Maturity of Fate
Is consummated equally
In Ages, or a Night –

A Hoary Boy, I've known to drop
Whole statured – by the side
Of Junior of Fourscore – 'twas Act
Not Period – that died.

c. 1865   *1894*

She sped as Petals of a Rose
Offended by the Wind –
A frail Aristocrat of Time
Indemnity to find –
Leaving on nature – a Default
As Cricket or as Bee –
But Andes in the Bosoms where
She had begun to lie –

c. 1865   *1932*

992*

The Dust behind I strove to join
Unto the Disk before –
But Sequence ravelled out of Sound
Like Balls upon a Floor –

c. 1865   *1955*

993

We miss Her, not because We see –
The Absence of an Eye –
Except its Mind accompany
Abridge Society

As slightly as the Routes of Stars –
Ourselves – asleep below –
We know that their superior Eyes
Include Us – as they go –

c. 1865   *1945*

994

Partake as doth the Bee,
Abstemiously.
The Rose is an Estate –
In Sicily.

c. 1865   *1945*

995

This was in the White of the Year –
That – was in the Green –
Drifts were as difficult then to think
As Daisies now to be seen –

Looking back is best that is left
Or if it be – before –

* See poem 937.

Retrospection is Prospect's half,
Sometimes, almost more.

c. *1865*   *1894*

996

We'll pass without the parting
So to spare
Certificate of Absence –
Deeming where

I left Her I could find Her
If I tried –
This way, I keep from missing
Those that died.

c. *1865*   *1894*

997

Crumbling is not an instant's Act
A fundamental pause
Dilapidation's processes
Are organized Decays.

'Tis first a Cobweb on the Soul
A Cuticle of Dust
A Borer in the Axis
An Elemental Rust –

Ruin is formal – Devil's work
Consecutive and slow –
Fail in an instant, no man did
Slipping – is Crash's law.

c. *1865*   *1945*

998

Best Things dwell out of Sight
The Pearl – the Just – Our Thought.

Most shun the Public Air
Legitimate, and Rare –

The Capsule of the Wind
The Capsule of the Mind

Exhibit here, as doth a Burr –
Germ's Germ be where?

c. 1865   1945

999

Superfluous were the Sun
When Excellence be dead
He were superfluous every Day
For every Day be said

That syllable whose Faith
Just saves it from Despair
And whose "I'll meet You" hesitates
If Love inquire "Where"?

Upon His dateless Fame
Our Periods may lie
As Stars that drop anonymous
From an abundant sky.

c. 1865   1896

1000

The Fingers of the Light
Tapped soft upon the Town
With "I am great and cannot wait
So therefore let me in."

"You're soon," the Town replied,
"My Faces are asleep –
But swear, and I will let you by,
You will not wake them up."

The easy Guest complied
But once within the Town

The transport of His Countenance
Awakened Maid and Man

The Neighbor in the Pool
Upon His Hip elate
Made loud obeisance and the Gnat
Held up His Cup for Light.

c. *1865*   *1945*

1001

The Stimulus, beyond the Grave
His Countenance to see
Supports me like imperial Drams
Afforded Day by Day.

c. *1865*   *1896*

1002

Aurora is the effort
Of the Celestial Face
Unconsciousness of Perfectness
To simulate, to Us.

c. *1865*   *1945*

1003

Dying at my music!
Bubble! Bubble!
Hold me till the Octave's run!
Quick! Burst the Windows!
Ritardando!
Phials left, and the Sun!

c. *1865*   *1945*

1004

There is no Silence in the Earth – so silent
As that endured

[465]

Which uttered, would discourage Nature
And haunt the World.

c. 1865   *1945*

1005

Bind me – I still can sing –
Banish – my mandolin
Strikes true within –

Slay – and my Soul shall rise
Chanting to Paradise –
Still thine.

c. 1865   *1945*

1006

The first We knew of Him was Death –
The second – was – Renown –
Except the first had justified
The second had not been.

c. 1865   *1945*

1007

Falsehood of Thee could I suppose
'Twould undermine the Sill
To which my Faith pinned Block by Block
Her Cedar Citadel.

c. 1865   *1945*

1008

How still the Bells in Steeples stand
Till swollen with the Sky
They leap upon their silver Feet
In frantic Melody!

c. 1865   *1896*

I was a Phoebe – nothing more –
A Phoebe – nothing less –
The little note that others dropt
I fitted into place –

I dwelt too low that any seek –
Too shy, that any blame –
A Phoebe makes a little print
Upon the Floors of Fame –

c. 1865   *1945*

Up Life's Hill with my little Bundle
If I prove it steep –
If a Discouragement withhold me –
If my newest step

Older feel than the Hope that prompted –
Spotless be from blame
Heart that proposed as Heart that accepted
Homelessness, for Home –

c. 1865   *1945*

She rose as high as His Occasion
Then sought the Dust –
And lower lay in low Westminster
For Her brief Crest –

c. 1865   *1945*

Which is best? Heaven –
Or only Heaven to come
With that old Codicil of Doubt?
I cannot help esteem

The "Bird within the Hand"
Superior to the one
The "Bush" may yield me
Or may not
Too late to choose again.

c. *1865*   *1945*

1013

Too scanty 'twas to die for you,
The merest Greek could that.
The living, Sweet, is costlier –
I offer even that –

The Dying, is a trifle, past,
But living, this include
The dying multifold – without
The Respite to be dead.

c. *1865*   *1945*

1014

Did We abolish Frost
The Summer would not cease –
If Seasons perish or prevail
Is optional with Us –

c. *1865*   *1945*

1015

Were it but Me that gained the Height –
Were it but They, that failed!
How many things the Dying play
Might they but live, they would!

c. *1865*   *1945*

1016

The Hills in Purple syllables
The Day's Adventures tell

[468]

To little Groups of Continents
Just going Home from School.

c. 1865   *1945*

1017

To die – without the Dying
And live – without the Life
This is the hardest Miracle
Propounded to Belief.

c. 1865   *1945*

1018

Who saw no Sunrise cannot say
The Countenance 'twould be.
Who guess at seeing, guess at loss
Of the Ability.

The Emigrant of Light, it is
Afflicted for the Day.
The Blindness that beheld and blest –
And could not find its Eye.

c. 1865   *1945*

1019

My Season's furthest Flower –
I tenderer commend
Because I found Her Kinsmanless,
A Grace without a Friend.

c. 1865   *1945*

1020

Trudging to Eden, looking backward,
I met Somebody's little Boy
Asked him his name – He lisped me "Trotwood" –
Lady, did He belong to thee?

Would it comfort – to know I met him –
And that He didn't look afraid?
I couldn't weep – for so many smiling
New Acquaintance – this Baby made –

c. *1865*   *1945*

1021

Far from Love the Heavenly Father
Leads the Chosen Child,
Oftener through Realm of Briar
Than the Meadow mild.

Oftener by the Claw of Dragon
Than the Hand of Friend
Guides the Little One predestined
To the Native Land.

c. *1865*   *1896*

1022

I knew that I had gained
And yet I knew not how
By Diminution it was not
But Discipline unto

A Rigor unrelieved
Except by the Content
Another bear its Duplicate
In other Continent.

c. *1865*   *1945*

1023

It rises – passes – on our South
Inscribes a simple Noon –
Cajoles a Moment with the Spires
And infinite is gone –

c. *1865*   *1945*

[470]

1024

So large my Will
The little that I may
Embarrasses
Like gentle infamy –

Affront to Him
For whom the Whole were small
Affront to me
Who know His Meed of all.

Earth at the best
Is but a scanty Toy –
Bought, carried Home
To Immortality.

It looks so small
We chiefly wonder then
At our Conceit
In purchasing.

c. 1865   1945

1025

The Products of my Farm are these
Sufficient for my Own
And here and there a Benefit
Unto a Neighbor's Bin.

With Us, 'tis Harvest all the Year
For when the Frosts begin
We just reverse the Zodiac
And fetch the Acres in.

c. 1865   1945

1026

The Dying need but little, Dear,
A Glass of Water's all,
A Flower's unobtrusive Face
To punctuate the Wall,

A Fan, perhaps, a Friend's Regret
And Certainty that one
No color in the Rainbow
Perceive, when you are gone.

c. 1865   *1896*

1027

My Heart upon a little Plate
Her Palate to delight
A Berry or a Bun, would be,
Might it an Apricot!

c. 1865   *1945*

1028

'Twas my one Glory –
Let it be
Remembered
I was owned of Thee –

c. 1865   *1945*

1029

Nor Mountain hinder Me
Nor Sea –
Who's Baltic –
Who's Cordillera?

c. 1865   *1945*

1030

That Such have died enable Us
The tranquiller to die –
That Such have lived,
Certificate for Immortality.

c. 1865   *1896*

Fate slew Him, but He did not drop –
She felled – He did not fall –
Impaled Him on Her fiercest stakes –
He neutralized them all –

She stung Him – sapped His firm Advance –
But when Her Worst was done
And He – unmoved regarded Her –
Acknowledged Him a Man.

c. 1865 *1896*

Who is the East?
The Yellow Man
Who may be Purple if He can
That carries in the Sun.

Who is the West?
The Purple Man
Who may be Yellow if He can
That lets Him out again.

c. 1865 *1945*

Said Death to Passion
"Give of thine an Acre unto me."
Said Passion, through contracting Breaths
"A Thousand Times Thee Nay."

Bore Death from Passion
All His East
He – sovereign as the Sun
Resituated in the West
And the Debate was done.

c. 1865 *1945*

His Bill an Auger is
His Head, a Cap and Frill
He laboreth at every Tree
A Worm, His utmost Goal.

c. 1865   *1896*

1035

Bee! I'm expecting you!
Was saying Yesterday
To Somebody you know
That you were due –

The Frogs got Home last Week –
Are settled, and at work –
Birds, mostly back –
The Clover warm and thick –

You'll get my Letter by
The seventeenth; Reply
Or better, be with me –
Yours, Fly.

c. 1865   *1945*

1036

Satisfaction – is the Agent
Of Satiety –
Want – a quiet Commissary
For Infinity.

To possess, is past the instant
We achieve the Joy –
Immortality contented
Were Anomaly.

c. 1865   *1945*

1037

Here, where the Daisies fit my Head
'Tis easiest to lie
And every Grass that plays outside
Is sorry, some, for me.

Where I am not afraid to go
I may confide my Flower –
Who was not Enemy of Me
Will gentle be, to Her.

Nor separate, Herself and Me
By Distances become –
A single Bloom we constitute
Departed, or at Home –

c. 1865   *1945*

1038

Her little Parasol to lift
And once to let it down
Her whole Responsibility –
To imitate be Mine.

A Summer further I must wear,
Content if Nature's Drawer
Present me from sepulchral Crease
As blemishless, as Her.

c. 1865   *1945*

1039

I heard, as if I had no Ear
Until a Vital Word
Came all the way from Life to me
And then I knew I heard.

I saw, as if my Eye were on
Another, till a Thing
And now I know 'twas Light, because
It fitted them, came in.

[475]

I dwelt, as if Myself were out,
My Body but within
Until a Might detected me
And set my kernel in.

And Spirit turned unto the Dust
"Old Friend, thou knowest me,"
And Time went out to tell the News
And met Eternity.

c. 1865   *1945*

1040

Not so the infinite Relations – Below
Division is Adhesion's forfeit – On High
Affliction but a Speculation – And Woe
A Fallacy, a Figment, We knew –

c. 1865   *1945*

1041

Somewhat, to hope for,
Be it ne'er so far
Is Capital against Despair –

Somewhat, to suffer,
Be it ne'er so keen –
If terminable, may be borne.

c. 1865   *1945*

1042

Spring comes on the World –
I sight the Aprils –
Hueless to me until thou come
As, till the Bee
Blossoms stand negative,
Touched to Conditions
By a Hum.

c. 1865   *1945*

1043

Lest this be Heaven indeed
An Obstacle is given
That always gauges a Degree
Between Ourself and Heaven.

c. 1865

1945

1044

A Sickness of this World it most occasions
When Best Men die.
A Wishfulness their far Condition
To occupy.

A Chief indifference, as Foreign
A World must be
Themselves forsake – contented,
For Deity.

c. 1865

1896

1045

Nature rarer uses Yellow
Than another Hue.
Saves she all of that for Sunsets
Prodigal of Blue

Spending Scarlet, like a Woman
Yellow she affords
Only scantly and selectly
Like a Lover's Words.

c. 1865

1891

1046

I've dropped my Brain – My Soul is numb –
The Veins that used to run
Stop palsied – 'tis Paralysis
Done perfecter on stone

Vitality is Carved and cool.
My nerve in Marble lies –
A Breathing Woman
Yesterday – Endowed with Paradise.

Not dumb – I had a sort that moved –
A Sense that smote and stirred –
Instincts for Dance – a caper part –
An Aptitude for Bird –

Who wrought Carrara in me
And chiselled all my tune
Were it a Witchcraft – were it Death –
I've still a chance to strain

To Being, somewhere – Motion – Breath –
Though Centuries beyond,
And every limit a Decade –
I'll shiver, satisfied.

c. 1865   *1945*

1047

The Opening and the Close
Of Being, are alike
Or differ, if they do,
As Bloom upon a Stalk.

That from an equal Seed
Unto an equal Bud
Go parallel, perfected
In that they have decayed.

c. 1865   *1945*

1048

Reportless Subjects, to the Quick
Continual addressed –
But foreign as the Dialect
Of Danes, unto the rest.

[478]

Reportless Measures, to the Ear
Susceptive – stimulus –
But like an Oriental Tale
To others, fabulous –

c. 1865

1945

1049

Pain has but one Acquaintance
And that is Death –
Each one unto the other
Society enough.

Pain is the Junior Party
By just a Second's right –
Death tenderly assists Him
And then absconds from Sight.

c. 1865

1945

1050

As willing lid o'er weary eye
The Evening on the Day leans
Till of all our nature's House
Remains but Balcony

c. 1865

1945

1051

I cannot meet the Spring unmoved –
I feel the old desire –
A Hurry with a lingering, mixed,
A Warrant to be fair –

A Competition in my sense
With something hid in Her –
And as she vanishes, Remorse
I saw no more of Her.

c. 1865

1945

1052

I never saw a Moor –
I never saw the Sea –
Yet know I how the Heather looks
And what a Billow be.

I never spoke with God
Nor visited in Heaven –
Yet certain am I of the spot
As if the Checks were given –

c. 1865   *1890*

1053

It was a quiet way –
He asked if I was his –
I made no answer of the Tongue
But answer of the Eyes –
And then He bore me on
Before this mortal noise
With swiftness, as of Chariots
And distance, as of Wheels.
This World did drop away
As Acres from the feet
Of one that leaneth from Balloon
Upon an Ether street.
The Gulf behind was not,
The Continents were new –
Eternity it was before
Eternity was due.
No Seasons were to us –
It was not Night nor Morn –
But Sunrise stopped upon the place
And fastened it in Dawn.

c. 1865   *1929*

1054

Not to discover weakness is
The Artifice of strength –
Impregnability inheres
As much through Consciousness

Of faith of others in itself
As Pyramidal Nerve
Behind the most unconscious clock
What skilful Pointers move –

c. 1865   *1945*

1055

The Soul should always stand ajar
That if the Heaven inquire
He will not be obliged to wait
Or shy of troubling Her

Depart, before the Host have slid
The Bolt unto the Door –
To search for the accomplished Guest,
Her Visitor, no more –

c. 1865   *1896*

1056

There is a Zone whose even Years
No Solstice interrupt –
Whose Sun constructs perpetual Noon
Whose perfect Seasons wait –

Whose Summer set in Summer, till
The Centuries of June
And Centuries of August cease
And Consciousness – is Noon.

c. 1865   *1945*

I had a daily Bliss
I half indifferent viewed
Till sudden I perceived it stir –
It grew as I pursued

Till when around a Height
It wasted from my sight
Increased beyond my utmost scope
I learned to estimate.

c. 1865   *1896*

1058

Bloom – is Result – to meet a Flower
And casually glance
Would scarcely cause one to suspect
The minor Circumstance

Assisting in the Bright Affair
So intricately done
Then offered as a Butterfly
To the Meridian –

To pack the Bud – oppose the Worm –
Obtain its right of Dew –
Adjust the Heat – elude the Wind –
Escape the prowling Bee

Great Nature not to disappoint
Awaiting Her that Day –
To be a Flower, is profound
Responsibility –

c. 1865   *1945*

1059

Sang from the Heart, Sire,
Dipped my Beak in it,
If the Tune drip too much
Have a tint too Red

Pardon the Cochineal –
Suffer the Vermilion –
Death is the Wealth
Of the Poorest Bird.

Bear with the Ballad –
Awkward – faltering –
Death twists the strings –
'Twasn't my blame –

Pause in your Liturgies –
Wait your Chorals –
While I repeat your
Hallowed name –

c. 1865   1945

1060

Air has no Residence, no Neighbor,
No Ear, no Door,
No Apprehension of Another
Oh, Happy Air!

Ethereal Guest at e'en an Outcast's Pillow –
Essential Host, in Life's faint, wailing Inn,
Later than Light thy Consciousness accost me
Till it depart, persuading Mine –

c. 1865   1945

1061

Three Weeks passed since I had seen Her –
Some Disease had vext
'Twas with Text and Village Singing
I beheld Her next

And a Company – our pleasure
To discourse alone –
Gracious now to me as any –
Gracious unto none –

[483]

Borne without dissent of Either
To the Parish night –
Of the Separated Parties
Which be out of sight?

c. 1865   *1896*

1062

He scanned it – staggered –
Dropped the Loop
To Past or Period –
Caught helpless at a sense as if
His Mind were going blind –

Groped up, to see if God was there –
Groped backward at Himself
Caressed a Trigger absently
And wandered out of Life.

c. 1865   *1945*

1063

Ashes denote that Fire was –
Revere the Grayest Pile
For the Departed Creature's sake
That hovered there awhile –

Fire exists the first in light
And then consolidates
Only the Chemist can disclose
Into what Carbonates.

c. 1865   *1896*

1064

To help our Bleaker Parts
Salubrious Hours are given
Which if they do not fit for Earth
Drill silently for Heaven –

c. 1865   *1896*

1065

Let down the Bars, Oh Death –
The tired Flocks come in
Whose bleating ceases to repeat
Whose wandering is done –

Thine is the stillest night
Thine the securest Fold
Too near Thou art for seeking Thee
Too tender, to be told.

c. 1865   *1891*

1066

Fame's Boys and Girls, who never die
And are too seldom born –

c. 1865   *1945*

1067

Except the smaller size
No lives are round –
These – hurry to a sphere
And show and end –
The larger – slower grow
And later hang –
The Summers of Hesperides
Are long.

c. 1866   *1891*

1068

Further in Summer than the Birds
Pathetic from the Grass
A minor Nation celebrates
Its unobtrusive Mass.

No Ordinance be seen
So gradual the Grace

A pensive Custom it becomes
Enlarging Loneliness.

Antiquest felt at Noon
When August burning low
Arise this spectral Canticle
Repose to typify

Remit as yet no Grace
No Furrow on the Glow
Yet a Druidic Difference
Enhances Nature now

c. 1866   *1891*

1069

Paradise is of the option.
Whosoever will
Own in Eden notwithstanding
Adam and Repeal.

c. 1866   *1931*

1070

To undertake is to achieve
Be Undertaking blent
With fortitude of obstacle
And toward encouragement

That fine Suspicion, Natures must
Permitted to revere
Departed Standards and the few
Criterion Sources here

c. 1865   *1932*

1071

Perception of an object costs
Precise the Object's loss –
Perception in itself a Gain
Replying to its Price –

[486]

The Object Absolute – is nought –
Perception sets it fair
And then upbraids a Perfectness
That situates so far –

c. 1866

1914

1072

Title divine – is mine!
The Wife – without the Sign!
Acute Degree – conferred on me –
Empress of Calvary!
Royal – all but the Crown!
Betrothed – without the swoon
God sends us Women –
When you – hold – Garnet to Garnet –
Gold – to Gold –
Born – Bridalled – Shrouded –
In a Day –
Tri Victory
"My Husband" – women say –
Stroking the Melody –
Is *this* – the way?

c. 1862

1924

1073

Experiment to me
Is every one I meet
If it contain a Kernel?
The Figure of a Nut

Presents upon a Tree
Equally plausibly,
But Meat within, is requisite
To Squirrels, and to Me.

c. 1865

1891

1074

Count not that far that can be had,
Though sunset lie between –
Nor that adjacent, that beside,
Is further than the sun.

1866   *1894*

1075

The Sky is low – the Clouds are mean.
A Travelling Flake of Snow
Across a Barn or through a Rut
Debates if it will go –

A Narrow Wind complains all Day
How some one treated him
Nature, like Us is sometimes caught
Without her Diadem.

c. 1866   *1890*

1076

Just Once! Oh least Request!
Could Adamant refuse
So small a Grace
So scanty put,
Such agonizing terms?
Would not a God of Flint
Be conscious of a sigh
As down His Heaven dropt remote
"Just Once" Sweet Deity?

c. 1862   *1924*

1077

These are the Signs to Nature's Inns –
Her invitation broad
To Whosoever famishing
To taste her mystic Bread –

These are the rites of Nature's House –
The Hospitality
That opens with an equal width
To Beggar and to Bee

For Sureties of her staunch Estate
Her undecaying Cheer
The Purple in the East is set
And in the North, the Star –

c. 1866

1929

1078

The Bustle in a House
The Morning after Death
Is solemnest of industries
Enacted upon Earth –

The Sweeping up the Heart
And putting Love away
We shall not want to use again
Until Eternity.

c. 1866

1890

1079

The Sun went down – no Man looked on –
The Earth and I, alone,
Were present at the Majesty –
He triumphed, and went on –

The Sun went up – no Man looked on –
The Earth and I and One
A nameless Bird – a Stranger
Were Witness for the Crown –

c. 1866

1929

1080

When they come back – if Blossoms do –
I always feel a doubt

[489]

If Blossoms can be born again
When once the Art is out –

When they begin, if Robins may,
I always had a fear
I did not tell, it was their last Experiment
Last Year,

When it is May, if May return,
Had nobody a pang
Lest in a Face so beautiful
He might not look again?

If I am there – One does not know
What Party – One may be
Tomorrow, but if I am there
I take back all I say –

c. 1866   *1929*

1081

Superiority to Fate
Is difficult to gain
'Tis not conferred of Any
But possible to earn

A pittance at a time
Until to Her surprise
The Soul with strict economy
Subsist till Paradise.

c. 1866   *1896*

1082

Revolution is the Pod
Systems rattle from
When the Winds of Will are stirred
Excellent is Bloom

But except its Russet Base
Every Summer be

[490]

The Entomber of itself,
So of Liberty –

Left inactive on the Stalk
All its Purple fled
Revolution shakes it for
Test if it be dead.

c. 1866   *1929*

1083

We learn in the Retreating
How vast an one
Was recently among us –
A Perished Sun

Endear in the departure
How doubly more
Than all the Golden presence
It was – before –

1866   *1896*

1084

At Half past Three, a single Bird
Unto a silent Sky
Propounded but a single term
Of cautious melody.

At Half past Four, Experiment
Had subjugated test
And lo, Her silver Principle
Supplanted all the rest.

At Half past Seven, Element
Nor Implement, be seen –
And Place was where the Presence was
Circumference between.

c. 1866   *1891*

If Nature smiles – the Mother must
I'm sure, at many a whim
Of Her eccentric Family –
Is She so much to blame?

c. 1866   *1929*

1086

What Twigs We held by –
Oh the View
When Life's swift River striven through
We pause before a further plunge
To take Momentum –
As the Fringe

Upon a former Garment shows
The Garment cast,
Our Props disclose
So scant, so eminently small
Of Might to help, so pitiful
To sink, if We had labored, fond
The diligence were not more blind

How scant, by everlasting Light
The Discs that satisfied Our Sight –
How dimmer than a Saturn's Bar
The Things esteemed, for Things that are!

c. 1866   *1935*

1087

We miss a Kinsman more
When warranted to see
Than when withheld of Oceans
From possibility

A Furlong than a League
Inflicts a pricklier pain,

[492]

Till We, who smiled at Pyrenees –
Of Parishes, complain.

c. *1866*   *1929*

1088

Ended, ere it begun –
The Title was scarcely told
When the Preface perished from Consciousness
The Story, unrevealed –

Had it been mine, to print!
Had it been yours, to read!
That it was not Our privilege
The interdict of God –

c. *1866*   *1932*

1089

Myself can read the Telegrams
A Letter chief to me
The Stock's advance and Retrograde
And what the Markets say

The Weather – how the Rains
In Counties have begun.
'Tis News as null as nothing,
But sweeter so – than none.

c. *1866*   *1945*

1090

I am afraid to own a Body –
I am afraid to own a Soul –
Profound – precarious Property –
Possession, not optional –

Double Estate – entailed at pleasure
Upon an unsuspecting Heir –

Duke in a moment of Deathlessness
And God, for a Frontier.

c. *1866*

1935

1091

The Well upon the Brook
Were foolish to depend –
Let Brooks – renew of Brooks –
But Wells – of failless Ground!

c. *1866*

1945

1092

It was not Saint – it was too large –
Nor Snow – it was too small –
It only held itself aloof
Like something spiritual –

c. *1866*

1929

1093

Because 'twas Riches I could own,
Myself had earned it – Me,
I knew the Dollars by their names –
It feels like Poverty

An Earldom out of sight to hold,
An Income in the Air,
Possession – has a sweeter chink
Unto a Miser's Ear –

c. *1866*

1935

1094

Themself are all I have –
Myself a freckled – be –
I thought you'd choose a Velvet Cheek

Or one of Ivory –
Would you – instead of Me?

c. *1866*   *1935*

1095

To Whom the Mornings stand for Nights,
What must the Midnights – be!

c. *1866*   *1935*

1096

These Strangers, in a foreign World,
Protection asked of me –
Befriend them, lest Yourself in Heaven
Be found a Refugee –

c. *1866*   *1945*

1097

Dew – is the Freshet in the Grass –
'Tis many a tiny Mill
Turns unperceived beneath our feet
And Artisan lies still –

We spy the Forests and the Hills
The Tents to Nature's Show
Mistake the Outside for the in
And mention what we saw.

Could Commentators on the Sign
Of Nature's Caravan
Obtain "Admission" as a Child
Some Wednesday Afternoon.

c. *1866*   *1914*

1098

Of the Heart that goes in, and closes the Door
Shall the Playfellow Heart complain

Though the Ring is unwhole, and the Company broke
Can never be fitted again?

c. *1866*   *1945*

                         1099

My Cocoon tightens – Colors tease –
I'm feeling for the Air –
A dim capacity for Wings
Demeans the Dress I wear –

A power of Butterfly must be –
The Aptitude to fly
Meadows of Majesty implies
And easy Sweeps of Sky –

So I must baffle at the Hint
And cipher at the Sign
And make much blunder, if at last
I take the clue divine –

c. *1866*   *1890*

                         1100

The last Night that She lived
It was a Common Night
Except the Dying – this to Us
Made Nature different

We noticed smallest things –
Things overlooked before
By this great light upon our Minds
Italicized – as 'twere.

As We went out and in
Between Her final Room
And Rooms where Those to be alive
Tomorrow were, a Blame

That Others could exist
While She must finish quite

                      [496]

A Jealousy for Her arose
So nearly infinite –

We waited while She passed –
It was a narrow time –
Too jostled were Our Souls to speak
At length the notice came.

She mentioned, and forgot –
Then lightly as a Reed
Bent to the Water, struggled scarce –
Consented, and was dead –

And We – We placed the Hair –
And drew the Head erect –
And then an awful leisure was
Belief to regulate –

c. *1866*   *1890*

1101

Between the form of Life and Life
The difference is as big
As Liquor at the Lip between
And Liquor in the Jug
The latter – excellent to keep –
But for ecstatic need
The corkless is superior –
I know for I have tried

c. *1866*   *1945*

1102

His Bill is clasped – his Eye forsook –
His Feathers wilted low –
The Claws that clung, like lifeless Gloves
Indifferent hanging now –
The Joy that in his happy Throat
Was waiting to be poured
Gored through and through with Death, to be
Assassin of a Bird

[497]

Resembles to my outraged mind
The firing in Heaven,
On Angels – squandering for you
Their Miracles of Tune –

c. 1866   1945

1103

The spry Arms of the Wind
If I could crawl between
I have an errand imminent
To an adjoining Zone –

I should not care to stop
My Process is not long
The Wind could wait without the Gate
Or stroll the Town among.

To ascertain the House
And is the soul at Home
And hold the Wick of mine to it
To light, and then return –

c. 1866   1945

1104

The Crickets sang
And set the Sun
And Workmen finished one by one
Their Seam the Day upon.

The low Grass loaded with the Dew
The Twilight stood, as Strangers do
With Hat in Hand, polite and new
To stay as if, or go.

A Vastness, as a Neighbor, came,
A Wisdom, without Face, or Name,
A Peace, as Hemispheres at Home
And so the Night became.

c. 1866   1896

1105

Like Men and Women Shadows walk
Upon the Hills Today –
With here and there a mighty Bow
Or trailing Courtesy
To Neighbors doubtless of their own
Not quickened to perceive
Minuter landscape as Ourselves
And Boroughs where we live –

c. *1867*   *1914*

1106

We do not know the time we lose –
The awful moment is
And takes its fundamental place
Among the certainties –

A firm appearance still inflates
The card – the chance – the friend –
The spectre of solidities
Whose substances are sand –

c. *1867*   *1932*

1107

The Bird did prance – the Bee did play –
The Sun ran miles away ·
So blind with joy he could not choose
Between his Holiday

The morn was up – the meadows out
The Fences all but ran,
Republic of Delight, I thought
Where each is Citizen –

From Heavy laden Lands to thee
Were seas to cross to come
A Caspian were crowded –
Too near thou art for Fame –

c. *1867*   *1945*

1108

A Diamond on the Hand
To Custom Common grown
Subsides from its significance
The Gem were best unknown –
Within a Seller's Shrine
How many sight and sigh
And cannot, but are mad for fear
That any other buy.

c. 1867   1932

1109

I fit for them –
I seek the Dark
Till I am thorough fit.
The labor is a sober one
With this sufficient sweet
That abstinence of mine produce
A purer food for them, if I succeed,
If not I had
The transport of the Aim –

c. 1867   1914

1110

None who saw it ever told it
'Tis as hid as Death
Had for that specific treasure
A departing breath –
Surfaces may be invested
Did the Diamond grow
General as the Dandelion
Would you serve it so?

c. 1867   1945

1111

Some Wretched creature, savior take
Who would exult to die

[500]

And leave for thy sweet mercy's sake
Another Hour to me

c. *1867*   *1945*

1112

That this should feel the need of Death
The same as those that lived
Is such a Feat of Irony
As never was – achieved –

Not satisfied to ape the Great
In his simplicity
The small must die, as well as He –
Oh the Audacity –

c. *1867*   *1945*

1113

There is a strength in proving that it can be borne
Although it tear –
What are the sinews of such cordage for
Except to bear
The ship might be of satin had it not to fight –
To walk on seas requires cedar Feet

c. *1867*   *1945*

1114

The largest Fire ever known
Occurs each Afternoon –
Discovered is without surprise
Proceeds without concern –
Consumes and no report to men
An Occidental Town,
Rebuilt another morning
To be burned down again.

c. *1864*   *1914*

The murmuring of Bees, has ceased
But murmuring of some
Posterior, prophetic,
Has simultaneous come.
The lower metres of the Year
When Nature's laugh is done
The Revelations of the Book
Whose Genesis was June.
Appropriate Creatures to her change
The Typic Mother sends
As Accent fades to interval
With separating Friends
Till what we speculate, has been
And thoughts we will not show
More intimate with us become
Than Persons, that we know.

c. 1868   *1947*

There is another Loneliness
That many die without –
Not want of friend occasions it
Or circumstance of Lot

But nature, sometimes, sometimes thought
And whoso it befall
Is richer than could be revealed
By mortal numeral –

c. 1868   *1914*

A Mine there is no Man would own
But must it be conferred,
Demeaning by exclusive wealth
A Universe beside –

Potosi never to be spent
But hoarded in the mind
What Misers wring their hands tonight
For Indies in the Ground!

c. 1868   1932

1118

Exhilaration is the Breeze
That lifts us from the Ground
And leaves us in another place
Whose statement is not found –

Returns us not, but after time
We soberly descend
A little newer for the term
Upon Enchanted Ground –

c. 1868   1914

1119

Paradise is that old mansion
Many owned before –
Occupied by each an instant
Then reversed the Door –
Bliss is frugal of her Leases
Adam taught her Thrift
Bankrupt once through his excesses –

c. 1868   1945
(unfinished)

1120

This slow Day moved along –
I heard its axles go
As if they could not hoist themselves
They hated motion so –

I told my soul to come –
It was no use to wait –

We went and played and came again
And it was out of sight –

c. *1868*   *1945*

1121

Time does go on –
I tell it gay to those who suffer now –
They shall survive –
There is a sun –
They don't believe it now –

c. *1868*   *1945*

1122

'Tis my first night beneath the Sun
If I should spend it here –
Above him is too low a height
For his Barometer
Who Airs of expectation breathes
And takes the Wind at prime –
But Distance his Delights confides
To those who visit him –

c. *1868*   *1945*

1123

A great Hope fell
You heard no noise
The Ruin was within
Oh cunning wreck that told no tale
And let no Witness in

The mind was built for mighty Freight
For dread occasion planned
How often foundering at Sea
Ostensibly, on Land

A not admitting of the wound
Until it grew so wide

That all my Life had entered it
And there were troughs beside

A closing of the simple lid
That opened to the sun
Until the tender Carpenter
Perpetual nail it down –

c. *1868*   *1945*

1124

Had we known the Ton she bore
We had helped the terror
But she straighter walked for Freight
So be hers the error –

c. *1868*   *1945*

1125

Oh Sumptuous moment
Slower go
That I may gloat on thee –
'Twill never be the same to starve
Now I abundance see –

Which was to famish, then or now –
The difference of Day
Ask him unto the Gallows led –
With morning in the sky –

c. *1868*   *1945*

1126

Shall I take thee, the Poet said
To the propounded word?
Be stationed with the Candidates
Till I have finer tried –

The Poet searched Philology
And when about to ring

[505]

For the suspended Candidate
There came unsummoned in –

That portion of the Vision
The Word applied to fill
Not unto nomination
The Cherubim reveal –

c. 1868   1945

1127

Soft as the massacre of Suns
By Evening's Sabres slain

c. 1868   1945

1128

These are the Nights that Beetles love –
From Eminence remote
Drives ponderous perpendicular
His figure intimate
The terror of the Children
The merriment of men
Depositing his Thunder
He hoists abroad again –
A Bomb upon the Ceiling
Is an improving thing –
It keeps the nerves progressive
Conjecture flourishing –
Too dear the Summer evening
Without discreet alarm –
Supplied by Entomology
With its remaining charm –

c. 1868   1945

1129

Tell all the Truth but tell it slant –
Success in Circuit lies
Too bright for our infirm Delight
The Truth's superb surprise

[506]

As Lightning to the Children eased
With explanation kind
The Truth must dazzle gradually
Or every man be blind –

c. *1868*   *1945*

1130

That odd old man is dead a year –
We miss his stated Hat.
'Twas such an evening bright and stiff
His faded lamp went out.

Who miss his antiquated Wick –
Are any hoar for him?
Waits any indurated mate
His wrinkled coming Home?

Oh Life, begun in fluent Blood
And consummated dull!
Achievement contemplating thee –
Feels transitive and cool.

c. *1868*   *1945*

1131

The Merchant of the Picturesque
A Counter has and sales
But is within or negative
Precisely as the calls –
To Children he is small in price
And large in courtesy –
It suits him better than a check
Their artless currency –
Of Counterfeits he is so shy
Do one advance so near
As to behold his ample flight –

c. *1868*   *1945*
(*unfinished*)

[507]

The smouldering embers blush –
Oh Hearts within the Coal
Hast thou survived so many years?
The smouldering embers smile –
Soft stirs the news of Light
The stolid seconds glow
One requisite has Fire that lasts
Prometheus never knew –

c. 1868
(unfinished)

1945

The Snow that never drifts –
The transient, fragrant snow
That comes a single time a Year
Is softly driving now –

So thorough in the Tree
At night beneath the star
That it was February's Foot
Experience would swear –

Like Winter as a Face
We stern and former knew
Repaired of all but Loneliness
By Nature's Alibi –

Were every storm so spice
The Value could not be –
We buy with contrast – Pang is good
As near as memory –

c. 1868

1945

The Wind took up the Northern Things
And piled them in the south –

Then gave the East unto the West
And opening his mouth

The four Divisions of the Earth
Did make as to devour
While everything to corners slunk
Behind the awful power –

The Wind – unto his Chambers went
And nature ventured out –
Her subjects scattered into place
Her systems ranged about

Again the smoke from Dwellings rose
The Day abroad was heard –
How intimate, a Tempest past
The Transport of the Bird –

c. *1868*   *1945*

1135

Too cold is this
To warm with Sun –
Too stiff to bended be,
To joint this Agate were a work –
Outstaring Masonry –

How went the Agile Kernel out
Contusion of the Husk
Nor Rip, nor wrinkle indicate
But just an Asterisk.

c. *1868*   *1914*

1136

The Frost of Death was on the Pane –
"Secure your Flower" said he.
Like Sailors fighting with a Leak
We fought Mortality.

Our passive Flower we held to Sea –
To Mountain – To the Sun –

Yet even on his Scarlet shelf
To crawl the Frost begun –

We pried him back
Ourselves we wedged
Himself and her between,
Yet easy as the narrow Snake
He forked his way along

Till all her helpless beauty bent
And then our wrath begun –
We hunted him to his Ravine
We chased him to his Den –

We hated Death and hated Life
And nowhere was to go –
Than Sea and continent there is
A larger – it is Woe –

c. 1869

1945

1137

The duties of the Wind are few,
To cast the ships, at Sea,
Establish March, the Floods escort,
And usher Liberty.

The pleasures of the Wind are broad,
To dwell Extent among,
Remain, or wander,
Speculate, or Forests entertain.

The kinsmen of the Wind are Peaks
Azof – the Equinox,
Also with Bird and Asteroid
A bowing intercourse.

The limitations of the Wind
Do he exist, or die,
Too wise he seems for Wakelessness,
However, know not I.

c. 1869

1945

1138

A Spider sewed at Night
Without a Light
Upon an Arc of White.

If Ruff it was of Dame
Or Shroud of Gnome
Himself himself inform.

Of Immortality
His Strategy
Was Physiognomy.

c. 1869   *1891*

1139

Her sovereign People
Nature knows as well
And is as fond of signifying
As if fallible –

c. 1869   *1952*

1140

The Day grew small, surrounded tight
By early, stooping Night –
The Afternoon in Evening deep
Its Yellow shortness dropt –
The Winds went out their martial ways
The Leaves obtained excuse –
November hung his Granite Hat
Upon a nail of Plush –

c. 1869   *1945*

1141

The Face we choose to miss –
Be it but for a Day

As absent as a Hundred Years,
When it has rode away.

c. 1869   *1914*

1142

The Props assist the House
Until the House is built
And then the Props withdraw
And adequate, erect,
The House support itself
And cease to recollect
The Auger and the Carpenter –
Just such a retrospect
Hath the perfected Life –
A past of Plank and Nail
And slowness – then the Scaffolds drop
Affirming it a Soul.

c. 1863   *1914*

1143

The Work of Her that went,
The Toil of Fellows done –
In Ovens green our Mother bakes,
By Fires of the Sun.

c. 1869   *1955*

1144

Ourselves we do inter with sweet derision.
The channel of the dust who once achieves
Invalidates the balm of that religion
That doubts as fervently as it believes.

1869?   *1894*

1145

In thy long Paradise of Light
No moment will there be

When I shall long for Earthly Play
And mortal Company –

c. 1869

1945

1146

When Etna basks and purrs
Naples is more afraid
Than when she shows her Garnet Tooth –
Security is loud –

c. 1869

1914

1147

After a hundred years
Nobody knows the Place
Agony that enacted there
Motionless as Peace

Weeds triumphant ranged
Strangers strolled and spelled
At the lone Orthography
Of the Elder Dead

Winds of Summer Fields
Recollect the way –
Instinct picking up the Key
Dropped by memory –

c. 1869

1891

1148

After the Sun comes out
How it alters the World –
Waggons like messengers hurry about
Yesterday is old –

All men meet as if
Each foreclosed a news –

Fresh as a Cargo from Batize
Nature's qualities –

c. 1869   1955

1149

I noticed People disappeared
When but a little child –
Supposed they visited remote
Or settled Regions wild –
Now know I – They both visited
And settled Regions wild
But did because they died
A Fact withheld the little child –

c. 1869
(unfinished)   1891

1150

How many schemes may die
In one short Afternoon
Entirely unknown
To those they most concern –
The man that was not lost
Because by accident
He varied by a Ribbon's width
From his accustomed route –
The Love that would not try
Because beside the Door
It must be competitions
Some unsuspecting Horse was tied
Surveying his Despair

c. 1869   1945

1151

Soul, take thy risk.
With Death to be

Were better than be not
With thee

c. *1869*

1945

1152

Tell as a Marksman – were forgotten
Tell – this Day endures
Ruddy as that coeval Apple
The Tradition bears –

Fresh as Mankind that humble story
Though a statelier Tale
Grown in the Repetition hoary
Scarcely would prevail –

Tell had a son – The ones that knew it
Need not linger here –
Those who did not to Human Nature
Will subscribe a Tear –

Tell would not bare his Head
In Presence
Of the Ducal Hat –
Threatened for that with Death – by Gessler –
Tyranny bethought

Make of his only Boy a Target
That surpasses Death –
Stolid to Love's supreme entreaty
Not forsook of Faith –

Mercy of the Almighty begging –
Tell his Arrow sent –
God it is said replies in Person
When the cry is meant –

c. *1869*

1945

1153

Through what transports of Patience
I reached the stolid Bliss

[515]

To breathe my Blank without thee
Attest me this and this –
By that bleak exultation
I won as near as this
Thy privilege of dying
Abbreviate me this –

c. 1874   1945

1154

A full fed Rose on meals of Tint
A Dinner for a Bee
In process of the Noon became –
Each bright Mortality
The Forfeit is of Creature fair
Itself, adored before
Submitting for our unknown sake
To be esteemed no more –

c. 1870   1955

1155

Distance – is not the Realm of Fox
Nor by Relay of Bird
Abated – Distance is
Until thyself, Beloved.

c. 1870   1914

1156

Lest any doubt that we are glad that they were born Today
Whose having lived is held by us in noble Holiday
Without the date, like Consciousness or Immortality –

c. 1870   1932

1157

Some Days retired from the rest
In soft distinction lie

The Day that a Companion came
Or was obliged to die

c. 1870   *1914*

1158

Best Witchcraft is Geometry
To the magician's mind –
His ordinary acts are feats
To thinking of mankind.

c. 1870   *1932*

1159

Great Streets of silence led away
To Neighborhoods of Pause –
Here was no Notice – no Dissent
No Universe – no Laws –

By Clocks, 'twas Morning, and for Night
The Bells at Distance called –
But Epoch had no basis here
For Period exhaled.

c. 1870   *1891*

1160

He is alive, this morning –
He is alive – and awake –
Birds are resuming for Him –
Blossoms – dress for His Sake.
Bees – to their Loaves of Honey
Add an Amber Crumb
Him – to regale – Me – Only –
Motion, and am dumb.

c. 1870   *1955*

1161

Trust adjusts her "Peradventure" –
Phantoms entered "and not you."

1870   1931

1162

The Life we have is very great.
The Life that we shall see
Surpasses it, we know, because
It is Infinity.
But when all Space has been beheld
And all Dominion shown
The smallest Human Heart's extent
Reduces it to none.

1870   1945

1163

God made no act without a cause,
   Nor heart without an aim,
Our inference is premature,
   Our premises to blame.

1870?   1894

1164

Were it to be the last
How infinite would be
What we did not suspect was marked –
Our final interview.

1870   1955

1165

Contained in this short Life
Are magical extents
The soul returning soft at night
To steal securer thence

[518]

As Children strictest kept
Turn soonest to the sea
Whose nameless Fathoms slink away
Beside infinity

c. 1870   1945

1166

Of Paul and Silas it is said
They were in Prison laid
But when they went to take them out
They were not there instead.

Security the same insures
To our assaulted Minds –
The staple must be optional
That an Immortal binds.

c. 1870   1945

1167

Alone and in a Circumstance
Reluctant to be told
A spider on my reticence
Assiduously crawled

And so much more at Home than I
Immediately grew
I felt myself a visitor
And hurriedly withdrew

Revisiting my late abode
With articles of claim
I found it quietly assumed
As a Gymnasium
Where Tax asleep and Title off
The inmates of the Air
Perpetual presumption took
As each were special Heir –
If any strike me on the street
I can return the Blow –

If any take my property
According to the Law
The Statute is my Learned friend
But what redress can be
For an offense nor here nor there
So not in Equity –
That Larceny of time and mind
The marrow of the Day
By spider, or forbid it Lord
That I should specify.

1870   1945

1168

As old as Woe –
How old is that?
Some eighteen thousand years –
As old as Bliss
How old is that
They are of equal years

Together chiefest they are found
But seldom side by side
From neither of them tho' he try
Can Human nature hide

c. 1870   1945

1169

Lest they should come – is all my fear
When sweet incarcerated here

c. 1870   1945

1170

Nature affects to be sedate
Upon occasion, grand
But let our observation shut
Her practices extend

[520]

To Necromancy and the Trades
Remote to understand
Behold our spacious Citizen
Unto a Juggler turned –

c. 1870   *1945*

1171

On the World you colored
Morning painted rose –
Idle his Vermilion
Aimless crept the Glows
Over Realms of Orchards
I the Day before
Conquered with the Robin –
Misery, how fair
Till your wrinkled Finger
Shored the sun away
Midnight's awful Pattern
In the Goods of Day –

c. 1870   *1945*

1172

The Clouds their Backs together laid
The North begun to push
The Forests galloped till they fell
The Lightning played like mice

The Thunder crumbled like a stuff
How good to be in Tombs
Where Nature's Temper cannot reach
Nor missile ever comes

c. 1870   *1890*

1173

The Lightning is a yellow Fork
From Tables in the sky

By inadvertent fingers dropt
The awful Cutlery

Of mansions never quite disclosed
And never quite concealed
The Apparatus of the Dark
To ignorance revealed.

c. 1870   1945

1174

There's the Battle of Burgoyne –
Over, every Day,
By the Time that Man and Beast
Put their work away
"Sunset" sounds majestic –
But that solemn War
Could you comprehend it
You would chastened stare –

c. 1870   1945

1175

We like a Hairbreadth 'scape
It tingles in the Mind
Far after Act or Accident
Like paragraphs of Wind

If we had ventured less
The Breeze were not so fine
That reaches to our utmost Hair
Its Tentacles divine.

c. 1870   1945

1176

We never know how high we are
Till we are asked to rise
And then if we are true to plan
Our statures touch the skies –

The Heroism we recite
Would be a normal thing
Did not ourselves the Cubits warp
For fear to be a King –

c. 1870 1896

1177

A prompt – executive Bird is the Jay –
Bold as a Bailiff's Hymn –
Brittle and Brief in quality –
Warrant in every line –

Sitting a Bough like a Brigadier
Confident and straight –
Much is the mien of him in March
As a Magistrate –

c. 1865 1914

1178

My God – He sees thee –
Shine thy best –
Fling up thy Balls of Gold
Till every Cubit play with thee
And every Crescent hold –
Elate the Acre at his feet –
Upon his Atom swim –
Oh Sun – but just a Second's right
In thy long Race with him!

c. 1871 1932

1179

Of so divine a Loss
We enter but the Gain,
Indemnity for Loneliness
That such a Bliss has been.

c. 1871 1914

"Remember me" implored the Thief!
Oh Hospitality!
My Guest "Today in Paradise"
I give thee guaranty.

That Courtesy will fair remain
When the Delight is Dust
With which we cite this mightiest case
Of compensated Trust.

Of all we are allowed to hope
But Affidavit stands
That this was due where most we fear
Be unexpected Friends.

c. 1871   *1914*

When I hoped I feared –
Since I hoped I dared
Everywhere alone
As a Church remain –
Spectre cannot harm –
Serpent cannot charm –
He deposes Doom
Who hath suffered him –

c. 1862   *1891*

Remembrance has a Rear and Front –
'Tis something like a House –
It has a Garret also
For Refuse and the Mouse.

Besides the deepest Cellar
That ever Mason laid –

Look to it by its Fathoms
Ourselves be not pursued –

c. *1871*

1896

1183

Step lightly on this narrow spot –
The broadest Land that grows
Is not so ample as the Breast
These Emerald Seams enclose.

Step lofty, for this name be told
As far as Cannon dwell
Or Flag subsist or Fame export
Her deathless Syllable.

c. *1871*

1891

1184

The Days that we can spare
Are those a Function die
Or Friend or Nature – stranded then
In our Economy

Our Estimates a Scheme –
Our Ultimates a Sham –
We let go all of Time without
Arithmetic of him –

c. *1871*

1932

1185

A little Dog that wags his tail
And knows no other joy
Of such a little Dog am I
Reminded by a Boy

Who gambols all the living Day
Without an earthly cause
Because he is a little Boy
I honestly suppose –

The Cat that in the Corner dwells
Her martial Day forgot
The Mouse but a Tradition now
Of her desireless Lot

Another class remind me
Who neither please nor play
But not to make a "bit of noise"
Beseech each little Boy –

c. 1871   1945

1186

Too few the mornings be,
Too scant the nights.
No lodging can be had
For the delights
That come to earth to stay,
But no apartment find
And ride away.

1871   1894

1187

Oh Shadow on the Grass,
Art thou a Step or not?
Go make thee fair my Candidate
My nominated Heart –
Oh Shadow on the Grass
While I delay to guess
Some other thou wilt consecrate –
Oh Unelected Face –

c. 1871   1929

1188

'Twas fighting for his Life he was –
That sort accomplish well –
The Ordnance of Vitality
Is frugal of its Ball.

It aims once – kills once – conquers once –
There is no second War
In that Campaign inscrutable
Of the Interior.

c. 1871

1945

1189

The Voice that stands for Floods to me
Is sterile borne to some –
The Face that makes the Morning mean
Glows impotent on them –

What difference in Substance lies
That what is Sum to me
By other Financiers be deemed
Exclusive Poverty!

c. 1871

1945

1190

The Sun and Fog contested
The Government of Day –
The Sun took down his Yellow Whip
And drove the Fog away –

c. 1871

1945

1191

The pungent atom in the Air
Admits of no debate –
All that is named of Summer Days
Relinquished our Estate –

For what Department of Delight
As positive are we
As Limit of Dominion
Or Dams – of Ecstasy –

c. 1871

1945

1192

An honest Tear
Is durabler than Bronze –
This Cenotaph
May each that dies –

Reared by itself –
No Deputy suffice –
Gratitude bears
When Obelisk decays

c. 1871   *1945*

1193

All men for Honor hardest work
But are not known to earn –
Paid after they have ceased to work
In Infamy or Urn –

c. 1871   *1945*

1194

Somehow myself survived the Night
And entered with the Day –
That it be saved the Saved suffice
Without the Formula.

Henceforth I take my living place
As one commuted led –
A Candidate for Morning Chance
But dated with the Dead.

c. 1871   *1935*

1195

What we see we know somewhat
Be it but a little –
What we don't surmise we do
Though it shows so fickle

I shall vote for Lands with Locks
Granted I can pick 'em –
Transport's doubtful Dividend
Patented by Adam.

c. 1871   1945

1196

To make Routine a Stimulus
Remember it can cease –
Capacity to Terminate
Is a Specific Grace –
Of Retrospect the Arrow
That power to repair
Departed with the Torment
Become, alas, more fair –

c. 1871   1947

1197

I should not dare to be so sad
So many Years again –
A Load is first impossible
When we have put it down –

The Superhuman then withdraws
And we who never saw
The Giant at the other side
Begin to perish now.

1871   1929

1198

A soft Sea washed around the House
A Sea of Summer Air
And rose and fell the magic Planks
That sailed without a care –
For Captain was the Butterfly
For Helmsman was the Bee

And an entire universe
For the delighted crew.

c. *1871*   *1945*

1199

Are Friends Delight or Pain?
Could Bounty but remain
Riches were good –

But if they only stay
Ampler to fly away
Riches are sad.

c. *1871*   *1896*

1200

Because my Brook is fluent
I know 'tis dry –
Because my Brook is silent
It is the Sea –

And startled at its rising
I try to flee
To where the Strong assure me
Is "no more Sea" –

c. *1871*   *1945*

1201

So I pull my Stockings off
Wading in the Water
For the Disobedience' Sake
Boy that lived for "or'ter"

Went to Heaven perhaps at Death
And perhaps he didn't
Moses wasn't fairly used –
Ananias wasn't –

c. *1871*   *1945*

The Frost was never seen –
If met, too rapid passed,
Or in too unsubstantial Team –
The Flowers notice first

A Stranger hovering round
A Symptom of alarm
In Villages remotely set
But search effaces him

Till some retrieveless Night
Our Vigilance at waste
The Garden gets the only shot
That never could be traced.

Unproved is much we know –
Unknown the worst we fear –
Of Strangers is the Earth the Inn
Of Secrets is the Air –

To analyze perhaps
A Philip would prefer
But Labor vaster than myself
I find it to infer.

c. 1871   1945

The Past is such a curious Creature
To look her in the Face
A Transport may receipt us
Or a Disgrace –

Unarmed if any meet her
I charge him fly
Her faded Ammunition
Might yet reply.

c. 1871   1896

1204

Whatever it is – she has tried it –
Awful Father of Love –
Is not Ours the chastising –
Do not chastise the Dove –

Not for Ourselves, petition –
Nothing is left to pray –
When a subject is finished –
Words are handed away –

Only lest she be lonely
In thy beautiful House
Give her for her Transgression
License to think of us –

c. 1871   *1945*

1205

Immortal is an ample word
When what we need is by
But when it leaves us for a time
'Tis a necessity.

Of Heaven above the firmest proof
We fundamental know
Except for its marauding Hand
It had been Heaven below.

c. 1872   *1896*

1206

The Show is not the Show
But they that go –
Menagerie to me
My Neighbor be –
Fair Play –
Both went to see –

c. 1872   *1891*

1207

He preached upon "Breadth" till it argued him narrow –
The Broad are too broad to define
And of "Truth" until it proclaimed him a Liar –
The Truth never flaunted a Sign –

Simplicity fled from his counterfeit presence
As Gold the Pyrites would shun –
What confusion would cover the innocent Jesus
To meet so enabled a Man!

c. 1872   *1891*

1208

Our own possessions – though our own –
'Tis well to hoard anew –
Remembering the Dimensions
Of Possibility.

c. 1872   *1894*

1209

To disappear enhances –
The Man that runs away
Is tinctured for an instant
With Immortality

But yesterday a Vagrant –
Today in Memory lain
With superstitious value
We tamper with "Again"

But "Never" far as Honor
Withdraws the Worthless thing
And impotent to cherish
We hasten to adorn –

Of Death the sternest function
That just as we discern

The Excellence defies us –
Securest gathered then

The Fruit perverse to plucking,
But leaning to the Sight
With the ecstatic limit
Of unobtained Delight –

c. 1872   1894

1210

The Sea said "Come" to the Brook –
The Brook said "Let me grow" –
The Sea said "Then you will be a Sea –
I want a Brook – Come now"!

The Sea said "Go" to the Sea –
The Sea said "I am he
You cherished" – "Learned Waters –
Wisdom is stale – to Me"

c. 1872   1947

1211

A Sparrow took a Slice of Twig
And thought it very nice
I think, because his empty Plate
Was handed Nature twice –

Invigorated, waded
In all the deepest Sky
Until his little Figure
Was forfeited away –

c. 1872   1945

1212

A word is dead
When it is said,
Some say.

I say it just
Begins to live
That day.

1872?   *1894*

1213

We like March.
His Shoes are Purple –
He is new and high –
Makes he Mud for Dog and Peddler,
Makes he Forests dry.
Knows the Adder Tongue his coming
And presents her Spot –
Stands the Sun so close and mighty
That our Minds are hot.

News is he of all the others –
Bold it were to die
With the Blue Birds exercising
On his British Sky.

version of 1872   *1955*

We like March – his shoes are Purple.
He is new and high –
Makes he Mud for Dog and Peddler –
Makes he Forests Dry –
Knows the Adder's Tongue his coming
And begets her spot –
Stands the Sun so close and mighty –
That our Minds are hot.
News is he of all the others –
Bold it were to die
With the Blue Birds buccaneering
On his British sky –

version of 1878   *1896*

1214

We introduce ourselves
To Planets and to Flowers

But with ourselves
Have etiquettes
Embarrassments
And awes

c. 1872   *1945*

1215

I bet with every Wind that blew
Till Nature in chagrin
Employed a Fact to visit me
And scuttle my Balloon –

c. 1872   *1914*

1216

A Deed knocks first at Thought
And then – it knocks at Will –
That is the manufacturing spot
And Will at Home and well

It then goes out an Act
Or is entombed so still
That only to the ear of God
Its Doom is audible –

c. 1872   *1891*

1217

Fortitude incarnate
Here is laid away
In the swift Partitions
Of the awful Sea –

Babble of the Happy
Cavil of the Bold
Hoary the Fruition
But the Sea is old   ٦

Edifice of Ocean
Thy tumultuous Rooms

[536]

Suit me at a venture
Better than the Tombs

c. 1872   *1945*

1218

Let my first Knowing be of thee
With morning's warming Light –
And my first Fearing, lest Unknowns
Engulf thee in the night –

c. 1878   *1945*

1219

Now I knew I lost her –
Not that she was gone –
But Remoteness travelled
On her Face and Tongue.

Alien, though adjoining
As a Foreign Race –
Traversed she though pausing
Latitudeless Place.

Elements Unaltered –
Universe the same
But Love's transmigration –
Somehow this had come –

Henceforth to remember
Nature took the Day
I had paid so much for –
His is Penury
Not who toils for Freedom
Or for Family
But the Restitution
Of Idolatry.

c. 1872   *1945*

1220

Of Nature I shall have enough
When I have entered these
Entitled to a Bumble bee's
Familiarities.

c. 1872   1945

1221

Some we see no more, Tenements of Wonder
Occupy to us though perhaps to them
Simpler are the Days than the Supposition
Their removing Manners
Leave us to presume

That oblique Belief which we call Conjecture
Grapples with a Theme stubborn as Sublime
Able as the Dust to equip its feature
Adequate as Drums
To enlist the Tomb.

c. 1872   1945

1222

The Riddle we can guess
We speedily despise –
Not anything is stale so long
As Yesterday's surprise –

c. 1870   1945

1223

Who goes to dine must take his Feast
Or find the Banquet mean –
The Table is not laid without
Till it is laid within.

For Pattern is the Mind bestowed
That imitating her

Our most ignoble Services
Exhibit worthier.

c. 1872

1945

1224

Like Trains of Cars on Tracks of Plush
I hear the level Bee –
A Jar across the Flowers goes
Their Velvet Masonry

Withstands until the sweet Assault
Their Chivalry consumes –
While He, victorious tilts away
To vanquish other Blooms.

c. 1872

1890

1225

Its Hour with itself
The Spirit never shows.
What Terror would enthrall the Street
Could Countenance disclose

The Subterranean Freight
The Cellars of the Soul –
Thank God the loudest Place he made
Is licensed to be still.

c. 1872

1929

1226

The Popular Heart is a Cannon first –
Subsequent a Drum –
Bells for an Auxiliary
And an Afterward of Rum –

Not a Tomorrow to know its name
Nor a Past to stare –

Ditches for Realms and a Trip to Jail
For a Souvenir –

c. 1872   1929

1227

My Triumph lasted till the Drums
Had left the Dead alone
And then I dropped my Victory
And chastened stole along
To where the finished Faces
Conclusion turned on me
And then I hated Glory
And wished myself were They.

What is to be is best descried
When it has also been –
Could Prospect taste of Retrospect
The tyrannies of Men
Were Tenderer – diviner
The Transitive toward.
A Bayonet's contrition
Is nothing to the Dead.

c. 1872   1935

1228

So much of Heaven has gone from Earth
That there must be a Heaven
If only to enclose the Saints
To Affidavit given.

The Missionary to the Mole
Must prove there is a Sky
Location doubtless he would plead
But what excuse have I?

Too much of Proof affronts Belief
The Turtle will not try

[540]

Unless you leave him – then return
And he has hauled away.

c. 1872   1947

1229

Because He loves Her
We will pry and see if she is fair
What difference is on her Face
From Features others wear.

It will not harm her magic pace
That we so far behind –
Her Distances propitiate
As Forests touch the Wind

Not hoping for his notice vast
But nearer to adore
'Tis Glory's far sufficiency
That makes our trying poor.

c. 1872   1945

1230

It came at last but prompter Death
Had occupied the House –
His pallid Furniture arranged
And his metallic Peace –

Oh faithful Frost that kept the Date
Had Love as punctual been
Delight had aggrandized the Gate
And blocked the coming in.

c. 1872   1945

1231

Somewhere upon the general Earth
Itself exist Today –
The Magic passive but extant
That consecrated me –

Indifferent Seasons doubtless play
Where I for right to be –
Would pay each Atom that I am
But Immortality –

Reserving that but just to prove
Another Date of Thee –
Oh God of Width, do not for us
Curtail Eternity!

c. 1872   1945

1232

The Clover's simple Fame
Remembered of the Cow –
Is better than enameled Realms
Of notability.
Renown perceives itself
And that degrades the Flower –
The Daisy that has looked behind
Has compromised its power –

c. 1872   1945

1233

Had I not seen the Sun
I could have borne the shade
But Light a newer Wilderness
My Wilderness has made –

c. 1872   1945

1234

If my Bark sink
'Tis to another sea –
Mortality's Ground Floor
Is Immortality –

c. 1872   1945

1235

Like Rain it sounded till it curved
And then I knew 'twas Wind –
It walked as wet as any Wave
But swept as dry as sand –
When it had pushed itself away
To some remotest Plain
A coming as of Hosts was heard
That was indeed the Rain –
It filled the Wells, it pleased the Pools
It warbled in the Road –
It pulled the spigot from the Hills
And let the Floods abroad –
It loosened acres, lifted seas
The sites of Centres stirred
Then like Elijah rode away
Upon a Wheel of Cloud.

c. 1872   *1945*

1236

Like Time's insidious wrinkle
On a beloved Face
We clutch the Grace the tighter
Though we resent the crease

The Frost himself so comely
Dishevels every prime
Asserting from his Prism
That none can punish him

c. 1872   *1945*

1237

My Heart ran so to thee
It would not wait for me
And I affronted grew
And drew away

For whatsoe'er my pace
He first achieve thy Face
How general a Grace
Allotted two –

Not in malignity
Mentioned I this to thee –
Had he obliquity
Soonest to share
But for the Greed of him –
Boasting my Premium –
Basking in Bethleem
Ere I be there –

c. 1878   1945

1238

Power is a familiar growth –
Not foreign – not to be –
Beside us like a bland Abyss
In every company –
Escape it – there is but a chance –
When consciousness and clay
Lean forward for a final glance –
Disprove that and you may –

c. 1872   1945

1239

Risk is the Hair that holds the Tun
Seductive in the Air –
That Tun is hollow – but the Tun –
With Hundred Weights – to spare –

Too ponderous to suspect the snare
Espies that fickle chair
And seats itself to be let go
By that perfidious Hair –

The "foolish Tun" the Critics say –
While that delusive Hair

Persuasive as Perdition,
Decoys its Traveller.

c. 1872

1945

1240

The Beggar at the Door for Fame
Were easily supplied
But Bread is that Diviner thing
Disclosed to be denied

c. 1872

1945

1241

The Lilac is an ancient shrub
But ancienter than that
The Firmamental Lilac
Upon the Hill tonight –
The Sun subsiding on his Course
Bequeaths this final Plant
To Contemplation – not to Touch –
The Flower of Occident.
Of one Corolla is the West –
The Calyx is the Earth –
The Capsules burnished Seeds the Stars
The Scientist of Faith
His research has but just begun –
Above his synthesis
The Flora unimpeachable
To Time's Analysis –
"Eye hath not seen" may possibly
Be current with the Blind
But let not Revelation
By theses be detained –

c. 1872

1945

1242

To flee from memory
Had we the Wings
Many would fly
Inured to slower things
Birds with surprise
Would scan the cowering Van
Of men escaping
From the mind of man

c. 1872   *1945*

1243

Safe Despair it is that raves –
Agony is frugal.
Puts itself severe away
For its own perusal.

Garrisoned no Soul can be
In the Front of Trouble –
Love is one, not aggregate –
Nor is Dying double –

c. 1873   *1914*

1244

The Butterfly's Assumption Gown
In Chrysoprase Apartments hung
This afternoon put on –

How condescending to descend
And be of Buttercups the friend
In a New England Town –

c. 1873   *1890*

1245

The Suburbs of a Secret
A Strategist should keep,

Better than on a Dream intrude
To scrutinize the Sleep.

c. 1873   1914

1246

The Butterfly in honored Dust
Assuredly will lie
But none will pass the Catacomb
So chastened as the Fly –

c. 1873   1915

1247

To pile like Thunder to its close
Then crumble grand away
While Everything created hid
This – would be Poetry –

Or Love – the two coeval come –
We both and neither prove –
Experience either and consume –
For None see God and live –

c. 1873   1914

1248

The incidents of love
Are more than its Events –
Investment's best Expositor
Is the minute Per Cents –

c. 1873   1914

1249

The Stars are old, that stood for me –
The West a little worn –
Yet newer glows the only Gold
I ever cared to earn –

Presuming on that lone result
Her infinite disdain
But vanquished her with my defeat
'Twas Victory was slain.

c. 1873   *1914*

1250

White as an Indian Pipe
Red as a Cardinal Flower
Fabulous as a Moon at Noon
February Hour –

c. 1873   *1932*

1251

Silence is all we dread.
There's Ransom in a Voice –
But Silence is Infinity.
Himself have not a face.

1873   *1932*

1252

Like Brooms of Steel
The Snow and Wind
Had swept the Winter Street –
The House was hooked
The Sun sent out
Faint Deputies of Heat –
Where rode the Bird
The Silence tied
His ample – plodding Steed
The Apple in the Cellar snug
Was all the one that played.

c. 1873   *1914*

1253

Had this one Day not been,
Or could it cease to be
How smitten, how superfluous,
Were every other Day!

Lest Love should value less
What Loss would value more
Had it the stricken privilege,
It cherishes before.

c. 1873   *1914*

1254

Elijah's Wagon knew no thill
Was innocent of Wheel
Elijah's horses as unique
As was his vehicle –

Elijah's journey to portray
Expire with him the skill
Who justified Elijah
In feats inscrutable –

c. 1873   *1914*

1255

Longing is like the Seed
That wrestles in the Ground,
Believing if it intercede
It shall at length be found.

The Hour, and the Clime –
Each Circumstance unknown,
What Constancy must be achieved
Before it see the Sun!

c. 1873   *1929*

1256

Not any higher stands the Grave
For Heroes than for Men –
Not any nearer for the Child
Than numb Three Score and Ten –

This latest Leisure equal lulls
The Beggar and his Queen
Propitiate this Democrat
A Summer's Afternoon –

c. 1873   *1896*

1257

Dominion lasts until obtained –
Possession just as long –
But these – endowing as they flit
Eternally belong.

How everlasting are the Lips
Known only to the Dew –
These are the Brides of permanence
Supplanting me and you.

c. 1873   *1932*

1258

Who were "the Father and the Son"
We pondered when a child,
And what had they to do with us
And when portentous told

With inference appalling
By Childhood fortified
We thought, at least they are no worse
Than they have been described.

Who are "the Father and the Son"
Did we demand Today
"The Father and the Son" himself
Would doubtless specify –

[550]

But had they the felicity
When we desired to know,
We better Friends had been, perhaps,
Than time ensue to be –

We start – to learn that we believe
But once – entirely –
Belief, it does not fit so well
When altered frequently –

We blush, that Heaven if we achieve –
Event ineffable –
We shall have shunned until ashamed
To own the Miracle –

c. 1873   *1914*

1259

A Wind that rose
Though not a Leaf
In any Forest stirred
But with itself did cold engage
Beyond the Realm of Bird –
A Wind that woke a lone Delight
Like Separation's Swell
Restored in Arctic Confidence
To the Invisible –

c. 1873   *1932*

1260

Because that you are going
And never coming back
And I, however absolute,
May overlook your Track –

Because that Death is final,
However first it be,
This instant be suspended
Above Mortality –

Significance that each has lived
The other to detect
Discovery not God himself
Could now annihilate

Eternity, Presumption
The instant I perceive
That you, who were Existence
Yourself forgot to live –

The "Life that is" will then have been
A thing I never knew –
As Paradise fictitious
Until the Realm of you –

The "Life that is to be," to me,
A Residence too plain
Unless in my Redeemer's Face
I recognize your own –

Of Immortality who doubts
He may exchange with me
Curtailed by your obscuring Face
Of everything but He –

Of Heaven and Hell I also yield
The Right to reprehend
To whoso would commute this Face
For his less priceless Friend.

If "God is Love" as he admits
We think that he must be
Because he is a "jealous God"
He tells us certainly

If "All is possible with" him
As he besides concedes
He will refund us finally
Our confiscated Gods –

c. 1873   1930

1261

A Word dropped careless on a Page
May stimulate an eye
When folded in perpetual seam
The Wrinkled Maker lie

Infection in the sentence breeds
We may inhale Despair
At distances of Centuries
From the Malaria –

c. 1873   1947

1262

I cannot see my soul but know 'tis there
Nor ever saw his house nor furniture,
Who has invited me with him to dwell;
But a confiding guest consult as well,
What raiment honor him the most,
That I be adequately dressed,
For he insures to none
Lest men specifical adorn
Procuring him perpetual drest
By dating it a sudden feast.

1873?   1894

1263

There is no Frigate like a Book
To take us Lands away
Nor any Coursers like a Page
Of prancing Poetry –
This Traverse may the poorest take
Without oppress of Toll –
How frugal is the Chariot
That bears the Human soul.

c. 1873   1894

1264

This is the place they hoped before,
Where I am hoping now.
The seed of disappointment grew
Within a capsule gay,
Too distant to arrest the feet
That walk this plank of balm –
Before them lies escapeless sea –
The way is closed they came.

c. 1873   *1894*

1265

The most triumphant Bird I ever knew or met
Embarked upon a twig today
And till Dominion set
I famish to behold so eminent a sight
And sang for nothing scrutable
But intimate Delight.
Retired, and resumed his transitive Estate –
To what delicious Accident
Does finest Glory fit!

c. 1873   *1894*

1266

When Memory is full
Put on the perfect Lid –
This Morning's finest syllable
Presumptuous Evening said –

c. 1873   *1951*

1267

I saw that the Flake was on it
But plotted with Time to dispute –
"Unchanged" I urged with a candor
That cost me my honest Heart –

But "you" – she returned with valor
Sagacious of my mistake
"Have altered – Accept the pillage
For the progress' sake" –

18731915

1268

Confirming All who analyze
In the Opinion fair
That Eloquence is when the Heart
Has not a Voice to spare –

c. 18731932

1269

I worked for chaff and earning Wheat
Was haughty and betrayed.
What right had Fields to arbitrate
In matters ratified?

I tasted Wheat and hated Chaff
And thanked the ample friend –
Wisdom is more becoming viewed
At distance than at hand.

c. 18731896

1270

Is Heaven a Physician?
They say that He can heal –
But Medicine Posthumous
Is unavailable –
Is Heaven an Exchequer?
They speak of what we owe –
But that negotiation
I'm not a Party to –

c. 18731891

September's Baccalaureate
A combination is
Of Crickets – Crows – and Retrospects
And a dissembling Breeze

That hints without assuming –
An Innuendo sear
That makes the Heart put up its Fun
And turn Philosopher.

c. *1873*   *1892*

So proud she was to die
It made us all ashamed
That what we cherished, so unknown
To her desire seemed –
So satisfied to go
Where none of us should be
Immediately – that Anguish stooped
Almost to Jealousy –

c. *1873*   *1896*

That sacred Closet when you sweep –
Entitled "Memory" –
Select a reverential Broom –
And do it silently.

'Twill be a Labor of surprise –
Besides Identity
Of other Interlocutors
A probability –

August the Dust of that Domain –
Unchallenged – let it lie –
You cannot supersede itself
But it can silence you –

c. *1873*   *1945*

The Bone that has no Marrow,
What Ultimate for that?
It is not fit for Table
For Beggar or for Cat.

A Bone has obligations –
A Being has the same –
A Marrowless Assembly
Is culpabler than shame.

But how shall finished Creatures
A function fresh obtain?
Old Nicodemus' Phantom
Confronting us again!

c. 1873   *1896*

The Spider as an Artist
Has never been employed –
Though his surpassing Merit
Is freely certified

By every Broom and Bridget
Throughout a Christian Land –
Neglected Son of Genius
I take thee by the Hand –

c. 1873   *1896*

'Twas later when the summer went
Than when the Cricket came –
And yet we knew that gentle Clock
Meant nought but Going Home –
'Twas sooner when the Cricket went
Than when the Winter came
Yet that pathetic Pendulum
Keeps esoteric Time.

c. 1873   *1890*

While we were fearing it, it came –
But came with less of fear
Because that fearing it so long
Had almost made it fair –

There is a Fitting – a Dismay –
A Fitting – a Despair –
'Tis harder knowing it is Due
Than knowing it is Here.

The Trying on the Utmost
The Morning it is new
Is Terribler than wearing it
A whole existence through.

c. *1873*   *1896*

The Mountains stood in Haze –
The Valleys stopped below
And went or waited as they liked
The River and the Sky.

At leisure was the Sun –
His interests of Fire
A little from remark withdrawn –
The Twilight spoke the Spire,

So soft upon the Scene
The Act of evening fell
We felt how neighborly a Thing
Was the Invisible.

c. *1873*   *1945*

The Way to know the Bobolink
From every other Bird
Precisely as the Joy of him –
Obliged to be inferred.

Of impudent Habiliment
Attired to defy,
Impertinence subordinate
At times to Majesty.

Of Sentiments seditious
Amenable to Law –
As Heresies of Transport
Or Puck's Apostacy.

Extrinsic to Attention
Too intimate with Joy –
He compliments existence
Until allured away

By Seasons or his Children –
Adult and urgent grown –
Or unforeseen aggrandizement
Or, happily, Renown –

By Contrast certifying
The Bird of Birds is gone –
How nullified the Meadow –
Her Sorcerer withdrawn!

c. 1873   *1945*

1280

The harm of Years is on him –
The infamy of Time –
Depose him like a Fashion
And give Dominion room.

Forget his Morning Forces –
The Glory of Decay
Is a minuter Pageant
Than least Vitality.

c. 1873   *1945*

A stagnant pleasure like a Pool
That lets its Rushes grow
Until they heedless tumble in
And make the Water slow

Impeding navigation bright
Of Shadows going down
Yet even this shall rouse itself
When freshets come along.

c. 1873   *1945*

Art thou the thing I wanted?
Begone – my Tooth has grown –
Supply the minor Palate
That has not starved so long –
I tell thee while I waited
The mystery of Food
Increased till I abjured it
And dine without Like God –

rough draft I

Art thou the thing I wanted?
Begone – my Tooth has grown –
Affront a minor palate
Thou could'st not goad so long –

I tell thee while I waited –
The mystery of Food
Increased till I abjured it
Subsisting now like God –

rough draft II
c. 1873   *1945*

Could Hope inspect her Basis
Her Craft were done –

Has a fictitious Charter
Or it has none –

Balked in the vastest instance
But to renew –
Felled by but one assassin –
Prosperity –

c. 1873   1945

1284

Had we our senses
But perhaps 'tis well they're not at Home
So intimate with Madness
He's liable with them

Had we the eyes within our Head –
How well that we are Blind –
We could not look upon the Earth –
So utterly unmoved –

c. 1873   1945

1285

I know Suspense – it steps so terse
And turns so weak away –
Besides – Suspense is neighborly
When I am riding by –

Is always at the Window
Though lately I descry
And mention to my Horses
The need is not of me –

c. 1873   1945

1286

I thought that nature was enough
Till Human nature came
But that the other did absorb
As Parallax a Flame –

Of Human nature just aware
There added the Divine
Brief struggle for capacity
The power to contain

Is always as the contents
But give a Giant room
And you will lodge a Giant
And not a smaller man

c. *1873*   *1945*

1287

In this short Life
That only lasts an hour
How much – how little – is
Within our power

c. *1873*   *1945*

1288

Lain in Nature – so suffice us
The enchantless Pod
When we advertise existence
For the missing Seed –

Maddest Heart that God created
Cannot move a sod
Pasted by the simple summer
On the Longed for Dead

c. *1873*   *1945*

1289

Left in immortal Youth
On that low Plain
That hath nor Retrospection
Nor Again –
Ransomed from years –
Sequestered from Decay

Canceled like Dawn
In comprehensive Day –

c. *1873*

1945

1290

The most pathetic thing I do
Is play I hear from you –
I make believe until my Heart
Almost believes it too
But when I break it with the news
You knew it was not true
I wish I had not broken it –
Goliah – so would you –

c. *1873*

1945

1291

Until the Desert knows
That Water grows
His Sands suffice
But let him once suspect
That Caspian Fact
Sahara dies

Utmost is relative –
Have not or Have
Adjacent sums
Enough – the first Abode
On the familiar Road
Galloped in Dreams –

c. *1873*

1945

1292

Yesterday is History,
'Tis so far away –
Yesterday is Poetry –
'Tis Philosophy –

[563]

Yesterday is mystery –
Where it is Today
While we shrewdly speculate
Flutter both away

c. 1873   *1945*

1293

The things we thought that we should do
We other things have done
But those peculiar industries
Have never been begun –

The Lands we thought that we should seek
When large enough to run
By Speculation ceded
To Speculation's Son –

The Heaven, in which we hoped to pause
When Discipline was done
Untenable to Logic
But possibly the one –

c. 1874   *1931*

1294

Of Life to own –
From Life to draw –
But never touch the reservoir –

1874   *1931*

1295

Two Lengths has every Day –
Its absolute extent
And Area superior
By Hope or Horror lent –

Eternity will be
Velocity or Pause

At Fundamental Signals
From Fundamental Laws.

To die is not to go –
On Doom's consummate Chart
No Territory new is staked –
Remain thou as thou art.

c. 1874   *1914*

1296

Death's Waylaying not the sharpest
Of the thefts of Time –
There Marauds a sorer Robber,
Silence – is his name –
No Assault, nor any Menace
Doth betoken him.
But from Life's consummate Cluster –
He supplants the Balm.

c. 1874   *1931*

1297

Go slow, my soul, to feed thyself
Upon his rare approach –
Go rapid, lest Competing Death
Prevail upon the Coach –
Go timid, should his final eye
Determine thee amiss –
Go boldly – for thou paid'st his price
Redemption – for a Kiss –

c. 1874   *1894*

1298

The Mushroom is the Elf of Plants –
At Evening, it is not –
At Morning, in a Truffled Hut
It stop upon a Spot

As if it tarried always
And yet its whole Career
Is shorter than a Snake's Delay
And fleeter than a Tare –

'Tis Vegetation's Juggler –
The Germ of Alibi –
Doth like a Bubble antedate
And like a Bubble, hie –

I feel as if the Grass was pleased
To have it intermit –
This surreptitious scion
Of Summer's circumspect.

Had Nature any supple Face
Or could she one contemn –
Had Nature an Apostate –
That Mushroom – it is Him!

c. *1874*   *1891*

1299

Delight's Despair at setting
Is that Delight is less
Than the sufficing Longing
That so impoverish.

Enchantment's Perihelion
Mistaken oft has been
For the Authentic orbit
Of its Anterior Sun.

c. *1874*   *1945*

1300

From his slim Palace in the Dust
He relegates the Realm,
More loyal for the exody
That has befallen him.

c. *1874*   *1945*

[566]

1301

I cannot want it more –
I cannot want it less –
My Human Nature's fullest force
Expends itself on this.

And yet it nothing is
To him who easy owns –
Is Worth itself or Distance
He fathoms who obtains.

c. 1874

1945

1302

I think that the Root of the Wind is Water –
It would not sound so deep
Were it a Firmamental Product –
Airs no Oceans keep –
Mediterranean intonations –
To a Current's Ear –
There is a maritime conviction
In the Atmosphere –

c. 1874

1914

1303

Not One by Heaven defrauded stay –
Although he seem to steal
He restitutes in some sweet way
Secreted in his will –

c. 1874

1914

1304

Not with a Club, the Heart is broken
Nor with a Stone –
A Whip so small you could not see it
I've known

[567]

To lash the Magic Creature
Till it fell,
Yet that Whip's Name
Too noble then to tell.

Magnanimous as Bird
By Boy descried –
Singing unto the Stone
Of which it died –

Shame need not crouch
In such an Earth as Ours –
Shame – stand erect –
The Universe is yours.

c. 1874   *1896*

1305

Recollect the Face of me
When in thy Felicity,
Due in Paradise today
Guest of mine assuredly –

Other Courtesies have been –
Other Courtesy may be –
We commend ourselves to thee
Paragon of Chivalry.

c. 1874   *1945*

1306

Surprise is like a thrilling – pungent –
Upon a tasteless meat
Alone – too acrid – but combined
An edible Delight.

c. 1874   *1945*

1307

That short – potential stir
That each can make but once –

[568]

That Bustle so illustrious
'Tis almost Consequence –

Is the éclat of Death –
Oh, thou unknown Renown
That not a Beggar would accept
Had he the power to spurn –

c. 1874   1890

1308

The Day she goes
Or Day she stays
Are equally supreme –
Existence has a stated width
Departed, or at Home –

c. 1874   1945

1309

The Infinite a sudden Guest
Has been assumed to be –
But how can that stupendous come
Which never went away?

c. 1874   1945

1310

The Notice that is called the Spring
Is but a month from here –
Put up my Heart thy Hoary work
And take a Rosy Chair.

Not any House the Flowers keep –
The Birds enamor Care –
Our salary the longest Day
Is nothing but a Bier.

c. 1874   1945

This dirty – little – Heart
Is freely mine.
I won it with a Bun –
A Freckled shrine –

But eligibly fair
To him who sees
The Visage of the Soul
And not the knees.

c. 1874   *1945*

To break so vast a Heart
Required a Blow as vast –
No Zephyr felled this Cedar straight –
'Twas undeserved Blast –

c. 1874   *1945*

Warm in her Hand these accents lie
While faithful and afar
The Grace so awkward for her sake
Its fond subjection wear –

c. 1874   *1945*

When a Lover is a Beggar
Abject is his Knee –
When a Lover is an Owner
Different is he –

What he begged is then the Beggar –
Oh disparity –
Bread of Heaven resents bestowal
Like an obloquy –

c. 1878   *1945*

1315

Which is the best – the Moon or the Crescent?
Neither – said the Moon –
That is best which is not – Achieve it –
You efface the Sheen.

Not of detention is Fruition –
Shudder to attain.
Transport's decomposition follows –
He is Prism born.

c. 1874

1945

1316

Winter is good – his Hoar Delights
Italic flavor yield –
To Intellects inebriate
With Summer, or the World –

Generic as a Quarry
And hearty – as a Rose –
Invited with Asperity
But welcome when he goes.

c. 1874

1945

1317

Abraham to kill him
Was distinctly told –
Isaac was an Urchin –
Abraham was old –

Not a hesitation –
Abraham complied –
Flattered by Obeisance
Tyranny demurred –

Isaac – to his children
Lived to tell the tale –

[571]

Moral – with a Mastiff
Manners may prevail.

c. *1874*   *1945*

1318

Frigid and sweet Her parting Face –
Frigid and fleet my Feet –
Alien and vain whatever Clime
Acrid whatever Fate.

Given to me without the Suit
Riches and Name and Realm –
Who was She to withhold from me
Penury and Home?

c. *1874*   *1945*

1319

How News must feel when travelling
If News have any Heart
Alighting at the Dwelling
'Twill enter like a Dart!

What News must think when pondering
If News have any Thought
Concerning the stupendousness
Of its perceiveless freight!

What News will do when every Man
Shall comprehend as one
And not in all the Universe
A thing to tell remain?

c. *1874*   *1945*

1320

Dear March – Come in –
How glad I am –
I hoped for you before –

Put down your Hat –
You must have walked –
How out of Breath you are –
Dear March, how are you, and the Rest –
Did you leave Nature well –
Oh March, Come right up stairs with me –
I have so much to tell –

I got your Letter, and the Birds –
The Maples never knew that you were coming – till I called
I declare – how Red their Faces grew –
But March, forgive me – and
All those Hills you left for me to Hue –
There was no Purple suitable –
You took it all with you –

Who knocks? That April.
Lock the Door –
I will not be pursued –
He stayed away a Year to call
When I am occupied –
But trifles look so trivial
As soon as you have come

That Blame is just as dear as Praise
And Praise as mere as Blame –

c. 1874   *1896*

1321

Elizabeth told Essex
That she could not forgive
The clemency of Deity
However – might survive –
That secondary succor
We trust that she partook
When suing – like her Essex
For a reprieving Look –

c. 1874   *1945*

1322

Floss won't save you from an Abyss
But a Rope will –
Notwithstanding a Rope for a Souvenir
Is not beautiful –

But I tell you every step is a Trough –
And every stop a Well –
Now will you have the Rope or the Floss?
Prices reasonable –

c. 1874   1945

1323

I never hear that one is dead
Without the chance of Life
Afresh annihilating me
That mightiest Belief,

Too mighty for the Daily mind
That tilling its abyss,
Had Madness, had it once or twice
The yawning Consciousness,

Beliefs are Bandaged, like the Tongue
When Terror were it told
In any Tone commensurate
Would strike us instant Dead

I do not know the man so bold
He dare in lonely Place
That awful stranger Consciousness
Deliberately face –

c. 1874   1945

1324

I send you a decrepit flower
That nature sent to me
At parting – she was going south
And I designed to stay –

Her motive for the souvenir
If sentiment for me
Or circumstance prudential
Withheld invincibly –

c. 1874

1945

1325

Knock with tremor –
These are Caesars –
Should they be at Home
Flee as if you trod unthinking
On the Foot of Doom –

These receded to accostal
Centuries ago –
Should they rend you with "How are you"
What have you to show?

c. 1874

1945

1326

Our little secrets slink away –
Beside God's shall not tell –
He kept his word a Trillion years
And might we not as well –
But for the niggardly delight
To make each other stare
Is there no sweet beneath the sun
With this that may compare –

c. 1874

1945

1327

The Symptom of the Gale –
The Second of Dismay –
Between its Rumor and its Face –
Is almost Revelry –

[575]

The Houses firmer root –
The Heavens cannot be found –
The Upper Surfaces of things
Take covert in the Ground –

The Mem'ry of the Sun
Not Any can recall –
Although by Nature's sterling Watch
So scant an interval –

And when the Noise is caught
And Nature looks around –
"We dreamed it"? She interrogates –
"Good Morning" – We propound?

c. 1874   *1955*

1328

The vastest earthly Day
Is shrunken small
By one Defaulting Face
Behind a Pall –

c. 1874   *1945*

1329

Whether they have forgotten
Or are forgetting now
Or never remembered –
Safer not to know –

Miseries of conjecture
Are a softer woe
Than a Fact of Iron
Hardened with I know –

c. 1874   *1945*

1330

Without a smile – Without a Throe
A Summer's soft Assemblies go
To their entrancing end

Unknown – for all the times we met –
Estranged, however intimate –
What a dissembling Friend –

c. 1874   1945

1331

Wonder – is not precisely Knowing
And not precisely Knowing not –
A beautiful but bleak condition
He has not lived who has not felt –

Suspense – is his maturer Sister –
Whether Adult Delight is Pain
Or of itself a new misgiving –
This is the Gnat that mangles men –

c. 1874   1945

1332

Pink – small – and punctual –
Aromatic – low –
Covert – in April –
Candid – in May –
Dear to the Moss –
Known to the Knoll –
Next to the Robin
In every human Soul –
Bold little Beauty
Bedecked with thee
Nature forswears
Antiquity –

c. 1875   1890

1333

A little Madness in the Spring
Is wholesome even for the King,
But God be with the Clown –

[577]

Who ponders this tremendous scene –
This whole Experiment of Green –
As if it were his own!

c. 1875   1914

1334

How soft this Prison is
How sweet these sullen bars
No Despot but the King of Down
Invented this repose

Of Fate if this is All
Has he no added Realm
A Dungeon but a Kinsman is
Incarceration – Home.

c. 1875   1951

1335

Let me not mar that perfect Dream
By an Auroral stain
But so adjust my daily Night
That it will come again.

Not when we know, the Power accosts –
The Garment of Surprise
Was all our timid Mother wore
At Home – in Paradise.

c. 1875   1947

1336

Nature assigns the Sun –
That – is Astronomy –
Nature cannot enact a Friend –
That – is Astrology.

c. 1875   1951

1337

Upon a Lilac Sea
To toss incessantly
His Plush Alarm
Who fleeing from the Spring
The Spring avenging fling
To Dooms of Balm –

c. 1875   *1945*

1338

What tenements of clover
Are fitting for the bee,
What edifices azure
For butterflies and me –
What residences nimble
Arise and evanesce
Without a rhythmic rumor
Or an assaulting guess.

1875?   *1894*

1339

A Bee his burnished Carriage
Drove boldly to a Rose –
Combinedly alighting –
Himself – his Carriage was –
The Rose received his visit
With frank tranquillity
Withholding not a Crescent
To his Cupidity –
Their Moment consummated –
Remained for him – to flee –
Remained for her – of rapture
But the humility.

c. 1875   *1945*

A Rat surrendered here
A brief career of Cheer
And Fraud and Fear.

Of Ignominy's due
Let all addicted to
Beware.

The most obliging Trap
Its tendency to snap
Cannot resist –

Temptation is the Friend
Repugnantly resigned
At last.

c. 1875   *1945*

Unto the Whole – how add?
Has "All" a further Realm –
Or Utmost an Ulterior?
Oh, Subsidy of Balm!

c. 1875   *1945*

"Was not" was all the Statement.
The Unpretension stuns –
Perhaps – the Comprehension –
They wore no Lexicons –

But lest our Speculation
In inanition die
Because "God took him" mention –
That was Philology –

c. 1875   *1945*

1343

A single Clover Plank
Was all that saved a Bee
A Bee I personally knew
From sinking in the sky –

'Twixt Firmament above
And Firmament below
The Billows of Circumference
Were sweeping him away –

The idly swaying Plank
Responsible to nought
A sudden Freight of Wind assumed
And Bumble Bee was not –

This harrowing event
Transpiring in the Grass
Did not so much as wring from him
A wandering "Alas" –

c. 1875   *1945*

1344

Not any more to be lacked –
Not any more to be known –
Denizen of Significance
For a span so worn –

Even Nature herself
Has forgot it is there –
Sedulous of her Multitudes
Notwithstanding Despair –

Of the Ones that pursued it
Suing it not to go
Some have solaced the longing
To accompany –

Some – rescinded the Wrench –
Others – Shall I say

[581]

Plated the residue of Adz
With Monotony.

c. 1875   1929

1345

An antiquated Grace
Becomes that cherished Face
As well as prime
Enjoining us to part
We and our pouting Heart
Good friends with time

c. 1875   1945

1346

As Summer into Autumn slips
And yet we sooner say
"The Summer" than "the Autumn," lest
We turn the sun away,

And almost count it an Affront
The presence to concede
Of one however lovely, not
The one that we have loved –

So we evade the charge of Years
On one attempting shy
The Circumvention of the Shaft
Of Life's Declivity.

c. 1875   1894

1347

Escape is such a thankful Word
I often in the Night
Consider it unto myself
No spectacle in sight

Escape – it is the Basket
In which the Heart is caught

When down some awful Battlement
The rest of Life is dropt –

'Tis not to sight the savior –
It is to be the saved –
And that is why I lay my Head
Upon this trusty word –

c. 1875   1945

1348

Lift it – with the Feathers
Not alone we fly –
Launch it – the aquatic
Not the only sea –
Advocate the Azure
To the lower Eyes –
He has obligation
Who has Paradise –

c. 1875   1945

1349

I'd rather recollect a setting
Than own a rising sun
Though one is beautiful forgetting –
And true the other one.

Because in going is a Drama
Staying cannot confer
To die divinely once a Twilight –
Than wane is easier –

c. 1875   1945

1350

Luck is not chance –
It's Toil –
Fortune's expensive smile
Is earned –

The Father of the Mine
Is that old-fashioned Coin
We spurned –

c. 1875   1945

1351

You cannot take itself
From any Human soul –
That indestructible estate
Enable him to dwell –
Impregnable as Light
That every man behold
But take away as difficult
As undiscovered Gold –

c. 1875   1945

1352

To his simplicity
To die – was little Fate –
If Duty live – contented
But her Confederate.

c. 1876   1931

1353

The last of Summer is Delight –
Deterred by Retrospect.
'Tis Ecstasy's revealed Review –
Enchantment's Syndicate.

To meet it – nameless as it is –
Without celestial Mail –
Audacious as without a Knock
To walk within the Veil.

c. 1876   1929

1354

The Heart is the Capital of the Mind –
The Mind is a single State –
The Heart and the Mind together make
A single Continent –

One – is the Population –
Numerous enough –
This ecstatic Nation
Seek – it is Yourself.

c. 1876   *1929*

1355

The Mind lives on the Heart
Like any Parasite –
If that is full of Meat
The Mind is fat.

But if the Heart omit
Emaciate the Wit –
The Aliment of it
So absolute.

c. 1876   *1932*

1356

The Rat is the concisest Tenant.
He pays no Rent.
Repudiates the Obligation –
On Schemes intent

Balking our Wit
To sound or circumvent –
Hate cannot harm
A Foe so reticent –
Neither Decree prohibit him –
Lawful as Equilibrium.

c. 1876   *1891*

1357

"Faithful to the end" Amended
From the Heavenly Clause –
Constancy with a Proviso
Constancy abhors –

"Crowns of Life" are servile Prizes
To the stately Heart,
Given for the Giving, solely,
No Emolument.

version I
c. 1876   *1932*

"Faithful to the end" Amended
From the Heavenly clause –
Lucrative indeed the offer
But the Heart withdraws –

"I will give" the base Proviso –
Spare Your "Crown of Life" –
Those it fits, too fair to wear it –
Try it on Yourself –

version II
c. 1876   *1945*

1358

The Treason of an accent
Might Ecstasy transfer –
Of her effacing Fathom
Is no Recoverer –

version I
c. 1876   *1931*

The Treason of an Accent
Might vilify the Joy –
To breathe – corrode the rapture
Of Sanctity to be –

version II
c. 1876   *1914*

[586]

1359

The long sigh of the Frog
Upon a Summer's Day
Enacts intoxication
Upon the Revery –
But his receding Swell
Substantiates a Peace
That makes the Ear inordinate
For corporal release –

c. 1876   1914

1360

I sued the News – yet feared – the News
That such a Realm could be –
"The House not made with Hands" it was –
Thrown open wide to me –

c. 1876   1931

1361

The Flake the Wind exasperate
More eloquently lie
Than if escorted to its Down
By Arm of Chivalry.

c. 1876   1931

1362

Of their peculiar light
I keep one ray
To clarify the Sight
To seek them by –

c. 1876   1931

1363

Summer laid her simple Hat
On its boundless Shelf –

[587]

Unobserved – a Ribbon slipt,
Snatch it for yourself.

Summer laid her supple Glove
In its sylvan Drawer –
Wheresoe'er, or was she –
The demand of Awe?

c. 1876   *1947*

1364

How know it from a Summer's Day?
Its Fervors are as firm –
And nothing in the Countenance
But scintillates the same –
Yet Birds examine it and flee –
And Vans without a name
Inspect the Admonition
And sunder as they came –

c. 1876   *1955*

1365

Take all away –
The only thing worth larceny
Is left – the Immortality –

c. 1876   *1891*

1366A

Brother of Ingots – Ah Peru –
Empty the Hearts that purchased you –

c. 1876   *1945*

1366B

Sister of Ophir –
Ah, Peru –

[588]

Subtle the Sum
That purchase you –

c. 1878   *1932*

1366C

Brother of Ophir
Bright Adieu,
Honor, the shortest route
To you.

c. 1880   *1894*

1367

"Tomorrow" – whose location
The Wise deceives
Though its hallucination
Is last that leaves –
Tomorrow – thou Retriever
Of every tare –
Of Alibi art thou
Or ownest where?

c. 1876   *1951*

1368

Love's stricken "why"
Is all that love can speak –
Built of but just a syllable
The hugest hearts that break.

c. 1876   *1894*

1369

Trusty as the stars
Who quit their shining working
Prompt as when I lit them
In Genesis' new house,
Durable as dawn
Whose antiquated blossom

[589]

Makes a world's suspense
Perish and rejoice.

1876?   *1894*

1370

Gathered into the Earth,
And out of story –
Gathered to that strange Fame –
That lonesome Glory
That hath no omen here – but Awe –

c. 1876   *1945*

1371

How fits his Umber Coat
The Tailor of the Nut?
Combined without a seam
Like Raiment of a Dream –

Who spun the Auburn Cloth?
Computed how the girth?
The Chestnut aged grows
In those primeval Clothes –

We know that we are wise –
Accomplished in Surprise –
Yet by this Countryman –
This nature – how undone!

c. 1876   *1945*

1372

The Sun is one – and on the Tare
He doth as punctual call
As on the conscientious Flower
And estimates them all –

c. 1876   *1945*

The worthlessness of Earthly things
The Ditty is that Nature Sings –
And then – enforces their delight
Till Synods are inordinate –

c. 1876

1945

A Saucer holds a Cup
In sordid human Life
But in a Squirrel's estimate
A Saucer hold a Loaf.

A Table of a Tree
Demands the little King
And every Breeze that run along
His Dining Room do swing.

His Cutlery – he keeps
Within his Russet Lips –
To see it flashing when he dines
Do Birmingham eclipse –

Convicted – could we be
Of our Minutiae
The smallest Citizen that flies
Is heartier than we –

c. 1876

1945

Death warrants are supposed to be
An enginery of equity
A merciful mistake
A pencil in an Idol's Hand
A Devotee has oft consigned
To Crucifix or Block

c. 1876

1945

1376

Dreams are the subtle Dower
That make us rich an Hour –
Then fling us poor
Out of the purple Door
Into the Precinct raw
Possessed before –

c. 1876   1945

1377

Forbidden Fruit a flavor has
That lawful Orchards mocks –
How luscious lies within the Pod
The Pea that Duty locks –

c. 1876   1896

1378

His Heart was darker than the starless night
For that there is a morn
But in this black Receptacle
Can be no Bode of Dawn

c. 1876   1945

1379

His Mansion in the Pool
The Frog forsakes –
He rises on a Log
And statements makes –
His Auditors two Worlds
Deducting me –
The Orator of April
Is hoarse Today –
His Mittens at his Feet
No Hand hath he –
His eloquence a Bubble
As Fame should be –

Applaud him to discover
To your chagrin
Demosthenes has vanished
In Waters Green –

c. 1876   1945

1380

How much the present moment means
To those who've nothing more –
The Fop – the Carp – the Atheist –
Stake an entire store
Upon a Moment's shallow Rim
While their commuted Feet
The Torrents of Eternity
Do all but inundate –

c. 1876   1945

1381

I suppose the time will come
Aid it in the coming
When the Bird will crowd the Tree
And the Bee be booming.

I suppose the time will come
Hinder it a little
When the Corn in Silk will dress
And in Chintz the Apple

I believe the Day will be
When the Jay will giggle
At his new white House the Earth
That, too, halt a little –

c. 1876   1945

1382

In many and reportless places
We feel a Joy –

Reportless, also, but sincere as Nature
Or Deity –

It comes, without a consternation –
Dissolves – the same –
But leaves a sumptuous Destitution –
Without a Name –

Profane it by a search – we cannot
It has no home –
Nor we who having once inhaled it –
Thereafter roam.

c. 1876   1945

1383

Long Years apart – can make no
Breach a second cannot fill –
The absence of the Witch does not
Invalidate the spell –

The embers of a Thousand Years
Uncovered by the Hand
That fondled them when they were Fire
Will stir and understand –

c. 1876   1945

1384

Praise it – 'tis dead –
It cannot glow –
Warm this inclement Ear
With the encomium it earned
Since it was gathered here –
Invest this alabaster Zest
In the Delights of Dust –
Remitted – since it flitted it
In recusance august.

c. 1876   1945

1385

"Secrets" is a daily word
Yet does not exist –
Muffled – it remits surmise –
Murmured – it has ceased –
Dungeoned in the Human Breast
Doubtless secrets lie –
But that Grate inviolate –
Goes nor comes away
Nothing with a Tongue or Ear –
Secrets stapled there
Will emerge but once – and dumb –
To the Sepulchre –

c. 1879   1945

1386

Summer – we all have seen –
A few of us – believed –
A few – the more aspiring
Unquestionably loved –

But Summer does not care –
She goes her spacious way
As eligible as the moon
To our Temerity –

The Doom to be adored –
The Affluence conferred –
Unknown as to an Ecstasy
The Embryo endowed –

c. 1876   1945

1387

The Butterfly's Numidian Gown
With spots of Burnish roasted on
Is proof against the Sun
Yet prone to shut its spotted Fan

And panting on a Clover lean
As if it were undone –

c. *1876*

1945

1388

Those Cattle smaller than a Bee
That herd upon the eye –
Whose tillage is the passing Crumb –
Those Cattle are the Fly –
Of Barns for Winter – blameless –
Extemporaneous stalls
They found to our objection –
On eligible walls –
Reserving the presumption
To suddenly descend
And gallop on the Furniture –
Or odiouser offend –
Of their peculiar calling
Unqualified to judge
To Nature we remand them
To justify or scourge –

c. *1876*

1945

1389

Touch lightly Nature's sweet Guitar
Unless thou know'st the Tune
Or every Bird will point at thee
Because a Bard too soon –

c. *1876*

1945

1390

These held their Wick above the West –
Till when the Red declined –
Or how the Amber aided it –
Defied to be defined –

Then waned without disparagement
In a dissembling Hue
That would not let the Eye decide
Did it abide or no –

c. 1877   *1951*

1391

They might not need me – yet they might –
I'll let my Heart be just in sight –
A smile so small as mine might be
Precisely their necessity –

c. 1877   *1894*

1392

Hope is a strange invention –
A Patent of the Heart –
In unremitting action
Yet never wearing out –

Of this electric Adjunct
Not anything is known
But its unique momentum
Embellish all we own –

c. 1877   *1931*

1393

Lay this Laurel on the One
Too intrinsic for Renown –
Laurel – veil your deathless tree –
Him you chasten, that is He!

c. 1877   *1891*

1394

Whose Pink career may have a close
Portentous as our own, who knows?

To imitate these Neighbors fleet
In awe and innocence, were meet.

c. 1877   1894

1395

After all Birds have been investigated and laid aside –
Nature imparts the little Blue-Bird – assured
Her conscientious Voice will soar unmoved
Above ostensible Vicissitude.

First at the March – competing with the Wind –
Her panting note exalts us – like a friend –
Last to adhere when Summer cleaves away –
Elegy of Integrity.

c. 1877   1932

1396

She laid her docile Crescent down
And this confiding Stone
Still states to Dates that have forgot
The News that she is gone –

So constant to its stolid trust,
The Shaft that never knew –
It shames the Constancy that fled
Before its emblem flew –

c. 1877   1896

1397

It sounded as if the Streets were running
And then – the Streets stood still –
Eclipse – was all we could see at the Window
And Awe – was all we could feel.

By and by – the boldest stole out of his Covert
To see if Time was there –

Nature was in an Opal Apron,
Mixing fresher Air.

c. 1877   *1891*

1398

I have no Life but this –
To lead it here –
Nor any Death – but lest
Dispelled from there –

Nor tie to Earths to come –
Nor Action new –
Except through this extent –
The Realm of you –

c. 1877   *1891*

1399

Perhaps they do not go so far
As we who stay, suppose –
Perhaps come closer, for the lapse
Of their corporeal clothes –

It may be know so certainly
How short we have to fear
That comprehension antedates
And estimates us there –

c. 1877   1947

1400

What mystery pervades a well!
That water lives so far –
A neighbor from another world
Residing in a jar

Whose limit none have ever seen,
But just his lid of glass –
Like looking every time you please
In an abyss's face!

The grass does not appear afraid,
I often wonder he
Can stand so close and look so bold
At what is awe to me.

Related somehow they may be,
The sedge stands next the sea –
Where he is floorless
And does no timidity betray

But nature is a stranger yet;
The ones that cite her most
Have never passed her haunted house,
Nor simplified her ghost.

To pity those that know her not
Is helped by the regret
That those who know her, know her less
The nearer her they get.

1877?   1896

1401

To own a Susan of my own
Is of itself a Bliss –
Whatever Realm I forfeit, Lord,
Continue me in this!

c. 1877   1932

1402

To the stanch Dust
We safe commit thee –
Tongue if it hath,
Inviolate to thee –
Silence – denote –
And Sanctity – enforce thee –
Passenger – of Infinity –

c. 1877   1914

My Maker – let me be
Enamored most of thee –
But nearer this
I more should miss –

c. 1877

1915

1404

March is the Month of Expectation.
The things we do not know –
The Persons of prognostication
Are coming now –
We try to show becoming firmness –
But pompous Joy
Betrays us, as his first Betrothal
Betrays a Boy.

c. 1877

1914

1405

Bees are Black, with Gilt Surcingles –
Buccaneers of Buzz.
Ride abroad in ostentation
And subsist on Fuzz.

Fuzz ordained – not Fuzz contingent –
Marrows of the Hill.
Jugs – a Universe's fracture
Could not jar or spill.

c. 1877

1945

1406

No Passenger was known to flee –
That lodged a night in memory –
That wily – subterranean Inn
Contrives that none go out again –

c. 1877

1945

1407

A Field of Stubble, lying sere
Beneath the second Sun –
Its Toils to Brindled People thrust –
Its Triumphs – to the Bin –
Accosted by a timid Bird
Irresolute of Alms –
Is often seen – but seldom felt,
On our New England Farms –

c. 1877   1932

1408

The Fact that Earth is Heaven –
Whether Heaven is Heaven or not
If not an Affidavit
Of that specific Spot
Not only must confirm us
That it is not for us
But that it would affront us
To dwell in such a place –

c. 1877   1945

1409

Could mortal lip divine
The undeveloped Freight
Of a delivered syllable
'Twould crumble with the weight.

c. 1877   1894

1410

I shall not murmur if at last
The ones I loved below
Permission have to understand
For what I shunned them so –
Divulging it would rest my Heart
But it would ravage theirs –

Why, Katie, Treason has a Voice –
But mine – dispels – in Tears.

c. *1877*

1945

1411

Of Paradise' existence
All we know
Is the uncertain certainty –
But its vicinity infer,
By its Bisecting
Messenger –

c. *1877*

1945

1412

Shame is the shawl of Pink
In which we wrap the Soul
To keep it from infesting Eyes –
The elemental Veil
Which helpless Nature drops
When pushed upon a scene
Repugnant to her probity –
Shame is the tint divine.

c. *1877*

1945

1413

Sweet Skepticism of the Heart –
That knows – and does not know –
And tosses like a Fleet of Balm –
Affronted by the snow –
Invites and then retards the Truth
Lest Certainty be sere
Compared with the delicious throe
Of transport thrilled with Fear –

c. *1877*

1945

1414

Unworthy of her Breast
Though by that scathing test
What Soul survive?
By her exacting light
How counterfeit the white
We chiefly have!

c. 1877   1945

1415

A wild Blue sky abreast of Winds
That threatened it – did run
And crouched behind his Yellow Door
Was the defiant sun –
Some conflict with those upper friends
So genial in the main
That we deplore peculiarly
Their arrogant campaign –

c. 1877   1945

1416

Crisis is sweet and yet the Heart
Upon the hither side
Has Dowers of Prospective
To Denizens denied

Inquire of the closing Rose
Which rapture she preferred
And she will point you sighing
To her rescinded Bud.

c. 1877   1914

1417

How Human Nature dotes
On what it can't detect.

The moment that a Plot is plumbed
Prospective is extinct –

Prospective is the friend
Reserved for us to know
When Constancy is clarified
Of Curiosity –

Of subjects that resist
Redoubtablest is this
Where go we –
Go we anywhere
Creation after this?

c. 1877   *1945*

1418

How lonesome the Wind must feel Nights –
When people have put out the Lights
And everything that has an Inn
Closes the shutter and goes in –

How pompous the Wind must feel Noons
Stepping to incorporeal Tunes
Correcting errors of the sky
And clarifying scenery

How mighty the Wind must feel Morns
Encamping on a thousand dawns
Espousing each and spurning all
Then soaring to his Temple Tall –

c. 1877   *1945*

1419

It was a quiet seeming Day –
There was no harm in earth or sky –
Till with the closing sun
There strayed an accidental Red
A Strolling Hue, one would have said
To westward of the Town –

But when the Earth began to jar
And Houses vanished with a roar
And Human Nature hid
We comprehended by the Awe
As those that Dissolution saw
The Poppy in the Cloud

c. 1877   1945

1420

One Joy of so much anguish
Sweet nature has for me
I shun it as I do Despair
Or dear iniquity –
Why Birds, a Summer morning
Before the Quick of Day
Should stab my ravished spirit
With Dirks of Melody
Is part of an inquiry
That will receive reply
When Flesh and Spirit sunder
In Death's Immediately –

c. 1877   1945

1421

Such are the inlets of the mind –
His outlets – would you see
Ascend with me the eminence
Of immortality –

c. 1877   1945

1422

Summer has two Beginnings –
Beginning once in June –
Beginning in October
Affectingly again –

Without, perhaps, the Riot
But graphicker for Grace –
As finer is a going
Than a remaining Face –

Departing then – forever –
Forever – until May –
Forever is deciduous –
Except to those who die –

c. 1877

1945

1423

The fairest Home I ever knew
Was founded in an Hour
By Parties also that I knew
A spider and a Flower –
A manse of mechlin and of Floss –

c. 1877

1945

1424

The Gentian has a parched Corolla –
Like azure dried
'Tis Nature's buoyant juices
Beatified –
Without a vaunt or sheen
As casual as Rain
And as benign –

When most is past – it comes –
Nor isolate it seems
Its Bond its Friend –
To fill its Fringed career
And aid an aged Year
Abundant end –

Its lot – were it forgot –
This Truth endear –

[607]

Fidelity is gain
Creation o'er –

c. *1877*   *1945*

1425

The inundation of the Spring
Enlarges every soul –
It sweeps the tenement away
But leaves the Water whole –

In which the soul at first estranged –
Seeks faintly for its shore
But acclimated – pines no more
For that Peninsula –

c. *1877*   *1914*

1426

The pretty Rain from those sweet Eaves
Her unintending Eyes –
Took her own Heart, including ours,
By innocent Surprise –

The wrestle in her simple Throat
To hold the feeling down
That vanquished her – defeated Feat –
Was Fervor's sudden Crown –

c. *1877*   *1945*

1427

To earn it by disdaining it
Is Fame's consummate Fee –
He loves what spurns him –
Look behind – He is pursuing thee.

So let us gather – every Day –
The Aggregate of

Life's Bouquet
Be Honor and not shame –

c. 1877   *1945*

1428

Water makes many Beds
For those averse to sleep –
Its awful chamber open stands –
Its Curtains blandly sweep –
Abhorrent is the Rest
In undulating Rooms
Whose Amplitude no end invades –
Whose Axis never comes.

c. 1877   *1945*

1429

We shun because we prize her Face
Lest sight's ineffable disgrace
Our Adoration stain

c. 1877   *1945*

1430

Who never wanted – maddest Joy
Remains to him unknown –
The Banquet of Abstemiousness
Defaces that of Wine –

Within its reach, though yet ungrasped
Desire's perfect Goal –
No nearer – lest the Actual –
Should disenthrall thy soul –

c. 1877   *1896*

1431

With Pinions of Disdain
The soul can farther fly

Than any feather specified
in Ornithology –
It wafts this sordid Flesh
Beyond its dull – control
And during its electric gale –
The body is a soul –
instructing by the same –
How little work it be –
To put off filaments like this
for immortality

c. 1877   1945

1432

Spurn the temerity –
Rashness of Calvary –
Gay were Gethsemane
Knew we of Thee –

c. 1878   1927

1433

How brittle are the Piers
On which our Faith doth tread –
No Bridge below doth totter so –
Yet none hath such a Crowd.

It is as old as God –
Indeed – 'twas built by him –
He sent his Son to test the Plank,
And he pronounced it firm.

c. 1878   1894

1434

Go not too near a House of Rose –
The depredation of a Breeze
Or inundation of a Dew
Alarms its walls away –

Nor try to tie the Butterfly,
Nor climb the Bars of Ecstasy,
In insecurity to lie
Is Joy's insuring quality.

c. 1878   *1894*

1435

Not that he goes – we love him more
Who led us while he stayed.
Beyond earth's trafficking frontier,
For what he moved, he made.

c. 1878   *1894*

1436

Than Heaven more remote,
For Heaven is the root,
But these the flitted seed,
More flown indeed
Than ones that never were,
Or those that hide, and are.

What madness, by their side,
A vision to provide
Of future days
They cannot praise.

My soul, to find them, come,
They cannot call, they're dumb,
Nor prove, nor woo,
But that they have abode
Is absolute as God,
And instant, too.

1878?   *1894*

1437

A Dew sufficed itself –
And satisfied a Leaf

[611]

And felt "how vast a destiny" –
"How trivial is Life!"

The Sun went out to work –
The Day went out to play
And not again that Dew be seen
By Physiognomy

Whether by Day Abducted
Or emptied by the Sun
Into the Sea in passing
Eternally unknown

Attested to this Day
That awful Tragedy
By Transport's instability
And Doom's celerity.

c. 1878   *1896*

1438

Behold this little Bane –
The Boon of all alive –
As common as it is unknown
The name of it is Love –

To lack of it is Woe –
To own of it is Wound –
Not elsewhere – if in Paradise
Its Tantamount be found –

c. 1878   *1945*

1439

How ruthless are the gentle –
How cruel are the kind –
God broke his contract to his Lamb
To qualify the Wind –

c. 1878   *1945*

1440

The healed Heart shows its shallow scar
With confidential moan –
Not mended by Mortality
Are Fabrics truly torn –
To go its convalescent way
So shameless is to see
More genuine were Perfidy
Than such Fidelity.

c. 1878   *1914*

1441

These Fevered Days – to take them to the Forest
Where Waters cool around the mosses crawl –
And shade is all that devastates the stillness
Seems it sometimes this would be all –

c. 1878   *1945*

1442

To mend each tattered Faith
There is a needle fair
Though no appearance indicate –
'Tis threaded in the Air –

And though it do not wear
As if it never Tore
'Tis very comfortable indeed
And spacious as before –

c. 1878   *1945*

1443

A chilly Peace infests the Grass
The Sun respectful lies –
Not any Trance of industry
These shadows scrutinize –

Whose Allies go no more astray
For service or for Glee –
But all mankind deliver here
From whatsoever sea –

c. 1878   1945

1444

A little Snow was here and there
Disseminated in her Hair –
Since she and I had met and played
Decade had gathered to Decade –

But Time had added not obtained
Impregnable the Rose
For summer too indelible
Too obdurate for Snows –

c. 1878   1945

1445

Death is the supple Suitor
That wins at last –
It is a stealthy Wooing
Conducted first
By pallid innuendoes
And dim approach
But brave at last with Bugles
And a bisected Coach
It bears away in triumph
To Troth unknown
And Kindred as responsive
As Porcelain.

c. 1878   1945

1446

His Mind like Fabrics of the East
Displayed to the despair

Of everyone but here and there
An humble Purchaser –
For though his price was not of Gold –
More arduous there is –
That one should comprehend the worth
Was all the price there was –

c. *1878*   *1945*

1447

How good his Lava Bed,
To this laborious Boy –
Who must be up to call the World
And dress the sleepy Day –

c. *1878*   *1945*

1448

How soft a Caterpillar steps –
I find one on my Hand
From such a velvet world it comes
Such plushes at command
Its soundless travels just arrest
My slow – terrestrial eye
Intent upon its own career
What use has it for me –

c. *1878*   *1945*

1449

I thought the Train would never come –
How slow the whistle sang –
I don't believe a peevish Bird
So whimpered for the Spring –
I taught my Heart a hundred times
Precisely what to say –
Provoking Lover, when you came
Its Treatise flew away

To hide my strategy too late
To wiser be too soon –
For miseries so halcyon
The happiness atone –

c. *1878*   *1945*

1450

The Road was lit with Moon and star –
The Trees were bright and still –
Descried I – by the distant Light
A Traveller on a Hill –
To magic Perpendiculars
Ascending, though Terrene –
Unknown his shimmering ultimate –
But he indorsed the sheen –

c. *1878*   *1945*

1451

Whoever disenchants
A single Human soul
By failure of irreverence
Is guilty of the whole.

As guileless as a Bird
As graphic as a star
Till the suggestion sinister
Things are not what they are –

c. *1878*   *1945*

1452

Your thoughts don't have words every day
They come a single time
Like signal esoteric sips
Of the communion Wine
Which while you taste so native seems
So easy so to be
You cannot comprehend its price
Nor its infrequency

c. *1878*   *1945*

1453

A Counterfeit – a Plated Person –
I would not be –
Whatever strata of Iniquity
My Nature underlie –
Truth is good Health – and Safety, and the Sky.
How meagre, what an Exile – is a Lie,
And Vocal – when we die –

c. 1879   1924

1454

Those not live yet
Who doubt to live again –
"Again" is of a twice
But this – is one –
The Ship beneath the Draw
Aground – is he?
Death – so – the Hyphen of the Sea –
Deep is the Schedule
Of the Disk to be –
Costumeless Consciousness –
That is he –

c. 1879   1932

1455

Opinion is a flitting thing,
But Truth, outlasts the Sun –
If then we cannot own them both –
Possess the oldest one –

c. 1879   1924

1456

So gay a Flower
Bereaves the Mind
As if it were a Woe –

[617]

Is Beauty an Affliction – then?
Tradition ought to know –

c. 1879

1914

1457

It stole along so stealthy
Suspicion it was done
Was dim as to the wealthy
Beginning not to own –

c. 1879

1915

1458

Time's wily Chargers will not wait
At any Gate but Woe's –
But there – so gloat to hesitate
They will not stir for blows –

c. 1879

1932

1459

Belshazzar had a Letter –
He never had but one –
Belshazzar's Correspondent
Concluded and begun
In that immortal Copy
The Conscience of us all
Can read without its Glasses
On Revelation's Wall –

c. 1879

1890

1460

His Cheek is his Biographer –
As long as he can blush
Perdition is Opprobrium –
Past that, he sins in peace –

c. 1879

1914

1461

"Heavenly Father" – take to thee
The supreme iniquity
Fashioned by thy candid Hand
In a moment contraband –
Though to trust us – seem to us
More respectful – "We are Dust" –
We apologize to thee
For thine own Duplicity –

c. 1879   1914

1462

We knew not that we were to live –
Nor when – we are to die –
Our ignorance – our cuirass is –
We wear Mortality
As lightly as an Option Gown
Till asked to take it off –
By his intrusion, God is known –
It is the same with Life –

c. 1879   1894

1463

A Route of Evanescence
With a revolving Wheel –
A Resonance of Emerald –
A Rush of Cochineal –
And every Blossom on the Bush
Adjusts its tumbled Head –
The mail from Tunis, probably,
An easy Morning's Ride –

c. 1879   1891

1464

One thing of it we borrow
And promise to return –

[619]

The Booty and the Sorrow
Its Sweetness to have known –
One thing of it we covet –
The power to forget –
The Anguish of the Avarice
Defrays the Dross of it –

c. 1879
1894

1465

Before you thought of Spring
Except as a Surmise
You see – God bless his suddenness –
A Fellow in the Skies
Of independent Hues
A little weather worn
Inspiriting habiliments
Of Indigo and Brown –
With specimens of Song
As if for you to choose –
Discretion in the interval
With gay delays he goes
To some superior Tree
Without a single Leaf
And shouts for joy to Nobody
But his seraphic self –

c. 1871
1891

1466

One of the ones that Midas touched
Who failed to touch us all
Was that confiding Prodigal
The reeling Oriole –

So drunk he disavows it
With badinage divine –
So dazzling we mistake him
For an alighting Mine –

A Pleader – a Dissembler –
An Epicure – a Thief –
Betimes an Oratorio –
An Ecstasy in chief –

The Jesuit of Orchards
He cheats as he enchants
Of an entire Attar
For his decamping wants –

The splendor of a Burmah
The Meteor of Birds,
Departing like a Pageant
Of Ballads and of Bards –

I never thought that Jason sought
For any Golden Fleece
But then I am a rural man
With thoughts that make for Peace –

But if there were a Jason,
Tradition bear with me
Behold his lost Aggrandizement
Upon the Apple Tree –

c. 1879   *1891*

1467

A little overflowing word
That any, hearing, had inferred
For Ardor or for Tears,
Though Generations pass away,
Traditions ripen and decay,
As eloquent appears –

c. 1879   *1924*

1468

A winged spark doth soar about –
I never met it near

[621]

For Lightning it is oft mistook
When nights are hot and sere —

Its twinkling Travels it pursues
Above the Haunts of men —
A speck of Rapture — first perceived
By feeling it is gone —
Rekindled by some action quaint

c. 1879   *1945*

1469

If wrecked upon the Shoal of Thought
How is it with the Sea?
The only Vessel that is shunned
Is safe — Simplicity —

c. 1879   *1945*

1470

The Sweets of Pillage, can be known
To no one but the Thief —
Compassion for Integrity
Is his divinest Grief —

c. 1879   *1914*

1471

Their Barricade against the Sky
The martial Trees withdraw
And with a Flag at every turn
Their Armies are no more.

What Russet Halts in Nature's March
They indicate or cause
An inference of Mexico
Effaces the Surmise —

Recurrent to the After Mind
That Massacre of Air —

[622]

The Wound that was not Wound nor Scar
But Holidays of War —

c. 1879   1945

1472

To see the Summer Sky
Is Poetry, though never in a Book it lie —
True Poems flee —

c. 1879   1945

1473

We talked with each other about each other
Though neither of us spoke —
We were listening to the seconds' Races
And the Hoofs of the Clock —
Pausing in Front of our Palsied Faces
Time compassion took —
Arks of Reprieve he offered to us —
Ararats — we took —

c. 1879   1945

1474

Estranged from Beauty — none can be —
For Beauty is Infinity —
And power to be finite ceased
Before Identity was leased.

c. 1879   1945

1475

Fame is the one that does not stay —
Its occupant must die
Or out of sight of estimate
Ascend incessantly —
Or be that most insolvent thing
A Lightning in the Germ —

Electrical the embryo
But we demand the Flame

c. 1879 *1945*

1476

His voice decrepit was with Joy –
Her words did totter so
How old the News of Love must be
To make Lips elderly
That purled a moment since with Glee –
Is it Delight or Woe –
Or Terror – that do decorate
This livid interview –

c. 1879 *1945*

1477

How destitute is he
Whose Gold is firm
Who finds it every time
The small stale Sum –
When Love with but a Pence
Will so display
As is a disrespect
To India.

c. 1879 *1914*

1478

Look back on Time, with kindly eyes –
He doubtless did his best –
How softly sinks that trembling sun
In Human Nature's West –

c. 1879 *1890*

1479

The Devil – had he fidelity
Would be the best friend –

Because he has ability –
But Devils cannot mend –
Perfidy is the virtue
That would but he resign
The Devil – without question
Were thoroughly divine

c. *1879*

1914

1480

The fascinating chill that music leaves
Is Earth's corroboration
Of Ecstasy's impediment –
'Tis Rapture's germination
In timid and tumultuous soil
A fine – estranging creature –
To something upper wooing us
But not to our Creator –

c. *1879*

1945

1481

The way Hope builds his House
It is not with a sill –
Nor Rafter – has that Edifice
But only Pinnacle –

Abode in as supreme
This superficies
As if it were of Ledges smit
Or mortised with the Laws –

c. *1879*

1945

1482

'Tis whiter than an Indian Pipe –
'Tis dimmer than a Lace –
No stature has it, like a Fog
When you approach the place –

Not any voice imply it here
Or intimate it there
A spirit – how doth it accost –
What function hath the Air?
This limitless Hyperbole
Each one of us shall be –
'Tis Drama – if Hypothesis
It be not Tragedy –

c. 1879   *1896*

1483

The Robin is a Gabriel
In humble circumstances –
His Dress denotes him socially,
Of Transport's Working Classes –
He has the punctuality
Of the New England Farmer –
The same oblique integrity,
A Vista vastly warmer –

A small but sturdy Residence,
A self denying Household,
The Guests of Perspicacity
Are all that cross his Threshold –
As covert as a Fugitive,
Cajoling Consternation
By Ditties to the Enemy
And Sylvan Punctuation –

c. 1880   *1894*

1484

We shall find the Cube of the Rainbow.
Of that, there is no doubt.
But the Arc of a Lover's conjecture
Eludes the finding out.

c. 1880   *1894*

1485

Love is done when Love's begun,
Sages say,
But have Sages known?
Truth adjourn your Boon
Without Day.

c. 1880   *1894*

1486

Her spirit rose to such a height
Her countenance it did inflate
Like one that fed on awe.
More prudent to assault the dawn
Than merit the ethereal scorn
That effervesced from her.

c. 1880   *1932*

1487

The Savior must have been
A docile Gentleman –
To come so far so cold a Day
For little Fellowmen –

The Road to Bethlehem
Since He and I were Boys
Was leveled, but for that 'twould be
A rugged billion Miles –

c. 1880   *1915*

1488

Birthday of but a single pang
That there are less to come –
Afflictive is the Adjective
But affluent the doom –

c. 1880   *1915*

1489

A Dimple in the Tomb
Makes that ferocious Room
A Home –

c. 1880   1931

1490

The Face in evanescence lain
Is more distinct than ours –
And ours surrendered for its sake
As Capsules are for Flower's –
Or is it the confiding sheen
Dissenting to be won
Descending to enamor us
Of Detriment divine?

c. 1880   1931

1491

The Road to Paradise is plain,
And holds scarce one.
Not that it is not firm
But we presume
A Dimpled Road
Is more preferred.
The Belles of Paradise are few –
Not me – nor you –
But unsuspected things –
Mines have no Wings.

c. 1880   1945

1492

"And with what body do they come?" –
Then they *do* come – Rejoice!
What Door – What Hour – Run – run – My Soul!
Illuminate the House!

"Body!" Then real – a Face and Eyes –
To know that it is them! –
Paul knew the Man that knew the News –
He passed through Bethlehem –

c. 1880   *1894*

1493

Could that sweet Darkness where they dwell
Be once disclosed to us
The clamor for their loveliness
Would burst the Loneliness –

                                                       1894

1494

The competitions of the sky
Corrodeless ply.

1880?   *1931*

1495

The Thrill came slowly like a Boon for
Centuries delayed
Its fitness growing like the Flood
In sumptuous solitude –
The desolation only missed
While Rapture changed its Dress
And stood amazed before the Change
In ravished Holiness –

c. 1880   *1945*

1496

All that I do
Is in review
To his enamored mind
I know his eye
Where e'er I ply
Is pushing close behind

[629]

Not any Port
Nor any flight
But he doth there preside
What omnipresence lies in wait
For her to be a Bride

c. 1880   *1945*

1497

Facts by our side are never sudden
Until they look around
And then they scare us like a spectre
Protruding from the Ground –

The height of our portentous Neighbor
We never know –
Till summoned to his recognition
By an Adieu –

Adieu for whence
The sage cannot conjecture
The bravest die
As ignorant of their resumption
As you or I –

c. 1880   *1945*

1498

Glass was the Street – in tinsel Peril
Tree and Traveller stood –
Filled was the Air with merry venture
Hearty with Boys the Road –

Shot the lithe Sleds like shod vibrations
Emphasized and gone
It is the Past's supreme italic
Makes this Present mean –

c. 1880   *1945*

How firm Eternity must look
To crumbling men like me
The only Adamant Estate
In all Identity –

How mighty to the insecure
Thy Physiognomy
To whom not any Face cohere –
Unless concealed in thee

c. 1880

1945

It came his turn to beg –
The begging for the life
Is different from another Alms
'Tis Penury in Chief –

I scanned his narrow realm
I gave him leave to live
Lest Gratitude revive the snake
Though smuggled his reprieve

c. 1880

1945

Its little Ether Hood
Doth sit upon its Head –
The millinery supple
Of the sagacious God –

Till when it slip away
A nothing at a time –
And Dandelion's Drama
Expires in a stem.

c. 1880

1945

1502

I saw the wind within her
I knew it blew for me –
But she must buy my shelter
I asked Humility

c. *1880*   *1955*

1503

More than the Grave is closed to me –
The Grave and that Eternity
To which the Grave adheres –
I cling to nowhere till I fall –
The Crash of nothing, yet of all –
How similar appears –

c. *1880*   *1945*

1504

Of whom so dear
The name to hear
Illumines with a Glow
As intimate – as fugitive
As Sunset on the snow –

c. *1880*   *1945*

1505

She could not live upon the Past
The Present did not know her
And so she sought this sweet at last
And nature gently owned her
The mother that has not a knell
for either Duke or Robin

c. *1880*   *1945*

1506

Summer is shorter than any one –
Life is shorter than Summer –
Seventy Years is spent as quick
As an only Dollar –

Sorrow – now – is polite – and stays –
See how well we spurn him –
Equally to abhor Delight –
Equally retain him –

c. 1880   *1945*

1507

The Pile of Years is not so high
As when you came before
But it is rising every Day
From recollection's Floor
And while by standing on my Heart
I still can reach the top
Efface the mountain with your face
And catch me ere I drop

c. 1880   *1945*

1508

You cannot make Remembrance grow
When it has lost its Root –
The tightening the Soil around
And setting it upright
Deceives perhaps the Universe
But not retrieves the Plant –
Real Memory, like Cedar Feet
Is shod with Adamant –
Nor can you cut Remembrance down
When it shall once have grown –
Its Iron Buds will sprout anew
However overthrown –

c. 1880   *1945*

1509

Mine Enemy is growing old –
I have at last Revenge –
The Palate of the Hate departs –
If any would avenge

Let him be quick – the Viand flits –
It is a faded Meat –
Anger as soon as fed is dead –
'Tis starving makes it fat –

c. *1881*   *1891*

1510

How happy is the little Stone
That rambles in the Road alone,
And doesn't care about Careers
And Exigencies never fears –
Whose Coat of elemental Brown
A passing Universe put on,
And independent as the Sun
Associates or glows alone,
Fulfilling absolute Decree
In casual simplicity –

c. *1881*   *1891*

1511

My country need not change her gown,
Her triple suit as sweet
As when 'twas cut at Lexington,
And first pronounced "a fit."

Great Britain disapproves, "the stars";
Disparagement discreet, –
There's something in their attitude
That taunts her bayonet.

c. *1881*   *1891*

1512

All things swept sole away
This – is immensity –

c. 1881   *1931*

1513

"Go traveling with us!"
Her travels daily be
By routes of ecstasy
To Evening's Sea –

c. 1881   *1931*

1514

An Antiquated Tree
Is cherished of the Crow
Because that Junior Foliage is disrespectful now
To venerable Birds
Whose Corporation Coat
Would decorate Oblivion's
Remotest Consulate.

c. 1881   *1945*

1515

The Things that never can come back, are several –
Childhood – some forms of Hope – the Dead –
Though Joys – like Men – may sometimes make a Journey –
And still abide –
We do not mourn for Traveler, or Sailor,
Their Routes are fair –
But think enlarged of all that they will tell us
Returning here –
"Here!" There are typic "Heres"–
Foretold Locations –
The Spirit does not stand –

Himself – at whatsoever Fathom
His Native Land –

c. *1881*   *1945*

1516

No Autumn's intercepting Chill
Appalls this Tropic Breast –
But African Exuberance
And Asiatic rest.

c. *1881*   *1914*

1517

How much of Source escapes with thee –
How chief thy sessions be –
For thou hast borne a universe
Entirely away.

1881   *1894*

1518

Not seeing, still we know –
Not knowing, guess –
Not guessing, smile and hide
And half caress –

And quake – and turn away,
Seraphic fear –
Is Eden's innuendo
"If you dare"?

c. *1881*   *1894*

1519

The Dandelion's pallid tube
Astonishes the Grass,
And Winter instantly becomes
An infinite Alas –

The tube uplifts a signal Bud
And then a shouting Flower, –
The Proclamation of the Suns
That sepulture is o'er.

c. 1881

1894

1520

The stem of a departed Flower
Has still a silent rank.
The Bearer from an Emerald Court
Of a Despatch of Pink.

c. 1881

1894

1521

The Butterfly upon the Sky,
That doesn't know its Name
And hasn't any tax to pay
And hasn't any Home
Is just as high as you and I,
And higher, I believe,
So soar away and never sigh
And that's the way to grieve –

c. 1881

1894

1522

His little Hearse like Figure
Unto itself a Dirge
To a delusive Lilac
The vanity divulge
Of Industry and Morals
And every righteous thing
For the divine Perdition
Of Idleness and Spring –

c. 1881

1915

We never know we go when we are going –
We jest and shut the Door –
Fate – following – behind us bolts it –
And we accost no more –

c. 1881   *1894*

A faded Boy – in sallow Clothes
Who drove a lonesome Cow
To pastures of Oblivion –
A statesman's Embryo –

The Boys that whistled are extinct –
The Cows that fed and thanked
Remanded to a Ballad's Barn
Or Clover's Retrospect –

c. 1881   *1945*

He lived the Life of Ambush
And went the way of Dusk
And now against his subtle name
There stands an Asterisk
As confident of him as we –
Impregnable we are –
The whole of Immortality intrenched
Within a star –

c. 1881   *1945*

His oriental heresies
Exhilarate the Bee,
And filling all the Earth and Air
With gay apostasy

* See poem 1616.

Fatigued at last, a Clover plain
Allures his jaded eye
That lowly Breast where Butterflies
Have felt it meet to die –

c. *1881*

1945

1527

Oh give it Motion – deck it sweet
With Artery and Vein –
Upon its fastened Lips lay words –
Affiance it again
To that Pink stranger we call Dust –
Acquainted more with that
Than with this horizontal one
That will not lift its Hat –

c. *1881*

1945

1528

The Moon upon her fluent Route
Defiant of a Road –
The Star's Etruscan Argument
Substantiate a God –

If Aims impel these Astral Ones
The ones allowed to know
Know that which makes them as forgot
As Dawn forgets them – now –

c. *1881*

1914

1529

'Tis Seasons since the Dimpled War
In which we each were Conqueror
And each of us were slain
And Centuries 'twill be and more
Another Massacre before
So modest and so vain –

Without a Formula we fought
Each was to each the Pink Redoubt –

c. *1881*   *1945*

1530

A Pang is more conspicuous in Spring
In contrast with the things that sing
Not Birds entirely – but Minds –
Minute Effulgencies and Winds –
When what they sung for is undone
Who cares about a Blue Bird's Tune –
Why, Resurrection had to wait
Till they had moved a Stone –

c. *1881*   *1945*

1531

Above Oblivion's Tide there is a Pier
And an effaceless "Few" are lifted there –
Nay – lift themselves – Fame has no Arms –
And but one smile – that meagres Balms –

c *1881*   *1945*

1532

From all the Jails the Boys and Girls
Ecstatically leap –
Beloved only Afternoon
That Prison doesn't keep

They storm the Earth and stun the Air,
A Mob of solid Bliss –
Alas – that Frowns should lie in wait
For such a Foe as this –

c. *1881*   *1892*

[640]

1533

On that specific Pillow
Our projects flit away –
The Night's tremendous Morrow
And whether sleep will stay
Or usher us – a stranger –
To situations new
The effort to comprise it
Is all the soul can do.

c. 1881

1945

1534

Society for me my misery
Since Gift of Thee –

c. 1881

1945

1535

The Life that tied too tight escapes
Will ever after run
With a prudential look behind
And spectres of the Rein –
The Horse that scents the living Grass
And sees the Pastures smile
Will be retaken with a shot
If he is caught at all –

c. 1881

1945

1536

There comes a warning like a spy
A shorter breath of Day
A stealing that is not a stealth
And Summers are away –

c. 1881

1945

1537

Candor – my tepid friend –
Come not to play with me –
The Myrrhs, and Mochas, of the Mind
Are its iniquity –

c. 1881   1914

1538

Follow wise Orion
Till you waste your Eye –
Dazzlingly decamping
He is just as high –

c. 1882   1914

1539

Now I lay thee down to Sleep –
I pray the Lord thy Dust to keep –
And if thou live before thou wake –
I pray the Lord thy Soul to make –

c. 1882   1924

1540

As imperceptibly as Grief
The Summer lapsed away –
Too imperceptible at last
To seem like Perfidy –
A Quietness distilled
As Twilight long begun,
Or Nature spending with herself
Sequestered Afternoon –
The Dusk drew earlier in –
The Morning foreign shone –
A courteous, yet harrowing Grace,
As Guest, that would be gone –

And thus, without a Wing
Or service of a Keel
Our Summer made her light escape
Into the Beautiful.

c. 1865   *1891*

1541

No matter where the Saints abide,
They make their Circuit fair
Behold how great a Firmament
Accompanies a Star.

1882?   *1914*

1542

   Come show thy Durham Breast
   To her who loves thee best,
   Delicious Robin –
   And if it be not me
   At least within my Tree
   Do the avowing –
   Thy Nuptial so minute
   Perhaps is more astute
   Than vaster suing –
   For so to soar away,
   Is our propensity
   The Day ensuing –

c. 1882   *1947*

1543

Obtaining but our own Extent
In whatsoever Realm –
'Twas Christ's own personal Expanse
That bore him from the Tomb –

c. 1882   *1894*

1544

Who has not found the Heaven – below –
Will fail of it above –
For Angels rent the House next ours,
Wherever we remove –

c. 1883   *1896*

1545

The Bible is an antique Volume –
Written by faded Men
At the suggestion of Holy Spectres –
Subjects – Bethlehem –
Eden – the ancient Homestead –
Satan – the Brigadier –
Judas – the Great Defaulter –
David – the Troubadour –
Sin – a distinguished Precipice
Others must resist –
Boys that "believe" are very lonesome –
Other Boys are "lost" –
Had but the Tale a warbling Teller –
All the Boys would come –
Orpheus' Sermon captivated –
It did not condemn –

c. 1882   *1924*

1546

Sweet Pirate of the heart,
Not Pirate of the Sea,
What wrecketh thee?
Some spice's Mutiny –
Some Attar's perfidy?
Confide in me.

c. 1882   *1894*

[644]

1547

Hope is a subtle Glutton –
He feeds upon the Fair –
And yet – inspected closely
What Abstinence is there –

His is the Halcyon Table –
That never seats but One –
And whatsoever is consumed
The same amount remain –

c. *1882*   *1896*

1548

Meeting by Accident,
We hovered by design –
As often as a Century
An error so divine
Is ratified by Destiny,
But Destiny is old
And economical of Bliss
As Midas is of Gold –

c. *1882*   *1945*

1549

My Wars are laid away in Books –
I have one Battle more –
A Foe whom I have never seen
But oft has scanned me o'er –
And hesitated me between
And others at my side,
But chose the best – Neglecting me – till
All the rest, have died –
How sweet if I am not forgot
By Chums that passed away –
Since Playmates at threescore and ten
Are such a scarcity –

c. *1882*   *1945*

1550

The pattern of the sun
Can fit but him alone
For sheen must have a Disk
To be a sun –

c. 1882   1945

1551

Those – dying then,
Knew where they went –
They went to God's Right Hand –
That Hand is amputated now
And God cannot be found –

The abdication of Belief
Makes the Behavior small –
Better an ignis fatuus
Than no illume at all –

c. 1882   1945

1552

Within thy Grave!
Oh no, but on some other flight –
Thou only camest to mankind
To rend it with Good night –

c. 1882   1945

1553

Bliss is the plaything of the child –
The secret of the man
The sacred stealth of Boy and Girl
Rebuke it if we can

c. 1882   1945

1554

"Go tell it" – What a Message –
To whom – is specified –
Not murmur – not endearment –
But simply – we – obeyed –
Obeyed – a Lure – a Longing?
Oh Nature – none of this –
To Law – said sweet Thermopylae
I give my dying Kiss –

c. 1882

1945

1555

I groped for him before I knew
With solemn nameless need
All other bounty sudden chaff
For this foreshadowed Food
Which others taste and spurn and sneer –
Though I within suppose
That consecrated it could be
The only Food that grows

c. 1882

1945

1556

Image of Light, Adieu –
Thanks for the interview –
So long – so short –
Preceptor of the whole –
Coeval Cardinal –
Impart – Depart –

c. 1882

1945

1557

Lives he in any other world
My faith cannot reply

[647]

Before it was imperative
'Twas all distinct to me –

c. 1882

1945

1558

Of Death I try to think like this –
The Well in which they lay us
Is but the Likeness of the Brook
That menaced not to slay us,
But to invite by that Dismay
Which is the Zest of sweetness
To the same Flower Hesperian,
Decoying but to greet us –

I do remember when a Child
With bolder Playmates straying
To where a Brook that seemed a Sea
Withheld us by its roaring
From just a Purple Flower beyond
Until constrained to clutch it
If Doom itself were the result,
The boldest leaped, and clutched it –

c. 1882

1945

1559

Tried always and Condemned by thee
Permit me this reprieve
That dying I may earn the look
For which I cease to live –

c. 1882

1945

1560

To be forgot by thee
Surpasses Memory
Of other minds

[648]

The Heart cannot forget
Unless it contemplate
What it declines
I was regarded then
Raised from oblivion
A single time
To be remembered what –
Worthy to be forgot
Is my renown

c. 1883

1945

1561

No Brigadier throughout the Year
So civic as the Jay –
A Neighbor and a Warrior too
With shrill felicity
Pursuing Winds that censure us
A February Day,
The Brother of the Universe
Was never blown away –
The Snow and he are intimate –
I've often seen them play
When Heaven looked upon us all
With such severity
I felt apology were due
To an insulted sky
Whose pompous frown was Nutriment
To their Temerity –
The Pillow of this daring Head
Is pungent Evergreens –
His Larder – terse and Militant –
Unknown – refreshing things –
His Character – a Tonic –
His Future – a Dispute –
Unfair an Immortality
That leaves this Neighbor out –

c. 1883

1891

1562

Her Losses make our Gains ashamed –
She bore Life's empty Pack
As gallantly as if the East
Were swinging at her Back.
Life's empty Pack is heaviest,
As every Porter knows –
In vain to punish Honey –
It only sweeter grows.

c. 1883   1894

1563

By homely gift and hindered Words
The human heart is told
Of Nothing –
"Nothing" is the force
That renovates the World –

c. 1883   1955

1564

Pass to thy Rendezvous of Light,
Pangless except for us –
Who slowly ford the Mystery
Which thou hast leaped across!

c. 1883   1924

1565

Some Arrows slay but whom they strike –
But this slew all *but* him –
Who so appareled his Escape –
Too trackless for a Tomb –

c. 1883   1932

1566

Climbing to reach the costly Hearts
To which he gave the worth,
He broke them, fearing punishment
He ran away from Earth –

c. 1883   *1931*

1567

The Heart has many Doors –
I can but knock –
For any sweet "Come in"
Impelled to hark –
Not saddened by repulse,
Repast to me
That somewhere, there exists,
Supremacy –

c. 1883   *1955*

1568

To see her is a Picture –
To hear her is a Tune –
To know her an Intemperance
As innocent as June –
To know her not – Affliction –
To own her for a Friend
A warmth as near as if the Sun
Were shining in your Hand.

c. 1883   *1945*

1569

The Clock strikes one that just struck two –
Some schism in the Sum –
A Vagabond for Genesis
Has wrecked the Pendulum –

c. 1883   *1894*

1570

Forever honored be the Tree
Whose Apple Winterworn
Enticed to Breakfast from the Sky
Two Gabriels Yestermorn.

They registered in Nature's Book
As Robins – Sire and Son –
But Angels have that modest way
To screen them from Renown.

c. 1883   *1914*

1571

How slow the Wind –
how slow the sea –
how late their Feathers be!

c. 1883   *1894*

1572

We wear our sober Dresses when we die,
But Summer, frilled as for a Holiday
Adjourns her sigh –

c. 1883   *1894*

1573

To the bright east she flies,
Brothers of Paradise
Remit her home,
Without a change of wings,
Or Love's convenient things,
Enticed to come.

Fashioning what she is,
Fathoming what she was,
We deem we dream –

[652]

And that dissolves the days
Through which existence strays
Homeless at home.

c. 1883   *1894*

1574

No ladder needs the bird but skies
To situate its wings,
Nor any leader's grim baton
Arraigns it as it sings.
The implements of bliss are few –
As Jesus says of *Him*,
"Come unto me" the moiety
That wafts the cherubim.

1883?   *1894*

1575

The Bat is dun, with wrinkled Wings –
Like fallow Article –
And not a song pervade his Lips –
Or none perceptible.

His small Umbrella quaintly halved
Describing in the Air
An Arc alike inscrutable
Elate Philosopher.

Deputed from what Firmament –
Of what Astute Abode –
Empowered with what Malignity
Auspiciously withheld –

To his adroit Creator
Ascribe no less the praise –
Beneficent, believe me,
His Eccentricities –

c. 1876   *1896*

The Spirit lasts – but in what mode –
Below, the Body speaks,
But as the Spirit furnishes –
Apart, it never talks –
The Music in the Violin
Does not emerge alone
But Arm in Arm with Touch, yet Touch
Alone – is not a Tune –
The Spirit lurks within the Flesh
Like Tides within the Sea
That make the Water live, estranged
What would the Either be?
Does that know – now – or does it cease –
That which to this is done,
Resuming at a mutual date
With every future one?
Instinct pursues the Adamant,
Exacting this Reply –
Adversity if it may be, or
Wild Prosperity,
The Rumor's Gate was shut so tight
Before my Mind was sown,
Not even a Prognostic's Push
Could make a Dent thereon –

c. *1883*   *1894*

Morning is due to all –
To some – the Night –
To an imperial few –
The Auroral light.

c. *1883*   *1931*

Blossoms will run away,
Cakes reign but a Day,

But Memory like Melody
Is pink Eternally.

c. *1883*   *1939*

1579

It would not know if it were spurned,
This gallant little flower –
How therefore safe to be a flower
If one would tamper there.

To enter, it would not aspire –
But may it not despair
That it is not a Cavalier,
To dare and perish there?

c. *1882*   *1945*

1580

We shun it ere it comes,
Afraid of Joy,
Then sue it to delay
And lest it fly,
Beguile it more and more –
May not this be
Old Suitor Heaven,
Like our dismay at thee?

c. *1882*   *1894*

1581

The farthest Thunder that I heard
Was nearer than the Sky
And rumbles still, though torrid Noons
Have lain their missiles by –
The Lightning that preceded it
Struck no one but myself –
But I would not exchange the Bolt
For all the rest of Life –

Indebtedness to Oxygen
The Happy may repay,
But not the obligation
To Electricity –
It founds the Homes and decks the Days
And every clamor bright
Is but the gleam concomitant
Of that waylaying Light –
The Thought is quiet as a Flake –
A Crash without a Sound,
How Life's reverberation
Its Explanation found –

c. *1883*   *1932*

1582

Where Roses would not dare to go,
What Heart would risk the way –
And so I send my Crimson Scouts
To sound the Enemy –

c. *1883*   *1945*

1583

Witchcraft was hung, in History,
But History and I
Find all the Witchcraft that we need
Around us, every Day –

c. *1883*   *1945*

1584

Expanse cannot be lost –
Not Joy, but a Decree
Is Deity –
His Scene, Infinity –
Whose rumor's Gate was shut so tight
Before my Beam was sown,

[656]

Not even a Prognostic's push
Could make a Dent thereon —

The World that thou hast opened
Shuts for thee,
But not alone,
We all have followed thee —
Escape more slowly
To thy Tracts of Sheen —
The Tent is listening,
But the Troops are gone!

c. 1883   *1955*

1585

The Bird her punctual music brings
And lays it in its place —
Its place is in the Human Heart
And in the Heavenly Grace —
What respite from her thrilling toil
Did Beauty ever take —
But Work might be electric Rest
To those that Magic make —

c. 1883   *1955*

1586

To her derided Home
A Weed of Summer came —
She did not know her station low
Nor Ignominy's Name —
Bestowed a summer long
Upon a fameless flower —
Then swept as lightly from disdain
As Lady from her Bower —

Of Bliss the Codes are few —
As Jesus cites of Him —

[657]

"Come unto me" the moiety
That wafts the Seraphim –

c. *1883*   *1945*

1587

He ate and drank the precious Words –
His Spirit grew robust –
He knew no more that he was poor,
Nor that his frame was Dust –

He danced along the dingy Days
And this Bequest of Wings
Was but a Book – What Liberty
A loosened spirit brings –

c. *1883*   *1890*

1588

This Me – that walks and works – must die,
Some fair or stormy Day,
Adversity if it may be
Or wild prosperity
The Rumor's Gate was shut so tight
Before my mind was born
Not even a Prognostic's push
Can make a Dent thereon –

c. *1883*   *1945*

1589

Cosmopolites without a plea
Alight in every Land
The compliments of Paradise
From those within my Hand

Their dappled Journey to themselves
A compensation fair

Knock and it shall be opened
Is their Theology

c. 1883   1945

1590

Not at Home to Callers
Says the Naked Tree –
Bonnet due in April –
Wishing you Good Day –

c. 1883   1924

1591

The Bobolink is gone –
The Rowdy of the Meadow –
And no one swaggers now but me –
The Presbyterian Birds
Can now resume the Meeting
He boldly interrupted that overflowing Day
When supplicating mercy
In a portentous way
He swung upon the Decalogue
And shouted let us pray –

c. 1883   1945

1592

The Lassitudes of Contemplation
Beget a force
They are the spirit's still vacation
That him refresh –
The Dreams consolidate in action –
What mettle fair

c. 1883   1945

1593

There came a Wind like a Bugle –
It quivered through the Grass

And a Green Chill upon the Heat
So ominous did pass
We barred the Windows and the Doors
As from an Emerald Ghost –
The Doom's electric Moccasin
That very instant passed –
On a strange Mob of panting Trees
And Fences fled away
And Rivers where the Houses ran
Those looked that lived – that Day –
The Bell within the steeple wild
The flying tidings told –
How much can come
And much can go,
And yet abide the World!

c. 1883   1891

1594

Immured in Heaven!
What a Cell!
Let every Bondage be,
Thou sweetest of the Universe,
Like that which ravished thee!

c. 1883   1914

1595

Declaiming Waters none may dread –
But Waters that are still
Are so for that most fatal cause
In Nature – they are full –

c. 1884   1932

1596

Few, yet enough,
Enough is One –
To that ethereal throng

Have not each one of us the right
To stealthily belong?

c. 1884   *1896*

1597

'Tis not the swaying frame we miss,
It is the steadfast Heart,
That had it beat a thousand years,
With Love alone had bent,
Its fervor the electric Oar,
That bore it through the Tomb,
Ourselves, denied the privilege,
Consolelessly presume –

c. 1884   *1932*

1598

Who is it seeks my Pillow Nights –
With plain inspecting face –
"Did you" or "Did you not," to ask –
'Tis "Conscience" – Childhood's Nurse –

With Martial Hand she strokes the Hair
Upon my wincing Head –
"All" Rogues "shall have their part in" what –
The Phosphorus of God –

c. 1884   *1914*

1599

Though the great Waters sleep,
That they are still the Deep,
We cannot doubt –
No vacillating God
Ignited this Abode
To put it out –

c. 1884   *1894*

[661]

Upon his Saddle sprung a Bird
And crossed a thousand Trees
Before a Fence without a Fare
His Fantasy did please
And then he lifted up his Throat
And squandered such a Note
A Universe that overheard
Is stricken by it yet –

c. 1884   1947

1601

Of God we ask one favor,
That we may be forgiven –
For what, he is presumed to know –
The Crime, from us, is hidden –
Immured the whole of Life
Within a magic Prison
We reprimand the Happiness
That too competes with Heaven.

c. 1884   1894

1602

Pursuing you in your transitions,
In other Motes –
Of other Myths
Your requisition be.
The Prism never held the Hues,
It only heard them play –

c. 1884   1931

1603

The going from a world we know
    To one a wonder still
Is like the child's adversity
    Whose vista is a hill,

Behind the hill is sorcery
And everything unknown,
But will the secret compensate
For climbing it alone?

c. 1884   *1894*

1604

We send the Wave to find the Wave –
An Errand so divine,
The Messenger enamored too,
Forgetting to return,
We make the wise distinction still,
Soever made in vain,
The sagest time to dam the sea is when the sea is gone –

c. 1884   *1894*

1605

Each that we lose takes part of us;
A crescent still abides,
Which like the moon, some turbid night,
Is summoned by the tides.

c. 1884   *1894*

1606

Quite empty, quite at rest,
The Robin locks her Nest, and tries her Wings.
She does not know a Route
But puts her Craft about
For *rumored* Springs –
She does not ask for Noon –
She does not ask for Boon,
Crumbless and homeless, of but one request –
The Birds she lost –

c. 1884   *1951*

1607

Within that little Hive
Such Hints of Honey lay
As made Reality a Dream
And Dreams, Reality –

c. 1884

1951

1608

The ecstasy to guess
Were a receipted bliss
If grace could talk.

1884?

1894

1609

Sunset that screens, reveals –
Enhancing what we see
By menaces of Amethyst
And Moats of Mystery.

c. 1884

1945

1610

Morning that comes but once,
Considers coming twice –
Two Dawns upon a single Morn,
Make Life a sudden price.

c. 1884

1945

1611

Their dappled importunity
Disparage or dismiss –
The Obloquies of Etiquette
Are obsolete to Bliss –

c. 1884

1945

1612

The Auctioneer of Parting
His "Going, going, gone"
Shouts even from the Crucifix,
And brings his Hammer down –
He only sells the Wilderness,
The prices of Despair
Range from a single human Heart
To Two – not any more –

c. 1884

1945

1613

Not Sickness stains the Brave,
Nor any Dart,
Nor Doubt of Scene to come,
But an adjourning Heart –

c. 1884

1894

1614

Parting with Thee reluctantly,
That we have never met,
A Heart sometimes a Foreigner,
Remembers it forgot –

c. 1884

1931

1615

Oh what a Grace is this,
What Majesties of Peace,
That having breathed
The fine – ensuing Right
Without Diminuet Proceed!

c. 1884

1931

1616*

Who abdicated Ambush
And went the way of Dusk,
And now against his subtle Name
There stands an Asterisk
As confident of him as we –
Impregnable we are –
The whole of Immortality
Secreted in a Star.

c. 1884   1894

1617

To try to speak, and miss the way
And ask it of the Tears,
Is Gratitude's sweet poverty,
The Tatters that he wears –

A better Coat if he possessed
Would help him to conceal,
Not subjugate, the Mutineer
Whose title is "the Soul."

c. 1884   1894

1618

There are two Mays
And then a Must
And after that a Shall.
How infinite the compromise
That indicates I will!

c. 1884   1955

1619

Not knowing when the Dawn will come,
I open every Door,

* See poem 1525.

[666]

Or has it Feathers, like a Bird,
Or Billows, like a Shore –

c. 1884   1896

1620

Circumference thou Bride of Awe
Possessing thou shalt be
Possessed by every hallowed Knight
That dares to covet thee

c. 1884   1932

1621

A Flower will not trouble her, it has so small a Foot,
And yet if you compare the Lasts,
Hers is the smallest Boot –

c. 1884   1955

1622

A Sloop of Amber slips away
Upon an Ether Sea,
And wrecks in Peace a Purple Tar,
The Son of Ecstasy –

c. 1884   1896

1623

A World made penniless by that departure
Of minor fabrics begs
But sustenance is of the spirit
The Gods but Dregs

c. 1885   1945

1624

Apparently with no surprise
To any happy Flower

The Frost beheads it at its play –
In accidental power –
The blonde Assassin passes on –
The Sun proceeds unmoved
To measure off another Day
For an Approving God.

c. 1884   1890

1625

Back from the cordial Grave I drag thee
He shall not take thy Hand
Nor put his spacious arm around thee
That none can understand

c. 1884   1945

1626

No Life can pompless pass away –
The lowliest career
To the same Pageant wends its way
As that exalted here –

How cordial is the mystery!
The hospitable Pall
A "this way" beckons spaciously –
A Miracle for all!

c. 1884   1891

1627

The pedigree of Honey
Does not concern the Bee,
Nor lineage of Ecstasy
Delay the Butterfly
On spangled journeys to the peak
Of some perceiveless thing –

[668]

The right of way to Tripoli
A more essential thing.

version I
c. *1884*

1945

The Pedigree of Honey
Does not concern the Bee –
A Clover, any time, to him,
Is Aristocracy –

version II
c. *1884*

1890

1628

A Drunkard cannot meet a Cork
Without a Revery –
And so encountering a Fly
This January Day
Jamaicas of Remembrance stir
That send me reeling in –
The moderate drinker of Delight
Does not deserve the spring –
Of juleps, part are in the Jug
And more are in the joy –
Your connoisseur in Liquors
Consults the Bumble Bee –

c. *1884*

1945

1629

Arrows enamored of his Heart –
Forgot to rankle there
And Venoms he mistook for Balms
disdained to rankle there –

c. *1884*

1945

1630

As from the earth the light Balloon
Asks nothing but release –

Ascension that for which it was,
Its soaring Residence.
The spirit looks upon the Dust
That fastened it so long
With indignation,
As a Bird
Defrauded of its song.

c. *1884*   *1945*

1631

Oh Future! thou secreted peace
Or subterranean woe –
Is there no wandering route of grace
That leads away from thee –
No circuit sage of all the course
Descried by cunning Men
To balk thee of thy sacred Prey –
Advancing to thy Den –

c. *1884*   *1945*

1632

So give me back to Death –
The Death I never feared
Except that it deprived of thee –
And now, by Life deprived,
In my own Grave I breathe
And estimate its size –
Its size is all that Hell can guess –
And all that Heaven was –

c. *1884*   *1945*

1633

Still own thee – still thou art
What surgeons call alive –
Though slipping – slipping I perceive
To thy reportless Grave –

Which question shall I clutch –
What answer wrest from thee
Before thou dost exude away
In the recallless sea?

c. 1884   1945

1634

Talk not to me of Summer Trees
The foliage of the mind
A Tabernacle is for Birds
Of no corporeal kind
And winds do go that way at noon
To their Ethereal Homes
Whose Bugles call the least of us
To undepicted Realms

c. 1884   1945

1635

The Jay his Castanet has struck
Put on your muff for Winter
The Tippet that ignores his voice
Is impudent to nature

Of Swarthy Days he is the close
His Lotus is a chestnut
The Cricket drops a sable line
No more from yours at present

c. 1884   1945

1636

The Sun in reining to the West
Makes not as much of sound
As Cart of man in road below
Adroitly turning round
That Whiffletree of Amethyst

c. 1884   1945

1637

Is it too late to touch you, Dear?
We this moment knew –
Love Marine and Love terrene –
Love celestial too –

c. 1885   *1894*

1638

Go thy great way!
The Stars thou meetst
Are even as Thyself –
For what are Stars but Asterisks
To point a human Life?

c. 1885   *1894*

1639

A Letter is a joy of Earth –
It is denied the Gods –

c. 1885   *1931*

1640

Take all away from me, but leave me Ecstasy,
And I am richer then than all my Fellow Men –
Ill it becometh me to dwell so wealthily
When at my very Door are those possessing more,
In abject poverty –

c. 1885   *1931*

1641

Betrothed to Righteousness might be
An Ecstasy discreet
But Nature relishes the Pinks
Which she was taught to eat –

c. 1885   *1945*

1642

"Red Sea," indeed! Talk not to me
Of purple Pharaoh –
I have a Navy in the West
Would pierce his Columns thro' –
Guileless, yet of such Glory fine
That all along the Line
Is it, or is it not, Marine –
Is it, or not, divine –
The Eye inquires with a sigh
That Earth sh'd be so big –
What Exultation in the Woe –
What Wine in the fatigue!

c. 1885   1945

1643

Extol thee – could I? Then I will
By saying nothing new –
But just the truest truth
That thou art heavenly.

Perceiving thee is evidence
That we are of the sky
Partaking thee a guaranty
Of immortality

c. 1885   1945

1644

Some one prepared this mighty show
To which without a Ticket go
The nations and the Days –

Displayed before the simplest Door
That all may witness it and more,
The pomp of summer Days.

1885   1945

1645

The Ditch is dear to the Drunken man
For is it not his Bed –
His Advocate – his Edifice?
How safe his fallen Head
In her disheveled Sanctity –
Above him is the sky –
Oblivion bending over him
And Honor leagues away.

c. 1885   *1945*

1646

Why should we hurry – why indeed?
When every way we fly
We are molested equally
By immortality.
No respite from the inference
That this which is begun,
Though where its labors lie
A bland uncertainty
Besets the sight
This mighty night –

c. 1885   *1945*

1647

Of Glory not a Beam is left
But her Eternal House –
The Asterisk is for the Dead,
The Living, for the Stars –

c. 1886   *1931*

1648

The immortality she gave
We borrowed at her Grave –

[674]

For just one Plaudit famishing,
The Might of Human love –

c. *1886*

1931

1649

A Cap of Lead across the sky
Was tight and surly drawn
We could not find the mighty Face
The Figure was withdrawn –

A Chill came up as from a shaft
Our noon became a well
A Thunder storm combines the charms
Of Winter and of Hell.

?

1914

1650

A lane of Yellow led the eye
Unto a Purple Wood
Whose soft inhabitants to be
Surpasses solitude
If Bird the silence contradict
Or flower presume to show
In that low summer of the West
Impossible to know –

?

1955

1651

A Word made Flesh is seldom
And tremblingly partook
Nor then perhaps reported
But have I not mistook
Each one of us has tasted
With ecstasies of stealth
The very food debated
To our specific strength –

A Word that breathes distinctly
Has not the power to die
Cohesive as the Spirit
It may expire if He –
"Made Flesh and dwelt among us"
Could condescension be
Like this consent of Language
This loved Philology.

?   1955

1652

Advance is Life's condition
The Grave but a Relay
Supposed to be a terminus
That makes it hated so –

The Tunnel is not lighted
Existence with a wall
Is better we consider
Than not exist at all –

?   1955

1653

As we pass Houses musing slow
If they be occupied
So minds pass minds
If they be occupied

?   1955

1654

Beauty crowds me till I die
Beauty mercy have on me
But if I expire today
Let it be in sight of thee –

?   1914

1655

Conferring with myself
My stranger disappeared
Though first upon a berry fat
Miraculously fared
How paltry looked my cares
My practise how absurd
Superfluous my whole career
Beside this travelling Bird

? 1955

1656

Down Time's quaint stream
Without an oar
We are enforced to sail
Our Port a secret
Our Perchance a Gale
What Skipper would
Incur the Risk
What Buccaneer would ride
Without a surety from the Wind
Or schedule of the Tide –

? 1955

1657

Eden is that old-fashioned House
We dwell in every day
Without suspecting our abode
Until we drive away.

How fair on looking back, the Day
We sauntered from the Door –
Unconscious our returning,
But discover it no more.

? 1914

1658

Endanger it, and the Demand
Of tickets for a sigh
Amazes the Humility
Of Credibility –

Recover it to Nature
And that dejected Fleet
Find Consternation's Carnival
Divested of its Meat.

?   *1955*

1659

Fame is a fickle food
Upon a shifting plate
Whose table once a
Guest but not
The second time is set.

Whose crumbs the crows inspect
And with ironic caw
Flap past it to the
Farmer's Corn –
Men eat of it and die.

?   *1914*

1660

Glory is that bright tragic thing
That for an instant
Means Dominion –
Warms some poor name
That never felt the Sun,
Gently replacing
In oblivion –

?   *1914*

1661

Guest am I to have
Light my northern room
Why to cordiality so averse to come
Other friends adjourn
Other bonds decay
Why avoid so narrowly
My fidelity –

?   *1955*

1662

He went by sleep that drowsy route
To the surmising Inn –
At day break to begin his race
Or ever to remain –

?   *1955*

1663

His mind of man, a secret makes
I meet him with a start
He carries a circumference
In which I have no part –

Or even if I deem I do
He otherwise may know
Impregnable to inquest
However neighborly –

?   *1914*

1664

I did not reach Thee
But my feet slip nearer every day
Three Rivers and a Hill to cross
One Desert and a Sea
I shall not count the journey one
When I am telling thee.

[679]

Two deserts, but the Year is cold
So that will help the sand
One desert crossed –
The second one
Will feel as cool as land
Sahara is too little price
To pay for thy Right hand.

The Sea comes last – Step merry, feet,
So short we have to go –
To play together we are prone,
But we must labor now,
The last shall be the lightest load
That we have had to draw.

The Sun goes crooked –
That is Night
Before he makes the bend.
We must have passed the Middle Sea –
Almost we wish the End
Were further off –
Too great it seems
So near the Whole to stand.

We step like Plush,
We stand like snow,
The waters murmur new.
Three rivers and the Hill are passed –
Two deserts and the sea!
Now Death usurps my Premium
And gets the look at Thee.

?   *1914*

1665

I know of people in the Grave
Who would be very glad
To know the news I know tonight
If they the chance had had.

'Tis this expands the least event
And swells the scantest deed –
My right to walk upon the Earth
If they this moment had.

? 1955

1666

I see thee clearer for the Grave
That took thy face between
No Mirror could illumine thee
Like that impassive stone –

I know thee better for the Act
That made thee first unknown
The stature of the empty nest
Attests the Bird that's gone.

? 1955

1667

I watched her face to see which way
She took the awful news –
Whether she died before she heard
Or in protracted bruise
Remained a few slow years with us –
Each heavier than the last –
A further afternoon to fail,
As Flower at fall of Frost.

? 1914

1668

If I could tell how glad I was
I should not be so glad –
But when I cannot make the Force,
Nor mould it into Word,
I know it is a sign
That new Dilemma be

From mathematics further off
Than from Eternity.

1914

1669

In snow thou comest –
Thou shalt go with the resuming ground,
The sweet derision of the crow,
And Glee's advancing sound.

In fear thou comest –
Thou shalt go at such a gait of joy
That man anew embark to live
Upon the depth of thee.

1955

1670

In Winter in my Room
I came upon a Worm –
Pink, lank and warm –
But as he was a worm
And worms presume
Not quite with him at home –
Secured him by a string
To something neighboring
And went along.

A Trifle afterward
A thing occurred
I'd not believe it if I heard
But state with creeping blood –
A snake with mottles rare
Surveyed my chamber floor
In feature as the worm before
But ringed with power –

The very string with which
I tied him – too
When he was mean and new
That string was there –

I shrank – "How fair you are"!
Propitiation's claw –
"Afraid," he hissed
"Of me"?
"No cordiality" –
He fathomed me –
Then to a Rhythm *Slim*
Secreted in his Form
As Patterns swim
Projected him.

That time I flew
Both eyes his way
Lest he pursue
Nor ever ceased to run
Till in a distant Town
Towns on from mine
I set me down
This was a dream.

?

1914

1671

Judgment is justest
When the Judged,
His action laid away,
Divested is of every Disk
But his sincerity.

Honor is then the safest hue
In a posthumous Sun –
Not any color will endure
That scrutiny can burn.

?

1955

1672

Lightly stepped a yellow star
To its lofty place –
Loosed the Moon her silver hat
From her lustral Face –
All of Evening softly lit
As an Astral Hall –
Father, I observed to Heaven,
You are punctual.

?

1914

1673

Nature can do no more
She has fulfilled her Dyes
Whatever Flower fail to come
Of other Summer days
Her crescent reimburse
If other Summers be
Nature's imposing negative
Nulls opportunity –

?

1955

1674

Not any sunny tone
From any fervent zone
Find entrance there –
Better a grave of Balm
Toward human nature's home –
And Robins near –
Than a stupendous Tomb
Proclaiming to the Gloom
How dead we are –

?

1914

1675

Of this is Day composed
A morning and a noon
A Revelry unspeakable
And then a gay unknown
Whose Pomps allure and spurn
And dower and deprive
And penury for Glory
Remedilessly leave.

?   *1914*

1676

Of Yellow was the outer Sky
In Yellower Yellow hewn
Till Saffron in Vermilion slid
Whose seam could not be shewn.

?   *1955*

1677

On my volcano grows the Grass
A meditative spot –
An acre for a Bird to choose
Would be the General thought –

How red the Fire rocks below –
How insecure the sod
Did I disclose
Would populate with awe my solitude.

?   *1914*

1678

Peril as a Possession
'Tis Good to bear
Danger disintegrates Satiety
There's Basis there –
Begets an awe

[685]

That searches Human Nature's creases
As clean as Fire.

?

1914

1679

Rather arid delight
If Contentment accrue
Make an abstemious Ecstasy
Not so good as joy –

But Rapture's Expense
Must not be incurred
With a tomorrow knocking
And the Rent unpaid –

?

1955

1680

Sometimes with the Heart
Seldom with the Soul
Scarcer once with the Might
Few – love at all.

?

1915

1681

Speech is one symptom of Affection
And Silence one –
The perfectest communication
Is heard of none –

Exists and its indorsement
Is had within –
Behold, said the Apostle,
Yet had not seen!

?

1914

1682

Summer begins to have the look
Peruser of enchanting Book
Reluctantly but sure perceives
A gain upon the backward leaves –

Autumn begins to be inferred
By millinery of the cloud
Or deeper color in the shawl
That wraps the everlasting hill.

The eye begins its avarice
A meditation chastens speech
Some Dyer of a distant tree
Resumes his gaudy industry.

Conclusion is the course of All
At *most* to be perennial
And then elude stability
Recalls to immortality.

? *1914*

1683

That she forgot me was the least
I felt it second pain
That I was worthy to forget
Was most I thought upon.

Faithful was all that I could boast
But Constancy became
To her, by her innominate,
A something like a shame.

? *1914*

1684

The Blunder is in estimate.
Eternity is there
We say, as of a Station –
Meanwhile he is so near

He joins me in my Ramble –
Divides abode with me –
No Friend have I that so persists
As this Eternity.

?   *1914*

1685

The butterfly obtains
But little sympathy
Though favorably mentioned
In Entomology –

Because he travels freely
And wears a proper coat
The circumspect are certain
That he is dissolute –

Had he the homely scutcheon
Of modest Industry
'Twere fitter certifying
For Immortality –

?   *1914*

1686

The event was directly behind Him
Yet He did not guess
Fitted itself to Himself like a Robe
Relished His ignorance.
Motioned itself to drill
Loaded and Levelled
And let His Flesh
Centuries from His soul.

?   *1955*

1687

The gleam of an heroic Act
Such strange illumination

The Possible's slow fuse is lit
By the Imagination.

?

1914

1688

The Hills erect their Purple Heads
The Rivers lean to see
Yet Man has not of all the Throng
A Curiosity.

?

1914

1689

The look of thee, what is it like
Hast thou a hand or Foot
Or Mansion of Identity
And what is thy Pursuit?

Thy fellows are they realms or Themes
Hast thou Delight or Fear
Or Longing – and is that for us
Or values more severe?

Let change transfuse all other Traits
Enact all other Blame
But deign this least certificate –
That thou shalt be the same.

?

1914

1690

The ones that disappeared are back
The Phoebe and the Crow
Precisely as in March is heard
The curtness of the Jay –
Be this an Autumn or a Spring
My wisdom loses way

One side of me the nuts are ripe
The other side is May.

?   1914

1691

The overtakelessness of those
Who have accomplished Death
Majestic is to me beyond
The majesties of Earth.

The soul her "Not at Home"
Inscribes upon the flesh –
And takes her fair aerial gait
Beyond the hope of touch.

?   1914

1692

The right to perish might be thought
An undisputed right –
Attempt it, and the Universe
Upon the opposite
Will concentrate its officers –
You cannot even die
But nature and mankind must pause
To pay you scrutiny.

?   1914

1693

The Sun retired to a cloud
A Woman's shawl as big –
And then he sulked in mercury
Upon a scarlet log –
The drops on Nature's forehead stood
Home flew the loaded bees –
The South unrolled a purple fan
And handed to the trees.

?   1955

1694

The wind drew off
Like hungry dogs
Defeated of a bone –
Through fissures in
Volcanic cloud
The yellow lightning shone –
The trees held up
Their mangled limbs
Like animals in pain –
When Nature falls upon herself
Beware an Austrian.

?

1914

1695

There is a solitude of space
A solitude of sea
A solitude of death, but these
Society shall be
Compared with that profounder site
That polar privacy
A soul admitted to itself –
Finite infinity.

?

1914

1696

These are the days that Reindeer love
And pranks the Northern star –
This is the Sun's objective,
And Finland of the Year.

?

1914

1697

They talk as slow as Legends grow
No mushroom is their mind
But foliage of sterility
Too stolid for the wind –

They laugh as wise as Plots of Wit
Predestined to unfold
The point with bland prevision
Portentously untold.

? 1955

1698

'Tis easier to pity those when dead
That which pity previous
Would have saved –
A Tragedy enacted
Secures Applause
That Tragedy enacting
Too seldom does.

? 1955

1699

To do a magnanimous thing
And take oneself by surprise
If oneself is not in the habit of him
Is precisely the finest of Joys –

Not to do a magnanimous thing
Notwithstanding it never be known
Notwithstanding it cost us existence once
Is Rapture herself spurn –

? 1955

1700

To tell the Beauty would decrease
To state the Spell demean –
There is a syllable-less Sea
Of which it is the sign –
My will endeavors for its word
And fails, but entertains

A Rapture as of Legacies –
Of introspective Mines –

? 1914

1701

To their apartment deep
No ribaldry may creep
Untumbled this abode
By any man but God –

? 1914

1702

Today or this noon
She dwelt so close
I almost touched her –
Tonight she lies
Past neighborhood
And bough and steeple,
Now past surmise.

? 1914

1703

'Twas comfort in her Dying Room
To hear the living Clock –
A short relief to have the wind
Walk boldly up and knock –
Diversion from the Dying Theme
To hear the children play –
But wrong the more
That these could live
And this of ours must *die*.

? 1914

1704

Unto a broken heart
No other one may go

Without the high prerogative
Itself hath suffered too.

1955

1705

Volcanoes be in Sicily
And South America
I judge from my Geography –
Volcanos nearer here
A Lava step at any time
Am I inclined to climb –
A Crater I may contemplate
Vesuvius at Home.

1914

1706

When we have ceased to care
The Gift is given
For which we gave the Earth
And mortgaged Heaven
But so declined in worth
'Tis ignominy now
To look upon –

1915

1707

Winter under cultivation
Is as arable as Spring.

1955

1708

Witchcraft has not a Pedigree
'Tis early as our Breath
And mourners meet it going out
The moment of our death –

1914

1709

With sweetness unabated
Informed the hour had come
With no remiss of triumph
The autumn started home

Her home to be with Nature
As competition done
By influential kinsmen
Invited to return –

In supplements of Purple
An adequate repast
In heavenly reviewing
Her residue be past –

?   *1955*

1710

A curious Cloud surprised the Sky,
'Twas like a sheet with Horns;
The sheet was Blue –
The Antlers Gray –
It almost touched the Lawns.

So low it leaned – then statelier drew –
And trailed like robes away,
A Queen adown a satin aisle
Had not the majesty.

?   *1945*

1711

A face devoid of love or grace,
A hateful, hard, successful face,
A face with which a stone
Would feel as thoroughly at ease
As were they old acquaintances –
First time together thrown.

?   *1896*

1712

A Pit – but Heaven over it –
And Heaven beside, and Heaven abroad,
And yet a Pit –
With Heaven over it.

To stir would be to slip –
To look would be to drop –
To dream – to sap the Prop
That holds my chances up.
Ah! Pit! With Heaven over it!

The depth is all my thought –
I dare not ask my feet –
'Twould start us where we sit
So straight you'd scarce suspect
It was a Pit – with fathoms under it –
Its Circuit just the same.
Seed – summer – tomb –
Whose Doom to whom?

?   1945

1713

As subtle as tomorrow
That never came,
A warrant, a conviction,
Yet but a name.

?   1945

1714

By a departing light
We see acuter, quite,
Than by a wick that stays.
There's something in the flight
That clarifies the sight
And decks the rays.

?   1945

1715

Consulting summer's clock,
But half the hours remain.
I ascertain it with a shock –
I shall not look again.
The second half of joy
Is shorter than the first.
The truth I do not dare to know
I muffle with a jest.

?   *1945*

1716

Death is like the insect
Menacing the tree,
Competent to kill it,
But decoyed may be.

Bait it with the balsam,
Seek it with the saw,
Baffle, if it cost you
Everything you are.

Then, if it have burrowed
Out of reach of skill –
Wring the tree and leave it,
'Tis the vermin's will.

?   *1896*

1717

Did life's penurious length
Italicize its sweetness,
The men that daily live
Would stand so deep in joy
That it would clog the cogs
Of that revolving reason
Whose esoteric belt
Protects our sanity.

?   *1945*

1718

Drowning is not so pitiful
As the attempt to rise.
Three times, 'tis said, a sinking man
Comes up to face the skies,
And then declines forever
To that abhorred abode,
Where hope and he part company –
For he is grasped of God.
The Maker's cordial visage,
However good to see,
Is shunned, we must admit it,
Like an adversity.

? 1896

1719

God is indeed a jealous God –
He cannot bear to see
That we had rather not with Him
But with each other play.

? 1945

1720

Had I known that the first was the last
I should have kept it longer.
Had I known that the last was the first
I should have drunk it stronger.
Cup, it was your fault,
Lip was not the liar.
No, lip, it was yours,
Bliss was most to blame.

? 1945

1721

He was my host – he was my guest,
I never to this day

If I invited him could tell,
Or he invited me.

So infinite our intercourse
So intimate, indeed,
Analysis as capsule seemed
To keeper of the seed.

?

1945

1722

Her face was in a bed of hair,
Like flowers in a plot –
Her hand was whiter than the sperm
That feeds the sacred light.
Her tongue more tender than the tune
That totters in the leaves –
Who hears may be incredulous,
Who witnesses, believes.

?

1945

1723

High from the earth I heard a bird,
He trod upon the trees
As he esteemed them trifles,
And then he spied a breeze,
And situated softly
Upon a pile of wind
Which in a perturbation
Nature had left behind.
A joyous going fellow
I gathered from his talk
Which both of benediction
And badinage partook.
Without apparent burden
I subsequently learned
He was the faithful father
Of a dependent brood.

And this untoward transport
His remedy for care.
A contrast to our respites.
How different we are!

? 1896

1724

How dare the robins sing,
When men and women hear
Who since they went to their account
Have settled with the year! –
Paid all that life had earned
In one consummate bill,
And now, what life or death can do
Is immaterial.
Insulting is the sun
To him whose mortal light
Beguiled of immortality
Bequeaths him to the night.
Extinct be every hum
In deference to him
Whose garden wrestles with the dew,
At daybreak overcome!

? 1896

1725

I took one Draught of Life –
I'll tell you what I paid –
Precisely an existence –
The market price, they said.

They weighed me, Dust by Dust –
They balanced Film with Film,
Then handed me my Being's worth –
A single Dram of Heaven!

? 1929

1726

If all the griefs I am to have
Would only come today,
I am so happy I believe
They'd laugh and run away.

If all the joys I am to have
Would only come today,
They could not be so big as this
That happens to me now.

?

1945

1727

If ever the lid gets off my head
And lets the brain away
The fellow will go where he belonged –
Without a hint from me,

And the world – if the world be looking on –
Will see how far from home
It is possible for sense to live
The soul there – all the time.

?

1945

1728

Is Immortality a bane
That men are so oppressed?

?

1945

1729

I've got an arrow here.
Loving the hand that sent it
I the dart revere.

Fell, they will say, in "skirmish"!
Vanquished, my soul will know

By but a simple arrow
Sped by an archer's bow.

1896

1730

"Lethe" in my flower,
Of which they who drink
In the fadeless orchards
Hear the bobolink!

Merely flake or petal
As the Eye beholds
Jupiter! my father!
I perceive the rose!

1945

1731

Love can do all but raise the Dead
I doubt if even that
From such a giant were withheld
Were flesh equivalent

But love is tired and must sleep,
And hungry and must graze
And so abets the shining Fleet
Till it is out of gaze.

1945

1732

My life closed twice before its close –
It yet remains to see
If Immortality unveil
A third event to me

So huge, so hopeless to conceive
As these that twice befell.

Parting is all we know of heaven,
And all we need of hell.

?

1896

1733

No man saw awe, nor to his house
Admitted he a man
Though by his awful residence
Has human nature been.

Not deeming of his dread abode
Till laboring to flee
A grasp on comprehension laid
Detained vitality.

Returning is a different route
The Spirit could not show
For breathing is the only work
To be enacted now.

"Am not consumed," old Moses wrote,
"Yet saw him face to face" –
That very physiognomy
I am convinced was this.

?

1945

1734

Oh, honey of an hour,
I never knew thy power,
Prohibit me
Till my minutest dower,
My unfrequented flower,
Deserving be.

?

1945

1735

One crown that no one seeks
And yet the highest head

Its isolation coveted
Its stigma deified

While Pontius Pilate lives
In whatsoever hell
That coronation pierces him
He recollects it well.

? 1945

1736

Proud of my broken heart, since thou didst break it,
Proud of the pain I did not feel till thee,

Proud of my night, since thou with moons dost slake it,
Not to partake thy passion, *my* humility.

Thou can'st not boast, like Jesus, drunken without companion
Was the strong cup of anguish brewed for the Nazarene

Thou can'st not pierce tradition with the peerless puncture,
See! I usurped *thy* crucifix to honor mine!

? 1947

1737

Rearrange a "Wife's" affection!
When they dislocate my Brain!
Amputate my freckled Bosom!
Make me bearded like a man!

Blush, my spirit, in thy Fastness –
Blush, my unacknowledged clay –
Seven years of troth have taught thee
More than Wifehood ever may!

Love that never leaped its socket –
Trust entrenched in narrow pain –
Constancy thro' fire – awarded –
Anguish – bare of anodyne!

Burden – borne so far triumphant –
None suspect me of the crown,

For I wear the "Thorns" till *Sunset* –
Then – my Diadem put on.

Big my Secret but it's *bandaged* –
It will never get away
Till the Day its Weary Keeper
Leads it through the Grave to thee.

? 					*1945*

1738

Softened by Time's consummate plush,
How sleek the woe appears
That threatened childhood's citadel
And undermined the years.

Bisected now, by bleaker griefs,
We envy the despair
That devastated childhood's realm,
So easy to repair.

? 					*1896*

1739

Some say goodnight – at night –
I say goodnight by day –
Good-bye – the Going utter me –
Goodnight, I still reply –

For parting, that is night,
And presence, simply dawn –
Itself, the purple on the height
Denominated morn.

? 					*1929*

1740

Sweet is the swamp with its secrets,
Until we meet a snake;
'Tis then we sigh for houses,
And our departure take

At that enthralling gallop
That only childhood knows.
A snake is summer's treason,
And guile is where it goes.

? 1896

1741

That it will never come again
Is what makes life so sweet.
Believing what we don't believe
Does not exhilarate.

That if it be, it be at best
An ablative estate –
This instigates an appetite
Precisely opposite.

? 1945

1742

The distance that the dead have gone
Does not at first appear –
Their coming back seems possible
For many an ardent year.

And then, that we have followed them,
We more than half suspect,
So intimate have we become
With their dear retrospect.

? 1896

1743

The grave my little cottage is,
Where "Keeping house" for thee
I make my parlor orderly
And lay the marble tea.

For two divided, briefly,
A cycle, it may be,

Till everlasting life unite
In strong society.

1744

The joy that has no stem nor core,
Nor seed that we can sow,
Is edible to longing,
But ablative to show.

By fundamental palates
Those products are preferred
Impregnable to transit
And patented by pod.

1745

The mob within the heart
Police cannot suppress
The riot given at the first
Is authorized as peace

Uncertified of scene
Or signified of sound
But growing like a hurricane
In a congenial ground.

1746

The most important population
Unnoticed dwell,
They have a heaven each instant
Not any hell.

Their names, unless you know them,
'Twere useless tell.

Of bumble-bees and other nations
The grass is full.

?   1945

1747

The parasol is the umbrella's daughter,
And associates with a fan
While her father abuts the tempest
And abridges the rain.

The former assists a siren
In her serene display;
But her father is borne and honored,
And borrowed to this day.

?   1945

1748

The reticent volcano keeps
His never slumbering plan –
Confided are his projects pink
To no precarious man.

If nature will not tell the tale
Jehovah told to her
Can human nature not survive
Without a listener?

Admonished by her buckled lips
Let every babbler be
The only secret people keep
Is Immortality.

?   1896

1749

The waters chased him as he fled,
Not daring look behind –
A billow whispered in his Ear,
"Come home with me, my friend –

My parlor is of shriven glass,
My pantry has a fish
For every palate in the Year" –
To this revolting bliss
The object floating at his side
Made no distinct reply.

?

1945

1750

The words the happy say
Are paltry melody
But those the silent feel
Are beautiful –

?

1945

1751

There comes an hour when begging stops,
When the long interceding lips
Perceive their prayer is vain.
"Thou shalt not" is a kinder sword
Than from a disappointing God
"Disciple, call again."

?

1945

1752

This docile one inter
While we who dare to live
Arraign the sunny brevity
That sparkled to the Grave

On her departing span
No wilderness remain
As dauntless in the House of Death
As if it were her own –

?

1945

1753

Through those old Grounds of memory,
The sauntering alone
Is a divine intemperance
A prudent man would shun.
Of liquors that are vended
'Tis easy to beware
But statutes do not meddle
With the internal bar.
Pernicious as the sunset
Permitting to pursue
But impotent to gather,
The tranquil perfidy
Alloys our firmer moments
With that severest gold
Convenient to the longing
But otherwise withheld.

?   1945

1754

To lose thee – sweeter than to gain
All other hearts I knew.
'Tis true the drought is destitute,
But then, I had the dew!

The Caspian has its realms of sand,
Its other realm of sea.
Without the sterile perquisite,
No Caspian could be.

?   1896

1755

To make a prairie it takes a clover and one bee,
One clover, and a bee,
And revery.
The revery alone will do,
If bees are few.

?   1896

1756

'Twas here my summer paused
What ripeness after then
To other scene or other soul
My sentence had begun.

To winter to remove
With winter to abide
Go manacle your icicle
Against your Tropic Bride.

? 				*1945*

1757

Upon the gallows hung a wretch,
Too sullied for the hell
To which the law entitled him.
As nature's curtain fell
The one who bore him tottered in, –
For this was woman's son.
" 'Twas all I had," she stricken gasped –
Oh, what a livid boon!

? 				*1896*

1758

Where every bird is bold to go
And bees abashless play,
The foreigner before he knocks
Must thrust the tears away.

? 				*1896*

1759

Which misses most,
The hand that tends,
Or heart so gently borne,
'Tis twice as heavy as it was
Because the hand is gone?

Which blesses most,
The lip that can,
Or that that went to sleep
With "if I could" endeavoring
Without the strength to shape?

? 1945

1760

Elysium is as far as to
The very nearest Room
If in that Room a Friend await
Felicity or Doom –

What fortitude the Soul contains,
That it can so endure
The accent of a coming Foot –
The opening of a Door –

c. 1882 1890

1761

A train went through a burial gate,
A bird broke forth and sang,
And trilled, and quivered, and shook his throat
Till all the churchyard rang;

And then adjusted his little notes,
And bowed and sang again.
Doubtless, he thought it meet of him
To say good-by to men.

? 1890

1762

Were nature mortal lady
    Who had so little time
To pack her trunk and order
    The great exchange of clime –

How rapid, how momentous –
What exigencies were –
But nature will be ready
    And have an hour to spare.

To make some trifle fairer
    That was too fair before –
Enchanting by remaining,
    And by departure more.

?   *1898*

1763

Fame is a bee.
    It has a song –
It has a sting –
    Ah, too, it has a wing.

?   *1898*

1764

The saddest noise, the sweetest noise,
    The maddest noise that grows, –
The birds, they make it in the spring,
    At night's delicious close.

Between the March and April line –
    That magical frontier
Beyond which summer hesitates,
    Almost too heavenly near.

It makes us think of all the dead
    That sauntered with us here,
By separation's sorcery
    Made cruelly more dear.

It makes us think of what we had,
    And what we now deplore.
We almost wish those siren throats
    Would go and sing no more.

An ear can break a human heart
    As quickly as a spear,

[713]

We wish the ear had not a heart
So dangerously near.

? 1898

1765

That Love is all there is,
Is all we know of Love;
It is enough, the freight should be
Proportioned to the groove.

? 1914

1766

Those final Creatures, – who they are –
That, faithful to the close,
Administer her ecstasy,
But just the Summer knows.

? 1914

1767

Sweet hours have perished here;
    This is a mighty room;
Within its precincts hopes have played, –
    Now shadows in the tomb.

? 1924

1768

Lad of Athens, faithful be
To Thyself,
And Mystery –
All the rest is Perjury –

c. 1883 1931

1769

The longest day that God appoints
Will finish with the sun.

[714]

Anguish can travel to its stake,
And then it must return.

?   *1894*

1770

Experiment escorts us last –
His pungent company
Will not allow an Axiom
An Opportunity

c. 1870   *1945*

1771

How fleet – how indiscreet an one –
How always wrong is Love –
The joyful little Deity
We are not scourged to serve –

c. 1881   *1945*

1772

Let me not thirst with this Hock at my Lip,
Nor beg, with Domains in my Pocket –

c. 1881   *1945*

1773

The Summer that we did not prize,
Her treasures were so easy
Instructs us by departing now
And recognition lazy –

Bestirs itself – puts on its Coat,
And scans with fatal promptness
For Trains that moment out of sight,
Unconscious of his smartness.

c. 1883   *1945*

1774

Too happy Time dissolves itself
And leaves no remnant by –
'Tis Anguish not a Feather hath
Or too much weight to fly –

c. 1870   1945

1775

The earth has many keys.
Where melody is not
Is the unknown peninsula.
Beauty is nature's fact.

But witness for her land,
And witness for her sea,
The cricket is her utmost
Of elegy to me.

?   1945

Acknowledgments

The Poems of Emily Dickinson, from which this text derives, was made possible, first, by the gift of Gilbert H. Montague to Harvard University Library of funds for the purchase of the poet's manuscripts and other papers from the heirs to the literary estate, the late Alfred Leete Hampson and his wife Mary Landis Hampson; and second, by the courtesy of Millicent Todd Bingham in making available for study all of the large number of Dickinson manuscripts in her possession, recently transferred by her to Amherst College.

This edition makes grateful and general acknowledgment to Harvard University Press and to Houghton Mifflin Company for permission to print here the Dickinson poems which are under copyright and have been published by them.

Thomas H. Johnson

Lawrenceville, New Jersey
4 April 1960

Previous Collections

The present edition derives from *The Poems of Emily Dickinson,* edited by Thomas H. Johnson (3 vols. Cambridge: the Belknap Press, Harvard University Press, 1955). Most of the poems here included appeared originally in the volumes named below. A few had their first publication in magazines and journals.

Ancestors' Brocades. By Millicent Todd Bingham. New York: Harper, 1945.

Bolts of Melody. Edited by Mabel Loomis Todd and Millicent Todd Bingham. New York: Harper, 1945.

The Complete Poems of Emily Dickinson. Edited by Martha Dickinson Bianchi and Alfred Leete Hampson. Boston: Little, Brown, 1924.

The Poems of Emily Dickinson. Edited by Martha Dickinson Bianchi and Alfred Leete Hampson. Boston: Little, Brown, 1930.

Emily Dickinson Face to Face: Unpublished Letters with Notes and Reminiscences. By Martha Dickinson Bianchi. Boston: Houghton Mifflin, 1932.

Emily Dickinson's Letters to Dr. and Mrs. Josiah Gilbert Holland. Edited by Theodora Van Wagenen Ward. Cambridge: Harvard University Press, 1951.

Further Poems of Emily Dickinson. Edited by Martha Dickinson Bianchi and Alfred Leete Hampson. Boston: Little, Brown, 1929.

Letters of Emily Dickinson. Edited by Mabel Loomis Todd. 2 vols. Boston: Roberts Brothers, 1894.

Letters of Emily Dickinson. New and enlarged edition. Edited by Mabel Loomis Todd. New York: Harper, 1931.

The Life and Letters of Emily Dickinson. By Martha Dickinson Bianchi. Boston: Houghton Mifflin, 1924.

Poems by Emily Dickinson. Edited by Mabel Loomis Todd and T. W. Higginson. Boston: Roberts Brothers, 1890.

Poems by Emily Dickinson, Second Series. Edited by T. W. Higginson and Mabel Loomis Todd. Boston: Roberts Brothers, 1891.

Poems by Emily Dickinson, Third Series. Edited by Mabel Loomis Todd. Boston: Roberts Brothers, 1896.

Poems by Emily Dickinson. Edited by Martha Dickinson Bianchi and Alfred Leete Hampson. Boston: Little, Brown, 1937.

The Single Hound. Edited by Martha Dickinson Bianchi. Boston: Little, Brown, 1914.

Unpublished Poems of Emily Dickinson. Edited by Martha Dickinson Bianchi and Alfred Leete Hampson. Boston: Little, Brown, 1935.

Indexes

Subject Index

The principal purpose of this index is to aid the reader in finding a desired poem. Since there are no titles, and the arrangement is chronological, the index of first lines alone does not provide adequate means of recognition. The subject index is not intended to fill the place of a concordance, nor should it be regarded as an attempt at interpretation of the poems. It is a classification based principally on key words in the poems themselves. In instances in which the whole content is stated in terms of imagery, the image itself, rather than the meaning, is used as a heading. An example of this is seen in the list of poems under the heading *Crown*.

It will be noted that certain large groups, such as those headed *Life*, *Love*, and *Death*, contain the bulk of the poems. In some instances, however, a poem listed under one of these headings will have also an entry under one or more categories. For example, "Death is a dialogue between/The spirit and the Dust" is entered under *Death*, *Spirit*, and *Dust*.

Under each main heading will be found first the numbers of the poems whose entire content is clearly on the subject given. These include poems of definition and description, and they are entered in numerical order, without subheadings. Following these, under separate subheadings, are the poems that represent special aspects of the main subject and those in which only a part of the content can be so classified. The order of the subheadings is governed by the numerical order of the poems they refer to, each new subheading being followed by the least number in its group, and the numerical sequence is followed also within the groups. When not more than five or six poems appear under a main subject, the subheadings have been for the most part eliminated, though sometimes a qualifying subheading has seemed desirable for the sake of clarity.

Another means of identification is offered under the headings *Names mentioned in the poems* and *Places mentioned in the poems.* Although names and places seldom represent the subjects of the poems, the author's use of such names as Cato and Carlo, Brazil and Himmaleh is often striking enough to linger in the memory. The heading *Names* rather than *Persons* was chosen since the list includes fictional and mythological as well as historical characters. The heading *Persons* has been used elsewhere with a more direct significance for a group of character sketches and verses dealing directly with personalities.

ACHIEVEMENT, 1070, 1315
Action, 361, 1216; heroic act, 1687
Affection, communication of, 1681
Affliction, 799, 951, 963
Age, old, 1280, 1345, 1346
Agony, 241, 414, 1243
Air, 647, 1060
Aloofness, 1092
Anemone, 31
Angels, 59, 78, 94, 231, 702, 895
Anguish, 264, 1769; pay for ecstasy, 125; the mail of, 165; sovereign, 167; smouldering, 175; drop of, 193; staggering mind, 859
Anticipation, 37
April, 65
Arbutus, 1332
Arcturus, 70
Arrows, 1565, 1729
Artist, 307
Asking, no less than skies, 352
Aster, 331
Asterisk, 1639, 1647
Atom, preferred, 664
Auctioneer, prices of despair, 1612
Aurora borealis, 290, 1002
Autumn, 12, 131, 656; falling leaves, 873; Indian summer, 1364, 1422; beginning of, 1682; end of, 1709
Awe, 1620, 1733

BALLET, 326
Balloon, 700
Balm, 238; dooms of, 1337

Banishment, 256
Bat, 1575
Beauty, 516, 988, 1474, 1654; and truth, 449; price of, 571; an affliction? 1456; nature's fact, 1775
Bee, 676, 916, 1224, 1405, 1522; and harebell, 213; and poet, 230; separation from rose, 620; liberty of, 661; becoming a, 869; traitor, 896; abstemious, 994; letter to, 1035; familiarities, 1220; and rose, 1339; and clover, 1343, 1526, 1627, 1755
Beetles, 1128
Being, repealless, 565
Belief, 1258; abdication of, 1551
Bells, 112, 1008
Bereavement, 87, 88, 104, 882, 1328; immortal friends, 645; part of us taken, 1605; which misses most? 1759. *See also* the Dead
Bible, 1545; First Corinthians, 62; Revelation, 168, 1115; Genesis, 1115
Birdling, 39
Birds, last refrain, 238; behavior of, 328, 1600, 1723; songs of, 526, 783, 1084, 1420, 1585, 1761, 1764; like down, 653; flight of, 703, 798; winged beggar, 760; lonesome glee, 774; earns the crumb, 880; dead, 1102; triumphant, 1265; magnanimous, 1304; career compared, 1655; needs no ladder, 1574. *See also* names of birds
Birthday greetings, 1156, 1488
Blackberry, 554

Bleakness, compensation for, 1064
Blindness, 327, 1018, 1284
Bliss, 1553; abyss? 340; compared, 343; gained by climbing, 359; like murder, 379; supreme, 756; pursued, 1057; stolid, 1153; and woe, 1168. *See also* Ecstasy, Happiness, Joy, Rapture, Transport
Blue Bird, 1395, 1465
Blue Jay, 1177, 1561, 1635
Bobolink, 755, 1279, 1591
Bone, marrow of, 1274
Books, antique, 371; enchantment of, 593; turning to, 604; as frigate, 1263; boon of, 1464; food for the spirit, 1587
Boon, delayed, 1495
Bounty, 771
Brain, funeral in, 280; current of, 556; size and weight, 632; haunted, 670; going where he belonged!, 728. *See also* Heart, Mind, Self, Soul, Spirit
Breath, simulated, 272
Bride, 461, 473, 508, 518, 817; omnipresence lies in wait for, 1497
Brook, 136, 1200, 1216
Butterfly, 129; system of aesthetics, 137; behavior of, 354, 517, 1521, 1685; two waltzed, 533; friend of buttercups, 1244; in honored dust, 1246; panting on a clover, 1387; spangled journeys, 1627

Caesars, 1325
Candle, 259
Candor, 1537
Cat, 61, 507, 1185
Caterpillar, 173, 1448
Century, 345
Chaff, 1269
Chance, 90, 879, 1150; game of, 21, 139, 172
Chestnut, 1371
Children, on lonely road, 9; death of, 146; boys, 166, 763, 1186, 1524; after school, 1532
Christ. *See* Jesus Christ
Circumference, 378, 633, 1620
Clematis, 440
Cloud, 1711; shadows of, 1105. *See also* Storm
Clover, 154, 380, 1232, 1755
Cocoon, 66, 893

Coffin, 943
Compassion, 481
Condescension, 385
Conjecture, 562, 1329; presence of, 286
Conscience, 1598
Consciousness, 822, 894, 1323; costumeless, 1454
Conservation of energy, 954
Consternation's carnival, 1658
Contemplation, 1592
Contentment, 495, 1679, 1772
Coronation, 151; triumph of, 942
Courage, 147
Courtesy, wordless, 932
Cricket, 1276
Crisis, 889, 948
Crocus, 671
Crow, 1514
Crown, 195, 336, 356, 508; Christ's, 1735
Crucifixion, newer, 553
Crumb, 791

Daffodil, 60, 927
Dandelion, 100, 1501, 1519
Danger, 1678
Darkness, 419
Day, 1676; times of, 197, 469, 931, 1095; turned away by, 425
Days, special: another, 42; endured, 410; when you praised, 659; Thanksgiving Day, 814; first and last, 902; This slow day, 1120; distinction of some, 1157; uncounted, 1184; this one day, 1253; fevered, 1441
Dead, the, 216, 409, 499, 529, 592, 813, 962, 981, 1288, 1724; their life after death, 24, 325, 417, 432, 665, 900, 1221, 1436, 1493, 1516, 1557; the body vacated, 45, 187, 519, 577, 758, 778, 1135; rising of, 89; music to awaken, 261; rapt forever, 282; recollections of, 360, 509, 610; sufferer polite, 388; face of, 482, 490; following, 542, 1742; apparitions of, 607; seeking for, 935, 949; their first repose, 942; new horizons for, 972; example of, 1030; endear in departure, 1083; praise for, 1384; thoughts of, 1390; come closer, 1399; restoration asked, 1527. *See also* Immortality, Resurrection
Death, 71, 153, 274, 524, 548, 654, 749, 960, 976, 1334, 1445, 1619,

Death (*Continued*)
1716; in nature, 28; foretold, 50; life as usual in spite of, 54; intervention of, 56; pomp of, 98, 1307; mystery of, 114; security of, 145, 1065; of children, 146, 717, 886; return from, 160, 830; majesty of, 171, 1691; nonchalance of, 194; drowning, 201, 923, 1718; doesn't hurt, 255; a clock stopped, 287; end of the track, 344; consciousness of, 358; gifts of, 382; in a house, 389, 1078; postponeless, 390; saluted, 412; tired lives, 423; in the autumn, 445; for beauty and truth, 449; choosing the manner of, 468; dying, 547, 623, 648, 692, 715, 1100, 1633; the common right, 583, 970; accidental, 614; unknown, 698, 1588, 1603; a drive with, 712; invited, 759; murder by degrees, 762; beginning of vitality, 816; leaving love behind, 831; saved from, 901; dying reorganizes estimate, 906; of little maid, 908; the white exploit, 922; freezing, 933; crisis of, 948; dying young, 990; of excellence, 999; the dying play, 1015; needs of the dying, 1026; and passion, 1033; of best men, 1044; suicide, 1062; plea for postponement, 1111; need of, 1112; as despoiling frost, 1136; doubt of our own, 1144; a child's view, 1149; fighting for life, 1188; values enhanced by, 1209; stubborn theme, 1221; more punctual than love, 1230; "God took him," 1342; span between living and dead, 1344; lonesome glory, 1370; death warrants, 1375; as night, 1533; one battle more, 1549; some other flight, 1552; likeness of the brook, 1558; miracle for all, 1626; back to, 1632; attacking from behind, 1686; publicity of, 1692; relief from dying theme, 1703. *See also* Immortality, Resurrection
Deer, 165
Defeat, 639
Delight, 257, 1186, 1191, 1299; republic of, 1107
Denial, 965
Deprivation, 773
Desire, 1430; outgrown, 1282
Despair, 305, 477, 1243; nature forgets, 768

Devil, the, 1479
Dew, 1437
Diamond, 395, 427, 1108
Dilapidation, 997
Disdain, 229
Disembodiment, 860
Disillusion, 747, 870
Disobedience, 1201
Dissolution, 236
Distance, 863, 1074, 1155; enhances, 439; between ourselves and the dead, 949
Dog, 1185
Doom, 475
Doubt, 1503, 1557
Dove, Noah's, 48
Dread, 770
Dreams, 450, 531, 1335, 1376; receding, 319; This was a dream, 1670
Drunkard, 1628, 1645
Dust, 153, 976, 1402, 1461

Eclipse, 415
Ecstasy, 125, 1640. *See also* Bliss, Happiness, Joy, Rapture, Transport
Eden, 211, 213, 1069, 1657
Electricity, 630
Elegy, mock, 1539
Elephant, 229
Eloquence, 1268
Emigrant, 821
Endings, 934
Enjoyment, 1131; sources of, 842
Enough, 1291, 1596
Escape, 77, 1347
Eternity, 350, 624, 695, 1499, 1684; as the sea, 76; face of, 461; fork in being's road, 615; miracle behind, 721; in time, 800; prepares for stupendous vision, 802; velocity or pause, 1295; that to which the grave adheres, 1504. *See also* Immortality, Infinity
Evening, 1278, 1672; twilight, 1104; autumn, 1140
Exhilaration, 383, 1118
Expanse, 1584
Expectation, 807
Experience, 875, 910
Experiment, 1770
Extinction, 587
Exultation, 76; bleak, 1153
Eyes, 327; meeting of, 752

Facts, 1215, 1329

Failure, 847
Faith, 185, 915, 1052, 1433; loss of, 377; of a child, 637; so vast depends, 766; in oneself, 969; cedar citadel of, 1007; of others, 1054; tattered, 1442
Fame, 866, 1066, 1475, 1531, 1659, 1763; beggar for, 1240; consummate fee of, 1427
Famine, 771; a finer, 872
Fancy, 562
Fate, 1524
Fear, 305, 608; icicles upon my soul, 768; overcome by suffering, 1181; anticipating, 1277; seraphic, 1518
Feather, 687
February, 1250
Fence, climbing the, 251
Fire, 1063; and flood, 530; that lasts, 1132
Firefly, 1468
Fitness, 1109
Flowers, 22, 133, 137, 404, 868, 1058; bulbs, 66; a flower described, 72, 978; so small a flower, 81; the dingle robbed, 91; for a grave, 95, 905; borrowing, 134; little beds of, 142; little arctic, 180; "not at home," 206; tended for the loved, 339; as jewels, 397; fading into Divinity, 682; plea for grace to, 707; as bauble, 805; good will of, 849; a maid would be a flower, 869; seed pod, 899; neighbors fleet, 1394; stem, 1520; weed, 1586; boon of, 1589; healing power of, 1735. See also names of flowers
Flowers, verses sent with, 32, 33, 44, 82, 86, 200, 202, 224, 308, 330, 334, 402, 434, 440, 447, 484, 558, 671, 730, 785, 845, 852, 903, 994, 1019, 1038, 1324, 1456, 1579, 1582, 1611, 1618, 1621
Fly, 1035, 1246
Food, savory at distance, 439; spiritual, 1555
Forgetting, 8, 33, 47, 267, 433, 1360
Forgiveness, 237
Fortitude, 310
Friends, 278, 1199, 1336, 1366; separation of, 5, 23, 710, 825, 881, 993, 1087, 1141; boon of, 20, 1464, 1643; fear for the life of, 734; humility asked of, 1502; messages to, 33, 123, 223, 691, 834, 1096, 1160, 1368, 1398, 1637; heart fit for rest, 84;

puzzling, 92; attacked, 118; doubting love of, 156; fear of hurting, 205; shutting the door, 220; service to, as thanks, 226; loss of, 245, 259, 953, 1219, 1318, 1754; emotional intensity of, 346, 446, 458; few deeply missed, 372; recollection of, 509; forgiveness of, 538; girls' confidences, 586; different futures, 631; arrival, 635; slighted by, 704; still precious, 727; in neighboring horizon, 752; prospective, 837; reunion with aged, 940; gulf between, 941; diverging flints, 958; separated by death, 1037; importance of, 1308; need of a smile, 1391; shunning, 1429; request for news of, 1432; hearing the name of, 1504; never met, 1614; forgotten by, 1683
Friendship, 55, 109; Destiny in, 1548; boon of, 1615. See also Love
Frog, 288, 1359, 1379
Frost, 337, 391, 1014, 1202, 1236, 1624
Fruit, forbidden, 1377
Future, office of, 672; inescapable, 1631

Gain, 522, 684, 843, 1179
Gap, 546
Garden, 116, 484; of the heart, 2
Gentian, 331, 442, 1424
Ghost, 274
Glee, 326, 774
Glory, 349, 1660
God, 357, 836, 1163, 1439, 1719; not caring, 376; no face, 564; attributes of, 576, 820, 1305, 1689; our old neighbor, 623; the Trinity, 626; His oath to sparrows, 690; worshiped in "small Deity," 694; His perturbless plan, 724; His test, 823; grace of, 839; interview with, 844; the creator, 848, 1528; awareness of, 867; light of, 871; eyes of, 894; of flint, 1076; Father and Son, 1258; safe distance from, 1403; intrusion of, 1462; His hand amputated, 1551; asking forgiveness of, 1601
Gold, 454; buried, 11
Grass, 333
Gratitude, 989, 1192, 1617
Grave, the, 829, 943, 1183, 1256, 1288, 1652; daisies and birds, 96; the thoughtful grave, 141; no chatter here, 408; color of, 411; playing on, 467;

Grave, the (*Continued*)
  precedes and follows, 784; feeling experienced at, 856; obtains all prizes, 897; blanketed with snow, 942; after a hundred years, 1147; and eternity, 1503; cordial, 1625; a living grave, 1632; illumines, 1666; "keeping house" in, 1743. *See also* Tomb
Graveyard, 51, 892, 1443, 1758
Grief, 561, 793; wading, 252; looking back on, 660; laugh and run away, 1726
Growth, 320, 563, 750, 1067
Guessing, 1608
Gun, loaded, 754

HAPPINESS, 787. *See also* Bliss, Ecstasy, Joy, Rapture, Transport
Harebell, 213
Harvest, vanished, 178
Haying, 529
Heart, as a gift, 26, 1027; admonition to, 47; poor, torn, 78; little, forsaken, 192; the hound within, 186; imperial, 217; in port, 249; largest woman's, 309; knocking at, 317, 1567; sequence of things asked, 536; heaviest, 688; like the sea, 928; ancient fashioned, 973; the tune too red, 1059; closes the door, 1098; extent of, 1162; popular, 1226; over-eager, 1237; broken, 1304, 1736; dirty but fair, 1311; vast, broken, 1312; and mind a continent, 1354; full of meat, 1355; skepticism of, 1413; dowers of prospective, 1416; truly torn, 1440; pirate of, 1546; adjourning, 1613; sympathy with broken, 1704; the mob within, 1745. *See also* Love
Heart's-ease, 176
Heaven, 370, 374, 413, 431, 489, 977, 1056, 1270, 1360; goal of experience, 7; "Zenith" now, 70; going to, 79; no bells nor factories, 112; beguiles the tired, 121; many mansions, 127; like the unattainable, 239; dissolved, 243; shut out of, 248; signalized by Hell, 459; unexpected, 513; sickening for, 559; symbols of, 575; lovers meeting in, 625; the house of supposition, 696; bashful Heaven, 703; how far?, 929; a prison?, 947; looking for the site of, 959; doubt of, 1012; obstacles between, 1043; above and below,

1205; to enclose the Saints, 1228; restitution by, 1303; not for us, 1408; finding it below, 1544; dismay at, 1580; immured in, 1594. *See also* Paradise
Heavens, the, 600
Hell, 929
Help, human and divine, 767; to the distressed, 919
Hemlock, 41, 525
History, troubled lives of, 295
Home, 589, 944; revisited, 609; no matter how late, 207
Honey, 676, 1607
Honor, 1193, 1366C, 1671
Hope, 254, 405, 1041, 1283, 1392, 1481, 1547; and fear, 768, 1181; end of, 913; and disappointment, 1264
Hosts, visitation by, 298
Houses, lonely, 289; deserted, 399
Human beings, 1663; gallant fight within, 126; lonesome exiles, 262; discern provincially, 285; each other's convert, 387; gentlewomen, 401; outer and inner, 451; silent man, 543; the art to save, 539; shame of nobleness, 551; greatness, 796; kings within, 803; infinite relations, 1040; meat within, 1073; differences, 1189; the show, 1206; human nature, 1286; curiosity, 1417, 1688; disenchantment of, 1451; a plated person, 1453; unknown, 1497; like escaping horse, 1535; minds of, 1653; slow minded, 1697; babblers, 1748
Hummingbird, 500, 1463

IDEALS, 428, 983
Identity, unalterable, 268; turned around, 351; secret, 835
Idolatry, 1219; adjusted, 765
Immensity, 1512
Immortality, 40, 679, 946, 1234, 1365, 1599, 1728; life and death lead to, 7; compensation of, 406; taught by time, 463; riddle of, 501; thirsting for, 726; miracle before me, 771; certificate for, 1030; physiognomy of, 1138; surmise about, 1195; reserved, 1231; life is one, 1454; the whole of, 1525; molested by, 1646. *See also* Eternity, Infinity
Importunity, 179
Impossibility, 838

Infinity, 1162, 1309; passenger of, 1402; beauty is, 1474; scene of Deity, 1584. *See also* Eternity, Immortality
Insects, 1068, 1388, 1746. *See also names of insects*

JESUS CHRIST, 85, 225, 317, 497, 698, 964, 1543; Where is Jesus gone?, 158; base as, 394; If Jesus was sincere, 432; loving as well as, 456; prayer to, 502; crucifixion, 553; He stooped, 833; His birthday, 1487; "Come unto me," 1574, 1586; cup of anguish, 1736
Jewel, 245
Jewel-weed, 697
Joy, 252, 1382, 1726; and pain inseparable, 582; too much, 313; likeness to grief, 329; loss of, 430; in bird songs, 1420; insecurity of, 1434; ineffable, 1744. *See also* Bliss, Ecstasy, Happiness, Rapture, Transport
Judge, 699
Judgment, 1671

KING, 103, 166
Knitting, 748

LANDSCAPE, 375
Lark, 143, 861
Laurel, 1393
Leaves, rustling of, 987; verse sent with, 1257
Leopard, 209, 492
Letters, 169, 441, 494, 636, 1313, 1639; to the Lord, 487
Liberty, 720, 728; inner, 613; left inactive, 1082
Life, 80, 159, 583, 601, 960, 1101, 1287, 1652, 1717; as a sea, 4; as a boat, 30; the Culprit, 108; our share, 113; little things, 189; the "narrow way," 234; reasoning about, 301; living hurts more than dying, 335; sudden eclipse, 415; darknesses in, 419; learning to cypher, 545; power in being alive, 677; goal of, 680; minor apparatus of, 706; created and effaced, 724; mixing bells and palls, 735; struggle, 806; beginning of vitality, 816; news and shows, 827; finite, 936; closing door, 953; the worst not repeated, 979; mortal consequence, 982; death in, 1017; opening and close of, 1047; pause to evaluate, 1086; another

hour of, 1111; like building a house, 1142; magical extents, 1165; speculation on, 1293; reservoir of, 1294; crown of, 1357; shortness of, 1506; moves forward, 1515; slowing of, 1571; reverberation of, 1581; as a show, 1644; time's stream, 1656; morning and noon, 1675; ceasing to care, 1706; ablative estate, 1741
Life and the individual, 351, 904; obscure problem, 10; seeing the rest of, 174; priceless hay, 178; asking too large, 352; a primer, 418; suspended, 443, 510; existence, 470; making one's toilette, 485; starved, 612; interrupted, 617; individual romance, 669; chasm in, 858; first and last days of a, 902; steep hill of, 1010; vital word, 1039; trying on the utmost, 1277; a pit, 1712; draught of, 1720; price of, 1725
Light, 862, 1233, 1556, 1714; awakens town, 1000; peculiar, 1362; Auroral, 1577
Lightning, 362, 1173
Lily, 392
Liquor, never brewed, 214; connoisseur in, 1628
Littleness, crumb would suffice, 651; of accomplishment, 1024; of Earth, 1024
Loneliness, 405, 532, 590, 777; another, 1116
Longing, 1255
Loss, 49, 181, 472, 840, 1179
Love, 453, 491, 809, 826, 917, 924, 1438, 1477, 1563, 1765, 1771; mother's, 164; cherishing, 521; test of, 573; legacy of love, 644; divine, 673; waiting, 781; outgrown, 887; narrow loving, 907; coeval with poetry, 1247; incidents of, 1248; boon of, 1485; achieved by few, 1680; tired, 1731
Love and the individual, led home, 190; separation, 240, 620, 640, 956, 1743; sharing, 246; renunciation, 271, 366; dedication, 273, 339, 603; totality, 275, 284, 1013; that stop-sensation, 293; anniversary, 296; sacred troth, 322; one port, 368; the guilty one, 394; veil between, 398; constancy, 400, 438, 464, 1005, 729, 1357, 1737; on earth preferred, 418; year by year, 434; loving how well?, 456; toil of, 478; reasons for loving, 480; identification, 491, 725; envy, 498; trans-

Love and the individual (*Continued*) figured by, 506; baptism of, 508; uncertainty, 511; remembering for two, 523; a sweeping river, 537; is life, 549; journey of, 550, 1664; not understood, 568; mutuality, 580, 909; as light, 611; sudden light, 638; decision, 643; rectifying, 646; liberation of, 728; unworthiness for, 751; loyalty, 754; reunion in Heaven, 788; waiting, 850; pride of, 914, 1736; struck, maimed, robbed by, 925; surrender, 966; growing fitter for, 968; discipline, 1022; being owned, 1028; exaltation, 1053; story unrevealed, 1088; knowing and fearing, 1218; paying all but immortality, 1231; reunion, 1383; how old the news, 1476; intimacy, 1721

Loved, the, as the Sun, 106; face of the loved, 247, 336, 815, 1001; guessing hurts, 253; death of the loved considered, 263, 577, 648, 1260; his rare life hid, 338; as moon to sea, 429; presents a claim, 463; footstep of, 570; lifting, 616; first visit recalled, 663; suiting the loved, 738; lessons taught by, 740; cannot be forfeited, 775; distance unimportant, 808; long absence, 877; service to, 961

Lovers, young lovers, 208; meeting in Paradise, 474, 625; glory's far sufficiency, 1229; beggar and owner, 1314; expected visit, 1449; mathematics of, 1484

Madness, 435, 1284; could it be?, 410
Magician, 1158
Magnanimity, 1699
Make-believe, 188, 1290
March, 736, 1213, 1320, 1404, 1669
Marriage, 1569; of the soul, 493
Martyrs, 260, 792
Memory, 939, 1182, 1266, 1273, 1406, 1578, 1753; fleeing from, 1242
Mind, posture of, 105; a plank in reason broke, 280; hermetic, 711; choosing against itself, 910; cleaving in, 937; banquet within, 1223; fat or emaciated, 1355; inlets and outlets, 1421; myrrhs and mochas of, 1537; foliage of, 1634. See also Brain, Heart, Self, Soul, Spirit
Misery, 787; this is misery, 462; wrinkled finger of, 1171; society for me, 1534
Moment, best, 393; sumptuous, 1125; present, 1380
Months, 386. See also names of months
Moon, 429, 629, 737; portrait in the, 504
Morning, 101, 232, 300, 304; dawn, 347; second dawn, 1610
Morning-glory, 1038
Mother, 1758
Mountains, 666, 667, 722, 975
Mouse, 61
Munificence, 323
Mushroom, 1298
Music, whistling, 83; heavenly, 157; unheard by dead, 261; translation of, 503; raised by, 505; as anodyne, 755; dying at, 1003; reportless measures, 1048; fascinating chill, 1480

Names mentioned in poems, Abraham, 1317; Adam, 3, 1119, 1195; John Alden, 357; Amphitrite, 284; Ananias, 1201; Major André, 468; Atropos, 11; Austin (William Austin Dickinson), 2; Beatrice, 371; Currer Bell (Charlotte Brontë), 148; Belshazzar, 1460; Bluebeard, 302; Bobadilla, 697; Daniel Boone, 3; Brontë (Charlotte Brontë), 148; Mr. Bryant (William Cullen Bryant), 131; Caesar, 102; Carlo, 186; Cato, 97; Cato's daughter (Portia), 102; Cinderella, 302; Columbus, 3; Dante, 371; David, 540, 1545; Dollie (Susan H. Dickinson), 51, 156, 158; Domenichino, 291; Elijah, 1254; Eliza (Eliza Coleman), 1; Elizabeth (Queen Elizabeth of England), 1321; Emeline (Emeline Kellogg), 1; Essex, 1321; Gabriel, 195, 336, 498, 673, 725, 1484, 1570; Gessler, 1152; Golia[t]h, 540, 1290; Guido (Guido Reni), 1; Hamlet, 741; Harriet (Harriet Merrill), 1; Herschel (Sir William Herschel), 835; Hesperides, 1067; Dr. Holland (Josiah Gilbert Holland), 163; Isaac, 1317; Iscariot (Judas Iscariot), 1298; Ishmael, 504; Israel, 597; Jacob, 59; Jason, 870, 1466; Jehovah, 415, 455, 626, 746, 982, 1748; John, 497; Judas, 1545; Juliet, 741; Jupiter, 1730; Katie (Kate Scott Anthon), 222,

Names mentioned in poems (*Continued*)
1410; William Kidd, 11, 555; Le Verriere (Urbain Leverrier), 149; Little John, 302; Lot, 702; Luna, 3; Mars, 3; Memnon, 261; Midas, 1466, 1548; Miles (Miles Standish), 357; Montcalm (General Louis Joseph Montcalm), 678; Moses, 168, 597, 1201, 1733; Mozart, 503; Napoleon, 159; Nicodemus, 140, 1274; Noah, 403; Orleans, 283; Orpheus, 1545; Pattie, 3; Paul, 597, 1166, 1492; Peter, 3, 193, 203; Peter Parley (Samuel Griswold Goodrich), 3, 65; Philip, 1202; Philip (Philip van Artevelde), 29; Pontius Pilate, 1735; Pizarro, 73; Plato, 371; Priscilla (Priscilla Mullens), 357; Prometheus, 1132; Puck, 1279; Richard (Richard Matthews), 445; Romeo, 741; Santa Claus, 445; Sappho, 371; Sarah (Sarah Taylor), 1; Satan, 1545; Shakespeare, 741; Shaw (Henry Shaw), 116; Shylock, 247; Silas, 1166; Sister Sue (Susan H. Dickinson), 14; Sophocles, 371; Soto (Hernando de Soto), 832; Stephen, 597; Susan (Susan H. Dickinson), 1400, 1401; Tell (William Tell), 1152; Thomas, 555, 861; Mr. Thomson (James Thomson), 131; Tim, 196; Titian, 291; Trotwood (David Copperfield), 1020; Vandyke, 606; Wolfe (General James Wolfe), 678

Nature, 668, 841, 1139, 1170, 1371, 1400; signs of, 97; mystery of, 128; effect on the poet, 155; aspects of, 258, 297, 627, 1075; ripening, 332; goes on, 714, 1338; without a syllable, 811; not a berry?, 846; forces of, 854; colors in, 1045; house of, 1050; doubt of, 1080; hospitality of, 1077; nature's show, 1097; change of mood, 1115; as mother, 1143; flowers and bees, 1220; permanence of, 1257; trusty, 1369; earthly things, 1373; the tunes of, 1389; imposing negative of, 1673; relishes the pinks, 1641; exchange of clime, 1762. *See also* Birds, Cloud, Flowers, Grass, Insects, Seasons, Sky, Storm, Sun, Trees, etc.; also names of trees, flowers, birds, insects, and other creatures

Nerve, 511

News, 1089, 1319, 1665; from immortality, 827
Night, 425, 471; nightfall, 416; tremendous morrow, 1534
Nobody, 288

Oak, 41
Object, loss of, 1071
Offerings, 38
Opinion, 1455
Opposites, 63, 73, 119, 135, 355, 689
Organ, 183
Oriole, 526, 1466
Owl, 699

Pain, 341, 599, 650, 806, 967; prepares for peace, 63; skill to instill, 177; makes work difficult, 244; old road through, 344; languor after, 396; viewing through, 572; legacy of, 644; cannot recollect, 650; hallowing of, 772; and death, 1049; a pang in spring, 1530
Painters, 505, 544
Paradise, 215, 1069, 1119, 1145; guest in, 1180, 1305; who has, 1348; vicinity of, 1411; road to, 1491
Parasol and umbrella, 1747
Parting, 996, 1614, 1732, 1739; auctioneer of, 1612
Past, the, 1203, 1498
Patience, 926
Peace, 912; elusive, 739
Pearl, 424, 452, 693; of great price, 270
Pencil, 921
Perception, 420, 1071
Persons, faces of, 353, 514, 1345, 1712; men, 43, 422, 865, 955, 1031, 1130, 1378, 1446, 1629; women, 84, 283, 479, 535, 732, 810, 1011, 1124, 1267, 1486, 1562, 1568, 1667, 1722; young lovers, 208; preacher, 315, 1207; quiet child, 486; "Thief," 1460
Phantoms, 1161
Philosophy, 301
Phoebe, 1009
Pilot, 4
Pine, 161, 797; pine needles, 602
Pirate, 1546
Pity, 588
Places mentioned in poems, Alps, 80, 124; Amherst, 179, 215; Apennine, 210, 300, 534; Ararat, 403; Arctic, 851; Athens, 1769; Auburn, 32; Ba-

Places mentioned in poems (*Continued*) hamas, 697; Baltic, 1029; Batize, 1148; Bethlehem, 85, 236, 1237, 1487, 1492, 1547; Brazil, 621, 841; Brussels, 602; Buenos Ayres, 299; Bunker Hill, 3; Burmah, 1466; Calvary, 313, 348, 364, 549, 553, 561, 577, 620, 725, 1072, 1432; Canaan, 597; Cashmere, 725; Caspian, 212, 276, 1291, 1754; Chimborazo, 453; Cordillera, 268, 534, 1029; Dnieper, 525; Don, 525; Doon, 3; Ethiopia, 492; Etna, 1146; Frankfort, 123, 214; Geneva, 287; Gethsemane, 148, 313, 553, 1432; Ghent, 29; Gibraltar, 350; Golconda, 299; Great Britain, 1512; Haworth, 148; Himmaleh, 252, 350, 481, 862; Hybla, 715; India, 299, 430; Indies, 1117; Italy, 80; Jordan, 59; Judea, 964; Kidderminster, 602; Lapland, 525; Libya, 681; Mediterranean, 628, 1302; Mexico, 1471; Naples, 601, 1146; Nebo, 597; North America, 243; Ophir, 1366; Paris, 138; Peru, 247, 299, 1366; Pompeii, 175; Popocatepetl, 422; Potomac, 596; Potosi, 119, 1117; Pyrenees, 1087; Red Sea, 1642; Rhine, 123, 214, 230, 383; Russia, 942; Sahara, 1291, 1664; San Domingo, 137, 697; Sicily, 994, 1705; South America, 1705; Teneriffe, 300, 666; Thermopylae, 1554; Thessaly, 715; Timbuctoo, 981; Tripoli, 1627; Tunis, 1464; Tuscarora, 3; Van Dieman's Land, 511; Venice, 138; Vera Cruz, 697; Vesuvius, 754, 1705; Vevay, 138, 206; Westminster, 1011; Yorkshire, 148; Zanzibar, 247

Planetary forces, 560
Plated wares, 747
Play, 244
Pleading, habitual, 731
Pleasure, 541, 782, 1281
Pledge, 46
Poetry, 441, 1247, 1472
Poets, 250, 448, 505, 544, 569, 883; the poet as carpenter, 488; choice of words, 1126
Portraits, 170
Possession, 1090; by right, 528
Possessions, 1208
Possibility, 657
Power, 1238
Prayer, unanswered, 376; apparatus of,

437; modest, 476; awed beyond my errand, 564; to Madonna, 918; denied, 1751
Predestination, 1021
Presentiment, 764
Prison, 652, 1166; magic, 1601
Privacy, 891
Problems, 69
Prosperity, interior sources, 395
Publication, 709
Purple, 776, 980

QUEEN, 373, 1710
Question, troubled, 48

RAGS, 117
Rainbow, 257
Rapture, 184; expense of, 1679. See also Bliss, Ecstasy, Joy, Transport
Rat, 61, 1340, 1356
Recollection, 367, 898, 1507
Remembrance, 1182, 1508; if remembering were forgetting, 33
Remorse, 744
Renown, 1006
Renunciation, 527, 745, 853. See also Love and the individual, renunciation
Reprieve, 1559
Request, 1076
Respite, 708
Resurrection, 62, 515, 984, 1492
Retrospection, 995
Revelation, 662, 685, 1241, 1459
Revenge, 1509
Revolution, 1082
Riches, 299, 454, 466, 791, 1093, 1640; unconscious of, 424; desire for, 801. See also Wealth
Riddle, 89, 1222
Ripeness, 332, 483, 1067
Risk, 1151, 1175, 1239; staking all, 971
River, to sea, 162
Robber, 289
Robin, 634, 828, 869, 1483, 1542, 1570; departure and return of, 5; in red cravat, 182; records the lady's name, 864; locks her nest, 1606
Room, mighty, 1767
Rope, 1322
Rose, 19, 35, 110, 138, 163; unexpected maid, 17; ordained, 34; attar from the, 675; and bee, 1154, 1339; "Lethe," 1730
Routine, 1196

SABBATH KEEPING, 324
Saints, their circuit, 1541
Satisfaction, 1036
Science, 70, 168
Sea, 520, 884, 1217; take me?, 162; drop in the, 284; and brook, 1210; undulating rooms, 1428
Seasons, 6, 403, 1381; shifting picture, 375; reversing the Zodiac, 1025; change of, 1682; Autumn or Spring, 1690. *See also names of seasons*
Secrets, 381, 1326; of the skies, 191; suburbs of, 1245; emerge but once, 1385; man's mind, 1663
Self, I — "Tim," 196; self-assault, 642; behind ourself, 670; self-esteem, 713; society in oneself, 746; columnar, 789; "Undiscovered Continent," 832; freckled, 1094; stature of the, 1177; survival of the, 1195; embarrassments, 1214; indestructible estate, 1351; ecstatic nation, 1354. *See also* Brain, Heart, Mind, Soul, Spirit
Sense, 435, 1727
September, 1271
Sequence, 992
Sewing, 617
Shadow, 1187
Shame, 1412
Ships, bark, 52, 1234; little boat, 107; brig, 723; frigate, 1263
Shipwreck, 619
Shrine, 918
Sickness, gain from, 574
Sight, clarified, 1362, 1714
Silence, 1004, 1251
Simplicity, 1469
Size, intrinsic, 641
Sky, 600, 1415, 1494
Sleds, 1498
Sleep, 13
Snake, 986, 1500, 1740
Snow, 36, 311; driven by wind, 1361
Society, in oneself, 746; the frown of, 874
Soldiers, 73, 147
Sorrow, 1197, 1368
Soul, lost boat, 107; throwing dice for, 139; lamp within, 233; soundness of, 242; at play, in pain, 244; reliance on death, 292; chooses one, 303, 664; awareness of immortality, 306; scalped, 315; storm within, 362; on the forge, 365; exhilaration of, 383; at liberty,

384; climax of agony, 414; ripening, 483; numbness of, 496; chaos in, 510; fright and escape of, 512; hunger of, 579; battle of, 594; unemployed, 618; moments of dominion, 627; imprisoned, 652; guest of, 674, 1055, 1262; in awe of itself, 683; as friend, 753; blankness in, 761; choice limited to one, 769; caverns of, 777; adventure unto itself, 822; entombed, 876; company within, 855; flower of, 945; gone to Heaven, 947; after suffering, 957; awareness of immortality, 974; an Emperor, 980; missing all, 985; paralysis of, 1046; earns subsistence, 1081; as butterfly, 1099; errand of, 1103; proving the sinews, 1113; wound not admitted, 1123; cellars of, 1225; scathing test of, 1414; inundated, 1425; electric gale of, 1431; welcomed as guest, 1661; polar privacy, 1695; sentenced to winter, 1756. *See also* Brain, Heart, Mind, Self, Spirit
Sovereign, offended, 235
Sparrow, 1211
Spider, 605, 1138, 1167, 1275, 1423
Spirit, 733, 1482, 1576; temple of, 578; and dust, 976; still vacation of, 1592; released, 1630. *See also* Brain, Heart, Mind, Self, Soul
Spring, 64, 74, 99, 140; light in, 812; from God, 844; hueless without the loved, 1042; the old desire, 1051; blossoms of, 1133; approach of, 1297; put up hoary work, 1310; experiment in green, 1333; a pang in, 1530
Squirrel, 1374
Stars and Planets, Arcturus, 70; Pleiads, 282, 851; Mercury, 835; Saturn, 1086; Orion, 1538
Stone, 1510
Stooping, 833
Storm, 198, 1235, 1419, 1593; after, 194; shower, 794; thunderstorm, 824, 1172, 1649; gale, 1327, 1397; threatening, 1694
Strawberries, 251
Stubble, 1407
Success, 67
Suffering, 405, 1041; cessation of, 584
Suicide, 1062; thoughts of, 277
Summer, 122, 342, 1198, 1386; no more astir, 16; death of, 18, 75, 1572; emotion in, 111; Indian Summer, 130,

Summer (*Continued*)
1364, 1422; recollection of, 302;
strives with frost, 337; deepened, 574;
a day in, 606; sympathy with, 743;
two Junes, 930; end of, 1330, 1536,
1540, 1773; last of, 1353; simple hat
of, 1363; half gone, 1715; final crea-
tures, 1766
Sun, 591, 878, 1023, 1372, 1447, 1550,
1636; flower at his feet, 106; touched
morning, 232; goes on, 714; compared
with earth, 888; following the, 920;
supercilious, 950; superfluous, 999;
witness for, 1079; beneath the, 1122;
massacre of suns, 1127; alters the
world, 1148; balls of gold, 1178; and
fog, 1190
Sunrise, and sunset, 204, 318, 1032; to
the doomed, 294
Sunset, 15, 120, 152, 219, 221, 228,
265, 266, 291, 552, 595, 628, 658,
716, 938, 1114, 1609, 1622, 1642,
1650, 1676, 1693; and sunrise, 204,
318, 1032; competition with, 308;
mountains at, 667, 757; on the hills,
1016; as revelation, 1241; drama of,
1349; and the dead, 1390
Surgeons, 108
Surmise, 1662
Surprise, 1306
Survival, 1121, 1194
Suspense, 705, 1285, 1331, 1760; vague
calamity, 971

Tears, 189, 877, 1192, 1426
Temples, building, 488
Tent, circus, 243
Thanksgiving Day, 814
Thief, 1470
Thirst, 132, 490, 726, 818
Thought, 210, 581, 701, 998, 1469; re-
portless subjects, 1048
Thoughtfulness, 818
Thunderbolt, 1581
Tiger, 566, 872
Time, 406, 624, 802, 1106, 1458, 1478;
passage of, 57, 1457; not a remedy,
686; admirations and contempts of,
906; relative, 1295; offered reprieve,
1473; too happy, 1774
Tippler, 214
Tomb, the, 115, 457, 911, 1701; ala-
baster chambers. 216; tells no secret,

408; no disturbance in, 1172; a dimple
in, 1489; stupendous, 1674
Tombstone, 1396
Tomorrow, 1367, 1713
Totality, 655, 819, 1341; venturing all,
172
Tragedy, 1698
Train, railroad, 585
Transitions, 1602
Transport, 184, 256. *See also* Bliss, Ec-
stasy, Happiness, Joy, Rapture
Traveler, 1450
Treason, 851
Treasure, hidden, 1110
Trees, 314, 742, 1471, 1590. *See also*
names of trees
Trial, 497
Tribulation, victors over, 325
Triumph, 455
Trouble, 269
Trust, 43, 555
Truth, 836, 1455; bold and cold, 281;
and beauty, 449; stirless, 780; blind-
ing, 1129; is good health, 1453
Tulip, 25

United states, 1511
Units, in a crowd, 565

Valentines, 1, 3
Values, 534, 696, 857, 1133, 1301, 1706
Veil, 421
Victory, possibility of, 42; definition of,
67; too late, 690; in retrospect, 1227;
slain, 1249
Violet, 557
Void, timeless, 1159
Volcanoes, 175, 601, 1146, 1677, 1705,
1748

Waking, 450
Want, 1036
War, 444; solemn, 1174; dimpled, 1529;
one battle more, 1549
Waters, deep, 598, 1599; still, 1595;
threatening, 1749
Wave, 1604
Wealth, 427, 1117. *See also* Riches
Wells, 460, 1091, 1400
Wheat, 1269
Whippoorwill, 161
Wife, 199, 732, 1072, 1737

Wind, 316, 321, 436, 1134, 1137, 1418; south, 719; of the spirit, 1259; root of, 1302; slow, 1571

Winter, 1252, 1316, 1708; solstice, 1696

Witchcraft, 1583, 1708

Withdrawal, 609, 635, 1098, 1169, 1410

Woe, 1136, 1168; knowing the worst, 281; Nature did not care, 364; respite from, 708; childhood's, 1738

Wonder, 37, 1331

Woodpecker, 1034

Woods, 41

Words, 952, 1212, 1261, 1409, 1452, 1467, 1750; can pierce, 8; one English phrase, 276; to every thought but one, 581; revealed not chosen, 1126; trusty word, 1347; treason of an accent, 1358; made flesh, 1651; failure of, 1668, 1700

Work, difficult in pain, 244; for sanity's sake, 443; unrewarded, 779; to fill the vacuum, 786; luck is toil, 1350

Worm, 885, 1670

Wound, probing the, 379

Wren, 143

YEAR, DEATH OF THE, 93; ribbons of, 873

Yesterday, 1292

Youth, immortal, 1289

Index of First Lines

Following the first lines of the poems are the poem numbers. No attempt is made to reproduce the exact punctuation or capitalization of the lines as they appear in the text.

A bee his burnished carriage, 1339
A bird came down the walk, 328
A burdock clawed my gown, 229
A cap of lead across the sky, 1649
A charm invests a face, 421
A chilly peace infests the grass, 1443
A clock stopped, 287
A cloud withdrew from the sky, 895
A coffin is a small domain, 943
A counterfeit, a plated person, 1453
A curious cloud surprised the sky, 1710
A darting fear, a pomp, a tear, 87
A day! Help! Help! Another day, 42
A death blow is a life blow to some, 816
A deed knocks first at thought, 1216
A dew sufficed itself, 1437
A diamond on the hand, 1108
A dimple in the tomb, 1489
A door just opened on a street, 953
A doubt if it be us, 859
A drop fell on the apple tree, 794
A drunkard cannot meet a cork, 1628
A dying tiger moaned for drink, 566
A face devoid of love or grace, 1711
A faded boy in sallow clothes, 1524
A feather from the whippoorwill, 161
A field of stubble lying sere, 1407
A first mute coming, 702
A flower will not trouble her, 1621
A full fed rose on meals of tint, 1154
A fuzzy fellow without feet, 173
A great hope fell, 1123
A happy lip breaks sudden, 353
A house upon the height, 399
A lady red amid the hill, 74
A lane of yellow led the eye, 1650
A letter is a joy of earth, 1639

A light exists in spring, 812
A little bread, a crust, a crumb, 159
A little dog that wags his tail, 1185
A little east of Jordan, 59
A little madness in the spring, 1333
A little overflowing word, 1467
A little road not made of man, 647
A little snow was here and there, 1444
A long, long sleep, a famous sleep, 654
A loss of something ever felt I, 959
A man may make a remark, 952
A mien to move a queen, 283
A mine there is no man would own, 1117
A moth the hue of this, 841
A murmur in the trees to note, 416
A narrow fellow in the grass, 986
A nearness to tremendousness, 963
A night there lay the days between, 471
A pang is more conspicuous in spring, 1530
A pit but heaven over it, 1712
A plated life diversified, 806
A poor torn heart, a tattered heart, 78
A precious mouldering pleasure 'tis, 371
A prison gets to be a friend, 652
A prompt executive bird is the jay, 1177
A rat surrendered here, 1340
A route of evanescence, 1463
A saucer holds a cup, 1374
A science so the savants say, 100
A secret told, 381
A sepal, petal, and a thorn, 19
A shade upon the mind there passes, 882
A shady friend for torrid days, 278
A sickness of this world it most occasions, 1044
A single clover plank, 1343
A single screw of flesh, 263
A slash of blue, 204
A sloop of amber slips away, 1622
A soft sea washed around the house, 1198
A solemn thing it was I said, 271
A solemn thing within the soul, 483
A something in a summer's day, 122
A south wind has a pathos, 719
A sparrow took a slice of twig, 1211
A spider sewed at night, 1138
A stagnant pleasure like a pool, 1281
A still volcano life, 601
A thought went up my mind today, 701
A throe upon the features, 71
A toad can die of light, 583
A tongue to tell him I am true, 400
A tooth upon our peace, 459
A train went through a burial gate, 1761
A transport one cannot contain, 184

A visitor in marl, 391
A weight with needles on the pounds, 264
A wife at daybreak I shall be, 461
A wild blue sky abreast of winds, 1415
A wind that rose, 1259
A winged spark doth soar about, 1468
A word dropped careless on a page, 1261
A word is dead, 1212
A word made flesh is seldom, 1651
A world made penniless by that departure, 1623
A wounded deer leaps highest, 165
Above oblivion's tide there is a pier, 1531
Abraham to kill him, 1317
Absence disembodies, so does death, 860
Absent place an April day, 927
Adrift! A little boat adrift, 30
Advance is life's condition, 1652
Afraid! Of whom am I afraid, 608
After a hundred years, 1147
After all birds have been investigated and laid aside, 1395
After great pain a formal feeling comes, 341
After the sun comes out, 1148
Again his voice is at the door, 663
Ah! Moon and star, 240
Ah! Necromancy sweet, 177
Ah, Teneriffe, 666
Air has no residence, no neighbor, 1060
All but death can be adjusted, 749
All circumstances are the frame, 820
All forgot for recollecting, 966
All I may if small, 819
All men for honor hardest work, 1193
All overgrown by cunning moss, 148
All that I do, 1496
All the letters I can write, 334
All these my banners be, 22
All things swept sole away, 1512
Alone and in a circumstance, 1167
Alone I cannot be, 298
Alter! When the hills do, 729
Although I put away his life, 366
Always mine, 839
Ambition cannot find him, 68
Ample make this bed, 829
An altered look about the hills, 140
An antiquated grace, 1345
An antiquated tree, 1514
An awful tempest mashed the air, 198
An everywhere of silver, 884
An honest tear, 1192
An hour is a sea, 825
An ignorance a sunset, 552
And this of all my hopes, 913
"And with what body do they come?", 1492

Angels in the early morning, 94
Answer July, 386
Apology for her, 852
Apparently with no surprise, 1624
"Arcturus" is his other name, 70
Are friends delight or pain, 1199
Arrows enamored of his heart, 1629
Art thou the thing I wanted, 1282
Artists wrestled here, 110
As by the dead we love to sit, 88
As children bid the guest "Good Night," 133
As far from pity as complaint, 496
As from the earth the light balloon, 1630
As frost is best conceived, 951
As if I asked a common alms, 323
As if some little arctic flower, 180
As if the sea should part, 695
As imperceptibly as grief, 1540
As old as woe, 1168
As one does sickness over, 957
As plan for noon and plan for night, 960
As sleigh bells seem in summer, 981
As subtle as tomorrow, 1713
As summer into autumn slips, 1346
As the starved maelstrom laps the navies, 872
As watchers hang upon the east, 121
As we pass houses musing slow, 1653
As willing lid o'er weary eye, 1050
Ashes denote that fire was, 1063
At half past three a single bird, 1084
At last to be identified, 174
At least to pray is left, is left, 502
At leisure is the soul, 618
Aurora is the effort, 1002
Autumn overlooked my knitting, 748
Awake ye muses nine, sing me a strain divine, 1
Away from home are some and I, 821

Back from the cordial grave I drag thee, 1625
Baffled for just a day or two, 17
Banish air from air, 854
Be mine the doom, 845
Beauty be not caused — it is, 516
Beauty crowds me till I die, 1654
Because he loves her, 1229
Because I could not stop for death, 712
Because my brook is fluent, 1200
Because that you are going, 1260
Because the bee may blameless hum, 869
Because 'twas riches I could own, 1093
Bee! I'm expecting you, 1035
Bees are black with gilt surcingles, 1405
Before he comes we weigh the time, 834
Before I got my eye put out, 327

Before the ice is in the pools, 37
Before you thought of spring, 1465
Behind me dips eternity, 721
Behold this little bane, 1438
Belshazzar had a letter, 1459
Bereaved of all, I went abroad, 784
Bereavement in their death to feel, 645
Besides the autumn poets sing, 131
Besides this May, 977
Best gains must have the losses' test, 684
Best things dwell out of sight, 998
Best witchcraft is geometry, 1158
Betrothed to righteousness might be, 1641
Better than music! For I who heard it, 503
Between my country and the others, 905
Between the form of Life and Life, 1101
Bind me, I still can sing, 1005
Birthday of but a single pang, 1488
Blazing in gold and quenching in purple, 228
Bless God, he went as soldiers, 147
Bliss is the plaything of the child, 1553
Bloom is result to meet a flower, 1058
Bloom upon the mountain stated, 667
Blossoms will run away, 1578
Bound a trouble, 269
Bring me the sunset in a cup, 128
Brother of ingots, ah Peru, 1366A
Brother of Ophir, 1366C
But little carmine hath her face, 558
By a departing light, 1714
By a flower, by a letter, 109
By chivalries as tiny, 55
By homely gift and hindered words, 1563
By my window have I for scenery, 797
By such and such an offering, 38

Candor, my tepid friend, 1537
Circumference thou bride of awe, 1620
Civilization spurns the leopard, 492
Climbing to reach the costly hearts, 1566
Cocoon above! Cocoon below, 129
Color, caste, denomination, 970
Come show thy Durham breast, 1542
Come slowly, Eden, 211
Conferring with myself, 1655
Confirming all who analyze, 1268
Conjecturing a climate, 562
Conscious am I in my chamber, 679
Consulting summer's clock, 1715
Contained in this short life, 1165
Cosmopolites without a plea, 1589
Could hope inspect her basis, 1283
Could I but ride indefinite, 661
Could I do more for thee, 447

Could I, then, shut the door, 220
Could live, did live, 43
Could mortal lip divine, 1409
Could that sweet darkness where they dwell, 1493
Count not that far that can be had, 1074
Crisis is a hair, 889
Crisis is sweet and yet the heart, 1416
Crumbling is not an instant's act, 997

Dare you see a soul at the white heat, 365
Dear March — Come in, 1320
Death is a dialogue between, 976
Death is like the insect, 1716
Death is potential to that man, 548
Death is the supple suitor, 1445
Death leaves us homesick, who behind, 935
Death sets a thing significant, 360
Death warrants are supposed to be, 1375
Death's waylaying not the sharpest, 1296
Declaiming waters none may dread, 1595
Defrauded I a butterfly, 730
Delayed till she had ceased to know, 58
Delight becomes pictorial, 572
Delight is as the flight, 257
Delight's despair at setting, 1299
Denial is the only fact, 965
Departed to the judgment, 524
Deprived of other banquet, 773
Despair's advantage is achieved, 799
Dew is the freshet in the grass, 1097
Did life's penurious length, 1717
Did our best moment last, 393
Did the harebell loose her girdle, 213
Did we abolish frost, 1014
Did we disobey him, 267
Did you ever stand in a cavern's mouth, 590
Distance is not the realm of fox, 1155
Distrustful of the gentian, 20
Do people moulder equally, 432
Dominion lasts until obtained, 1257
Don't put up my thread and needle, 617
Doom is the house without the door, 475
Doubt me! My dim companion, 275
Down time's quaint stream, 1656
Drab habitation of whom, 893
Drama's vitallest expression is the common day, 741
Dreams are the subtle dower, 1376
Dreams are well, but waking's better, 450
Dropped into the ether acre, 665
Drowning is not so pitiful, 1718
Dust is the only secret, 153
Dying at my music, 1003
Dying! Dying in the night, 158
Dying! To be afraid of thee, 831

Each life converges to some centre, 680
Each scar I'll keep for him, 877
Each second is the last, 879
Each that we lose takes part of us, 1605
Eden is that old-fashioned house, 1657
Elijah's wagon knew no thill, 1254
Elizabeth told Essex, 1321
Elysium is as far as to, 1760
Embarrassment of one another, 662
Empty my heart, of thee, 587
Endanger it, and the demand, 1658
Ended, ere it begun, 1088
Endow the living with the tears, 521
Escape is such a thankful word, 1347
Escaping backward to perceive, 867
Essential oils are wrung, 675
Estranged from beauty none can be, 1474
Except the heaven had come so near, 472
Except the smaller size, 1067
Except to heaven, she is nought, 154
Exhilaration is the breeze, 1118
Exhilaration is within, 383
Expanse cannot be lost, 1584
Expectation is contentment, 807
Experience is the angled road, 910
Experiment escorts us last, 1770
Experiment to me, 1073
Extol thee, could I? Then I will, 1643
Exultation is the going, 76

Facts by our side are never sudden, 1497
Fairer through fading, as the day, 938
"Faith" is a fine invention, 185
Faith is the pierless bridge, 915
"Faithful to the end" amended, 1357
Falsehood of thee could I suppose, 1007
Fame is a bee, 1763
Fame is a fickle food, 1659
Fame is the one that does not stay, 1475
Fame is the tint that scholars leave, 866
Fame of myself to justify, 713
Fame's boys and girls, who never die, 1066
Far from love the Heavenly Father, 1021
Fate slew him, but he did not drop, 1031
Few, yet enough, 1596
Finding is the first act, 870
Finite to fail, but infinite to venture, 847
Fitter to see him, I may be, 968
Floss won't save you from an abyss, 1322
Flowers — Well if anybody, 137
Follow wise Orion, 1538
For death or rather, 382
For each ecstatic instant, 125
For every bird a nest, 143

For largest woman's heart I knew, 309
For this accepted breath, 195
Forbidden fruit a flavor has, 1377
Forever at his side to walk, 246
Forever honored be the tree, 1570
Forever is composed of nows, 624
Forget! The lady with the amulet, 438
Fortitude incarnate, 1217
Four trees upon a solitary acre, 742
Frequently the woods are pink, 6
Frigid and sweet her parting face, 1318
From all the jails the boys and girls, 1532
From blank to blank, 761
From cocoon forth a butterfly, 354
From his slim palace in the dust, 1300
From us she wandered now a year, 890
Funny to be a century, 345
Further in summer than the birds, 1068

Garlands for queens may be, 34
Gathered into the earth, 1370
Give little anguish, 310
Given in marriage unto thee, 817
Glass was the street in tinsel peril, 1498
Glee — The great storm is over, 619
Glory is that bright tragic thing, 1660
Glowing is her bonnet, 72
Go not too near a house of rose, 1434
Go slow, my soul, to feed thyself, 1297
"Go tell it" — What a message, 1554
Go thy great way, 1638
"Go traveling with us!", 1513
God gave a loaf to every bird, 791
God is a distant, stately lover, 357
God is indeed a jealous God, 1719
God made a little gentian, 442
God made no act without a cause, 1163
God permits industrious angels, 231
Going to heaven, 79
Going to Him! Happy letter, 494
Good morning, midnight, 425
Good night, because we must, 114
Good night! Which put the candle out, 259
Good to hide and hear 'em hunt, 842
Gratitude is not the mention, 989
Great Caesar! Condescend, 102
Great streets of silence led away, 1159
Grief is a mouse, 793
Growth of man like growth of nature, 750
Guest am I to have, 1661

Had I known that the first was the last, 1720
Had I not seen the sun, 1233
Had I not this or this, I said, 904

Had I presumed to hope, 522
Had this one day not been, 1253
Had we known the ton she bore, 1124
Had we our senses, 1284
Have any like myself, 736
Have you got a brook in your little heart, 136
He ate and drank the precious words, 1587
He forgot and I remembered, 203
He fought like those who've nought to lose, 759
He found my being, set it up, 603
He fumbles at your soul, 315
He gave away his life, 567
He is alive this morning, 1160
He lived the life of ambush, 1525
He outstripped time with but a bout, 865
He parts himself like leaves, 517
He preached upon "breadth" till it argued him narrow, 1207
He put the belt around my life, 273
He scanned it, staggered, 1062
He strained my faith, 497
He told a homely tale, 763
He touched me, so I live to know, 506
He was my host, he was my guest, 1721
He was weak, and I was strong, then, 190
He went by sleep that drowsy route, 1662
He who in himself believes, 969
Heart not so heavy as mine, 83
Heart! We will forget him, 47
"Heaven" has different signs to me, 575
Heaven is so far of the mind, 370
"Heaven" is what I cannot reach, 239
"Heavenly Father" take to thee, 1461
Her breast is fit for pearls, 84
Her face was in a bed of hair, 1722
Her final summer was it, 795
Her grace is all she has, 810
Her "last Poems," 312
Her little parasol to lift, 1038
Her losses make our gains ashamed, 1562
Her smile was shaped like other smiles, 514
Her sovereign people, 1139
Her spirit rose to such a height, 1486
Her sweet turn to leave the homestead, 649
Her sweet weight on my heart a night, 518
Here where the daisies fit my head, 1037
Herein a blossom lies, 899
High from the earth I heard a bird, 1723
His bill an auger is, 1034
His bill is clasped, his eye forsook, 1102
His cheek is his biographer, 1460
His feet are shod with gauze, 916
His heart was darker than the starless night, 1378
His little hearse like figure, 1522
His mansion in the pool, 1379

His mind like fabrics of the east, 1446
His mind of man a secret makes, 1663
His oriental heresies, 1526
His voice decrepit was with joy, 1476
Hope is a strange invention, 1392
Hope is a subtle glutton, 1547
"Hope" is the thing with feathers, 254
"Houses" — so the wise men tell me, 127
How brittle are the piers, 1433
How dare the robins sing, 1724
How destitute is he, 1477
How far is it to heaven, 929
How firm eternity must look, 1499
How fits his umber coat, 1371
How fleet, how indiscreet an one, 1771
How fortunate the grave, 897
How good his lava bed, 1447
How happy I was if I could forget, 898
How happy is the little stone, 1510
How human nature dotes, 1417
How know it from a summer's day, 1364
How lonesome the wind must feel nights, 1418
How many flowers fail in wood, 404
How many schemes may die, 1150
How many times these low feet staggered, 187
How much of source escapes with thee, 1517
How much the present moment means, 1380
How news must feel when travelling, 1319
How noteless men and pleiads stand, 282
How ruthless are the gentle, 1439
How sick to wait in any place but thine, 368
How slow the wind, 1571
How soft a caterpillar steps, 1448
How soft this prison is, 1334
How still the bells in steeples stand, 1008
How the old mountains drip with sunset, 291
How the waters closed above him, 923
How well I knew her not, 837

I am afraid to own a body, 1090
I am alive I guess, 470
I am ashamed, I hide, 473
I asked no other thing, 621
I bet with every wind that blew, 1215
I breathed enough to take the trick, 272
I bring an unaccustomed wine, 132
I came to buy a smile today, 223
I can wade grief, 252
I cannot be ashamed, 914
I cannot buy it, 'tis not sold, 840
I cannot dance upon my toes, 326
I cannot live with you, 640
I cannot meet the spring unmoved, 1051
I cannot see my soul but know 'tis there, 1262

I cannot want it more, 1301
I can't tell you but you feel it, 65
I cautious scanned my little life, 178
I could bring you jewels had I a mind to, 697
I could die to know, 570
I could not drink it, sweet, 818
I could not prove the years had feet, 563
I could suffice for him, I knew, 643
I counted till they danced so, 36
I cried at pity, not at pain, 588
I cross till I am weary, 550
I did not reach thee, 1664
I died for beauty, but was scarce, 449
I dreaded that first robin so, 348
I dwell in possibility, 657
I envy seas whereon he rides, 498
I fear a man of frugal speech, 543
I felt a cleaving in my mind, 937
I felt a funeral in my brain, 280
I felt my life with both my hands, 351
I fit for them, 1109
I found the words to every thought, 581
I gained it so, 359
I gave myself to him, 580
I got so I could take his name, 293
I groped for him before I knew, 1555
I had a daily bliss, 1057
I had a guinea golden, 23
I had been hungry all the years, 579
I had no cause to be awake, 542
I had no time to hate, 478
I had not minded walls, 398
I had some things that I called mine, 116
I had the glory — that will do, 349
I have a bird in spring, 5
I have a king who does not speak, 103
I have never seen "Volcanoes," 175
I have no like but this, 1398
I haven't told my garden yet, 50
I heard a fly buzz when I died, 465
I heard as if I had no ear, 1039
I held a jewel in my fingers, 245
I hide myself within my flower, 903
I keep my pledge, 46
I knew that I had gained, 1022
I know a place where summer strives, 337
I know lives, I could miss, 372
I know of people in the grave, 1665
I know some lonely houses off the road, 289
I know suspense — it steps so terse, 1285
I know that he exists, 338
I know where wells grow, droughtless wells, 460
I learned at least what home could be, 944
I like a look of agony, 241

I like to see it lap the miles, 585
I live with him, I see his face, 463
I lived on dread, 770
I lost a world the other day, 181
I made slow riches but my gain, 843
I make his crescent fill or lack, 909
I many times thought peace had come, 739
I meant to find her when I came, 718
I meant to have but modest needs, 476
I measure every grief I meet, 561
I met a king this afternoon, 166
I never felt at home below, 413
I never hear that one is dead, 1323
I never hear the word "escape," 77
I never lost as much but twice, 49
I never saw a moor, 1052
I never told the buried gold, 11
I noticed people disappeared, 1149
I often passed the village, 51
I pay in satin cash, 402
I play at riches to appease, 801
I prayed at first a little girl, 576
I read my sentence steadily, 412
I reason earth is short, 301
I reckon when I count at all, 569
I robbed the woods, 41
I rose because he sank, 616
I saw no way — the heavens were stitched, 378
I saw that the flake was on it, 1267
I saw the wind within her, 1502
I see thee better in the dark, 611
I see thee clearer for the grave, 1666
I send two sunsets, 308
I send you a decrepit flower, 1324
I shall keep singing, 250
I shall know why, when time is over, 193
I shall not murmur if at last, 1410
I should have been too glad, I see, 313
I should not dare to be so sad, 1197
I should not dare to leave my friend, 205
I showed her heights she never saw, 446
I sing to use the waiting, 850
I sometimes drop it, for a quick, 708
I started early, took my dog, 520
I stepped from plank to plank, 875
I stole them from a bee, 200
I sued the news, yet feared the news, 1360
I suppose the time will come, 1381
I taste a liquor never brewed, 214
I tend my flowers for thee, 339
I think I was enchanted, 593
I think just how my shape will rise, 237
I think that the root of the wind is water, 1302
I think the hemlock likes to stand, 525

I think the longest hour of all, 635
I think to live may be a bliss, 646
I thought that nature was enough, 1286
I thought the train would never come, 1449
I tie my hat, I crease my shawl, 443
I took my power in my hand, 540
I took one draught of life, 1725
I tried to think a lonelier thing, 532
"I want" — it pleaded all its life, 731
I was a phoebe, nothing more, 1009
I was the slightest in the house, 486
I watched her face to see which way, 1667
I watched the moon around the house, 629
I went to heaven, 374
I went to thank her, 363
I worked for chaff and earning wheat, 1269
I would distil a cup, 16
I would not paint a picture, 505
I years had been from home, 609
I'd rather recollect a setting, 1349
Ideals are the fairy oil, 983
If all the griefs I am to have, 1726
If any sink, assure that this, now standing, 358
If anybody's friend be dead, 509
If blame be my side, forfeit me, 775
If ever the lid gets off my head, 1727
If he dissolve, then there is nothing more, 236
If he were living, dare I ask, 734
If I can stop one heart from breaking, 919
If I could bribe them by a rose, 179
If I could tell how glad I was, 1668
If I may have it when it's dead, 577
If I should cease to bring a rose, 56
If I should die, 54
If I shouldn't be alive, 182
If I'm lost now, 256
If it had no pencil, 921
If my bark sink, 1234
If nature smiles, the mother must, 1085
If pain for peace prepares, 63
If recollecting were forgetting, 33
If she had been the mistletoe, 44
If the foolish call them "flowers," 168
If this is "fading," 120
If those I loved were lost, 29
If what we could were what we would, 407
If wrecked upon the shoal of thought, 1469
If you were coming in the fall, 511
If your nerve deny you, 292
I'll clutch and clutch, 427
I'll send the feather from my hat, 687
I'll tell you how the sun rose, 318
I'm ceded, I've stopped being theirs, 508
I'm nobody! Who are you, 288

I'm saying every day, 373
I'm sorry for the dead today, 529
I'm the little "Heart's Ease," 176
I'm "wife" — I've finished that, 199
Image of light, adieu, 1556
Immortal is an ample word, 1205
Immured in heaven, 1594
Impossibility like wine, 838
In ebon box, when years have flown, 169
In falling timbers buried, 614
In lands I never saw, they say, 124
In many and reportless places, 1382
In rags mysterious as these, 117
In snow thou comest, 1669
In this short life, 1287
In thy long paradise of light, 1145
In winter in my room, 1670
Inconceivably solemn, 582
Is bliss then such abyss, 340
Is heaven a physician, 1270
Is immortality a bane, 1728
Is it too late to touch you, dear, 1637
Is it true, dear Sue, 218
It always felt to me a wrong, 597
It bloomed and dropt, a single noon, 978
It came at last but prompter death, 1230
It came his turn to beg, 1500
It can't be "summer," 221
It ceased to hurt me, though so slow, 584
It did not surprise me, 39
It don't sound so terrible, quite, as it did, 426
It dropped so low in my regard, 747
It feels a shame to be alive, 444
It is a lonesome glee, 774
It is an honorable thought, 946
It is dead — find it, 417
It is easy to work when the soul is at play, 244
It knew no lapse nor diminution, 560
It knew no medicine, 559
It makes no difference abroad, 620
It might be lonelier, 405
It rises, passes on our south, 1023
It sifts from leaden sieves, 311
It sounded as if the streets were running, 1397
It stole along so stealthy, 1457
It struck me every day, 362
It tossed and tossed, 723
It troubled me as once I was, 600
It was a grave, yet bore no stone, 876
It was a quiet seeming day, 1419
It was a quiet way, 1053
It was given to me by the gods, 454
It was not death, for I stood up, 510
It was not saint — it was too large, 1092

It was too late for man, 623
It will be summer eventually, 342
It would have starved a gnat, 612
It would never be common more, I said, 430
It would not know if it were spurned, 1579
It's all I have to bring today, 26
It's coming, the postponeless creature, 390
It's easy to invent a life, 724
Its hour with itself, 1225
It's like the light, 297
Its little ether hood, 1501
It's such a little thing to weep, 189
It's thoughts and just one heart, 495
I've dropped my brain — my soul is numb, 1046
I've got an arrow here, 1729
I've heard an organ talk sometimes, 183
I've known a heaven like a tent, 243
I've none to tell me to but thee, 881
I've nothing else to bring, you know, 224
I've seen a dying eye, 547

Jesus! thy crucifix, 225
Joy to have merited the pain, 788
Judgment is justest, 1671
Just as he spoke it from his hands, 848
Just lost, when I was saved, 160
Just once! Oh least request, 1076
Just so — Jesus raps, 317

Kill your balm and its odors bless you, 238
Knock with tremor, 1325
Knows how to forget, 433

Lad of Athens, faithful be, 1768
Lain in nature, so suffice us, 1288
Lay this laurel on the one, 1393
Least bee that brew, 676
Least rivers docile to some sea, 212
Left in immortal youth, 1289
Lest any doubt that we are glad that they were born today, 1156
Lest they should come is all my fear, 1169
Lest this be heaven indeed, 1043
Let down the bars, oh death, 1065
Let me not mar that perfect dream, 1335
Let me not thirst with this hock at my lip, 1772
Let my first knowing be of thee, 1218
Let us play yesterday, 728
"Lethe" in my flower, 1730
Life and death and giants, 706
Life is what we make it, 698
Lift it with the feathers, 1348
Light is sufficient to itself, 862
Lightly stepped a yellow star, 1672
Like brooms of steel, 1252

Like eyes that looked on wastes, 458
Like flowers that heard the news of dews, 513
Like her the saints retire, 60
Like men and women shadows walk, 1105
Like mighty foot lights burned the red, 595
Like rain it sounded till it curved, 1235
Like some old fashioned miracle, 302
Like time's insidious wrinkle, 1236
Like trains of cars on tracks of plush, 1224
Lives he in any other world, 1557
Long years apart can make no, 1383
Longing is like the seed, 1255
Look back on time with friendly eyes, 1478
Love can do all but raise the dead, 1731
Love is anterior to life, 917
Love is done when love's begun, 1485
Love is that later thing than death, 924
Love reckons by itself alone, 826
Love thou art high, 453
Love's stricken "why," 1368
Low at my problem bending, 69
Luck is not chance, 1350

Make me a picture of the sun, 188
Mama never forgets her birds, 164
Many a phrase has the English language, 276
Many cross the Rhine, 123
March is the month of expectation, 1404
Me, change! Me, alter, 268
Me, come! My dazzled face, 431
Me from myself to banish, 642
Me prove it now, whoever doubt, 537
Meeting by accident, 1548
Midsummer was it when they died, 962
Mine by the right of the white election, 528
Mine enemy is growing old, 1509
More life went out when he went, 422
More than the grave is closed to me, 1503
Morning is due to all, 1577
Morning is the place for dew, 197
"Morning" means "milking" to the farmer, 300
Morning that comes but once, 1610
Morns like these we parted, 27
Most she touched me by her muteness, 760
Much madness is divinest sense, 435
Musicians wrestle everywhere, 157
Must be a woe, 571
Mute thy coronation, 151
My best acquaintances are those, 932
My cocoon tightens, colors tease, 1099
My country need not change her gown, 1511
My eye is fuller than my vase, 202
My faith is larger than the hills, 766
My first well day since many ill, 574

My friend attacks my friend, 118
My friend must be a bird, 92
My garden like the beach, 484
My God, he sees thee, 1178
My heart ran so to thee, 1237
My heart upon a little plate, 1027
My life closed twice before its close, 1732
My life had stood a loaded gun, 754
My maker let me be, 1403
My nosegays are for captives, 95
My period had come for prayer, 564
My portion is defeat today, 639
My reward for being was this, 343
My river runs to thee, 162
My season's furthest flower, 1019
My soul accused me and I quailed, 753
My triumph lasted till the drums, 1227
My wars are laid away in books, 1549
My wheel is in the dark, 10
My worthiness is all my doubt, 751
Myself can read the telegrams, 1089
Myself was formed a carpenter, 488

Nature affects to be sedate, 1170
Nature and God — I neither knew, 835
Nature assigns the sun, 1336
Nature can do no more, 1673
"Nature" is what we see, 668
Nature rarer uses yellow, 1045
Nature sometimes sears a sapling, 314
Nature the gentlest mother is, 790
Never for society, 746
New feet within my garden go, 99
No autumn's intercepting chill, 1516
No bobolink reverse his singing, 755
No brigadier throughout the year, 1561
No crowd that has occurred, 515
No ladder needs the bird but skies, 1574
No life can pompless pass away, 1626
No man can compass a despair, 477
No man saw awe, nor to his house, 1733
No matter now, sweet, 704
No matter where the saints abide, 1541
No notice gave she, but a change, 804
No other can reduce, 982
No passenger was known to flee, 1406
No prisoner be, 720
No rack can torture me, 384
No romance sold unto, 669
Nobody knows this little rose, 35
None can experience stint, 771
None who saw it ever told it, 1110
Noon is the hinge of day, 931
Nor mountain hinder me, 1029

Not all die early, dying young, 990
Not any higher stands the grave, 1256
Not any more to be lacked, 1344
Not any sunny tone, 1674
Not at home to callers, 1590
Not in this world to see his face, 418
Not knowing when the dawn will come, 1619
Not one by heaven defrauded stay, 1303
Not probable — the barest chance, 346
Not "Revelation" 'tis that waits, 685
Not seeing, still we know, 1518
Not sickness stains the brave, 1613
Not so the infinite relations — below, 1040
Not that he goes — we love him more, 1435
Not to discover weakness is, 1054
Not what we did shall be the test, 823
Not with a club the heart is broken, 1304
Now I knew I lost her, 1219
Now I lay thee down to sleep, 1539

Obtaining but our own extent, 1543
Of all the souls that stand create, 664
Of all the sounds despatched abroad, 321
Of being is a bird, 653
Of bronze and blaze, 290
Of Brussels it was not, 602
Of consciousness her awful mate, 894
Of course I prayed, 376
Of death I try to think like this, 1558
Of glory not a beam is left, 1647
Of God we ask one favor, 1601
Of life to own, 1294
Of nature I shall have enough, 1220
Of nearness to her sundered things, 607
Of paradise' existence, 1411
Of Paul and Silas it is said, 1166
Of silken speech and specious shoe, 896
Of so divine a loss, 1179
Of the heart that goes in and closes the door, 1098
Of their peculiar light, 1362
Of this day composed, 1675
Of tolling bell I ask the cause, 947
Of tribulation these are they, 325
Of whom so dear, 1504
Of yellow was the outer sky, 1676
Oh future! thou secreted peace, 1631
Oh give it motion, deck it sweet, 1527
Oh, honey of an hour, 1734
Oh shadow on the grass, 1187
Oh sumptuous moment, 1125
Oh, what a grace is this, 1615
On a columnar self, 789
On my volcano grows the grass, 1677
On such a night, or such a night, 146

On that dear frame the years had worn, 940
On that specific pillow, 1533
On the world you colored, 1171
On this long storm the rainbow rose, 194
On this wondrous sea, 4
Once more, my now bewildered dove, 48
One and one are one, 769
One anguish in a crowd, 565
One blessing had I than the rest, 756
One crown that no one seeks, 1735
One crucifixion is recorded only, 553
One day is there of the series, 814
One dignity delays for all, 98
One joy of so much anguish, 1420
One life of so much consequence, 270
One need not be a chamber to be haunted, 670
One of the ones that Midas touched, 1466
One sister have I in our house, 14
One thing of it we borrow, 1464
One year ago jots what, 296
Only a shrine, but mine, 918
Only God detect the sorrow, 626
Opinion is a flitting thing, 1455
Our journey had advanced, 615
Our little kinsmen after rain, 885
Our little secrets slink away, 1326
Our lives are Swiss, 80
Our own possessions, though our own, 1208
Our share of night to bear, 113
Ourselves we do inter with sweet derision, 1144
Ourselves were wed one summer, dear, 631
Out of sight? What of that, 703
Over and over, like a tune, 367
Over the fence, 251

Pain expands the time, 967
Pain has an element of blank, 650
Pain has but one acquaintance, 1049
Papa above, 61
Paradise is of the option, 1069
Paradise is that old mansion, 1119
Partake as doth the bee, 994
Parting with thee reluctantly, 1614
Pass to thy rendezvous of light, 1564
Patience has a quiet outer, 926
Peace is a fiction of our faith, 912
Perception of an object costs, 1071
Perhaps I asked too large, 352
Perhaps they do not go so far, 1399
Perhaps you think me stooping, 833
Perhaps you'd like to buy a flower, 134
Peril as a possession, 1678
Pigmy seraphs gone astray, 138
Pink, small, and punctual, 1332

Poor little heart, 192
Portraits are to daily faces, 170
Power is a familiar growth, 1238
Praise it, 'tis dead, 1384
Prayer is the little implement, 437
Precious to me she still shall be, 727
Presentiment is that long shadow on the lawn, 764
Promise this when you be dying, 648
Proud of my broken heart, since thou didst break it, 1736
Publication is the auction, 709
Purple is fashionable twice, 980
Pursuing you in your transitions, 1602
Put up my lute, 261

Quite empty, quite at rest, 1606

Rather arid delight, 1679
Read, sweet, how others strove, 260
Rearrange a "wife's" affection, 1737
Recollect the face of me, 1305
"Red Sea" indeed! Talk not to me, 1642
Rehearsal to ourselves, 379
"Remember me" implored the thief, 1180
Remembrance has a rear and front, 1182
Remorse is memory awake, 744
Removed from accident of loss, 424
Renunciation is a piercing virtue, 745
Reportless subjects to the quick, 1048
Rests at night, 714
Reverse cannot befall, 395
Revolution is the pod, 1082
Ribbons of the year, 873
Risk is the hair that holds the tun, 1239
Robbed by death, but that was easy, 971

Safe despair it is that raves, 1243
Safe in their alabaster chambers, 216
Said Death to Passion, 1033
Sang from the heart, sire, 1059
Satisfaction is the agent, 1036
Savior! I've no one else to tell, 217
"Secrets" is a daily word, 1385
September's baccalaureate, 1271
Severer service of myself, 786
Sexton! my master's sleeping here, 96
Shall I take thee, the poet said, 1126
Shame is the shawl of pink, 1412
She bore it till the simple veins, 144
She could not live upon the past, 1505
She dealt her pretty words like blades, 479
She died at play, 75
She died — this was the way she died, 150
She dwelleth in the ground, 671
She hideth her the last, 557

She laid her docile crescent down, 1396
She lay as if at play, 369
She rose as high as his occasion, 1011
She rose to his requirement, dropt, 732
She sights a bird, she chuckles, 507
She slept beneath a tree, 25
She sped as petals of a rose, 991
She staked her feathers, gained an arc, 798
She sweeps with many-colored brooms, 219
She went as quiet as the dew, 149
Shells from the coast mistaking, 693
She's happy, with a new content, 535
Should you but fail at sea, 226
"Sic transit gloria mundi," 3
Silence is all we dread, 1251
Sister of Ophir, 1366B
Size circumscribes — it has no room, 641
Sleep is supposed to be, 13
Smiling back from coronation, 385
Snow beneath whose chilly softness, 942
So bashful when I spied her, 91
So from the mould, 66
So gay a flower, 1456
So give me back to death, 1632
So glad we are, a stranger'd deem, 329
So has a daisy vanished, 28
So I pull my stockings off, 1201
So large my will, 1024
So much of heaven has gone from earth, 1228
So much summer, 651
So proud she was to die, 1272
So set its sun in thee, 808
So the eyes accost and sunder, 752
So well that I can live without, 456
Society for me my misery, 1534
Soft as the massacre of suns, 1127
Softened by time's consummate plush, 1738
Soil of flint, if steady tilled, 681
Some arrows slay but whom they strike, 1565
Some days retired from the rest, 1157
Some keep the Sabbath going to church, 324
Some one prepared this mighty show, 1644
Some rainbow coming from the fair, 64
Some say goodnight at night, 1739
Some such butterfly be seen, 541
Some things that fly there be, 89
Some too fragile for winter winds, 141
Some we see no more, tenements of wonder, 1221
Some work for immortality, 406
Some wretched creature savior take, 1111
Somehow myself survived the night, 1194
Sometimes with the heart, 1680
Somewhat to hope for, 1041
Somewhere upon the general earth, 1231

Soto! Explore thyself, 832
Soul, take thy risk, 1151
Soul, wilt thou toss again, 139
South winds jostle them, 86
"Sown in dishonor," 62
Speech is a prank of parliament, 688
Speech is one symptom of affection, 1681
Split the lark and you'll find the music, 861
Spring comes on the world, 1042
Spring is the period, 844
Spurn the temerity, 1432
Step lightly on this narrow spot, 1183
Still own thee, still thou art, 1633
Strong draughts of their refreshing minds, 711
Struck was I, not yet by lightning, 925
Success is counted sweetest, 67
Such are the inlets of the mind, 1421
Such is the force of happiness, 787
Summer begins to have the look, 1682
Summer for thee, grant I may be, 31
Summer has two beginnings, 1422
Summer is shorter than any one, 1506
Summer laid her simple hat, 1363
Summer we all have seen, 1386
Sunset at night is natural, 415
Sunset that screens reveals, 1609
Superfluous were the sun, 999
Superiority to fate, 1081
Surgeons must be very careful, 108
Surprise is like a thrilling pungent, 1306
Suspense is hostiler than death, 705
Sweet hours have perished here, 1767
Sweet is the swamp with its secrets, 1740
Sweet mountains, ye tell me no lie, 722
Sweet pirate of the heart, 1546
Sweet, safe houses, 457
Sweet skepticism of the heart, 1413
Sweet to have had them lost, 901
Sweet, you forgot but I remembered, 523

Take all away, 1365
Take all away from me, 1640
Take your heaven further on, 388
Taken from men this morning, 53
Taking up the fair ideal, 428
Talk not to me of summer trees, 1634
Talk with prudence to a beggar, 119
Teach him, when he makes the names, 227
Tell all the truth but tell it slant, 1129
Tell as a marksman were forgotten, 1152
Than heaven more remote, 1436
That after horror, that 'twas us, 286
That distance was between us, 863
That first day, when you praised me, sweet, 659

That I did always love, 549
That is solemn we have ended, 934
That it will never come again, 1741
That love is all there is, 1765
That odd old man is dead a year, 1130
That sacred closet when you sweep, 1273
That she forgot me was the least, 1683
That short potential stir, 1307
That such have died enable us, 1030
That this should feel the need of death, 1112
The admirations and contempts of time, 906
The angle of a landscape, 375
The auctioneer of parting, 1612
The bat is dun with wrinkled wings, 1575
The battle fought between the soul, 594
The bee is not afraid of me, 111
The beggar at the door for fame, 1240
The beggar lad dies early, 717
The Bible is an antique volume, 1545
The bird did prance, the bee did play, 1107
The bird her punctual music brings, 1585
The bird must sing to earn the crumb, 880
The birds begun at four o'clock, 783
The birds reported from the south, 743
The blackberry wears a thorn in his side, 554
The blunder is in estimate, 1684
The bobolink is gone, 1591
The body grows without, 578
The bone that has no marrow, 1274
The brain is wider than the sky, 632
The brain within its groove, 556
The bustle in a house, 1078
The butterfly in honored dust, 1246
The butterfly obtains, 1685
The butterfly upon the sky, 1521
The butterfly's assumption grown, 1244
The butterfly's Numidian gown, 1387
The chemical conviction, 954
The child's faith is new, 637
The clock strikes one that just struck two, 1569
The clouds their backs together laid, 1172
The clover's simple fame, 1232
The color of a queen is this, 776
The color of the grave is green, 411
The competitions of the sky, 1494
The court is far away, 235
The crickets sang, 1104
The daisy follows soft the sun, 106
The dandelion's pallid tube, 1519
The day came slow till five o'clock, 304
The day grew small surrounded tight, 1140
The day she goes, 1308
The day that I was crowned, 356
The day undressed herself, 716

The days that we can spare, 1184
The definition of beauty is, 988
The devil had he fidelity, 1479
The difference between despair, 305
The distance that the dead have gone, 1742
The ditch is dear to the drunken man, 1645
The doomed regard the sunrise, 294
The drop that wrestles in the sea, 284
The dust behind I strove to join, 992
The duties of the wind are few, 1137
The dying need but little, dear, 1026
The earth has many keys, 1775
The ecstasy to guess, 1608
The event was directly behind him, 1686
The face I carry with me last, 336
The face in evanescence lain, 1490
The face we choose to miss, 1141
The fact that earth is heaven, 1408
The fairest home I ever knew, 1423
The farthest thunder that I heard, 1581
The fascinating chill that music leaves, 1480
The feet of people walking home, 7
The fingers of the light, 1000
The first day that I was a life, 902
The first day's night had come, 410
The first we knew of him was death, 1006
The flake the wind exasperate, 1361
The flower must not blame the bee, 206
The frost of death was on the pane, 1136
The frost was never seen, 1202
The future never spoke, 672
The gentian has a parched corolla, 1424
The gentian weaves her fringes, 18
The gleam of an heroic act, 1687
The going from a world we know, 1603
The good will of a flower, 849
The grace myself might not obtain, 707
The grass so little has to do, 333
The grave my little cottage is, 1743
The guest is gold and crimson, 15
The hallowing of pain, 772
The harm of years is on him, 1280
The healed heart shows its shallow scar, 1440
The heart asks pleasure first, 536
The heart has many doors, 1567
The heart has narrow banks, 928
The heart is the capital of the mind, 1354
The heaven vests for each, 694
The hills erect their purple heads, 1688
The hills in purple syllables, 1016
The Himmaleh was known to stoop, 481
The hollows round his eager eyes, 955
The immortality she gave, 1648
The incidents of love, 1248

The infinite a sudden guest, 1309
The inundation of the spring, 1425
The jay his castanet has struck, 1635
The joy that has no stem nor core, 1744
The judge is like the owl, 699
The juggler's hat her country is, 330
The lady feeds her little bird, 941
The lamp burns sure within, 233
The largest fire ever known, 1114
The lassitudes of contemplation, 1592
The last night that she lived, 1100
The last of summer is delight, 1353
The leaves like women interchange, 987
The life that tied too tight escapes, 1535
The life we have is very great, 1162
The lightning is a yellow fork, 1173
The lightning playeth all the while, 630
The lilac is an ancient shrub, 1241
The loneliness one dare not sound, 777
The lonesome for they know not what, 262
The long sigh of the frog, 1359
The longest day that God appoints, 1769
The look of thee, what is it like, 1689
The love a life can show below, 673
The luxury to apprehend, 815
The Malay took the pearl, 452
The manner of its death, 468
The martyr poets did not tell, 544
The merchant of the picturesque, 1131
The mind lives on the heart, 1355
The missing all prevented me, 985
The mob within the heart, 1745
The months have ends, the years a knot, 423
The moon is distant from the sea, 429
The moon upon her fluent route, 1528
The moon was but a chin of gold, 737
The morning after woe, 364
The morns are meeker than they were, 12
The most important population, 1746
The most pathetic thing I do, 1290
The most triumphant bird I ever knew or met, 1265
The mountain sat upon the plain, 975
The mountains grow unnoticed, 757
The mountains stood in haze, 1278
The murmur of a bee, 155
The murmuring of bees has ceased, 1115
The mushroom is the elf of plants, 1298
The name of it is "Autumn," 656
The nearest dream recedes unrealized, 318
The night was wide and furnished scant, 589
The notice that is called the spring, 1310
The one who could repeat the summer day, 307
The ones that disappeared are back, 307
The only ghost I ever saw, 274

The only news I know, 827
The opening and the close, 1047
The outer from the inner, 451
The overtakelessness of those, 1691
The parasol is the umbrella's daughter, 1747
The past is such a curious creature, 1203
The pattern of the sun, 1550
The pedigree of honey, 1627
The pile of years is not so high, 1507
The poets light but lamps, 883
The popular heart is a cannon first, 1226
The power to be true to you, 464
The pretty rain from those sweet eaves, 1426
The products of my farm are these, 1025
The props assist the house, 1142
The province of the saved, 539
The pungent atom in the air, 1191
The rainbow never tells me, 97
The rat is the concisest tenant, 1356
The red blaze is the morning, 469
The reticent volcano keeps, 1748
The riddle we can guess, 1222
The right to perish might be thought, 1692
The road to paradise is plain, 1491
The road was lit with moon and star, 1450
The robin for the crumb, 864
The robin is a Grabriel, 1483
The robin is the one, 828
The robin's my criterion for tune, 285
The rose did caper on her cheek, 208
The saddest noise, the sweetest noise, 1764
The savior must have been, 1487
The sea said "Come" to the brook, 1210
The service without hope, 779
The show is not the show, 1206
The skies can't keep their secret, 191
The sky is low, the clouds are mean, 1075
The smouldering embers blush, 1132
The snow that never drifts, 1133
The soul has bandaged moments, 512
The soul selects her own society, 303
The soul should always stand ajar, 1055
The soul that hath a guest, 674
The soul unto itself, 683
The soul's distinct connection, 974
The soul's superior instants, 306
The spider as an artist, 1275
The spider holds a silver ball, 605
The spirit is the conscious ear, 733
The spirit lasts, but in what mode, 1576
The spry arms of the wind, 1103
The stars are old that stood for me, 1249
The stem of a departed flower, 1520
The stimulus beyond the grave, 1001

The suburbs of a secret, 1245
The summer that we did not prize, 1773
The sun and fog contested, 1190
The sun and moon must make their haste, 871
The sun in reining to the west, 1636
The sun is gay or stark, 878
The sun is one, and on the tare, 1372
The sun just touched the morning, 232
The sun kept setting, setting still, 692
The sun wept stooping, stooping low, 152
The sun retired to a cloud, 1693
The sun went down — no man looked on, 1079
The sunrise runs for both, 710
The sunset stopped on cottages, 950
The sweetest heresy received, 387
The sweets of pillage can be known, 1470
The symptom of the gale, 1327
The test of love is death, 573
The things that never can come back are several, 1515
The things we thought that we should do, 1293
The thought beneath so slight a film, 210
The thrill came slowly like a boon, 1495
The tint I cannot take is best, 627
The treason of an accent, 1358
The trees like tassels hit and swung, 606
The truth is stirless, 780
The vastest earthly day, 1328
The veins of other flowers, 811
The voice that stands for floods to me, 1189
The waters chased him as he fled, 1749
The way hope builds his house, 1481
The way I read a letter's this, 636
The way to know the bobolink, 1279
The well upon the brook, 1091
The whole of it came not at once, 762
The wind begun to knead the grass, 824
The wind didn't come from the orchard today, 316
The wind drew off, 1694
The wind tapped like a tired man, 436
The wind took up the northern things, 1134
The winters are so short, 403
The words the happy say, 1750
The work of her that went, 1143
The world feels dusty, 715
The world stands solemner to me, 493
The worthlessness of earthly things, 1373
The zeroes taught us phosphorus, 689
Their barricade against the sky, 1471
Their dappled importunity, 1611
Their height in heaven comforts not, 696
Themself are all I have, 1094
There are two Mays, 1618
There are two ripenings — one of sight, 332
There came a day at summer's full, 322

There came a wind like a bugle, 1593
There comes a warning like a spy, 1536
There comes an hour when begging stops, 1751
There is a finished feeling, 856
There is a flower that bees prefer, 380
There is a June when corn is cut, 930
There is a languor of the life, 396
There is a morn by men unseen, 24
There is a pain so utter, 599
There is a shame of nobleness, 551
There is a solitude of space, 1695
There is a strength in proving that it can be borne, 1113
There is a word, 8
There is a zone whose even years, 1056
There is an arid pleasure, 782
There is another loneliness, 1116
There is another sky, 2
There is no frigate like a book, 1263
There is no silence in the earth so silent, 1004
There's a certain slant of light, 258
There's been a death in the opposite house, 389
There's something quieter than sleep, 45
There's the battle of Burgoyne, 1174
These are the days that reindeer love, 1696
These are the days when birds come back, 130
These are the nights that beetles love, 1128
These are the signs to nature's inns, 1077
These fevered days — to take them to the forest, 1441
These held their wick above the west, 1390
These saw visions, 758
These strangers in a foreign world, 1096
These tested our horizon, 886
They ask but our delight, 868
They called me to the window, for, 628
They dropped like flakes, 409
They have a little odor, that to me, 785
"They have not chosen me," he said, 85
They leave us with the infinite, 350
They might not need me, yet they might, 1391
They put us far apart, 474
They say that "Time assuages," 686
They shut me up in prose, 613
They talk as slow as legends grow, 1697
They won't frown always, some sweet day, 874
This bauble was preferred of bees, 805
This chasm, sweet, upon my life, 858
This consciousness that is aware, 822
This dirty little heart, 1311
This docile one inter, 1752
This dust and its feature, 936
This heart that broke so long, 145
This is a blossom of the brain, 945
This is my letter to the world, 441
This is the land the sunset washes, 266

This is the place they hoped before, 1264
This me, that walks and works, must die, 1588
This merit hath the worst, 979
This quiet dust was gentlemen and ladies, 813
This slow day moved along, 1120
This that would greet an hour ago, 778
This was a Poet — It is that, 448
This was in the white of the year, 995
This world is not conclusion, 501
Those cattle smaller than a bee, 1388
Those dying then, 1551
Those fair, fictitious people, 499
Those final creatures — who they are, 1766
Those not live yet, 1454
Those who have been in the grave the longest, 922
Tho' I get home how late — how late, 207
Tho' my destiny be fustian, 163
Though the great waters sleep, 1599
Three times we parted, breath and I, 598
Three weeks passed since I had seen her, 1061
Through lane it lay, through bramble, 9
Through the dark sod, as education, 392
Through the strait pass of suffering, 792
Through those old grounds of memory, 1753
Through what transports of patience, 1153
Tie the strings to my life, my Lord, 279
Till death is narrow loving, 907
Time does go on, 1121
Time feels so vast that were it not, 802
Time's wily chargers will not wait, 1458
'Tis anguish grander than delight, 984
'Tis customary as we part, 440
'Tis easier to pity those when dead, 1698
'Tis good — the looking back on grief, 660
'Tis little I could care for pearls, 466
'Tis my first night beneath the sun, 1122
'Tis not that dying hurts us so, 335
'Tis not the swaying frame we miss, 1597
'Tis one by one the Father counts, 545
'Tis opposites entice, 355
'Tis seasons since the dimpled war, 1529
'Tis so appalling, it exhilarates, 281
'Tis so much joy! 'Tis so much joy, 172
'Tis sunrise, little maid. Hast thou, 908
'Tis true they shut me in the cold, 538
'Tis whiter than an Indian pipe, 1482
Title divine is mine, 1072
To be alive is power, 677
To be forgot by thee, 1560
To break so vast a heart, 1312
To die takes just a little while, 255
To die without the dying, 1017
To disappear enhances, 1209
To do a magnanimous thing, 1699

To earn it by disdaining it, 1427
To fight aloud is very brave, 126
To fill a gap, 546
To flee from memory, 1242
To hang our head ostensibly, 105
To hear an oriole sing, 526
To help our bleaker parts, 1064
To her derided home, 1586
To his simplicity, 1352
To interrupt his yellow plan, 591
To know just how he suffered would be dear, 622
To learn the transport by the pain, 167
To lose one's faith, surpass, 377
To lose thee, sweeter than to gain, 1754
To love thee year by year, 434
To make a prairie it takes a clover and one bee, 1755
To make one's toilette after death, 485
To make routine a stimulus, 1196
To mend each tattered faith, 1442
To my quick ear the leaves conferred, 891
To my small hearth his fire came, 638
To offer brave assistance, 767
To one denied to drink, 490
To own a Susan of my own, 1401
To own the art within the soul, 855
To pile like thunder to its close, 1247
To put this world down, like a bundle, 527
To see her is a picture, 1568
To see the summer sky, 1472
To tell the beauty would decrease, 1700
To the bright east she flies, 1573
To the stanch dust, 1402
To their apartment deep, 1701
To this world she returned, 830
To try to speak and miss the way, 1617
To undertake is to achieve, 1070
To venerate the simple days, 57
To wait an hour is long, 781
To whom the mornings stand for nights, 1095
Today or this noon, 1702
"Tomorrow" — whose location, 1367
Too cold is this, 1135
Too few the mornings be, 1186
Too happy time dissolves itself, 1774
Too little way the house must lie, 911
Too scanty 'twas to die for you, 1013
Touch lightly nature's sweet guitar, 1389
Tried always and condemned by thee, 1559
Triumph may be of several kinds, 455
Trudging to Eden, looking backward, 1020
Trust adjusts her "peradventure," 1161
Trust in the unexpected, 555
Trusty as the stars, 1369
Truth is as old as God, 836

'Twas a long parting, but the time, 625
'Twas awkward, but it fitted me, 973
'Twas comfort in her dying room, 1703
'Twas crisis — All the length had passed, 948
'Twas fighting for his life he was, 1188
'Twas here my summer paused, 1756
'Twas just this time last year I died, 445
'Twas later when the summer went, 1276
'Twas like a maelstrom with a notch, 414
'Twas love, not me, 394
'Twas my one glory, 1028
'Twas such a little, little boat, 107
'Twas the old road through pain, 344
'Twas warm, at first, like us, 519
Twice had summer her fair verdure, 846
Two butterflies went out at noon, 533
Two lengths has every day, 1295
Two swimmers wrestled on the spar, 201
Two travellers perishing in snow, 933
Two were immortal twice, 800
'Twould ease a butterfly, 682

Unable are the loved to die, 809
Uncertain lease develops lustre, 857
Under the light, yet under, 949
Undue significance a starving man attaches, 439
Unfulfilled to observation, 972
Unit, like death, for whom, 408
Until the desert knows, 1291
Unto a broken heart, 1704
Unto like story trouble has enticed me, 295
"Unto me?" I do not know you, 964
Unto my books so good to turn, 604
Unto the whole how add, 1341
Unworthy of her breast, 1414
Up life's hill with my little bundle, 1010
Upon a lilac sea, 1337
Upon concluded lives, 735
Upon his saddle sprung a bird, 1600
Upon the gallows hung a wretch, 1757

Victory comes late, 690
Volcanoes be in Sicily, 1705

Wait till the majesty of death, 171
Warm in her hand these accents lie, 1313
"Was not" was all the statement, 1342
Water is taught by thirst, 135
Water makes many beds, 1428
We, bee and I, live by the quaffing, 230
We can but follow to the sun, 920
We cover thee, sweet face, 482
We do not know the time we lose, 1106
We do not play on graves, 467

We don't cry, Tim and I, 196
We dream — it is good we are dreaming, 531
We grow accustomed to the dark, 419
We introduce ourselves, 1214
We knew not that we were to live, 1462
We learn in the retreating, 1083
We learned the whole of love, 568
We like a hairbreadth 'scape, 1175
We like March, 1213
We lose because we win, 21
We met as sparks, diverging flints, 958
We miss a kinsman more, 1087
We miss her, not because we see, 993
We never know how high we are, 1176
We never know we go when we are going, 1523
We outgrow love like other things, 887
We play at paste, 320
We pray to heaven, 489
We see comparatively, 534
We send the wave to find the wave, 1604
We shall find the cube of the rainbow, 1484
We should not mind so small a flower, 81
We shun because we prize her face, 1429
We shun it ere it comes, 1580
We talked as girls do, 586
We talked with each other about each other, 1473
We thirst at first — 'tis nature's act, 726
We wear our sober dresses when we die, 1572
We'll pass without the parting, 996
Went up a year this evening, 93
Were it but me that gained the height, 1015
Were it to be the last, 1164
Were nature mortal lady, 1762
Wert thou but ill, that I might show thee, 961
What care the dead for chanticleer, 592
What did they do since I saw them, 900
What I can do I will, 361
What I see not, I better see, 939
What if I say I shall not wait, 277
What inn is this, 115
What is "Paradise," 215
What mystery pervades a well, 1400
What shall I do, it whimpers so, 186
What shall I do when the summer troubles, 956
What soft, cherubic creatures, 401
What tenements of clover, 1338
What twigs we held by, 1086
What we see we know somewhat, 1195
What would I give to see his face, 247
Whatever it is, she has tried it, 1204
When a lover is a beggar, 1314
When bells stop ringing, church begins, 633
When diamonds are a legend, 397
When Etna basks and purrs, 1146

When I count the seeds, 40
When I have seen the sun emerge, 888
When I hoped I feared, 1181
When I hoped, I recollect, 768
When I was small, a woman died, 596
When Katie walks, this simple pair accompany her side, 222
When memory is full, 1266
When night is almost done, 347
When one has given up one's life, 853
When roses cease to bloom, sir, 32
When the astronomer stops seeking, 851
When they come back, if blossoms do, 1080
When we have ceased to care, 1706
When we stand on the tops of things, 242
Where bells no more affright the morn, 112
Where every bird is bold to go, 1758
Where I have lost, I softer tread, 104
Where roses would not dare to go, 1582
Where ships of purple gently toss, 265
Where thou art, that is home, 725
Whether my bark went down at sea, 52
Whether they have forgotten, 1329
Which is best? Heaven, 1012
Which is the best — the moon or the crescent, 1315
Which misses most, 1759
While asters, 331
While it is alive, 491
While we were fearing it, it came, 1277
White as an Indian pipe, 1250
Who abdicated ambush, 1616
Who court obtain within himself, 803
Who giants know, with lesser men, 796
Who goes to dine must take his feast, 1223
Who has not found the heaven below, 1544
Who is it seeks my pillow nights, 1598
Who is the east, 1032
Who never lost are unprepared, 73
Who never wanted maddest joy, 1430
Who occupies this house, 892
Who saw no sunrise cannot say, 1018
Who were "the Father and the Son," 1258
Whoever disenchants, 1451
Whole gulfs of red, and fleets of red, 658
Whose are the little beds, I asked, 142
Whose cheek is this, 82
Whose pink career may have a close, 1394
"Why do I love" you, sir, 480
Why do they shut me out of heaven, 248
Why make it doubt, it hurts it so, 462
Why should we hurry, why indeed, 1646
Wild nights — wild nights, 249
Will there really be a "Morning," 101
Winter is good — his hoar delights, 1316
Winter under cultivation, 1707

Witchcraft has not a pedigree, 1708
Witchcraft was hung in history, 1583
With pinions of disdain, 1431
With sweetness unabated, 1709
With thee in the desert, 209
Within my garden rides a bird, 500
Within my reach, 90
Within that little hive, 1607
Within thy grave, 1552
Without a smile, without a throe, 1330
Without this there is nought, 655
Wolfe demanded during dying, 678
Wonder is not precisely knowing, 1331
Would you like summer? Taste of ours, 691

Yesterday is history, 1292
You cannot make remembrance grow, 1508
You cannot put a fire out, 530
You cannot take itself, 1351
You constituted time, 765
You know that portrait in the moon, 504
You left me, sire, two legacies, 644
You love me, you are sure, 156
You love the Lord you cannot see, 487
You said that I "was great" one day, 738
You see I cannot see — your lifetime, 253
You taught me waiting with myself, 740
You'll find it when you try to die, 610
You'll know her by her foot, 634
You'll know it as you know 'tis noon, 420
Your riches taught me poverty, 299
Your thoughts don't have words every day, 1452
You're right — "the way is narrow," 234
You've seen balloons set, haven't you, 700